D1562148

BIOLOGICAL
WARFARE

BIOLOGICAL
WARFARE
MODERN OFFENSE
AND DEFENSE

EDITED BY
RAYMOND A. ZILINSKAS

LYNNE
RIENNER
PUBLISHERS

BOULDER
LONDON

Published in the United States of America in 2000 by
Lynne Rienner Publishers, Inc.
1800 30th Street, Boulder, Colorado 80301
www.rienner.com

and in the United Kingdom by
Lynne Rienner Publishers, Inc.
3 Henrietta Street, Covent Garden, London WC2E 8LU

Library of Congress Cataloging-in-Publication Data
Biological warfare : modern offense and defense / edited by Raymond A. Zilinskas.
    p. cm.
   Includes bibliographical references and index.
   ISBN 1-55587-761-3 (alk. paper)
   1. Biological warfare. 2. Biological arms control.
I. Zilinskas, Raymond A.
UG447.8.B565   1999
327.1'745—dc21   99-12065
                                                CIP

British Cataloguing in Publication Data
A Cataloguing in Publication record for this book
is available from the British Library.

5 4 3 2

To my mother, Elena Warren;
always loving, always supporting

Contents

Acknowledgments

I am indebted to many persons who offered me expert assistance and encouragement while I worked to complete this book. I ask for their forebearance in not being able to name them all here. I limit myself to acknowledging those who directly affected how the final product reads and looks. In particular, I am thankful to the several experts who reviewed individual chapters and, even more so, to the few who reviewed the entire book. The reviewers were Kathleen Bresnahan (U.S. government), Tom Dashiell (former consultant, now deceased), David Franz (Southern Research Institute), Del Freeman (U.S. government), Alan Holmberg (Eli Lily and Company), David Huxsoll (Louisiana State University), Steven S. Morse (Columbia University), James Poupart (SmithKline Beecham Company), Phillip Russell (Johns Hopkins University), Edmund Tramont (University of Maryland Biotechnology Institute), Ken Ward (U.S. Arms Control and Disarmament Agency), and Alan Zelicoff (Sandia National Laboratory).

Of course, the project could not have been done without the support of the Smith Richardson Foundation and the helpfulness of the foundation's staff. In this regard, I am most thankful to Marin Strmecki, who probably is the one person most responsible for this project having become a reality, and Nadia Schadlow, who provided valuable guidance and assistance.

The project would have meant little if its findings and results remained unpublished. It is to the credit of Lynne Rienner Publishers that its editors saw what we tried to accomplish and the value of making project accomplishments available to the wider public. I am in particular indebted to Dan Eades, Leanne Anderson, and Lesli Athanasoulis.

Finally, when developments were slow and things got very frustrating, my family never faltered in their belief that I would be able to finish the project. To my mother, Elena Warren, and two brothers, Gene and Victor Zilinskas, a heartfelt thank you. But the greatest credit for the emotional support that I so much needed toward the end of an interminable editing process goes to my wife, Helen. Thank you, thank you.

Raymond A. Zilinskas

Introduction

RAYMOND A. ZILINSKAS

It is an odd characteristic of biological weapons that military generals tend to view them with distaste, but civilian bioscientists often have lobbied for their development and deployment. There are, of course, understandable reasons for this oddity; generals find that these weapons do not fit neatly into tactical or strategic military doctrines of attack or defense, whereas researchers have observed that transforming microbes into weapons presents interesting scientific challenges whose solution governments have been willing to pay well for. Another oddity is that whenever biological weapons have been employed in battle, they have proven militarily ineffectual, yet bellicose national leaders persevere in seeking to acquire them. There is also a facile explanation for this anomaly, namely, that although pathogens are all too willing to invade prospective hosts, human ingenuity so far has failed to devise reliable methods for effectively conveying a large number of pathogens to the population targeted for annihilation by disease. This repeated failure has not deterred leaders; again and again they become allured by the potential destructive power of biological weapons. Perhaps trusting science too much, they direct government scientists to develop them, believing that this time a usable weapon of mass destruction will be achieved. Their belief so far has been thwarted, but is it possible that within the foreseeable future the potential of biological weapons will be realized and that the effect of a biological bomb, missile, or aerosolized cloud can be as readily predetermined as that of a bomb or missile carrying a conventional or nuclear warhead?

There are many who believe that today's bioscientists and chemical engineers working in unison and wielding the techniques of molecular biology developed since the early 1970s could, if so commanded, develop mili-

1

tarily effective biological weapons within a fairly short time. If this supposition is correct, our perception of biological weapons as being undependable, uncontrollable, and unreliable must change. The reason is simple: if these weapons are demonstrated to possess properties that make it possible for commanders to effect controlled, confined mass destruction on command, all governments would be forced to construct defenses against them and some undoubtedly would be tempted to arm their military with these weapons that would be both powerful and relatively inexpensive to acquire. Ironically, as tougher international controls are put into place to deter nations from seeking to acquire chemical and nuclear weapons, leaders may be even more drawn to biological arms as the most accessible form of weapon of mass destruction.

Before beginning a consideration of the implications of molecular biology for biological warfare (BW) and defense, it is worthwhile to briefly review the history of microbiology. It has passed through two eras, and we presently are in its third era. The first was the "pre-Pasteur" era; when the underlying science of fermentation was unknown, so microbiology was applied strictly on an empirical basis. Although undoubtedly many fine beers and wines, as well as breads and other fermented foods, were produced through the use of empirically developed fermentation techniques, no finely controlled production of chemicals was possible. During this era, BW was also empirically based. Common tactics included contaminating water sources with bloated animal carcasses and catapulting infected cadavers into citadels (Poupard and Miller, 1992).

Once Louis Pasteur demonstrated the vital role of microbes in the fermentation process, the foundation for the "applied microbiology" era was laid. During this period the bacteria and yeast used in industrial processes were improved through the now classical techniques of mutation, selection, and breeding. Through the judicious application of these techniques, industrial microbiologists were able to improve the capacity of microorganisms to convert raw material into finished product, whether an antibiotic or bulk chemical. For example, since it first was employed for production in the 1930s, the capacity of penicillin-producing *Penicillium notatum* has been enhanced by 5,000 percent.

The few national BW programs initiated during the applied microbiology era used the same techniques of mutation, selection, and breeding to weaponize biological agents (that is, to develop pathogens or toxins for purposes of warfare). Thus, before, during, and after World War II, BW programs were operated by Japan (USSR, 1950; Williams and Wallace, 1989), the Soviet Union (Leitenberg, 1992; Meselson et al., 1994), the United Kingdom (Carter, 1992a; Bryden, 1989), and the United States (U.S. Department of the Army, 1977a). In the course of these programs, a large variety of pathogens (such as bacterial species causing anthrax, plague, and typhoid fever) and toxins (such as botulinum toxin and staphylococcus enterotoxin B) were researched and developed for weapons applications. No special equipment or facilities needed to be developed for this purpose because fermenters, grinders, dryers, and other equipment readily available for purchase in civilian markets could be used for this purpose. One of the largest problems of biological arms control, and one that remains to this day, is that instruments and machinery employed by civilian researchers and developers can just as easily be used by their military counterparts for purposes of biological warfare.

In the early 1970s, when genetic engineering techniques were first developed, the era of "molecular biology" commenced. In the intervening twenty-five years or so, a panoply of ever more powerful techniques has been developed, which are being employed by an ever-growing number of scientists and engineers at research institutes and bioindustries located throughout the world. The consequences of this chain of scientific progress have been profound. Bioscientists have used techniques derived from molecular biology and genetics to clarify some of the most mysterious and complex of life's processes, including aspects of the genetic control over metabolism and heredity (Meselson, 1999). Engineers have harnessed the power of the microbe to mass-produce substances for the pharmaceutical and food industries whose existence until recently was barely known. However, the power of biotechnology so evident in civilian endeavors may also have equally profound effects on developments related to biological weapons and defenses. After all, in the pre-Pasteur and applied microbiology eras, developments in the civilian sphere were mirrored in the military sector; we would be wise to assume the same for the era of molecular biology.

It is notable that wide-ranging, thorough assessments of the implications of the biotechnology revolution on biological warfare and defense are lacking. This is in marked contrast to what occurred in the applied microbiology era; from 1969 to 1973 four important studies were completed that heavily influenced how national leaders and their diplomatic representatives viewed biological weaponry and biological arms control (United Nations, 1969; Interdepartmental Political-Military Group, 1969; WHO, 1970; SIPRI, 1971, 1973a, 1973b). These studies simultaneously described the horrific potential of biological weapons and elucidated their scant military utility as constructed at the time. The potential is horrific because biological weapons, similar to chemical weapons, are most effective when directed against defenseless and vulnerable civilian populations. Soldiers usually would both be vaccinated against common BW agents and have ready access to personal and communal protective equipment. Troop formations, therefore, were likely to sustain only light casualties, whereas civilian populations would be decimated. These technical findings added to the moral outrage many persons felt about biological weapons and gave impetus to President Richard M. Nixon's decisions to dismantle the United

States' offensive BW program in 1969 (Nixon, 1971) and to adopt, with the majority of the world's governments, the Convention on the Prohibition of the Development, Production and Stockpiling of Bacteriological (Biological) and Toxin Weapons, and on Their Destruction (BWC) in 1972 (BWC, 1975).

With the coming into force of the BWC in 1975, many believed that the specter of BW disappeared. Unfortunately, this was not the case; during 1979–1981 incidents at Sverdlovsk in the Soviet Union and throughout Indochina indicated that illicit BW-related activity was continuing (Sims, 1988). We now know that the Soviet Union not only continued its national BW program after having ratified the BWC but also actually substantially increased its size (Alibek, 1998a, 1998b, 1998c, 1999). Other nations also seemed to have been lured by the potential of biological weaponry; the number of nations believed to possess biological weapons or seek to acquire them has increased since the BWC entered into effect, from four to possibly twelve (U.S. Congress, 1993c). The proliferation of BW was most dramatically demonstrated when it was revealed that Iraq had begun a BW program in 1978 and, by the time Desert Storm took place in January 1991, had produced biologically-laden ballistic missiles, bombs, rockets, and artillery shells, all deployed and ready for use (Zilinskas, 1997b; Barton, 1998).

Whereas it appears that Soviet weapon scientists used molecular biology techniques in research to produce ever more deadly agents (Alibek, 1999), neither the Soviets nor the Iraqis have (as far as is known) deployed genetically engineered microorganisms in their biological weapons; in fact both programs were firmly anchored in the applied microbiology era. As such, the relevance of these programs to this volume has mostly to do with two issues: intent (why governments seek to acquire BW) and implications for biological arms control (how to deter nations from acquiring biological weapons and how to detect existing BW programs). The first aspect remains conjectural (because no government has explained why it decided to acquire these weapons), whereas the second aspect is well grounded in lessons derived from the experience of the United Nations Special Commission (UNSCOM) in Iraq (Barton, 1998). As is set forth in several chapters of this volume, much has been learned from the UNSCOM experience about the detection of BW-related weaponry, equipment, and facilities; the deterrence of future acquisition of biological weapons through continuous monitoring; and the accessing by intergovernmental oversight organizations of information collected by national intelligence agencies. These lessons should prove valuable when confronting illicit BW-related research, development, and production, regardless of whether classical applied microbiological methods or molecular biology techniques are employed by the perpetrators.

As mentioned above, the main purpose of this book is to consider whether advances in molecular biology have substantially affected BW and defenses against it. To achieve this objective, we need to consider the following complex questions: (1) Will the use of molecular biology techniques allow the development and deployment of a militarily potent new generation of biological weaponry? (2) Has our ability to detect BW agents been significantly enhanced through applications of molecular biology techniques? (3) If advances in molecular biology have not substantially affected BW-related developments to date, are they likely to do so within the foreseeable future?

When this study began, the answers to these questions were not at all clear. The range of opinions held by security experts varied widely. At one end of the spectrum were those who believed that nature cannot be improved upon. They hold that although molecular biology techniques might be useful tools to incrementally improve the capabilities of existing pathogens as BW agents, they do not qualitatively alter BW capability. If this assessment is correct, the gradual approach taken during the applied microbiology era to strengthen the BWC should continue, and no drastic new measures are needed for international arms control. Conversely, many held the opinion that since it is possible to genetically engineer microorganisms for specific industrial purposes, it is just as feasible to genetically engineer bacteria and viruses for BW purposes. If so, effective, controllable, and dependable biological weapons are now possible, and the present arms control regime is inadequate, unlikely to be able to suppress their global proliferation.

In approaching the questions listed above, the authors begin with the working hypothesis that molecular biology is profoundly affecting BW-related developments or will be doing so in the immediate future. If this hypothesis proves correct, there are important implications for biological arms control and for civil defense. Further, if scientific developments have led to or will lead to the development and deployment of biological weapons by a larger number of nations or subnational groups, we must also consider whether modern bioscience has enhanced our abilities to protect populations from infectious disease or can treat diseases resulting from biological attacks.

In order to address this broad range of issues, the book is divided into three parts: (1) "Biological Weapons and Warfare," (2) "Defense and Prophylaxis," and (3) "International Control." Part 1 begins with a chapter by Robert P. Kadlec and Alan P. Zelicoff, who analyze the utility of biological and toxin weapons both for today's military forces and for terrorist organizations in light of new technologies, the changing dynamics of the modern battlefield, and the changing nature of terrorist operations, and discuss the scientific developments that allow the design and production of biological weaponry that were not possible in previous eras. In particular, they consider whether molecular biology techniques endow microbiologists

with new capabilities to design and develop agents for the specific purpose
of biological warfare. In Chapter 2, Jonathan B. Tucker analyzes the motivations of various countries that either sought to acquire biological
weapons or chose to spurn them.

Part 2 addresses defense; that is, the means that governments have to
defend their human, animal, and plant populations against biological
attacks by hostile nations or terrorists. In Chapter 3, Graham S. Pearson
argues that nations must conduct accurate assessments of the biological
threats to human, animal, and plant populations. He makes clear that biological threat assessment is a complex exercise, demanding the services of
experts knowledgeable in microbiology, epidemiology, infectious disease,
technology assessment, scientific capabilities of suspect nations, terrorist
organizations, and geopolitics. If the threat assessment is successful and a
nation is able to determine which infectious diseases its human, animal, or
plant populations might be exposed to, that nation's government is in a
good position to design and implement appropriate defenses.

As is the case with most powerful technologies, they can be employed
for good or evil. Several of the techniques of molecular biology are being
employed to detect and identify potentially dangerous chemicals and
microorganisms. As Stephen S. Morse discusses in Chapter 4, sophisticated
new immunological procedures add to the existing arsenal of classical techniques for the detection of toxins and pathogenic microorganisms.
Nevertheless, as he explains, there are severe limitations to these techniques that limit their usefulness to soldiers in the battlefield and to inspectors conducting on-site inspections.

There is more to investigating disease outbreaks than wielding sophisticated methods and techniques. As Mark L. Wheelis makes clear in
Chapter 5, in the initial stages of investigations no one will know if the etiology of the outbreak in question is nature or laboratory. Investigators of
outbreaks usually will find it very difficult to determine where the pathogenic or toxin agent came from and the mechanisms whereby it came to
infect the stricken hosts. Wheelis describes epidemiological and other techniques that can be applied in disease investigations and discusses their possibilities and limitations for biological arms control.

In Chapter 6, Stanley L. Wiener considers the consequences of a biological attack that succeeds, including the response of military and civilian
health delivery systems to such a catastrophe. He argues that we are poorly
prepared to meet the challenges of such an event and that such steps as
issuing light portable masks to the general population should be given high
priority.

Part 3 addresses biological arms control, which encompasses many different types of activities. In Chapter 7, Marie I. Chevrier considers classical
arms control via multilateral treaty. In the case of BW, the most important
treaty is the BWC. As of May 3, 1997, 159 governments had signed it; 141

of these had also ratified the convention, thus making them BWC state parties. Chevrier first determines what constitutes a "strong" arms control treaty and then considers the adequacy of ongoing efforts to strengthen the BWC. These include the separate but interconnected initiatives for confidence building and establishing a treaty compliance regime. She also reviews the different roles that governments, industry, and nongovernmental organizations can play in strengthening the treaty.

In Chapter 8, Will D. Carpenter and Michael Moodie argue that an effective, technically valid, and verifiable biological arms control treaty requires the active participation of industry. A precedent for industry involvement in an arms control treaty can be found in the successful participation of the chemical industry in negotiations that led to the adoption of the Chemical Weapons Convention (CWC), which entered into force April 1997. The authors explain how many of the aspects of the chemical industry's participation in the CWC negotiating process are translatable to ongoing efforts to strengthen the BWC, including the effort to establish a treaty compliance regime.

Yet another approach to achieving biological arms control is the implementation of counterproliferation programs. W. Seth Carus notes in Chapter 9 that these efforts are designed to detect, track, identify, intercept, and destroy or otherwise neutralize all biological weapons regardless of their delivery means. They might also include counterforce operations, such as developing military capabilities to target and destroy biological weapons, launch forms, and their production facilities. Such action can be launched from air, sea, space, or land and be conducted by conventional or special operations forces. The U.S. government is also devoting significant resources to developing the necessary technical means to counter covert delivery and terrorist threats. Much of this effort, explains Carus, is focused on intelligence programs and response teams.

One of the important features of biological weapons development and production is its lack of "signature"; that is, there is no unique sign or indication that divulges BW activity. Thus, inspectors investigating compliance concerns would find it difficult to distinguish between peacefully directed activities and biological weapons development since both use the same equipment and similar facilities. This being the case, secret BW work is likely to remain secret unless (1) an accident reveals it (such as occurred in 1979 in Sverdlovsk, USSR); (2) a nation's defeat leads to information about its BW program being uncovered by the victors (such as happened with Japan after World War II and Iraq after the Gulf War); or (3) data collected from various sources by an intelligence service indicates the existence of the secret program. As Tim Trevan notes in Chapter 10, UNSCOM was the first intergovernmental agency to have intelligence data conveyed to it that had been collected by national intelligence agencies. Since future treaty compliance regimes, beginning with the CWC compliance regime, will be required to investigate suspicious activities or facilities, they will need intelligence to carry out their work effectively. Trevan notes that these regimes should be able to benefit from UNSCOM's experience with national intelligence agencies, including how to establish contacts, train international civil servants to maintain confidentiality, best utilize intelligence information, and maintain credibility while protecting sources.

In Chapter 11, Rita R. Colwell and Raymond A. Zilinskas argue that if peace is to be secured for the long term in the Middle East, it is vital that Iraqi bioscientists be reintegrated into the international scientific community and imbued with a humanitarian ethic. However, the authors note that the involvement of Iraqi scientists in their nation's BW program is not a unique phenomenon; scientists in other countries have been promoters of national programs to acquire biological weapons in the past. In this chapter, the authors describe events in history when scientists promoted BW, examine why they did so, consider the specific case of Iraqi scientists' involvement with BW, analyze mechanisms for reintegrating Iraqi scientists into the international scientific community, and discuss steps that the international community can take to deter scientists in general from fostering BW.

In the Conclusion, the editor seeks to synthesize the information presented in the preceding chapters in order to answer the questions posed at the outset. This analysis is offered in the hope that it will lead to more effective treaties and compliance regimes and, ultimately, to a world in which the threat of biological warfare, if not eliminated, is contained so that the probability of it occurring is infinitesimal.

PART 1
Biological Weapons and Warfare

1

Implications of the Biotechnology Revolution for Weapons Development and Arms Control

ROBERT P. KADLEC AND ALAN P. ZELICOFF

In 1970, Joshua Lederberg, Nobel Laureate in molecular biology, was one of the first scientists to express concern over the possible misuse of the dramatic advances in molecular biology that were on the horizon. He observed, for example, that it might soon be possible to create infectious agents against which there would be no defense (Geissler, 1984). Soon afterwards, in 1973, Stanley Cohen and Herbert Boyer demonstrated for the first time that it was possible for scientists to deliberately mediate the exchange of genetic information between different strains of bacteria. Using a technique called recombinant DNA (rDNA), they successfully transferred DNA coding for resistance to penicillin from one bacterial genus, *Staphylococcus aureus,* to another, *Escherichia coli* (Jaurin et al., 1987). Subsequent generations of the altered *E. coli* inherited the "foreign" DNA and exhibited penicillin resistance, thereby attesting to the effectiveness of the procedure.

Although advocates have publicized the many benefits of civilian biotechnology—noting, for example, that genetic engineering contributes to solving world food shortages, allows for the creation of potent new medicines, and aids in environmental remediation (BIO, 1990)—other researchers have followed Lederberg's example and expressed fears about the lethal agents that could be created if these revolutionary capabilities were co-opted to enhance clandestine and illicit biological warfare (BW) programs (Hendricks, 1989; Atlas, 1998).

By coincidence, at the same time that the powerful new techniques of genetic engineering were first being demonstrated, the world community was negotiating the Convention on the Prohibition of the Development, Production and Stockpiling of Bacteriological (Biological) and Toxin Weapons, and on Their Destruction (BWC). As it became apparent that the techniques of modern biotechnology had the potential to be diverted to aid in the design of offensive BW weapons, biological arms control experts began to share the concerns expressed by some of the scientists.

Fears of military expropriation of civilian biotechnology research and development have been nurtured over the years by allegations that nations have indeed attempted to create new infectious agents and toxins for use as weapons. Most of these allegations have been made for propaganda purposes and have not been grounded in fact. For example, the Soviet-supported disinformation campaign of the mid-1980s, claiming that HIV and the ensuing AIDS epidemic resulted from genetic engineering experiments conducted by the U.S. Army laboratory at Fort Detrick, Maryland, clearly had no merit (Grmek, 1990).

Other allegations, concerning the Soviet Union and Iraq, had to be taken more seriously. In the late 1980s, the Soviet Union raised suspicions about its intentions when officials publicly stated that they would counter perceived U.S. technical military superiority by exploiting genetic engineering to create pathogens with BW potential (Odom, 1989; Lewis, 1987). This story gained credibility when, according to newspaper accounts, Russian defectors claimed that efforts had indeed been made to develop plague bacteria with enhanced virulence and resistance to antibiotics (Urban, 1993; Gertz, 1992). These claims about the Soviet BW program have been independently verified (Alibek, 1999). In the case of Iraq, even though it has been clearly established that the Iraqis weaponized infectious and toxin agents prior to the Gulf War, it has not been determined that they used rDNA techniques to enhance their biological agents.

Therefore, despite the long-standing fears of arms control experts and biotechnology researchers and despite various claims and allegations to the contrary, there is no hard evidence so far that advances in molecular biology have been diverted for BW applications. Nevertheless, the potential for misuse remains, adding urgency to efforts currently underway to strengthen language in the BWC treaty relating to monitoring and compliance. In this chapter, we investigate the implications for biological arms control of the extraordinary advances in biotechnology that have occurred over the past two and a half decades. First, we review the new techniques available to bioscientists; second, we examine how these methods could be applied to the development of biological weapons; and third, we discuss the challenges faced by negotiators as they attempt to strengthen the BWC in light of these new possibilities.

GENETICS: RECOMBINANT DNA AND OTHER TOOLS OF THE TRADE

Before the rDNA revolution, microbiologists studied the genetic constituents of test organisms through iterative analyses of mutations generated through application of physical (for example, radiation) or chemical stresses. Using this methodology, scientists were able to match properties to genes, make progress in mapping chromosome structure, and generate additional hypotheses for further testing. Over the past twenty-five years, however, new techniques have emerged that have dramatically accelerated the rate of progress and led to deeper understanding of genetic mechanisms. Researchers now can design targeted experiments in which specific genes are cloned, sequenced, and inserted into new organisms. In this way, the properties of the genes in question can be determined with precision by observing the effects on the host cells to which they are transferred. Genetic engineering permits a rapid and controlled means of creating unique variants of microorganisms that was not possible with classical methods (Old and Primrose, 1994). Geneticists can now produce quantities of specific DNA molecules, proteins, and other products and, through the use of rDNA, impart altered characteristics to host organisms (Sims, 1988).

As a result, researchers have been able to map entire genetic codes of various microorganisms. One example of such an effort is the recent multinational collaboration to sequence the DNA of the variola (smallpox) virus before a final decision is made to destroy the last remaining stocks. Much can be learned both from the process of mapping an entire genetic code and from the fully sequenced DNA itself. For example, during the course of the twenty-year effort to complete a comparative analysis of the DNA sequences that code for protein production in the two distinct strains of variola that were responsible for smallpox outbreaks in India in 1967 and Bangladesh in 1975, scientists were able to identify 200 potential proteins that could be produced by each virus (Shchelkunov, Massung, and Esposito, 1995). In combination with independent studies of the Bangladesh-1975 variola virus, this work revealed protein production similar to that encoded in the DNA of the vaccinia virus used as a smallpox vaccine. These variant proteins in the Bangladesh-1975 virus are believed to have augmented the transmissibility and virulence of the virus in humans (Massung et al., 1993, 1994). Although naturally occurring smallpox has been eliminated as a threat, knowledge gained through such analysis allows scientists to identify the mechanisms by which other disease-causing microorganisms infect human hosts, thereby revealing new strategies for prevention and treatment.

The new rDNA methodologies also have important pharmaceutical applications. Proteins possessing enhanced, beneficial bioactive properties are being developed (Old and Primrose, 1994), and the genes coding for production of these compounds have been inserted into new host organisms. For example, *E. coli* have been genetically engineered to produce commercial quantities of valuable complex proteins, including human growth hormones, interferon, insulin, hepatitis B surface antigens, and angiotensin.

Human insulin production through genetic engineering is a dramatic example of the benefits that can accrue to society from civilian use of modern biotechnology. Before the development of these techniques, animal insulin was used in the treatment of diabetes in humans. Now a reliable source of true human insulin is available. In 1978, rDNA techniques first permitted successful laboratory production of human insulin, and in 1982 the Food and Drug Administration (FDA) approved the product for human use. Since then, metric tons of the life-saving protein have been produced and distributed worldwide. Furthermore, in 1995 continued research into human insulin's bioactivity led to the development of a structural analog with a faster absorption rate, resulting in a more rapid onset of lower blood glucose levels in patients receiving this advanced treatment (Howey et al., 1995; Wiefels et al., 1995; Nielsen et al., 1995).

Despite the impressive record in medicine and pharmacology, the greatest practical results of rDNA techniques have been achieved in agriculture. The more mature state of commercial agricultural applications of rDNA biotechnology is reflected in the number of plants and animals that have been subjected to successful genetic engineering and the level of market penetration of these products. U.S. farmers already plant, harvest, and bring to market crops such as tomatoes, tobacco, strawberries, and cotton that are "hardened" through insertion of foreign genes against the adverse effects of disease, insects, and temperature variations (Old and Primrose, 1994). Work is also being done to improve the quality of animal products. In April 1996, Genzyme Transgenics Corporation successfully bred a goat that had been genetically altered to produce milk containing a human protein with anticarcinogenic properties (Johannes, 1996). Progress has also been made, for example, in developing pigs with leaner meat and cows with higher levels of milk production.

IN SEARCH OF THE PERFECT BIOLOGICAL WARFARE AGENT

The relevance to biological warfare of the advances in rDNA capability is that the same insights that lead to improved medical, pharmaceutical, and agricultural products can be used to characterize and exploit human vulnerabilities to toxins and infectious diseases. Experts point out that researchers could overcome the perceived deficiencies of "classical" BW agents by using rDNA techniques to create more potent and more effective weaponized agents (Geissler, 1984). Before discussing the characteristics of an ideal BW agent, we review the applicability to BW design and delivery of the techniques described in the previous section.

First, these powerful new cellular and molecular investigative techniques have expanded the range of toxin agents and harmful bioactive proteins that can be developed. In the past fifteen years, scientists have determined the primary sequence and crystal structure of recognized toxins, improved their understanding of the molecular mechanisms by which infectious agents act on the host, and have discovered new, previously unknown toxins and virulence factors (Hewlett, 1995). Biotechnological progress is rapidly overcoming technical obstacles that served as de facto safeguards against the development of new pathogens. As recently as 1980, a study commissioned by the nations designated as depositories of the BWC treaty (United States, United Kingdom, and the Soviet Union) to explore the potential ramifications of rDNA techniques and other advances in biotechnology prior to the 1981 BWC Review Conference found that the likelihood of creating a fundamentally new agent or toxin was "least likely" because it "would represent a problem of insurmountable complexity" (Sims, 1988: 107). Clearly, this finding must be reassessed in light of new advances.

Second, progress in understanding the mechanisms that promote the virulence and transmissibility of infectious microorganisms could be diverted by BW developers to enhance rather than retard their impact on human hosts. It has been observed, for example, that the exhaustive analysis described above of the smallpox outbreaks in India and Bangladesh in the 1960s and 1970s provides data and insights that could make "unequivocal contributions" to BW development (Geissler, 1984). In a similar vein, researchers have learned to exploit new bioactive proteins that affect the human immune response to infections. For example, in June 1996, the Xoma Corporation was granted a patent for a recombinant protein called bactericidal permeability increasing (BPI) that enhances the effectiveness of widely used antibiotics (*Wall Street Journal*, 1996; Fisher, 1996). According to the company, BPI, which is found naturally in humans, reverses the resistance of some bacteria to certain antibiotics. This development opens the door to the elucidation of new antibiotic targets (Fisher, 1996; Chopra et al., 1996) and could potentially allow for the creation of BW agents with the power to disable host immune responses in target human populations (Geissler, 1984).

Third, new production techniques add to the risk that advanced biological weapons could be developed. Until recently, for example, experts considered that the large-scale use of toxins would be effectively limited by the difficulties associated with natural fermentation. However, advances in industrial fermentation, separation, and purification may be used to overcome these barriers, thereby increasing the diversity and quantity of toxins and harmful bioactive proteins available for military use (Patrick, 1994a).

The biological arms control literature contains several viewpoints on what constitutes the ideal BW agent. In this context, the studies of smallpox already mentioned have particular relevance because the causative virus has many of the properties a BW program might seek when developing antihuman weapons: it is simple to grow, is easily aerosolized, causes a disease with high mortality, and is stable both in storage and after release into the environment. Of course, the characteristics selected by BW weapons designers will vary depending upon the outcome desired. Possible applications of a microbial or toxin agent run the gamut from large-scale tactical and strategic uses in time of war to localized acts of terrorism and assassination. Weapons designers may have the ability to manipulate the intensity of the reaction in the targeted population (ranging from incapacitation to mortality) and the incubation period (the time between agent delivery and onset of symptoms). Further, it must be kept in mind that BW may be waged against a variety of organisms; for example, biological weapons can be designed to attack livestock or agricultural crops as a component of economic warfare.

Given these variables, the list of possible BW agents is a lengthy one (Wiener and Barrett, 1986; Royal Society, 1994; Cordesman, 1990). Table 1.1 lists attributes possessed by known pathogens that a BW weapons designer could modify through genetic engineering or other advanced methods to create more effective agents. In particular, experts agree that rDNA methodologies could be used to enhance the following traits: the virulence of the agents, the resistance of the agents to therapeutic or prophylactic defensive actions in the target populations, the stability and longevity of the agents both in storage and after release, and the rate and efficiency of production (Wiener and Barrett, 1986; Royal Society, 1994; Cordesman, 1990).

Classical BW agents (i.e., those that have been developed and weaponized in the course of past BW programs) have displayed some but not all of the qualities listed in Table 1.1 and have possessed them at

Table 1.1 Biological Warfare Agent Attributes Considered Targets for Genetic Engineering

Attribute to Be Modified	Zilinskas (1986)	Geissler (1986)	Novick and Shulman (1990)	Utgoff (1993)
Virulence	X	X	X	X
Drug resistance	X	X	X	X
Production, storage, and dissemination	X	X	X	X
Protection of own forces	X	X		X
Antigenic structure	X	X	X	
Diagnostic markers		X	X	
Environmental resistance	X	X		X
Efficient vectors		X		
Control of agents	X			X

varying degrees of strength. BW weapons designers who apply the techniques of genetic engineering may attempt to create agents that possess all of the identified attributes and manifest each trait with maximized potency. Next, we consider several desirable characteristics of BW agents (from the point of view of the attacker) and assess the likelihood that recent developments in biotechnology could be applied to enhance these qualities.

Virulence

As mentioned earlier, newspaper reports have alleged that during the early 1980s the Soviet Union pursued offensive BW research utilizing rDNA methodology to develop strains of plague-causing bacteria with enhanced virulence and resistance to antibiotics (Urban, 1993; Gertz, 1992). As noted, these allegations remain speculative; they have not been reliably confirmed. As far as we know, only natural evolutionary mechanisms have been successful in creating organisms with enhanced virulence. Natural selection, however, operates through the modification of genetic code, and as humans acquire the ability to make these modifications on demand, we also acquire the capability to create dangerous new infectious agents.

Microorganisms vary as to their susceptibility to genetic manipulation. Bacteria, for example, have a more stable genetic content than viruses (Lederberg, 1993). The code that determines virulence in bacteria is complex and multifactorial, involving a multitude of genes. The nature of the processes that control changes in virulence has been the subject of several hypotheses. The recent outbreaks of "flesh-eating" streptococci provide a case in point. Some scientists believe that the introduction of viral DNA coding for production of a toxin known as a superantigen into the M1 strain of Group A streptococcus endowed this otherwise manageable bacterium with the capability to cause life-threatening, invasive infections and shock syndromes (Rennie, 1994).

This example is not unique. Recent outbreaks of *E. coli* 0:157 infections in Japan and the northwestern United States caused hemorrhagic uremic syndrome, resulting in acute illness and death in children. The reason for the severity of disease symptoms in these cases was that this strain of *E. coli* produces the so-called Shiga toxin. Before 1982, as far as was known, this toxin was produced exclusively by the bacterial species *Shigella dysenteriae*. As the result of natural DNA exchanges, however, *E. coli* 0:157 acquired the gene coding for Shiga toxin production and, thus, were immediately transformed into a dangerous pathogen characterized by increased virulence.

Viruses manifest an even greater propensity to acquire new genetic material. The "very essence" of a virus results in a "fundamental entanglement with the genetic and metabolic machinery of the host" (Lederberg, 1993: 3). This continual exchange of DNA between virus and host increases the probability of changes in virulence. The influenza virus is a good example of a virus that undergoes frequent changes in its level of virulence as a result of genetic mutations. In a given year, the virulence of a particular strain of influenza may vary significantly from the strain that was prevalent the year before. This variability is thought to result from complex patterns of genetic exchange among the reservoirs of the virus that exist in its various hosts, including aquatic birds, several species of animals, and human beings (Webster, 1993). A recurrence of the deadly influenza pandemic of 1918, which resulted in more than twenty-five million deaths worldwide, remains a possibility (Webster, 1993).

The outbreak of the Sin Nombre Hantavirus in the southwestern U.S. provides another example of the unexpected changes that can occur in the virulence of a virus. Hantavirus is recognized as a globally distributed pathogen typically causing a hemorrhagic syndrome associated with kidney failure. In contrast, the primary symptom in the New Mexico outbreak was fulminant respiratory distress syndrome virulent enough to cause 50 percent mortality in previously healthy young adults. Epidemiological investigations finally identified the offending pathogen as a type of Hantavirus found in the local deer mouse population. The mice excrete the virus in their urine and feces. Humans become infected incidentally when the aerosolized excreta is inhaled.

The Sin Nombre Hantavirus has a significantly different and more lethal symptom complex than strains previously identified in other areas of the world. Retrospective analysis of stored serum collected from acute respiratory distress syndrome (ARDS) cases demonstrated that Sin Nombre had caused disease sporadically in the United States for many years. Since the New Mexico outbreak, medical epidemiologists have identified a second Hantavirus variant in Argentina that also causes pulmonary distress. Despite this similarity, the Argentinean strain varies from the North American Sin Nombre type in that it apparently spreads via human-to-human contact (Wells, 1997).

These examples demonstrate that well-known and manageable infectious agents can be transformed naturally into organisms with markedly increased virulence. The unexpected emergence of natural pathogens with enhanced potency underscores the dangerous potential of illicit use of genetic engineering for BW purposes. Even if the complexity of host/agent dynamics and genetic control of virulence make it unlikely that a country pursuing a BW program could succeed in creating novel pathogens with enhanced virulence in the short run, this should not give rise to complacency. First, as mentioned above, the extraordinary pace of developments in biotechnology means that presently existing technical barriers may soon be overcome. Second, BW programs may be able to take advantage of the naturally occurring pathogens with enhanced virulence that emerge from time to time. In fact, published reports suggest that both the Soviet Union and the Japanese cult, Aum Shinrikyo, sought to obtain viral isolates during recent outbreaks in Africa of Lassa fever and Ebola fever (Kaplan and Marshall, 1996; Garrett, 1995). The concept of "bioprospecting," that is, searching for microbial species that produce natural substances with desirable properties, is not new. Pharmaceutical companies scour the world's soil and waters seeking animals, plants, and microorganisms that produce bioactive compounds with possible applications in the pharmacological and chemical industries (Mukerjee, 1994). It is not surprising that others with sinister motives would bioprospect for organisms that possess disease-causing, lethal properties.

Beyond the possibility of direct use of emerging disease-causing microorganisms, their genetic material could be appropriated as a source of DNA coding for particular traits with BW relevance. Virulence factors could be isolated and inserted into existing pathogens with known epidemiological properties to create more potent disease variations. The Sin Nombre Hantavirus may represent nature's version of this phenomenon. This virus acquired an unidentified virulence factor, probably from another microbe, that altered its disease expression. BW developers may attempt to replicate this type of hybridization to create weaponizable agents, taking advantage of the propensity of viruses to integrate foreign genetic material and express production of new proteins (Geissler, 1984, 1986).

In summary, three methods are available to BW weapons developers seeking pathogens characterized by increased virulence. First, they may attempt to use genetic engineering to design new infectious or toxin agents; second, they may seek to employ naturally emerging variants without modification; third, they may combine the first two methods to use emerging diseases as a source of virulence factors that can be transferred to known pathogens. Though the first may be beyond the capability of scientific knowledge at present, the second and third pose immediate threats that cannot be ignored.

Stability

The lack of environmental stability has traditionally been perceived as the primary factor limiting the military effectiveness of most BW agents. Ambient conditions, such as ultraviolet light or high relative humidity, act to degrade BW agents, thereby negatively affecting their ability to survive in the open environment and infect intended target populations. Only the anthrax spore, with its protective coat, is considered an environmentally hardened BW agent. BW weapons developers may now be able to overcome the limitations caused by environmental effects through the application of modern biotechnology, including genetic engineering. Two examples are illustrative.

The first example relates to advances in the longevity and potency of a biopesticide used in agriculture throughout the world. The bacterial species *Bacillus thuringiensis* (Bt) produces a toxin that is lethal to certain insect pests. In its natural state, however, Bt toxin quickly loses potency after being sprayed on the crops to be protected. Researchers have overcome Bt toxin's limited effective lifespan by inserting the gene coding for its production into a new microbial host, *Pseudomonas fluorescens*. During fermentation, *P. fluorescens* endowed with the introduced gene produces Bt toxin in a crystalline form within its cell wall. The *P. fluorescens* cell then is killed with a fixative, encapsulating the toxin molecules within the cell wall. In this form, the Bt toxin has a significantly longer environmental half-life (Frenc, 1994).

In a second example, researchers have developed a process to encapsulate the vegetative cells of *Pseudomonas aeruginosa* in alginate, a natural product of algae. In their unaltered form, *P. aeruginosa* cells have no protective spore coat and, when released into the environment, have a relatively short lifespan since they are adversely affected by chemicals in the soil. In contrast, the genetically engineered, encapsulated cells manifest both increased resistance to chemical disinfectants and increased longevity (Weir, Lee, and Trevors, 1996).

The implication of these developments is that techniques applicable to peaceful pursuits may be used by those intent on developing agents for BW to enhance their environmental stability. In doing so, BW agents would persist longer at the site of dispersal, increasing the danger of infection to anyone passing through the affected site.

Antigenic Structure

Infectious agents generally display antigenic characteristics; that is, they stimulate an immune system response in the host. Medical and public health officials exploit this effect to protect uninfected populations through immunization campaigns. Once exposed to antigenic markers of a pathogen (usually through the use of weakened or inactive strains in a vaccine), the immune system of the vaccinated individual creates antibodies coded to defend against the particular agent. If BW developers were able to alter these markers through genetic engineering, it is conceivable that the redesigned pathogens would be able to circumvent the immune system defenses of the target population. In such a scenario, even individuals immunized against common childhood diseases (e.g., diphtheria or whooping cough) would be susceptible to infectious microorganisms whose antigenic structure had been slightly altered.

The influenza virus is an example of a naturally occurring organism that alters its antigenic markers frequently through a process called antigenic drift. As a result, vaccines against the disease have to be reformulated periodically to ensure that the immune systems of those vaccinated will recognize the virus and produce protective antibodies. Certain bacteria have also demonstrated the ability to change antigenic markers. For example, a strain of *Streptococcus pneumoniae* was recently discovered to have acquired two surface-protein genes from a related strain through natural genetic recombination that permitted it to elude immune system surveillance (Borysiewicz et al., 1996).

Medical researchers have learned to create similar effects through genetic engineering; the antigenic or immune-stimulating characteristics of viral agents have been modified to express foreign antigenic markers. This technique is being exploited to create novel vaccines that protect against diseases for which no preventative inoculation previously existed, such as cancer, or that stimulate defenses against multiple diseases in a single treatment (Marwick, 1994). In the cancer treatment, carrier viruses express tumor markers that allow the human immune system to develop a response against the cancer cells. An example of a new, multipathogen vaccine is the vaccinia virus, previously used to immunize against smallpox, which has been modified to express the antigenic markers for such diseases as rabies, influenza, AIDS, measles, hepatitis B, and malaria (Smith, Mackett, and Moss, 1983; Brochier et al., 1994; Moelans et al., 1995; Gallate, Beauverger, and Wild, 1995; Suplee, 1996).

These examples suggest that it is at least theoretically possible to use rDNA to create organisms with altered antigenic markers that could circumvent the protective effect of vaccine-induced immunity. It is also possible that such altered organisms could evade detection by existing technologies that use antibody-based tests to identify the presence of BW agents in various environmental and medical samples (see Chapter 4).

Production and Delivery

Other challenges faced by designers of "classical" BW weapons included restricted production capacity and difficulties relating to delivery and dispersal of the agent. Modern advances in computer science and biotechnology threaten to remove these limitations as well. For example, sophisticated new computer technology, including both hardware and software, has permitted an exponential increase in the rates at which potentially dangerous microorganisms can be produced. The combination of improved growth media and more precise control of other essential growth factors has made continuous fermentation possible (Huxsoll, 1994). As a result, microbial production yield is now 100 to 1,000 times greater than it was thirty years ago.

Simultaneously, the commercialization of biopesticides has led to the integration of enhanced production and deployment mechanisms. These advances include industrial-scale fermentation, efficient microencapsulation, improved methods for transferring genes that code for toxin production, and more effective techniques for large-scale aerosol dissemination (Huxsoll, 1994).

Military experts emphasize that biological weapons are complex, integrated systems shaped by the interaction between tactical and strategic requirements and constraints inherent in the design and production process. Particularly in the case of biological warfare, the whole is greater than the sum of its parts; effective BW weapons are much more than merely biological material. Military effectiveness can also be influenced by command and control structures, targeting decisions, efficiency of delivery devices, and operator safety. Moreover, the special properties of biological agents (e.g., the inability to tolerate ultraviolet light or explosive shock) and their human targets (e.g., respiratory susceptibility and skin impermeability) directly affect weapon functioning. Application of advances in a range of disciplines, including respiratory physiology, immune system response, aerosol physics, large-volume drying and sizing of particles, microencapsulation, and meteorology are required in order to produce effective biological weapon systems.

Terrorists and nation-states clearly have differing requirements and expectations for biological weapons that can determine the nature of the attack (Henderson, 1999). Delivery devices can take a number of forms: spray tanks mounted on aircraft, bomblets, modified agricultural field-foggers, packages left on subway cars, or even small, covert assassination weapons, such as the famous umbrella adapted to inject a ricin-filled bead from its tip into the leg of Bulgarian expatriate Georgi Markov in the London Underground in 1977.

Although targeting decisions and delivery capability may vary, all the characteristics desirable in the BW agent itself—virulence, stability, disguised antigen structure, and production efficiency—may be subject to enhancement through genetic engineering. In the next section, we examine how the biological arms community has attempted to respond to these challenges.

THE IMPLICATIONS FOR BIOLOGICAL ARMS CONTROL

For almost two decades, arms control experts have been concerned with the possible application of advances in biotechnology to BW development. After the first review conference in 1981, the BWC state parties agreed that efforts to genetically engineer BW agents were prohibited by Article I of the convention as written (Sims, 1988; Geissler, 1984). Article I states that it is illegal to engage in research, development, or production of biological agents or their byproducts for any purpose other than peaceful or prophylactic applications. However, many signatory nations have since come to believe that the convention must be strengthened and that the prohibition against the use of recombinant technologies must be made explicit and subject to credible monitoring for compliance. As ratified in 1975, the BWC does not incorporate legally binding measures to ensure compliance by its participants.

As a first step in this direction, the BWC state parties created an Ad Hoc Group at a special conference held during September 1994. It was charged with the mandate "to consider appropriate measures, including possible verification measures, and draft proposals to strengthen the Convention" that would be legally binding (BWC, 1994). It is generally agreed that the BWC as written applies to agents enhanced using rDNA techniques, but the challenge remains to draft, adopt, and implement credible verification protocols to ensure that advances in biotechnology are not diverted for illicit purposes.

One facet of current negotiations is the effort to make declaration of so-called special interest activities mandatory. This would require nations to disclose any research with potential BW relevance being conducted at either military or civilian facilities (e.g., biodefense institutions or vaccine manufacturers, with still other categories being considered). The major stumbling block to agreement on such a provision is that it would be too broad and thus impossible to enforce; in some cases, even high school biology classes now utilize recombinant techniques in laboratory demonstrations (Iovine, 1994). One possible way to narrow the wording would be to restrict the disclosure requirement to those institutions working with a specified lists of agents with known BW applicability (e.g., agents that cause anthrax, plague, etc.). Any effort to generate a limited list of potentially dangerous agents, however, is likely to present problems because modern techniques may make it possible to modify almost any pathogen for BW purposes. Exclusion of particular toxins or pathogenic substances from the list could effectively limit the application of Article I. Furthermore, the Ad Hoc Group charged with drafting a legally binding protocol has not yet decided whether the appropriate target for regulation should be the microorganism itself or the genetic material it contains.

No matter how these issues are decided, complex, technical problems relating to verification will remain (Zilinskas, 1998a). First, in order to verify any declaration of a listed recombinant activity, techniques have to be developed to allow monitoring agencies to characterize the genetic constituents of sample organisms and verify legitimate use. Given the potential political consequences of an inaccurate determination, these analytical methodologies would have to undergo significant technical validation to ensure sufficient sensitivity and specificity to limit the likelihood of false negatives or positives. Just as there is now an international "arms race" between athletes and investigative bodies charged with discovering the use of illegal performance enhancers, nations attempting to hide their BW programs would seek to mask the true nature and intent of their research. Any system established through the BWC to monitor biotechnology activities on a global scale would of necessity require an enormous political and scientific infrastructure and would almost certainly be subject to cheating and subversion.

CONCLUSION

In the twenty-five years since the pioneering experiment of Cohen and Boyer first demonstrated the power of genetic engineering, beneficial civilian applications of modern biotechnology have led to dramatic improvements in agriculture, pharmaceuticals, and medicine. Fortunately, as far as we know, the fears of misuse first expressed by Joshua Lederberg have not been realized. Nevertheless, the possibility of resurgent biological warfare programs built around toxin and pathogenic agents enhanced through genetic recombination will be a threat to world security as long as nations or terrorist groups seek to develop weapons of mass destruction. Revelations from the former Soviet Union, Iraq, and Aum Shinrikyo are frightening reminders that despite modern sensibilities and the ratification of the BWC, there are still those who attempt to exploit disease as a weapon of war.

The use of biological weapons is prohibited by the Geneva Protocol of 1925, and mere possession of biological materials incompatible with "prophylactic, protective or other peaceful purposes" is prohibited by the BWC. The BWC has no verification regime, however, nor are any reliable means available for detecting national BW programs (let alone small-scale rogue terrorist operations). The United Nations Special Commission (UNSCOM) has only succeeded in characterizing Iraq's BW program (to the extent that it has succeeded) through the combination of a long-term, repetitive regime of intrusive inspections and the fortuitous acquisition of information from a high-level Iraqi defector. It is likely that several nations have accomplished all but the final step in the development of BW programs, opting for a covert, "just-in-time" concept for deployment of an array of biological weaponry if the need arises. The UNSCOM experience in Iraq illustrates the enormous difficulty of uncovering such activities.

It is quite possible that genetically enhanced biological weapons will be used in our lifetimes—by terrorists; in limited, tactical battlefield encounters; or as a component of broad, strategic attacks against enemy populations and economic assets. In the absence of credible means to detect and deter the development of BW, threatened nations must develop and maintain a strong technical and public policy BW defense posture.

BW defense is based on physical protection and immunization prior to attacks, rapid detection and identification of disseminated toxins and pathogens during biological strikes, and effective treatment in the aftermath of exposure. Efforts are constantly underway to improve all three components. Actions in the public policy realm should support a strong technical defense posture. These include supporting international nonproliferation accords, maintaining an intense intelligence focus on potential BW aggressors, and contributing to regular assessments of the global threat of BW programs (e.g., the yearly Pell report [ACDA, 1996a]).

The international community should make vigorous use of international arms control agreements such as the BWC to strengthen international norms against the acquisition of biological materials for nonpeaceful purposes. It is unlikely that state parties to the BWC will agree to intrusive inspection measures such as those adopted in the Chemical Weapons Convention because of the inherent dual-use ambiguity of agents, technologies, and research infrastructure at declared sites (Zelicoff, 1995). Nevertheless, under certain circumstances, such as unusual disease outbreaks or credible allegations of contravened activities, inspections would quickly yield unequivocal verdicts on the presence or absence of illicit materials as defined by the BWC (Tucker, 1996b; Wheelis, 1992) and should be permitted under the aegis of a BWC protocol.

As dramatic progress in civilian biotechnology goes forward, technical obstacles that have prevented development of enhanced BW agents continue to fall. The expanding reaches of global information resources, such as the Internet, compound the risk. Scientists in all fields benefit enormously from broadened opportunities for communication with their peers and instantaneous access to new developments, but the downside is that it is impossible to guard the secrets of dual-use technologies that could be exploited in clandestine BW programs. Even countries or organizations with modest means and relatively unsophisticated scientific resources can master the technologies needed to produce biological weapons for military or terrorist purposes. The potential danger posed by the synergy of these two revolutions—biotechnology and computerized information—has yet to be fully recognized or assessed by those charged with monitoring BW proliferation.

While arms control authorities proceed with efforts to strengthen the language of the BWC, the scientific and medical communities in the civilian sector must accept responsibility for ensuring that the spirit of the convention is also upheld, by conforming to worldwide norms against BW research and development. Adherence to ethical standards by researchers with the specialized training and experience necessary to manipulate rDNA is the first and most important defense against the misuse of these techniques (see Chapter 11). While work to draft a binding protocol to the BWC continues, we must remember that the ultimate success of efforts to prevent misuse of modern biotechnology depends as much on what happens in the laboratory as on what takes place around the negotiating table.

2

Motivations For and Against Proliferation: The Case of the Middle East

Jonathan B. Tucker

If policies to halt and reverse the spread of biological weapons are to be effective, they must be grounded in an understanding of the external and internal factors that motivate countries to acquire these weapons. Of particular interest is why only a small minority of countries that possess the technological infrastructure needed for biological weapons production have actually pursued this option. The available evidence suggests that multiple incentives and disincentives, acting in combination, have the net effect of motivating countries to seek an offensive biological warfare (BW) program or to refrain from doing so.

States suspected of having ongoing BW programs are clustered in two conflict-ridden regions of the world. Six are located in North Africa and the Middle East (Egypt, Iraq, Iran, Israel, Libya, and Syria) and another five are concentrated in East Asia (Burma, China, North Korea, South Korea, and Taiwan). Other alleged BW proliferators include Russia, which may not have fully eliminated the vast program inherited from the former Soviet Union, and South Africa, which during the apartheid era had an active BW program that was reportedly dismantled in 1993 (Taylor, 1995). Cuba, India, Laos, Pakistan, and Vietnam also appear on some lists of suspected BW proliferators (U.S. Congress, 1993c: 82; Collins, 1994: 2; Carus, 1998a).

Based on the assumption that a state's decision whether or not to acquire biological weapons derives from a calculus of incentives and disincentives, this chapter lays out a typology of plausible motivating factors. The analysis then compares this typology with the limited open-source data available on suspected BW proliferators in the Middle East. Discrepancies between proliferation behavior predicted by the model and that actually observed are then explained by suggesting a number of domestic *predisposing factors* that may encourage governments to pursue or renounce a BW capability despite external incentives or disincentives that may be pushing in the opposite direction.

TECHNICAL PREREQUISITES FOR A BW CAPABILITY

Two technical prerequisites for the acquisition of biological weapons are the availability of a suitable technological infrastructure, either indigenous or imported, and scientific and technical expertise in the fields of microbiology and industrial fermentation. Compared to nuclear or even chemical weapons, a low-tech BW capability is relatively affordable and can be achieved without highly specialized equipment and know-how. Indeed, any country with a basic fermentation industry capable of producing beer, wine, single-cell protein, biopesticides, vaccines, or antibiotics has sufficient expertise to make crude preparations of BW agents such as anthrax or botulinum toxin, particularly if the proliferant state is prepared to cut corners on worker safety and environmental protection (U.S. Congress, 1993d: 85). The chief technical hurdle involves "weaponizing" biological agents to ensure effective dissemination over a large area, although the United States and the Soviet Union largely solved these problems during the early 1960s (Patrick, 1994b).

Of the more than 100 countries that possess dual-use fermentation or pharmaceutical plants capable of producing BW agents, only about twelve have reportedly done so (U.S. Congress, 1993c: 82). This observation suggests that "demand-side" factors play the dominant role in driving the proliferation of biological weapons, although it is also true that some states seeking a BW capability have been constrained by a lack of technical expertise, particularly with respect to weaponization.

INCENTIVES FOR PROLIFERATION

The dense veil of secrecy surrounding BW programs suggests that biological weapons do not have the same prestige value as nuclear weapons. It therefore appears that the decision to acquire a BW capability is based most often on the perception of an acute security threat, accompanied by a deficit in the ability of the state to counter that threat with alternative means. Security-related incentives and disincentives for the acquisition of biological weapons are summarized in Table 2.1 and are discussed in greater detail next.

Table 2.1   Security Incentives and Disincentives for Acquiring Biological Weapons

Incentives
1. To deter chemical, biological, or nuclear attack by regional or extraregional powers
2. As a force-multiplier against regional or extraregional powers possessing superior conventional capabilities
3. To achieve regional hegemony by intimidating neighboring states
4. As a tactical weapon for battlefield use
5. For covert warfare or economic sabotage against enemy states
6. For state-supported terrorism
7. For counterinsurgency warfare against internal groups
8. For assassination and harassment of political opponents

Disincentives
1. Absence of a perceived security deficit or the existence of a credible security guarantee
2. Limited deterrent value compared with nuclear arms or the perception that BW lacks military utility
3. Risk of provoking offsetting weapons programs by other states or presumptive military action
4. Security problems associated with maintaining a BW capability
5. International norms against acquisition and use
6. Global and regional arms control regimes, if backed up with political or economic sanctions
7. Availability of effective defenses
8. Opportunity costs and resource trade offs with conventional arms

In-kind Deterrence

Most countries that possess or seek a BW capability apparently do not intend to use it tactically on the battlefield but instead view it as a strategic deterrent. The goal may be to restrain adversaries from attacking cities and high-value military targets, to limit the adversary's military options, or to prevent total military defeat by retaining an escalatory option as a last resort. Because of the dynamic of competitive armament, as soon as one country acquires a BW capability, its potential adversaries may seek to fill the resulting security deficit by developing an in-kind retaliatory capability, giving rise to a chain reaction of proliferation moves. This phenomenon is not inevitable, however, since states may choose an alternative means of defense and deterrence, such as threatening retaliation with some other weapon of mass destruction (WMD) or joining a military alliance.

Deterrence of Nuclear Weapons Use

Some countries may view BW as a means to deter the use against them of other WMD, particularly nuclear. The mating of biological weapons to long-range delivery systems such as ballistic missiles or tactical aircraft makes it possible to launch strategic BW attacks against enemy population centers. Since biological weapons have the potential to inflict mass casualties on the same scale as a nuclear attack, countries that feel threatened by nuclear-armed adversaries may seek a BW capability to provide rough strategic parity (Carus, 1991: 35). Accordingly, a BW capability may be attractive to countries that seek a means of strategic deterrence or coercion but for whom nuclear weapons are technically or financially out of reach.

In general, the list of suspected BW proliferators can be divided into two categories based on the technical and financial resources at their disposal. More developed states, such as China, Russia, Iran, and Iraq, have pursued the full panoply of weapons of mass destruction, with a primary emphasis on nuclear arms. In contrast, less-developed states such as Libya, for whom the nuclear option remains technically and financially inaccessible, have focused their efforts on the acquisition of chemical and biological weapons. Countries that seek nuclear weapons may also pursue biological weapons as an interim strategic deterrent—for example, to deter preemptive strikes against their nuclear installations—until they can build and deploy secure nuclear forces.

During the Cold War, the Soviet Union's reluctance to extend its nuclear umbrella to Arab client-states in the Middle East such as Egypt, Iraq, Libya, and Syria may have led Moscow to assist some of these countries in acquiring an indigenous BW capability. With the end of the Cold War, the disappearance of Soviet security guarantees may have given these states new reasons to *retain* a BW capability. Having lost Moscow as a security guarantor and principal supplier of conventional arms, Egypt (after 1974), Iraq, Libya, and Syria have since placed an increasing emphasis on nonconventional weapons to maintain a strategic balance with Israel or Iran.

An apparent paradox concerning the value of biological weapons for deterrence is that countries generally do not admit to possessing them. The high level of secrecy surrounding BW programs naturally raises the question of how an undeclared capability can provide a credible deterrent. One possible explanation is that such weapons do not have to be formally declared to be effective for deterrence. As Israel's undeclared nuclear program has shown, states can hint effectively at a "bomb in the basement" without officially acknowledging its existence (Cohen, 1998). Suspicions that a given state possesses biological weapons are particularly difficult to prove, given the current lack of a verification regime for the 1972 Convention on the Prohibition of the Development, Production and Stockpiling of Bacteriological (Biological) and Toxin Weapons, and on Their Destruction (BWC) and the reluctance of national intelligence agencies to release sensitive information obtained by clandestine means. For these reasons, BW proliferators may obtain the benefits of deterrence or coercion vis-à-vis potential adversaries without exposing themselves to international opprobrium.

Asymmetric Strategy

Some developing countries, having learned the lessons of Iraq's defeat in the 1991 Gulf War and Serbia's debacle in Kosovo in 1999, may pursue an "asymmetric strategy" in which they seek to pit their military strengths against the vulnerabilities of advanced industrialized states that are vastly superior in conventional military power. Since biological weapons can inflict mass casualties yet are far cheaper than conventional bombs and delivery systems, they offer a potential means for poor countries to offset the advantage provided by high-technology conventional weapons. The goal of this strategy would be either to deter outside intervention altogether or to prevent the stronger side from bringing to bear the full weight of its conventional military power. For example, Syria's chemical and biological warfare capabilities may have played a role in restraining Israel's response to a provocative Syrian troop redeployment near Israeli positions on the Golon Heights in August 1996. According to Israeli defense analyst Dany Shoham, "The fact that there is a Syrian [chemical/biological] arsenal . . . affects the balance of power with Israel" (Rodan, 1996).

In regions of geostrategic importance such as the oil-rich Middle East, actors pursuing regional ambitions may affect the interests of the great powers, creating the potential for outside military intervention. This threat has become more acute since the end of the Cold War and the breakup of the Soviet Union. Countries that formerly relied on Moscow to deter U.S. intervention in the region have lost their superpower patron and must place greater reliance on their own military resources. Military intervention involves an inherent imbalance of interests and motivation between the intervening state and the regional power because the physical security of the intervening state is not at risk, whereas the very survival of the attacked country may be in jeopardy. For this reason, a credible threat of biological warfare could be effective in deterring or curtailing intervention by regional or extra-regional powers (Roberts, 1994: 56).

Tactical Military Use

A few states (such as Iraq and Libya) appear to view biological weapons as a "force-multiplier" to compensate for the weakness of conventional military capabilities in the face of a numerically or technologically superior adversary. For most battlefield applications, biological weapons have limited utility because they are hard to disseminate in a controlled manner and produce incapacitating effects only after an incubation period lasting several hours to days. Nevertheless, biological weapons might be employed tactically in a limited range of military operations for which immediate results are not required and the risk of exposing friendly troops is low. Such contingencies include attacks against fixed enemy positions in a drawn-out war of attrition; special-operations missions against targets deep behind enemy lines such as airfields, supply dumps, port facilities, command centers, logistical staging areas, and reserve forces; and attacks against large naval vessels passing through choke points (Zilinskas, 1990).

Iraq, for example, conceived of biological weapons as a war-fighting capability against Iran, as well as a strategic deterrent against Israel. After a failed effort to produce biological weapons in the mid-1970s, Iraq revived its BW program during the Iran-Iraq War. In 1983, one of Iraq's most eminent microbiologists, Nassir al-Hindawi, wrote a secret paper for top officials of the ruling Ba'ath political party in which he outlined how production of biological weapons could become a major military asset. A key goal of the Iraqi BW program was to develop inexpensive weapons capable of killing thousands of Iranian soldiers and sowing panic in the enemy's ranks (Smith, 1997).

The military utility of biological weapons is obviously greater if the adversary lacks effective detectors or defensive gear. Biological warfare also may have a potent psychological impact, including the potential to induce terror and undermine the morale of enemy troops. There are also operational benefits to be gained by forcing enemy troops into cumbersome protective gear, which degrades military performance and slows the tempo of combat operations.

Pursuit of Regional Hegemony

Some states, such as Iraq, have acquired biological weapons and other WMD as a means of intimidating their neighbors and achieving regional hegemony. Before the 1991 Gulf War, Baghdad aspired to political leadership of the Arab world by offering to extend its deterrent capabilities to friendly states in the region. In a speech in June 1990, Iraqi president Saddam Hussein stated, "We will strike at them [Israel] with all the arms in our possession if they attack Iraq or the Arabs. . . . Whoever strikes at the Arabs, we will strike back from Iraq" (Baghdad Radio, 1990). The use of the term "all the arms in our possession" implies that asymmetrical WMD responses were being considered, although biological weapons were never explicitly mentioned. To benefit from Iraq's protection, however, other Arab states would first have to accept Iraqi leadership. Thus, Iraq's offer of extended deterrence sought to position Saddam at the forefront of the defense of the Arab nation.

Sabotage and Terrorism

Biological weapons could be acquired for covert warfare, such as sabotage actions behind enemy lines by special-operations forces and attacks against civilians by state-sponsored terrorists (Tucker, 1996). Plant and animal disease agents may be employed covertly against enemy crops and livestock to cause starvation or economic hardship and to undermine civilian morale. Biological weapons are well suited to covert use because they are effective in small amounts, cause acute symptoms only after a delay of hours or days, and can be selected to simulate a natural outbreak of disease, giving the attacker "plausible deniability" to avoid responsibility and retribution.

Counterinsurgency and Assassination

In civil conflicts, BW attacks could be employed in counterinsurgency operations to kill, incapacitate, or terrorize unprotected rebels and their families and drive them out of contested areas. The internal use of biological warfare poses little risk of retaliation in kind and could also be conducted covertly, reducing the risk of international condemnation or sanctions. Biological and toxin weapons have also been employed by the secret services of a few states (e.g., communist Bulgaria and apartheid South Africa) for the assassination of political dissidents or armed rebels.

DISINCENTIVES FOR PROLIFERATION

Absence of a Perceived Security Deficit

Many states do not perceive a need to acquire WMD of any kind, either because they do not face an acute security deficit or because they benefit from a credible security guarantee on the part of a powerful regional hegemon or global superpower. Other states possess powerful conventional forces that they consider sufficient for their security or have other WMD (e.g., nuclear weapons) that could deter the use of biological weapons against them.

Uncertain Military Utility

Although biological and toxin agents are potentially capable of inflicting massive casualties, they cannot destroy military hardware or infrastructure, and their dissemination and persistence are strongly affected by atmospheric and meteorological conditions. A BW proliferator would face significant technical difficulties in developing an efficient means of delivery and preserving the virulence of microbial pathogens stored for long periods as a deterrent. (In contrast, militarily significant quantities of a BW agent for offensive use might be produced "to order" shortly before a planned attack.) Another disincentive is that the large-scale production of BW agents could threaten the health of key scientists and the proliferator's own population. For example, an accidental release of anthrax spores from a Soviet military biological facility in 1979 led to a major outbreak of human anthrax in the Russian city of Sverdlovsk (Leitenberg, 1992).

Limited Deterrent Value

It seems unlikely that biological weapons could provide the same level of deterrence as nuclear weapons. Nuclear retaliation would be immediate and devastating and would destroy military equipment and infrastructure as well as troops (Freedman, 1983). In contrast, biological weapons could potentially kill or incapacitate large numbers of enemy soldiers and civilians but are slow, uncertain in their effects, and incapable of destroying military hardware and buildings. Moreover, whereas nuclear weapons have already been used twice in war to devastating effect, the horrors of a large-scale BW attack remain (thankfully) hypothetical. Because of this lack of historical experience, a BW-based deterrent may be somewhat less credible.

Risk of Provoking Countermeasures

Acquiring a BW capability may prove counterproductive by raising tensions with neighboring states and causing them to deploy offsetting capabilities, triggering a regional arms race and increasing the risk of war. Countries may also hesitate to pursue a BW capability for fear of provoking massive retaliation from a hegemonic power. Prior to the 1991 Gulf War, U.S. secretary of state James A. Baker III met with Iraq's deputy prime minister Tariq Aziz and "purposely left the impression that the use of chemical or biological agents by Iraq could invite tactical nuclear retaliation" (Baker, 1995a: 359). This action was a bluff intended to deter Baghdad from employing its nonconventional arsenal, since President George Bush had already ruled out U.S. nuclear retaliation if the Iraqis launched chemical or biological attacks. In March 1996, however, U.S. defense secretary William Perry sought to establish a broader deterrent threat by warning that the United States would answer any chemical or biological attack with "overwhelming force" while refusing to rule out the use of nuclear weapons (Seiff, 1996).

Security Problems Associated with a BW Capability

The acquisition of any type of WMD necessitates the creation of strict command-and-control arrangements for their handling, deployment, and release. In a highly centralized state, such arrangements are problematic

because of the unavoidable trade-off between delegation of release authority, which increases the risk of unauthorized or accidental use, and tight central control, which increases the vulnerability of the command structure to
"decapitation" in a preemptive attack (Fever, 1992–1993). Moreover, autocratic leaders who do not trust their own armed forces may be reluctant to
delegate control of biological weapons to subordinate commanders, for fear
that the weapons might be used against them in a coup d'état.

Availability of Defenses

The military utility of biological weapons depends to a large extent on the
ability of likely adversaries to detect an attack and to defend themselves
effectively. Since nearly all BW agents cannot penetrate the skin and must
be inhaled to cause infection, a simple mask offers adequate protection—
provided troops are warned of an imminent attack in time to don their protective gear. Thus, the attractiveness of biological weapons for battlefield
use is considerably reduced if the opposing troops are equipped with defensive equipment such as standoff detectors, individual protective masks, and
collective shelters.

Legal and Moral Constraints

Biological weapons are widely considered abhorrent and have been formally banned under international law. This behavioral norm appears to be
deeply rooted in an innate human fear of infectious disease. Although many
states consider nuclear deterrence—as distinct from actual use—as morally
defensible, the possession of biological weapons is widely viewed with
repugnance. Given the choice, then, most aspiring proliferators would prefer to acquire nuclear rather than biological weapons of mass destruction
and appear to have pursued the latter as a less desirable or transitional
alternative.

Nevertheless, the legal ban on development, production, stockpiling,
and transfer of biological weapons enshrined in the BWC can help con-
strain proliferation only if violations are punished with tough political and
economic sanctions. During the 1980–1988 Iran-Iraq War, the norm against
BW use was seriously weakened by the muted international condemnation
that followed Iraq's large-scale employment of chemical weapons in blatant
violation of the 1925 Geneva Protocol. William Webster, then U.S. Director
of Central Intelligence, expressed concern that the international community's failure to punish Iraq for its use of chemical weapons also meant that
"the moral barrier to biological warfare has been breached" (U.S. Senate,
1989: 30). The norm against acquisition of biological weapons has been
further eroded by the lack of verification and enforcement measures in the

BWC and allegations that major powers such as Russia and China have systematically violated the treaty. In an effort to strengthen the BWC, an Ad Hoc Group of state parties is currently negotiating a legally binding compliance protocol (Tucker, 1998).

CASE STUDIES

Biological weapons proliferation in the Middle East is a function both of the Arab-Israeli strategic competition and of other regional conflicts and rivalries. As defense analyst Peter Jones has pointed out, "Israel's nuclear policy may in some cases serve as a convenient public shield for other programs that may have gone ahead regardless of Israel's status. In looking closely at the chemical and biological weapons programs of other regional states—and at the actual cases of use of such weapons—one sees a pattern of development and use for reasons largely having to do with inter-Arab and Arab-Iranian conflicts, as well as with internal security in some countries" (Jones, 1998). The following case studies examine six countries in North Africa and the Middle East that are believed to have some type of BW capability, ranging from latent to weaponized, and two that do not.

Egypt

Capabilities. Egypt has a substantial capability in civilian biotechnology and appears to have an offensive BW program. According to the 1996 arms control compliance report published by the U.S. Arms Control and Disarmament Agency (ACDA), "The United States believes that Egypt has [*sic*] developed biological warfare agents by 1972. There is no evidence to indicate that Egypt had eliminated this capability and it remains likely that the Egyptian capability to conduct BW continues to exist" (ACDA, 1997a: 87).

Motivations. Although Egypt does not admit to possessing biological weapons, Egyptian officials have stated that, *in principle,* their acquisition by Arab states is justified by the need to offset Israel's undeclared nuclear capability, as well as its suspected BW potential. In 1972, President Anwar Sadat warned that "we have the instruments of biological warfare in the refrigerator and we will not use them unless they [the Israelis] begin to use them" (SIPRI, 1973a: 241). This statement indicates that Egypt believed Israel possessed biological weapons or had the industrial potential to produce them rapidly.

In 1976, Egyptian minister of war General Muhammad Abd al-Gani al-Gamasy warned that "weapons of mass extermination are not limited to nuclear weapons. Egypt has enough of the other types of weapons of mass extermination and it has the capability of retaliating to an Israeli nuclear blow by making use of these weapons" (Feldman, 1982: 69). In July 1988, the former head of Egypt's chemical warfare program, Mamdouh Ateya, also hinted that Egypt had acquired chemical and biological warfare capabilities to neutralize the coercive power of Israel's nuclear arsenal. "A chemical and biological Arab force could provide a temporary protective umbrella until we achieve nuclear parity with Israel," he said. "With that force at our disposal, I believe Israel will think twice about embarking on any hostile act against the Arabs" (Reuters, 1988). It is unclear, however, whether Ateya's statement reflected official Egyptian government policy or was merely a personal opinion.

Although Egypt currently maintains a "cold peace" with Israel, Cairo may view its undeclared BW capability as a political counterweight to Israel's nuclear arsenal, as a hedge against future adverse shifts in the regional security environment (with respect both to Israel and Egypt's unpredictable neighbor, Libya), or as a weapon of last resort to preclude total military defeat. Given the lack of hard evidence, these motivations must remain speculative.

Iraq

Capabilities. Iraq is one country for which there is unequivocal evidence of a major BW program involving large-scale production and weaponization of both microbial and toxin agents (Tucker, 1993). Although Iraq did not employ biological weapons during the Iran-Iraq War of the 1980s, Baghdad may have already had a BW capability that was held in reserve. The U.S. Armed Forces Medical Intelligence Center assessed in 1990 that "if the Iran-Iraq war had lasted another year, BW weapons would have been employed by Iraq" (Defense Intelligence Agency, 1990).

By the time of the 1991 Gulf War, Iraq's BW program was the largest and most advanced in the Arab world (U.S. Department of Defense, 1992: 15). Iraq has acknowledged having mass-produced four BW agents: botulinum toxin, anthrax bacteria, aflatoxin, and *Clostridium perfringens* ("gas gangrene") toxin. The first three were poured into aerial bombs and missile warheads for the Al-Hussein, an extended-range version of the Soviet Scud B. Iraq also researched other lethal and incapacitating agents that it claims were never produced in quantity, including a plant toxin called ricin, fungal toxins known as trichothecene mycotoxins, and several lethal and incapacitating viruses (UN Security Council, 1995a: 26–27).

Motivations. Historically, Iraq has sought to balance military threats from Iran and Israel while attaining hegemony over the Gulf region and expanding its room for strategic maneuver. In the aftermath of the Israeli air raid against the Osirak nuclear reactor on June 7, 1981, which dealt a major setback to the Iraqi nuclear weapons program, Baghdad sought to deploy a strategic retaliatory capability that would deter Israel from future preemptive strikes against Iraqi targets. The desire to match the chemical/biological capabilities of Syria—its traditional rival for primacy in the region—has also provided an incentive for Iraq's strategic buildup (Eisenstadt, 1990: 3).

In April 1990, Saddam boasted that Iraq had developed binary chemical munitions and the capability to deliver them against Israeli cities (Zanders, 1995: 22). In contrast to these open threats of chemical warfare, however, Iraq's BW arsenal remained a closely guarded secret. Iraqi president Saddam Hussein may have viewed biological weapons as an option of last resort—a trump card against total military defeat and occupation—and sought to keep them under wraps until the appropriate moment.

Before the outbreak of the Gulf War in January 1991, Iraq deployed BW agent–filled bombs and Al-Hussein missile warheads at remote airfields and missile launch sites in western Iraq, within range of Israeli population centers. Launch authority was reportedly predelegated to the Iraqi base commanders where the weapons were stored, so that if the central military command structure in Baghdad were "decapitated" by an Israeli nuclear first strike, Iraq would still be able to retaliate (Reuters, 1995). Yet according to a report by the United Nations Special Commission, Iraq's claim of predelegation "does not exclude the alternative use of such a capability and therefore does not constitute proof of only intentions concerning second use" (UN Security Council, 1995a: 10).

Iraq may have also planned for tactical use of biological weapons against coalition forces in the belief that large numbers of dead and injured troops would generate political pressures on the U.S. administration to end the war on terms favorable to Baghdad (Trainor, 1996). Possible insights into Iraq's offensive BW doctrine can be drawn from an Iraqi military manual titled *Chemical, Biological and Nuclear Operations,* published by the Iraqi Chemical Corps in 1984, in the midst of the Iran-Iraq War. This manual discusses the use of BW agents to produce fatal and nonfatal casualties as a means of overburdening the enemy's medical infrastructure and weakening troop morale (AFMIC, 1992b: 6). Another manual, published in 1987 by the Iraqi Ministry of Defense, discusses covert BW operations as follows: "It is possible to undertake small attacks and sabotage operations through the use of vehicles and small boats in coastal areas. The use of these quick attacks before beginning the general offensive requires its protection and secrecy" (AFMIC, 1992a: 14). It is unclear, however, whether these manuals reflect unique Iraqi concepts or were copied from standard documents produced in the Soviet Union or elsewhere.

Iran

Capabilities. Iran began its BW program in the mid-1980s, in response to Iraq's massive use of chemical weapons during the Iran-Iraq War. According to one assessment, Iran "probably is researching such standard agents as anthrax and botulinum toxin and it has shown interest in acquiring materials which could be used to produce ricin and mycotoxins" (Eisenstadt, 1995). A 1995 article in the London *Sunday Times* asserted that Iran's BW production facilities are located in Tehran and in Damghan, a site about 300 kilometers east of the capital. The article also alleged that Russian experts had helped Iran make a "quantum leap forward" in the development of biological weapons, enabling Tehran to proceed directly from basic research to production and the acquisition of an effective delivery system (London *Sunday Times,* 1995).

In July 1996, in response to questions submitted by the U.S. Senate Select Committee on Intelligence, the Central Intelligence Agency (CIA) stated that Iran's scientific and technical infrastructure was advanced enough to develop and field biological weapons without foreign assistance and that Tehran had probably stockpiled BW agents (Boulden, 1996: 32). In August 1996, the London *Sunday Times* cited reports from Israeli intelligence sources that Iran had stockpiled anthrax and botulinum toxin in Tabriz, a city northwest of Tehran, and could quickly produce more of these agents. Israeli sources also claimed that the Iranians had developed a number of delivery systems, including a portable aerosolizer suitable for terrorist use, Scud missile warheads, and aerial sprayers mounted on Soviet-era Sukoi attack aircraft (Mahnaimi and Adams, 1996). The 1996 ACDA compliance report concluded that "Iran probably has produced biological warfare agents and has weaponized a small quantity of those agents" and that the Iranian BW program "has been embedded within Iran's extensive biotechnology and pharmaceutical industries so as to obscure its activities" (ACDA, 1997a: 87). A 1997 Pentagon report found that "while only small quantities of usable agent may exist now, within 10 years, Iran's military forces may be able to deliver biological agents effectively" (U.S. Office of the Secretary of Defense, 1997: 27).

Motivations. Tehran's primary strategic objectives are to deter future attacks by Iraq armed with a reconstituted WMD arsenal; to strengthen its political, economic, and military position as a regional power; and to limit the influence of the West (especially the United States) in the Middle East. Iran's threat perceptions focus primarily on Iraq, but it remains a sworn enemy of Israel. For Tehran, the bitter lesson of the muted international response to Iraqi chemical warfare during the Iran-Iraq War was that such weapons can be employed with impunity as long as big-power interests are not adversely affected. After the August 1988 cease-fire with Iraq, Iranian president Hashami Rafsanjani openly described chemical and biological weapons as the "poor man's atomic bombs [which] we should at least consider . . . for our defense. . . . although the use of such weapons is inhumane, the [Iran-Iraq] war taught us that international laws are only drops of ink on paper" (Tehran IRNA, 1988).

The largely successful efforts by the United States and other supplier states to limit Iran's access to nuclear technology and materials also motivated Tehran to pursue the BW option. Given the uncertainties confronting its nuclear weapons program, a BW capability provides Iran with a transitional, strategic weapon that can deter attack until it acquires a nuclear arsenal (Eisenstadt, 1995). Beyond the desire to counter Israel, Iran may have pursued a BW capability as part of an asymmetric strategy to deter intervention by the United States and its allies. According to a U.S. military analyst, "The Iranian military leadership knows that it cannot challenge the United States in a direct confrontation, but it can raise the stakes of U.S. actions by making access to the Gulf more dangerous and more difficult, and by adding more militarily significant factors for U.S. defense planners to worry about" (Twing, 1996: 81). Tehran may calculate that if the costs of intervention can be raised high enough to mobilize U.S. public opinion (e.g., by threatening high U.S. casualties), the United States could be deterred from intervening in another regional war in the Gulf.

Israel

Capabilities. Available evidence indicates a long-standing Israeli interest in biological weapons. According to journalist Seymour Hersh, in 1960 the CIA tracked Israeli scientists to a French chemical and biological weapons testing site in the Algerian desert and concluded that the Israelis were "looking at CBW as a stopgap until they got the bomb" (Hersh, 1991: 64). Hersh also contends that Levi Eshkol, the Israeli prime minister from 1963 to 1969, had "no ambivalence about continuing Israel's ongoing chemical and biological weapons programs" (Hersh, 1991: 136).

It is widely believed that the heavily guarded Israel Institute for Biological Research near the town of Ness Ziona, about 10 miles south of Tel Aviv, "plays a pivotal role" in Israel's suspected BW program (Kumaraswamy, 1996: 21). Established in 1953 as a laboratory for basic and applied research in chemistry and biology, the institute has a staff of about 300 scientists (Hunt, 1998: 84). According to a book by two Israeli journalists, "As early as 1973, the institute [in Ness Ziona] was linked by foreign researchers to 'topics related to chemical and biological warfare.' United States intelligence analysts concluded that Israel, at the very least, was developing defensive measures . . . [including] stocks of vaccines and the means to monitor air and water against potential chemical or biological aggression" (Raviv and Melman, 1990: 234).

From 1957 to 1979, one of the principal researchers at Ness Ziona was Marcus Klingberg, an internationally known epidemiologist. In 1983, Israel's security service arrested Klingberg and charged him with spying for the Soviet Union. He was convicted in a secret trial and sentenced to eighteen years in Ashekelon Prison. According to one source, Klingberg was a colonel in the Soviet army and a "world-class" expert in biological warfare who was "planted" in Israel by the KGB (Soviet intelligence agency) and worked on top-secret projects at Ness Ziona until his arrest. In 1996, Klingberg petitioned to be released from prison because of ill health, but this request was denied on the grounds that he still posed a grave threat to national security (Hunt, 1998: 93). He was finally released in September 1998, but remains under tight surveillance.

In 1993, a Russian Foreign Intelligence Service report stated that Israel was implementing "a ramified program of biological research of a general nature, in which elements of a military-applied purpose are present" (Russian Foreign Intelligence Service, 1993). Israel is known to have a large biological defense research program, including joint projects with military laboratories in the United States, and it has an advanced civilian biotechnology base that could be converted rapidly to offensive BW agent production if the decision were made to do so. According to a report published by the Jaffee Centre for Strategic Studies at Tel Aviv University, citing U.S. intelligence sources, "although Israel has the capability to produce [biological agents] at will, it has not stockpiled operational weapons" (Kumaraswamy, 1998: 22).

Motivations. Israel possesses an undeclared nuclear arsenal and has refused to sign the Nuclear Non-Proliferation Treaty until it is satisfied that Iran, Iraq, Libya, and Syria no longer pose a threat to its existence. Israel also enjoys an overwhelming qualitative edge in conventional military capabilities over its Arab rivals because of extensive U.S. military assistance, but Israel does not wish to depend for its ultimate survival on the United States, a potentially unreliable ally. Although little is known about Israeli intentions in the BW field, Israel may wish to maintain an in-kind deterrent (perhaps in the form of a mobilizable production capacity) to neutralize the BW threat posed by Iraq, Iran, Libya, and Syria without having to rely solely on nuclear deterrence, which might not appear sufficiently credible.

Libya

Capabilities. The U.S. Department of Defense has alleged that Libya is researching biological weapons inside a hollowed-out mountain near the town of Tarhuna, 50 miles southeast of Tripoli (Gertz, 1996). Most accounts suggest that Libya's BW program is still at an early stage of development because Tripoli lacks the technology base to process biological agents and fill them into munitions and warheads, a capability it has attained with chemicals (Sinai, 1998). According to the 1996 ACDA compliance report, "evidence indicates that Libya has the expertise to produce small quantities of biological equipment for its BW program" and is "seeking to move its research program into a program of weaponized BW agents" (ACDA, 1997a: 88). The Pentagon's 1997 proliferation report concurs with this assessment: "While Libya has had a biological warfare program for many years, it remains in the early research and development stages, primarily because Libya lacks an adequate scientific and technical base" (U.S. Office of the Secretary of Defense, 1997: 37).

Tripoli has sought to acquire foreign expertise and equipment to massproduce and weaponize BW agents. The 1993 Russian Foreign Intelligence Service report noted that Libya was "displaying particular interest in information on work involving biological agents overseas. In contacts with representatives of other Arab countries, Libyan specialists are expressing a readiness to fund joint biological programs, [including those] of a militaryapplied purpose . . . provided they are not undertaken on Libyan territory" (Russian Foreign Intelligence Service, 1993: 64). In February 1995, the London *Sunday Times* reported that Libya had recruited two South African scientists who had worked on biological weapons during the apartheid period (Adams, 1995). And in April 1996, press accounts indicated that German companies had sold Libya fermentors suitable for production of BW agents (*Der Spiegel,* 1996). As a potential delivery system, Libya reportedly is developing an intermediate-range ballistic missile called the Al-Fatah (Waller, 1996a: 228).

Motivations. Ever since seizing power in 1969, Libyan leader Colonel Muammar Qaddafi has sought to acquire weapons of mass destruction. Although Libya is a relatively minor player in the overall Middle East power balance, Qaddafi aspires to regional leadership. According to one analysis, "Geography dictates that Libya will never be more than a marginal Mediterranean power, a reality which meshes awkwardly with Qaddafi's ambitions. Since he cannot set the Mediterranean agenda, he has vowed to disrupt it" (Waller, 1996a: 229). To this end, Qaddafi has tried to subvert and destabilize his Arab and African neighbors, undermine the

Arab-Israeli peace process, and launch terrorist attacks against Western targets.

Libya's pursuit of biological weapons is primarily a means of bolstering its military capabilities, since the country lacks effective conventional land, air, or naval forces (Sinai, 1997: 92). Libyan troops were soundly defeated in a series of military engagements: a border skirmish with Egypt in July 1977, an intervention in support of the Ugandan regime of Idi Amin in 1978, and an invasion of neighboring Chad during its civil war of 1983–1987 (Terrill, 1994: 54). In the latter case, the Libyan army suffered a humiliating defeat at the hands of Chadian forces equipped by the United States and France. These military setbacks have fostered a deep sense of vulnerability in Tripoli and led the Libyan government to seek nonconventional weapons as an equalizer, particularly vis-à-vis Israel. On March 30, 1996, the official Libyan news agency reported a speech by Qaddafi in which he urged Arab states to acquire chemical and biological capabilities to offset Israel's nuclear arsenal. "Arabs have the right to own toxic gas and biological bombs as long as the Israelis own these internationally banned arms and nobody can force them to abandon their destructive arsenal," he said (Reuters, 1996).

Libya may also seek biological weapons as a deterrent to military intervention by the United States, France, and Italy. On April 14, 1986, U.S. warplanes bombed the Libyan cities of Tripoli and Benghazi after Washington said it had irrefutable evidence linking Libya to the bombing of a Berlin discotheque frequented by U.S. military personnel. Libya claimed that thirty-seven civilians died in the U.S. air raids (Aldinger, 1996). In retaliation, Qaddafi ordered the launching of two Scud missiles at the Italian island of Lampedusa (Jacobs, 1986). Although both missiles fell short, the attack put Rome and other U.S. allies in the region on notice that they would run significant risks by supporting Washington in any future confrontation with Tripoli.

Qaddafi has supplied arms and explosives to terrorist groups in the past, and he might consider providing them with BW agents for covert attacks against Israel or the United States. In July 1996, Qaddafi hinted at such a strategy when he observed, "There is no longer any logic between us [Libya and the United States], no common denominator or rationality. We are looking for ways to frighten America so that it retreats" (Waller, 1996b: 523). At the same time, Qaddafi has worried about the prospect of U.S. retaliation.

Finally, the prestige factor has played an important role in Libyan security policy. Qaddafi is determined to keep pace with his Arab rivals in missiles and weapons of mass destruction, both to lend credibility to his foreign policy pronouncements and to bolster his domestic standing (Wyllie, 1995). Given the secrecy surrounding the BW program, however, it is unlikely that Libya is seeking to acquire biological weapons for prestige purposes.

Syria

Capabilities. After Syria's humiliating defeat in the 1973 Arab-Israeli war, Damascus launched a chemical weapons program that by the mid-1980s had reached an advanced stage (Diab, 1997). With respect to biological weapons, the 1996 ACDA compliance report states that "it is highly probable that Syria is developing an offensive biological warfare capability" (ACDA, 1997a: 87). According to a 1997 Pentagon report, "Syria probably has an adequate biotechnical infrastructure to support a small biological warfare program, although the Syrians are not believed to have begun any major weaponization or testing related to biological warfare. Without significant foreign assistance, it is unlikely that Syria could advance to the manufacture of biological weapons for several years" (U.S. Office of the Secretary of Defense, 1997: 39).

Nevertheless, Israeli military planners are deeply concerned by what they assert is a new Syrian capability to produce biological warheads and place them on Scud B and Scud C surface-to-surface missiles. The Israelis claim that Syria has received assistance from Russian scientists on its BW program, which is being conducted in hardened underground facilities (Rodan, 1996). An article in the *Wall Street Journal* also refers to "the virtual strategic cooperation between Syria and Iran in developing biological and chemical weapons," including exchanges of scientific and technical personnel (Marcus, 1996).

Other reports suggest that Syria has received assistance from Chinese and German firms in developing biological warheads for its long-range missiles (Eisenstadt, 1993: 168). According to one account, "U.S. intelligence sources fear that Chinese equipment may be involved in what they think is an underground chemical/biological weapons factory outside Damascus, much like the one Libya is said to be building near Tarhuna. Their belief that such a project exists is based on documents seized last summer from two Germans arrested in Germany and charged with illegal equipment sales" (Yost, 1996).

Motivations. Historically, Syria's security preoccupations have been divided among Israel, Turkey, and Iraq. Recognizing that nuclear weapons are beyond its financial and technical reach, Damascus may be pursuing a BW capability as a strategic deterrent against Israel's nuclear arsenal and as a weapon of last resort in the event of a major conventional war with Israel or Iraq. According to Michael Eisenstadt, "Syria's strategic forces serve as a deterrent to offset Israel's nuclear capabilities, counter the threat posed by Israel's ground and air forces, and act as a hedge against defeat in wartime" (Eisenstadt, 1993: 168). By threatening Israeli cities with biological attack, Syria may wish to establish a mutual-deterrence relationship that would preclude Israeli preemptive strikes against high-value Syrian targets.

Jordan and Morocco

Capabilities. Jordan and Morocco do not possess biological weapons and have not sought to acquire them, even though they have the basic technical and industrial infrastructure needed to do so. These two countries therefore provide useful counterexamples to the other cases discussed above.

Motivations. Both countries face less acute security threats than the BW proliferators in the region. The governments of Jordan and Morocco enjoy good relations with the United States, other Western countries, and Israel and do not fear military intervention by outside powers. Morocco is primarily concerned with subduing a guerrilla war in the south of the country, for which weapons of mass destruction are not required, and its tensions with Algeria and the Polisario Front are offset by its close security cooperation with the United States. Jordan, for its part, has worked out a modus vivendi with neighboring Iraq that delivers economic benefits to both countries and diminishes the potential military threat from Baghdad. Finally, both Jordan and Morocco are enmeshed in extensive and growing political, economic, and security relations with the West that would be jeopardized were they to seek weapons of mass destruction.

At the domestic level, neither king may trust his own military with weapons of mass destruction. Although both Jordan and Morocco are monarchies, they are relatively benign and open societies compared to the autocratic and brutal regimes of Iraq, Libya, and Syria. For this reason, public opinion and international norms may play a stronger role in constraining military developments.

ANALYSIS OF THE CASE STUDIES

According to the simple typology introduced at the outset, a net balance among proliferation incentives and disincentives in a country's security environment should determine whether it decides to pursue a BW capability. As summarized in Table 2.2, the case studies indicate that insecurity is a major factor driving the proliferation process but also suggest the need for

Table 2.2 Security Incentives and Disincentives for BW Proliferation in the Middle East

Country	Incentives	Disincentives	Offensive Program
Egypt	Deter Israel from resorting to first use of nuclear weapons; hedge against adverse shifts in security environment	International opprobrium, increased tension with Israel	Yes
Iraq	Counter Israeli nuclear threat; intimidate Iran, Kuwait, and Saudi Arabia; extend hegemony over Gulf; deter U.S. intervention	Could provoke Israeli or U.S. preemptive strike, international sanctions	Yes
Iran	Strengthen position as a regional power; deter Iraq and Israel; deter U.S. intervention	Could provoke Israeli or U.S. preemptive strikes	Yes
Israel	Deter Arab or Iranian BW use through the threat of in-kind retaliation without resorting to nuclear weapons	International opprobrium, possible cut-off of U.S. assistance	Latent?
Libya	Compensate for weakness of conventional forces; deter outside intervention	Deployed capability might provoke a preemptive strike	Yes
Jordan and Morocco	No acute security deficit warranting acquisition of WMD	International opprobrium; possible cut-off of U.S. assistance	No
Syria	Deter Israel's nuclear capability, serve as hedge against total defeat in wartime	Increased tensions with Iraq, Israel, and Turkey	Yes

additional explanatory variables. On the basis of the data, one can make four observations.

First, BW proliferation in the Middle East is linked to the spread of other weapons of mass destruction, as well as the reciprocal threat perceptions of Israel, Iran, and the Arab states. Mideast analyst Geoffrey Kemp has emphasized the "strategic connectivity" of chemical and biological weapons with nuclear weapons (Kemp, 1991: 111). Although Egypt, Libya, and Syria do not admit to possessing BW capabilities, they insist on the right to acquire them as a counter to Israel's undeclared nuclear arsenal.

Second, although no additional countries in the Middle East appear to be seeking biological weapons, the existing proliferators are improving their production and delivery capabilities. There may also be a certain amount of "latent" proliferation, since countries do not necessarily make a single, irrevocable decision to acquire biological weapons. Aware that a weaponized BW capability would entail significant political costs, some states may prefer to acquire dual-use capabilities and perform basic research and development (easily attributed to defensive or peaceful purposes) to keep the BW option open. Other states (possibly including Israel) may go a step further, acquiring a mobilizable production capacity for BW agents within their civilian industrial base and perhaps developing and testing suitable delivery systems. In the event of a war threatening national survival, this latent capacity could be converted fairly rapidly to the production and stockpiling of an offensive BW arsenal.

Third, the Middle Eastern countries pursuing biological weapons are a subset of those already known to possess chemical warfare (CW) capabilities. Indeed, these two types of weapons programs appear to be linked, at least at the policy level (Carus, 1991: 29). One possible explanation is that proliferant states may view chemical and biological weapons as complementary: whereas chemical weapons have greater tactical utility on the battlefield, biological weapons are potentially more effective for strategic attacks against population centers and for covert operations.

Fourth, the observation that neighboring states such as Iraq and Jordan respond quite differently to external security threats suggests that domestic factors play an important role in determining how states react to proliferation incentives and disincentives. Such country-specific factors include history, form of government, foreign policy objectives, and the personality of the national leader. Also important are the cognitive and bureaucratic processes by which national governments perceive and respond to external threats. For example, it may be a fallacy to assume that the acquisition of biological weapons is always driven by a coherent strategic rationale. Some leaders seeking to maximize their authority and power, such as Iraq's Saddam Hussein, may simply pursue all forms of highly potent weaponry without a clear preconception of their military utility. The domestic factors that influence BW proliferation behavior can be grouped into two categories: *predisposing* and *precipitating*.

Predisposing Factors

Predisposing factors are historical, cultural, and political variables that affect a state's general disposition toward weapons of mass destruction. For example, democratic countries such as Sweden, Japan, and the United States are more sensitive to nonproliferation norms because domestic public opinion would strongly oppose a decision to acquire or retain a capability prohibited under international law. Yet this constraint is weak or nonexistent in authoritarian regimes, where military matters are shrouded in secrecy, and the population enjoys few if any freedoms of the press or of individual expression. Examples of other factors that may predispose toward BW proliferation include the following:

1. The state has an autocratic structure with a top-down policymaking process and a government-controlled press.
2. Military policymaking is rigidly compartmentalized and nontransparent, so that the existence of a BW program remains a closely guarded secret.
3. The state's cultural and historical traditions cause it to perceive nonproliferation norms as discriminatory or even as a conspiracy on the part of Western powers.
4. The state has an expansionist, irredentist, or revolutionary ideology rather than a status-quo foreign policy.

Bureaucratic and institutional factors may also play a role in the decision to acquire or retain biological weapons. Although little hard information is available in the BW area, historical case studies of conventional and nuclear weapons acquisition have shown that large procurement programs engender organizational structures that can entrench a military capability long after its strategic rationale has disappeared (York, 1973). Senior civilian and military officials involved in the development of a new weapon tend to acquire a personal and institutional stake in its perpetuation, such as career goals, status, and perks. The U.S. Army Chemical Corps, for example, was a powerful institutional defender of chemical and biological weapons. Similar bureaucratic obstacles appear to have slowed the elimination of Russia's BW capabilities. Despite President Boris Yeltsin's 1992 decree halting the offensive BW program inherited from the former Soviet Union, the implementation of this order has faced bureaucratic resistance (Smith, 1994). A lobby within the Russian government, including senior Defense Ministry officials, appears to have prevented the complete demilitarization and conversion of Russia's former offensive BW facilities (Rimmington, 1996: 81).

Bureaucratic *disincentives* for the acquisition of BW may arise from competition among government ministries for coveted missions and scarce resources. Within the defense sector, military officials may prefer to spend money to procure conventional weapons such as tanks and fighter aircraft, which have greater utility on the battlefield and support traditional armed services roles and missions. The degree of assimilation of a particular type of weaponry into mainstream military doctrine also plays an important role. Frederic Brown's classic study of the nonuse of chemical weapons during World War II concludes that a major explanatory factor was the reluctance of both German and Allied forces to integrate offensive chemical warfare into their military strategy and tactics (Brown, 1968).

Precipitating Factors

Precipitating factors are short-term international or domestic events that can catalyze a decision to proliferate. William Potter has argued that the choice to acquire nuclear weapons may be triggered by "situational variables," such as an international crisis that provides the opportunity to forge a bureaucratic consensus, the acquisition of a nuclear capability by a hostile state, or a major change in political leadership (Potter, 1982: 143–144; Potter, 1995: 30). Short-term events that may influence a state's decision to acquire biological weapons include the following:

1. the outbreak of war or the emergence of an acute security threat or imminent military intervention;
2. the known or suspected acquisition by a regional adversary of a nuclear, chemical, or biological capability;
3. the sudden disappearance of a superpower patron or the breakdown of a regional security arrangement or alliance;
4. a rapid and unexpected change of regime (e.g., by military coup rather than democratic election) or the election of an aggressively nationalist government;
5. a large-scale, lethal use of chemical or biological weapons that is not met with strong international sanctions.

The case studies suggest that given the availability of an adequate technology and industrial base and the existence of a perceived security deficit, BW proliferation is more likely if predisposing or precipitating domestic factors or both are also present. Table 2.3 illustrates the strong correlation between the presence of predisposing factors and a state's tendency to acquire biological weapons. The main anomaly is Israel. Although its

Table 2.3 Predisposing Domestic Factors for BW Proliferation (at time program began)

Factors	Egypt	Iraq	Iran	Israel	Libya	Jordan and Morocco	Syria
Autocratic/dictatorial regime	X	X	X		X	X	X
Isolation or pariah status				X	X		
Aggressive foreign policy		X					
Extreme military secrecy	X	X	X		X		X
Sociopathic national leader		X					X
Restricted press and speech	X	X	X		X		X
BW capability	Yes	Yes	Yes	Latent	Yes	No	Yes

democratic form of government and relatively free press create disincentives to BW proliferation, the security threat that Israel faces from neighboring states may exert a more than offsetting influence. As stated previously, however, Israel appears to have a latent rather than weaponized BW capability. It should also be noted that existential security threats may cause democracies to adopt extreme countermeasures, including the acquisition of biological arms. During World War II, for example, both the United States and Great Britain developed, produced, and stockpiled biological weapons, and Winston Churchill seriously considered using anthrax bombs in a strategic bombing campaign against German cities (Bernstein, 1987a).

In summary, two types of domestic factors—predisposing and precipitating—appear to influence how a given state responds to the proliferation incentives and disincentives in its security environment. It is also possible that a state may be motivated to *acquire* biological weapons by one set of factors and to *retain* them by a different set. Indeed, the incentive structure of key states in the Middle East has evolved significantly in response to major shifts in the external security environment, such as the end of the Cold War and the vicissitudes of the Arab-Israeli peace process, as well as domestic political transitions.

Another interesting issue is how the incentive structure of a state changes *after* it has acquired biological weapons. Ironically, it appears that proliferant countries generally end up less secure than they were before. The acquisition of a BW capability by one state may have severe repercussions on its neighbors, provoking them to acquire offsetting weapons and exacerbating regional tensions and threat perceptions. As a result, national leaders in zones of endemic conflict may find themselves trapped in a vicious circle, investing ever more resources in weapons of mass destruction that bring ever less security.

POLICY IMPLICATIONS

Since the sources of BW proliferation are multidimensional and operate at different levels, nonproliferation strategies must do the same. The model presented in this chapter suggests that a state's tendency to proliferate can be modified by a wide range of variables, including a change in its form of government, the creation of new regional security structures, or the strengthening of global norms.

"Supply-side" measures such as export controls are designed to target the basic technical prerequisites for a BW program, such as access to biological fermentation equipment and know-how. Given the rapid diffusion of dual-capable technologies throughout the developing world, supply-side strategies, although useful in slowing the pace of proliferation, do not offer a long-term solution to the problem. Similarly, outside countries generally have little influence over domestic precipitating factors, such as a coup d'état that brings a nationalist regime to power. For these reasons, nonproliferation strategies may be most effective if they focus on predisposing factors that influence how a state perceives and responds to its security environment.

Demand-side approaches to halting and ultimately reversing BW proliferation should therefore emphasize five areas. First, the strengthening and enforcement of international norms is vital for stemming the spread of biological weapons. The lack of international condemnation and sanctions in response to Iraq's use of chemical weapons during the Iran-Iraq War weakened the taboo against both chemical and biological warfare. This debacle underlines the need both to strengthen the BWC by negotiating an effective and legally binding compliance regime and to mobilize the international political will to punish violators.

Second, scientists and engineers must be educated about the behavioral norms enshrined in the BWC, with the ultimate aim of building a nonproliferation culture in countries of concern. Such training may be accomplished in part through Internet Web sites such as the Program on Monitoring Emerging Diseases (ProMED), as well as international laboratory exchange programs and collaborative research efforts to improve global epidemiological surveillance and combat deadly infectious diseases (Woodall, 1998). Criminalization of BW acquisition and use would further reinforce the norm.

Third, since chronic regional conflict and tension tend to foster BW proliferation, the United States should actively promote regional security arrangements including military alliances, security guarantees, and confidence-building and transparency measures. Such policies would facilitate the negotiation of zones free of weapons of mass destruction.

Fourth, democratic regimes are more responsive to public opinion and hence less likely to acquire biological weapons. In general, the more open the society, the more difficult it is to acquire a prohibited military capability. For this reason, every effort should be made to enhance the processes of political liberalization and democratization throughout the Middle East region.

Finally, deterrent postures aimed at discouraging the acquisition and use of biological weapons should not threaten nuclear retaliation in response to a biological attack, since this linkage would undermine the nuclear nonproliferation regime and repudiate the negative security assurances provided to nonnuclear-weapon states under the Nuclear Non-Proliferation Treaty. Instead, deterrent threats should focus on the asset that leaders of proliferant regimes value most: their continued grasp on power.

To this end, the United States and other like-minded states should pledge that any national leader who resorts to biological warfare will be removed from power by whatever means necessary and tried before an international tribunal as a war criminal.

PART 2
Defense and Prophylaxis

3

The Essentials of Biological Threat Assessment

GRAHAM S. PEARSON

One of the primary functions of governments is to ensure the security of their nations. Traditionally, governments have tended to regard security primarily in terms of safeguarding their nationals from violence, maintaining their territorial integrity, and protecting vital economic interests. The array of measures governments employ to preserve security is wide, ranging from collecting information that bears on the capabilities and intentions of possible adversaries to dispatching military forces to deter or subdue foes. Measures to ensure the protection of citizens from infectious diseases usually have not been part of this array. However, there are at least four cogent reasons why governments ought to regard the protection of their populations from disease as tantamount to ensuring security.

First, as a consequence of greatly expanded international trade and travel, more opportunities have arisen for pathogens causing disease in one part of the world to be introduced into another. No doubt, most such introductions will be accidental, that is, pathogens will be transported from one site to another as a consequence of the movement of a host who carries them. However, a foreign government ill disposed toward a particular nation could seek to damage it by biological sabotage or terrorism; that is, it might instruct its representatives to deliberately introduce pathogens onto its enemy's territory for the express purpose of sickening its human, animal, or plant populations. It is important to recognize that since the etiology of an introduced disease would be unknown when it first becomes manifest, the government of the attacked nation would employ standard epidemiological methods to investigate the outbreak. Thus, the initial response of a government to address this type of biological threat would be identical whether the causative organism emerged from nature or was deliberately created in the laboratory to cause mayhem. At an early stage of disease emergence, the public health and security issues are the same.

Second, there exists the possibility that some states have acquired or will seek to acquire biological weapons that may be used against humans, animals, or plants. In particular, following the indefinite extension of the Nuclear Non-Proliferation Treaty in April 1995 and the entry into force of the Chemical Weapons Convention (CWC) in April 1997, governments may find it so difficult to acquire nuclear and chemical weapons that they will forgo attempting to do so. If so, some of them may find it worthwhile to initiate programs to obtain biological weapons. As is discussed elsewhere in this volume, activities to this end are relatively easy to conceal, are less costly than would be the case with other weapon systems, and are likely to result in the proliferant country gaining a weapon of mass destruction within a short time. If and when a biological weapon is used, disease afflicting humans, animals, or plants will ensue. Activities taken to prevent such an occurrence or, should such an occurrence take place, to mitigate its effects would necessarily include security and public health measures.

Third, governments responding to international calls to provide military capabilities for peacekeeping in foreign countries would be remiss unless they took steps to protect their personnel from diseases that may be indigenous to countries or regions to which they are deployed or biological weapons wielded by local militias or other forces. This is particularly important because dispatched persons are likely to be immunologically ill prepared to resist infections by indigenous pathogens and biological warfare (BW) agents unless they have been appropriately vaccinated. However, before appropriate vaccines can be prepared and administered, it is necessary for the dispatching government to possess the capability to assess the status of indigenous infectious diseases and local BW capabilities in the region where its troops will operate.

Fourth, public health services, as well as parallel organizations with respect to animal and plant health, are established by governments to secure the health of their nationals. These services and organizations collaborate with their international counterparts in order to exchange information on infectious diseases in other parts of the world and monitor their spread. They can then advise their nationals traveling to other parts of the world about health risks they might face. Similarly, persons engaged in trade involving exotic animals and plants need to be aware of the measures aiming to protect home countries from importation of disease from other parts of the world. These activities are particularly important now, in this age of virtually instantaneous air travel, when it is all too easy for persons, animals, or plants infected at one site to travel afar within hours to an uninfected area and there give rise to an outbreak of disease.

Common to all these reasons is the need for governments to possess the capability to assess biological threats emanating from abroad. To be complete, this capability must encompass biological threats of all types, be they directed against military personnel or civilians, animals or plants. In this chapter I address the biological threat assessment process and how this is best done. To accomplish this, four topics are considered. First, biological threats are outlined. Second, the assessment of biological threats is addressed, including the need to distinguish between natural and deliberate outbreaks of disease. Third, three particular cases involving BW programs—Iraq, Russia, and Aum Shinrikyo—are discussed. Last, the issue of how biological threat assessment can and should be strengthened is considered.

BIOLOGICAL THREATS

Biological threats can arise from one of three sources: nature, accidental releases from facilities, or the use of biological weapons. Each is considered in turn.

Natural Outbreaks of Disease

Awareness of the susceptibility of humans, animals, and plants to disease is increasing. Hiroshi Nakajima, director general of the World Health Organization (WHO) said in 1996 "we stand on the brink of a global crisis in infectious diseases. No country is safe from them. No country can any longer afford to ignore their threat" (WHO, 1996a). Headline reports of plague in India in September 1994 and of Ebola in Zaire in April 1995 show how outbreaks of disease can produce widespread, if not worldwide, alarm and concern because of fears about how far these may spread and confusion as to what restrictions should be placed on travel into and out of the affected areas. A WHO team visited India in October 1994 and reported that there had been an outbreak of bubonic plague in the town of Beed some distance inland from Bombay, followed by an outbreak of pneumonic plague in the city of Surat on the coast, some 250 kilometers (km) north of Bombay (*Nature,* 1994). In the Ebola outbreak, the WHO reported ninety-three infections and eighty-six deaths less than two months after the start of the outbreak, a pattern similar to that in the earlier 1976 outbreak in which 290 died out of 318 infected—a 90 percent mortality rate (*The Economist,* 1995a, 1995b). Animals and plants are no less vulnerable than humans to infectious disease.

Steps have also recently been taken by the WHO to improve the epidemiological surveillance of disease. Worldwide concern about new and emerging disease was recognized at the May 1995 World Health Assembly, which passed a resolution urging member states to strengthen national and local programs of active surveillance for infectious diseases; to enhance communications between national and international services involved in disease detection, early notification, surveillance, control, and response; and to control outbreaks and promote accurate and timely reporting of cases at national and international levels (WHO, 1995: 2). It also urged "other specialized agencies of the United Nations system, bilateral development agencies, nongovernmental organizations and other groups concerned to increase their cooperation in the recognition, prevention and control of new, emerging, and re-emerging infectious diseases both through continued support for general social and health development and through specific support to national and international programs to recognize and respond to those diseases." The WHO Division of Emerging and Other Communicable Diseases Surveillance and Control is actively engaged in the implementation of this World Health Assembly resolution.

There is increasing worldwide concern about new and emerging diseases (Garrett, 1994). Disease has caused more casualties in all wars than the actual weapons of war. As the world population continues to increase, new areas of land are occupied and greater overcrowding occurs of existing areas with ever greater demands for both plants and animals as sources of food. This overcrowding provides greater opportunities for new or old diseases to spread in humans, animals, or plants, with damaging socioeconomic effects for the countries involved.

Accidental Release

Pathogens or toxins handled or produced in biological laboratories or production plants may be accidentally released from contained facilities. Such facilities can also provide a source of the pathogen or toxin for malevolent persons to deliberately release. The need to take steps to improve safety is increasingly being recognized internationally following the entry into force in December 1993 of the Convention on Biological Diversity (United Nations, 1992), which discusses in Article 19 the "Handling of Biotechnology and Distribution of Its Benefits":

> The Parties shall consider the need for modalities of a protocol setting out appropriate procedures, including, in particular, advance informed agreement, in the field of the safe transfer, handling and use of any living modified organism resulting from biotechnology that may have adverse effect on the conservation and sustainable use of biological diversity.

An open-ended Ad Hoc Working Group was established at the second annual Conference of Parties held in Djakarta in November 1995 to negotiate in "the field of the safe transfer, handling and use of living modified organisms, a protocol on biosafety, specifically focusing on transboundary movement, of any living modified organism resulting from modern biotechnology that may have adverse effects on the conservation and sustainable use of biological diversity" (UN Environment Programme, 1995: 46). The decision also made it clear that the United Nations Environment Programme (UNEP) International Technical Guidelines on Safety in Biotechnology may be used as an interim mechanism during the development of the protocol and to complement it after its completion.

Deliberate Outbreaks of Disease

The probability that disease will be used as a weapon of war is increasing. The director of the U.S. Arms Control and Disarmament Agency (ACDA) said in November 1996 that the United States believed that twice as many countries now have or are actively pursuing offensive biological weapons programs as when the Convention of the Prohibition of the Development, Production and Stockpiling of Bacteriological (Biological) and Toxin Weapons, and on Their Destruction (BWC) went into force in 1975 (Holum, 1996). Also in 1996, the heads of state of the Group of 7 (G7) meeting in France asserted, "Special attention should be paid to the threat of utilization of nuclear, biological and chemical materials, as well as toxic substances, for terrorist purposes" (UN General Assembly, 1996a). Increased attention is being given to possible counters to such use (Tucker, 1996), including, in the United States, tight controls on the transfers of biological pathogens (U.S. Congress, 1996; *U.S. Federal Register,* 1996).

U.S. president Bill Clinton has clearly expressed his concern, saying, "We must do more to protect our people against those who would use disease as a weapon of war" (UN General Assembly, 1996c). Similar views have been put forth by the United Kingdom and the Russian Federation, the other two co-depositary governments of the BWC. The United Kingdom said in November 1996 that "the ban on biological weapons had been flagrantly violated. The Biological Weapons Convention needs teeth. It needs systematic and reliable mechanisms to detect, and hence deter, proliferators. . . . Time for trusting to luck has run out" (Davis, 1996: 7). And Yevgeni Primakov, then director of the Foreign Intelligence Service (FIS) of the Russian Federation, wrote the following in a report released in 1993:

> Special studies conducted by the FIS show that the observed tendency towards broad dissemination of biotechnologies (having a dual use, as a rule) and difficulties in controlling the production and use of biological agents and toxins increase the likelihood of the use of biological weapons by Third World countries in local military conflicts as well as for subversive and terrorist purposes. In this regard, the advantage of biological weapons is emphasized over nuclear and chemical weapons from the point of view of the opportunity to inflict serious damage to an enemy's

economy through covert use of biological weapons against plants and livestock in his agriculture. Nor can these actions be ruled out in peacetime for purposes of "economic war." (Primakov, 1993: 15)

Unlike chemical weapons, whose application requires the production of relatively large stockpiles of appropriate toxic substances, most biological agents are self-reproducing. With a small initial stockpile of biomaterial and access to modern methods of industrial microbiology and biotechnology, large-scale production of biological agents can be set up over the course of several weeks. In addition, the infrastructure for production of biological weapons is barely noticeable through visual means.

This international concern about biological weapon capabilities recognizes that the quantities of biological agents needed to cause significant harm are considerably less than for chemical agents. One of the earliest comparisons of biological, chemical, and nuclear weapons was made in 1969 by a group of international experts on behalf of the United Nations Secretary-General (United Nations, 1969). It compared the weapons that could then be carried by "a single strategic bomber" and showed that a biological weapon weighing 10 tons (it was not specified whether this figure referred to the agent alone or to the entire weapon) could affect up to 100,000 km², whereas the corresponding areas for chemical weapons (15 tons of nerve agent) and nuclear weapons (1 megaton) were up to 60 and 300 km², respectively. A more recent study compared the fatalities that might be caused by a missile with a 1-ton warhead attacking a large city with an average population density of thirty unprotected citizens per hectare (Fetter, 1991). It showed that a biological warhead would produce 20,000 to 80,000 deaths, whereas the corresponding figures for conventional, chemical, and nuclear warheads were 5, 200–3,000, and 40,000 respectively. Similar figures were produced by the U.S. Office of Technology Assessment, namely, that a biological attack by a single aircraft delivering 100 kilograms (kg) of anthrax spores against Washington, D.C., would produce 1 to 3 million deaths, whereas an attack with a chemical agent (1,000 kg of sarin) would produce 3,000 to 8,000 deaths, and a 1-megaton hydrogen bomb would cause 570,000 to 1,900,000 deaths (U.S. Congress, 1993c). It is therefore hardly surprising that General Colin Powell, as chairman of the Joint Chiefs of Staff in 1993, said, "The one that scares me to death, perhaps even more so than tactical nuclear weapons, and the one that we have least capability against is biological weapons. And this was my greatest concern during Operation Desert Storm, knowing that the Iraqis had been working on such a capability" (U.S. Congress, 1993e: 112).

The possibility that biological materials may become attractive to substate actors such as splinter groups or terrorists cannot be discounted (Henderson, 1999). The incidents in the Tokyo subway in March 1995, in which the Aum Shinrikyo sect placed small containers of the nerve gas sarin on baggage racks or on the floor of subway trains and then punctured these containers to release the sarin, has heightened international awareness that substate actors might seek to use chemicals to further their aims (U.S. Senate, 1995).

Clearly, there is a very real concern worldwide about the danger that disease, whether occurring naturally or deliberately, presents to the people, animals, and plants of states. How, then, can the nature of the threat be assessed?

ASSESSMENT OF THE BIOLOGICAL THREAT

Assessment of the biological threat must be done by analysts with technical knowledge about biological agents and toxins and the ability to analyze the threat posed by potential aggressors or terrorist groups. Assuming that analysts with such expertise are available, the assessment process involves two phases: analysis and validation. In addition, a third phase is frequently important: the interpretation of the significance of the assessed threat. In this section, the technical knowledge and analytical ability required are addressed first, and then analysis, validation, and interpretation are considered.

Technical Knowledge of Biological Agents

Because BW is the deliberate use of infectious or toxin agents to cause harm in a target population, be it human, animal, or plant, analysts need to possess specialized skills and knowledge about how pathogens or toxins may be employed to deliberately cause harm, including the following:

- Agent characteristics: Are agents available to adversaries that possess the capabilities necessary for BW? Important characteristics include optimal size for retention in the lungs and the abilities to survive physical and meteorological forces and to retain virulence after storage and dispersal.
- Agent production: Can the candidate agents be produced relatively easily in sufficient quantity to be useful by adversaries?
- Agent stability: Will the candidate agents be sufficiently stable to survive dissemination?
- Agent dissemination: Is the adversary likely to be able to disseminate the agent, whether as a wet slurry or as a dry powder, and deliver enough material to infect the target population?

Agent characteristics. Any assessment of the biological threat, whether natural or deliberate, requires an understanding of the nature of the pathogens that can cause infectious disease and of toxins that can cause toxinosis. The principal groups or classes of potential biological agents are

- Bacteria: These are the causative agents that produce diseases such as anthrax, plague, and tularemia. Many can be readily grown in artificial media using facilities akin to those used in the brewing industry. Although many pathogenic bacteria are susceptible to treatment by antibiotic drugs, strains can be selected that are antibiotic resistant and occur naturally.
- Viruses: There are large numbers of viruses that produce disease, such as the Venezuelan equine encephalitis (VEE) virus. Since these must be grown on living tissue, they need a host such as fertilized eggs.
- Rickettsia: These are intermediate between viruses and bacteria and must be grown in living tissue. An example is *Coxiella burnetii,* the organism that produces Q-fever.
- Fungi: Relatively few fungal species appear to have potential for deliberate use against humans, although many more have potential against plants. An example of a human pathogen is *Coccidioides immitis,* the causative agent of coccidioidomycosis.
- Toxins: These are the nonliving products of microorganisms such as botulinum toxin or staphylococcal enterotoxin B; of plants, such as ricin from castor beans; or of living creatures, such as saxitoxin from shellfish.

The sorts of pathogens and toxins that are of potential concern as biological agents have been listed in many publications as well as in papers produced by the Ad Hoc Group of State Parties to the BWC. It has produced lists of human, animal, and plant pathogens and human toxins together with criteria for identification of materials to be included in such lists (BWC, 1995a, 1995b, 1997). The criteria for human pathogens and toxins are (1) agents known to have been developed, produced, stockpiled, or used as weapons; (2) low infectious dose or high toxicity; (3) high level of morbidity; (4) high level of contagiousness in population; (5) infection or intoxication by respiratory route; (6) high level of incapacity or mortality; (7) no effective prophylaxis (i.e., immune sera, vaccines, antibiotics) or therapy commonly available and widely in use; (8) stability in the atmosphere; (9) difficulty of detection or identification; and (10) ease of production (BWC, 1999).

Although the Ad Hoc Group states that the criteria are "proposed to be used in combination" (p. 155), it has to be emphasized that the criteria listed are not absolute requirements but factors that may be relevant. For example, the criterion of "high level of contagiousness in the population" is not necessarily a requirement; the UK and U.S. offensive BW programs, which ceased in the late 1950s and 1969, respectively, had focused on agents that were not transmissible within a population. Again, the criteria regarding the availability of prophylaxis and therapy need not be relevant. In addition, it has to be recognized that the factors leading a terrorist group to select an agent may be very different from those influencing a potential adversary state—a terrorist group may, for example, prefer to cause infection through ingestion and thereby more accurately target a particular group.

Understanding the nature and characteristics of biological agents requires knowledge of a large number of factors, including

- Infective dose, or ID_{50}: the number of organisms that will cause 50 percent of the exposed population to be infected with the disease. The infective dose can vary depending on the age and susceptibility of the target population.
- Time to effect, or incubation time: the time between exposure to the organisms and the appearance of the symptoms of the disease.
- Method of attack of the target population, whether by inhalation, ingestion, or through the bite of an insect vector and whether the disease can be spread from one member of the target population to another.
- Methods of production of the agent, and whether sufficient quantity can be produced relatively easily and in sufficient concentration to be effective.
- Method of dispersion of the agent, the particle sizes produced and their ability to be retained by the target population, and the efficiency of dissemination.
- Stability of the agent before and after dispersion. Microorganisms are fragile and can be killed by exposure to the natural environment—to heat, sunlight, or ultraviolet radiation—in the dissemination process or subsequently.
- Practicability of achieving an infectious dose in the target population. This requires an evaluation of the dispersion in the atmosphere, which will depend on the atmospheric stability, wind direction, and speed.

Similar considerations apply to toxins, but because toxins are nonliving, they cannot produce a transmissible disease. Toxins are much more closely related to chemical warfare agents; unlike some biological agents, toxins can only affect those exposed to the agent. The characteristics of some illustrative biological agents are summarized in Table 3.1 (United Nations, 1969).

Table 3.1   Characteristics of Some Potential Biological Warfare Agents

Agent	Dose to Effect[a]	Time to Effect	Mortality	Transmissibility
Bacteria				
Bacillus anthracis				
(anthrax)	20,000	1–5 days	fatal	negligible
Yersinia pestis				
(plague)	3,000	2–5 days	fatal	high
Francisella tularensis				
(tularemia)	>25	1–10 days	low	negligible
Brucella species				
(brucellosis)	1,300	1–3 weeks	low	none
Viruses				
VEE virus				
(encephalitis)	25	2–5 days	low	none
Rickettsia				
Coxiella burnetii				
(Q-fever)	1	10–21 days	low	none
Fungi				
Coccidioides immitis				
(coccidioimycosis)	1,350	1–3 weeks	low	none
Toxins				
Botulinum toxin	0.12 micrograms	1/2–3 days	fatal	none
Staphylococcal				
enterotoxin B	0.1 micrograms/kg intravenous	1 hour	low	none
Ricin	0.1 micrograms/kg intramuscular	1–3 days	fatal	none

Source: United Nations, 1969.
Note: a. The units are in viable cells for bacteria and fungi and in infectious units for viruses and rickettsia. The dose to effect is by the aerosol route unless otherwise stated.

Agent production. An understanding is necessary of the ways in which pathogens and toxins can be produced and the time required for sufficient quantities to be produced to meet the requirements of the state or terrorist group seeking the BW capability. This needs to include an appreciation of the various ways in which pathogens can be cultured, the sort of media needed to culture the pathogen, the conditions required for such culturing, and how the pathogen can be harvested after culturing. Both the capabilities of modern fermentation technology as well as the traditional flask culture techniques have to be understood.

Agent stability. This has to be understood from at least two standpoints. First, after the pathogen is cultured and harvested, how stable is it in storage? Although there will probably not be any need to store biological agents for extended periods (as was the requirement when the United

States was engaged in producing a retaliatory capability that was to be stored ready for use until required), it will generally be necessary to store the agent for at least some days or weeks. Second, will the agent be stable while it is being dispersed and subsequently carried downwind? Dispersion techniques can include explosive or other methods that can cause the fragile microorganisms to die. Subsequent to dispersion, exposure to the environment—to the ambient temperature, ultraviolet radiation, or sunlight—may also cause the microorganisms to die. The rate at which such microorganisms decay in the environment needs to be understood.

Agent dissemination. An essential capability is an understanding of the way in which disease can be spread. Some pathogens are contagious, thus, persons suffering from infectious disease are frequently isolated. However, some diseases are not contagious; many of the pathogens studied by the United States and UK as part of their past BW programs were not contagious. Only those inhaling a sufficient quantity of the dispersed pathogens would catch the disease. For example, spores of the bacterial pathogen *Bacillus anthracis* can be relatively easily spread by aerosol. Persons who inhale a sufficient number of spores (ID_{50}) are likely to contract pulmonary anthrax, the most lethal form of anthrax. However, it is one of this disease's characteristics that infected persons are not able to pass on the organism to others by the aerosol route.

The other area that needs to be understood is how such agents might be delivered. The means of delivery needs to be tailored so as to deliver a quantity of agent sufficient to cause disease in the target population. One example was the BW capability acquired by the UK in World War II in order to retaliate should BW be used against it. This was an antianimal capability based on cattle cakes laced with anthrax spores that would have been disseminated over Germany through flare chutes of aircraft. German cattle that ate these cakes would develop anthrax and die. Because the dispersal of cattle cakes at night over pastureland would be difficult to detect, this example also illustrates the point that the delivery means seldom have any particular signature indicating BW.

Another possible delivery system for antipersonnel agents could be to disperse biological agents into the atmosphere as aerosol particles that would be carried downwind and inhaled by the target population. Dispersion from an aircraft, vehicle, or boat traveling across the wind is likely to be effective. The way in which such aerosol particles might be dispersed so as to reach the target population needs to be understood so that the characteristics of potential delivery vehicles can be recognized and the apparent lack of signature countered. The distance downwind at which a dangerous concentration of agent will be experienced will depend on factors such as the meteorological conditions at the time and the nature of the agent.

Ability to Analyze Threats

If sufficient information exists about some of these factors, the competent analyst can make a reasonable determination of the technical threat posed by the potential adversary or terrorist group. However, such an assessment would be incomplete without analysis of the technological capability and the motivation of the would-be possessor. In addition, the analyst has to be able to evaluate whether an outbreak of disease is the result of a natural or deliberate release. Consequently, assessment of the biological threat to a particular state requires several additional capabilities:

- Technological capability: What technological capability does the potential aggressor or terrorist groups have?
- Motivation: What motivation might the potential aggressor or terrorist groups have to select, develop, and use BW?
- Analysis of outbreaks: Are the characteristics from outbreaks of disease or intoxinations indicative of natural outbreaks or deliberate releases?

Each of these capabilities will be considered in turn.

Technological capabilities. The ability to assess the likely threat from a potential adversary country or terrorist group also requires an appreciation of their technological capabilities, what agents are likely to be available, what relevant expertise they are likely to have, and what their proven relevant capability is. Because of the increasing importance of biotechnology throughout the world, the necessary technological capabilities are likely to be available. The bilateral and multilateral programs that have aided the spread of biotechnology were given a fresh international impetus when the UN Conference on Environment and Development (the Earth Summit) held in Rio de Janeiro June 5–14, 1992, produced a Declaration of Principles and Agenda 21, a series of aspirations relating to all aspects of the environment and development (United Nations, 1992). In addition, two legally binding Conventions—the Convention on Biological Diversity (CBD) and the Convention on Climate Change (CCC)—were opened for signature. Both Agenda 21 and CBD promote the peaceful uses of microbiology and biotechnology. The worldwide spread of biotechnology for peaceful purposes means that the possibilities of accidental release or the deliberate misuse of disease as a weapon of war are greater than before.

The assessment of the biological threat requires the creation over time of an appreciation of the pattern of microbiological and biotechnological activities within a country and a region against which variations can be identified and evaluated. The BWC state parties agreed in 1986 to a set of politically binding confidence-building measures (CBMs) (BWC, 1986b), which were improved and extended in 1991 (BWC, 1992); these CBMs are designed to improve transparency about microbiological and biotechnological activities of relevance to the convention being carried out in BWC state parties and thereby build confidence that state parties are indeed in compliance with the convention. The declarations provided under the CBMs, together with other available information, help to build a national pattern of microbiological and biotechnological activity against which judgments can be reached as to the likely significance of variations from the pattern.

Motivation. An equally important capability is the ability to analyze whether the potential adversary or terrorist group might wish to utilize BW in order to achieve its aims. The adversary will need an appreciation of the nature of BW and of the risk that using such agents may cause harm to supporters and opponents alike. The political, military, economic, and historical aspects of the potential adversary all need to be evaluated.

Analysis of outbreaks. The first indication of a biological threat may be the outbreak of disease in a particular location. This could be a natural outbreak, which can occur in areas previously free from the particular disease, or it could be the first manifestation of a potentially hostile biological weapons program arising from an accidental release, a field trial of candidate BW agents, or a small-scale use against a particular target population.

Outbreaks of disease occur worldwide with distressing frequency. In order to determine whether such outbreaks have occurred naturally, accidentally, or deliberately, an understanding is needed of the natural patterns of disease in the various regions of the world as well as what diseases are endemic in a particular area, their mechanisms of spread in that area, and their local symptoms. Over time a good appreciation can be gained about the typical pattern for outbreaks of endemic disease—whether in humans, animals, or plants—for some diseases in particular locations. It is then possible to compare subsequent outbreaks of disease with the typical pattern and identify variations that may be indicative of a deliberate outbreak or accidental release.

In a typical pattern involving an endemic disease, cases will continue to occur throughout the outbreak, and the location of cases will be widespread. Indicators of an unusual outbreak could include an outbreak of a disease that is not endemic in the area, a number of cases developing symptoms at the same time, or cases located in a particular area, all of which could be indicative of an accidental or deliberate release.

It is, however, apparent that not all unusual outbreaks will differ sharply from natural outbreaks, especially if a transmissible disease is involved, in which case the pattern of spread and location will be much more diffuse. Nevertheless, there is little doubt that study and investigation of unusual outbreaks of disease and similar occurrences caused by toxins can provide valuable information that will contribute to the biological threat assessment.

Analysis of the Biological Threat

The analyst carrying out an assessment of a biological threat has to draw together several strands:

- Information on national microbiological and biotechnological activity, primarily from open sources, together with an appreciation of the political-military situation in the particular country. This information can be analyzed to discover any variations from the national or regional pattern that appear to be unusual or unexplained.
- Information on any unusual outbreaks of disease or similar occurrences caused by toxins and any indications as to whether these resulted from a deliberate or accidental release.
- Evaluation of any information from any source regarding an alleged BW capability, together with an assessment of the credibility and effectiveness of the alleged agents and delivery means.

The analyst can identify the types of agent and delivery systems that are likely to be selected by a state considering the acquisition of a BW capability. For example, information is available as to which agents were studied and type-classified by the United States in its BW program (U.S. Department of the Army, 1977b), which was terminated in 1969. These included both antipersonnel and anticrop agents (Perry Robinson, 1981). Antipersonnel agents (all were nontransmissible) included anthrax, tularemia, brucellosis, Q-fever, VEE, yellow fever, botulinum toxin, saxitoxin, and staphylococcal enterotoxin B. Anticrop agents included wheat stem rust, rye stem rust, and rice blast. A variety of delivery systems were studied by the United States (Perry Robinson, 1981), including:

- Line source spray tanks (A/B45Y-1, A/B45Y-2, A/B45Y-4, Aero X2A)
- Cluster bombs (500-lb. M33 and M115, 750-lb. E86)

- Burster-type munitions
- Submunitions (4.5-inch spherical bomblet for air dispensers; 3.4-inch spherical bomblet for the Sergeant missile)
- Portable generators (E32R1, M32)
- Special Forces devices (E2, M5, M4)

Although the UK and Canada had had earlier BW programs, which terminated in the 1950s, the types of agent and delivery systems were similar to those at the start of the much broader U.S. program, and all three countries cooperated closely (Carter and Pearson, 1996).

A potential aggressor is likely to start by considering the above agents and delivery systems because they have all been demonstrated in trials—and, indeed, have been proven to a greater extent than had nuclear weapons before they were used at Nagasaki and Hiroshima. An aggressor can choose other agents and other delivery systems, but there is far less information available as to whether these would actually be effective—and consequently, there would be a much higher risk that the capability to wage BW would be ineffective and that the delivery systems, which are generally scarce and in much demand in any conflict, might be wasted in attempting to deliver biological weapons instead of being used to deliver conventional war-heads. Alternatively, if the uncertainty is reduced by carrying out trials of the alternative agents and delivery systems, there is an increased risk that such trials will be detected and trigger international reactions and responses.

A similar argument can apply to considerations of whether to use genetically manipulated or modified agents. A potential aggressor may choose to modify an agent with a view to improving some characteristic such as its virulence, but this modification may result in an undesirable change to some other important characteristic, such as agent stability in the atmosphere. The risk that the capability to wage BW would be ineffective could be increased, and if trials were carried out to determine whether the capability was effective, they might be detected.

However, any assessment of the most likely agent and delivery system that might be used by a potential aggressor must recognize that a would-be aggressor will not necessarily follow a logical approach or make the same choices as the assessing nation might think to be likely. Consequently, although it would be reasonable to focus protective measures against the sort of agents and delivery systems indicated above, it would also be prudent to bear in mind that other agents, including genetically modified agents, and other delivery systems might well be used. The aim in developing protective measures must be to adopt generic techniques that will be effective against as wide a range of biological agents and delivery systems as possible (Pearson, 1995).

Validation of the Biological Threat

In assessing such information, particular attention needs to be given to whether the information from different sources is consistent, both internally and externally (i.e., one piece of information from one source does not contradict that obtained from a quite different source). As much as possible, the information on which the assessment is based needs to be validated and verified; all data must be scientifically and technically credible. Care needs to be taken throughout to avoid the dangers of mirror imaging—of assuming that another country will necessarily follow the same logic or make the same choices as would the assessing state. The assessment will be more robust if different agencies are responsible for different parts of the evaluation and arrive at a common assessment.

Interpretation of the Biological Threat

The third important phase of assessment is the interpretation of the significance of the biological threat. This is sometimes known as hazard evaluation and is a technical assessment of the implications of the assessed threat. In many respects, hazard evaluation should be regarded as part of the biological threat assessment because the credibility of any threat needs to be evaluated. Clearly, if a threat can be shown technically to present no hazard, then it will not be a threat—assuming that the hazard evaluation is sound and has not made any invalid assumptions.

Hazard evaluation requires knowledge of the characteristics of the agent, its effect on the target population (whether human, animal, or plant), and the means of dispersion and transport of the agent from the device to the target. The information about the agent needs to include an appreciation as to how it might be produced, the ease of its production, the nature and the stability of the product, and whether or not it needs to be purified or concentrated to obtain an effective concentration. As to the effect on the target population, knowledge is required of the infective (or in the case of toxins, the lethal) dose necessary to affect the target population, together with the characteristics of the way in which the disease will become apparent. The ability of the agent to survive dispersion in the natural environment must be known to assess whether the agent can indeed be used as a biological agent dispersed as an aerosol and carried on the wind to the target, or whether some other route of attack will be necessary. A knowledge of the delivery means together with information on the survivability of the agent enables an evaluation to be made of the extent of the downwind areas that would be exposed to a harmful concentration. The concentrations at various distances downwind from the delivery means can be used to calculate the challenge levels at these distances, which in turn determines the protection levels needed to protect the target.

A careful hazard evaluation enables the effect of various protective measures to be compared, and thus an optimum protective stance can be developed that will be invaluable in targeting the efforts of those responsible for the development of effective protective measures. In broad terms, such hazard evaluations can determine the optimum location for biological agent detection capabilities upwind of those to be protected, so that there is time to warn them to adopt respiratory protection. Such respiratory protection may take the form of oro-nasal masks or full respirators; oro-nasal masks may provide a protection factor of 100 or so, thereby necessitating a much higher challenge level if the biological agent attack is to be effective (Danzig, 1996; Lowe et al., 1996). Physical protection needs to be complemented by medical countermeasures—both prophylaxis before exposure, such as vaccinations and therapy, and treatment after exposure, such as antibiotics.

Decontamination generally presents less of a postattack hazard; a useful rule is that about 1 percent of the biological challenge will fall out and deposit on the surface over which the challenge is carried on the wind. A strong wind could re-aerosolize deposited agents, but if this was to occur, it would be at a low level of efficiency. Consequently, the challenge level would have to be very high indeed—about 10,000 infective doses in order to present a re-aerosolization hazard—and such a challenge level is improbable. Some agent will still be present on surfaces after a biological attack, but its concentration will not present a hazard.

THREE CASE STUDIES: IRAQ, RUSSIA, AND AUM SHINRIKYO

Three recent case studies in which there is clear evidence that a BW capability had been acquired are considered to see what lessons can be drawn for the assessment and evaluation of the biological threat. In the case of Iraq, the coalition forces in Operations Desert Shield and Desert Storm faced the prospect that Iraq might use chemical or biological weapons against them. The perception of the Iraqi capability at the outset of the conflict and that which became apparent as a result of investigations performed by the United Nations Special Commission (UNSCOM) on Iraq are compared. The second case study covers Russia, which as the former Soviet Union had been a co-depositary of the 1972 BWC yet had continued an offensive biological weapons program until 1992. Since then the United Kingdom, United States, and Russian Federation have been working together under the terms of a joint statement made September 14, 1992, with the aim of ensuring that the offensive program has indeed been terminated and that the Russian Federation is in compliance with the BWC. The third case study considers Aum Shinrikyo, which had been seeking to acquire both chemical and biological weapons capabilities and used the chemical agent sarin in its attack on the Tokyo subway in March 1995.

Iraq

On August 2, 1990, Iraq invaded Kuwait. Within hours, the invasion had been condemned by the United Nations Security Council, which unanimously adopted Resolution 660 (UN Security Council, 1990). On August 7, 1990, in response to requests from Kuwait, Saudi Arabia, Bahrain, and other governments in the region, the United States, United Kingdom, and other European countries started dispatching air and naval forces to the region. This multinational force eventually involved more than thirty nations.

This section consists of three parts: first, the assessment of the Iraqi biological threat at the outset of Desert Storm; second, the actual threat as disclosed by the efforts of UNSCOM; and third, in view of what is now known about the Iraqi biological capabilities, the accuracy of the assessment. This analysis is complicated by the difficulty of determining precisely the nature of the threat assessment prior to Desert Storm and by the continuing efforts of Iraq to conceal the full extent of its program and capabilities.

Biological threat assessment. The coalition forces were greatly concerned about Iraqi chemical and biological weapons capabilities. The UK annual defense white paper issued after the cease-fire in 1991 stated that "Iraq was known to possess stocks of chemical weapons, and to have used them during the Iran-Iraq war and against its own citizens. There was evidence too that Iraq had been seeking to develop nuclear and biological weapons. The allies therefore placed great importance on deterring Iraq from using any such weapons. Alliance leaders made it clear they would take the gravest view of any Iraqi use of weapons of mass destruction" (Ministry of Defence, 1991: 17). Likewise, the UK joint commander stated that "we had to be prepared for a preemptive Iraqi attack including the use of Scud short range ballistic missiles and perhaps armed with chemical or biological warheads" (Hine, 1991: 639). Finally, the U.S. Department of Defense Final Report to Congress stated, "By the time of the invasion of Kuwait, Iraq had developed biological weapons. Its advanced and aggressive BW program was the most extensive in the Arab world. The program . . . concentrated on development of two agents—botulinum toxin and anthrax bacteria. Delivery means for biological agents ranged from simple aerial bombs and artillery rockets to surface-to-surface missiles" (U.S. Department of Defense, 1991: 18).

The coalition forces consequently took action to ensure that they had protective measures against the threat of both chemical and biological attacks, but they were "ill-prepared at the start for defense against BW, even though [they knew] Saddam had developed biological agents" (U.S. Department of Defense, 1991: 19). In addition, the objectives of the air campaign by the coalition forces were to "disrupt Iraq's command, control and communications, to destroy Iraq's nuclear, biological and chemical warfare capability, to establish air superiority. . . . Production and development facilities were attacked with precision-guided munitions using tactics designed to minimize any risk of contamination outside the sites. The equipment that Iraq would have used to deliver such weapons—artillery pieces, rockets, aircraft or helicopters—were also priority targets" (Ministry of Defence, 1991: 17). It is also apparent that the armed forces were vaccinated against the biological agents thought to be in the Iraqi biological weapons capability: anthrax, botulinum toxin, and plague (Cordingley, 1996).

The 1991 assessment of the Iraqi biological threat was that the coalition forces faced an Iraqi biological weapons threat comprising anthrax, botulinum toxin, and plague in delivery systems ranging from simple aircraft bombs and artillery rockets to surface-to-surface missiles, including Scud short-range ballistic missiles. Insofar as biological facilities are concerned, little detailed information has become available about facilities known to the coalition forces other than Salman Pak and a "baby milk factory" in Baghdad, both of which were attacked.

Iraqi biological weapons capability. Following the suspension of combat operations at midnight on February 27, 1991, the United Nations Security Council negotiated and adopted on April 3, 1991, Security Council Resolution 687 (UN Security Council, 1991) that established UNSCOM, which was charged with destroying, removing, or rendering harmless all Iraqi chemical and biological weapons, all stocks of agents, and all research, development, support, and manufacturing facilities. UNSCOM also drew up plans for ongoing monitoring and verification to ensure that Iraq did not reacquire any proscribed capabilities.

UNSCOM's investigations of the Iraqi biological weapons program have been fraught with difficulty throughout. The first Iraqi disclosure on its biological weapons program in April 1991 simply said, "Iraq does not possess any biological weapons or related items as mentioned" in Resolution 687 (Al-Anbari, 1991: 1). The situation improved only in mid-1995, when UNSCOM pressed Iraq to account for large imports of growth media and specialized dual-purpose equipment. Iraq then disclosed the production of significant quantities of biological weapons agents and later of their weaponization and deployment. However, UNSCOM reports of 1997 and 1998 make it clear that Iraq's latest declarations of its biological program are incomplete, containing many gaps and inconsistencies (UN Security Council, 1997; UNSCOM, 1999a). The UNSCOM evaluation of the Iraqi biological weapons capability cannot be regarded as being complete, especially because UNSCOM had said in 1992, in commenting on Iraq's full, final, and complete disclosures of its proscribed weapons programs, that "the information so far provided is tailored to what the Iraqi authorities consider UNSCOM to know already, rather than constituting a frank and open disclosure of all the true facts" (UN Security Council, 1992: 2). More recently, Iraq has admitted that it had mounted a deliberate concealment program to hide its capabilities from the UNSCOM inspectors (UNSCOM, 1999a). Consequently, the UNSCOM evaluation of the Iraq biological weapons capability comes with a warning—the capability is that which has thus far been disclosed by Iraq.

According to Iraq, its BW program (UN Security Council, 1995a) started in 1975 and continued until early January 1991, with a pause between 1978 and 1985. The agents were anthrax and botulinum toxin, together with work on *Clostridium perfringens* (gas gangrene), aflatoxin, trichothecene mycotoxins, and ricin; on viruses including camelpox virus; and on wheat cover smut fungus. There was significant concentrated agent production of 19,000 liters of botulinum toxin, 8,500 liters of anthrax, and 2,200 liters of aflatoxin, and weaponization systems included spray tanks, unmanned aerial vehicles, aerial bombs, missiles, and rockets. In December 1990, more than 160 aerial bombs and twenty-five Al-Hussein warheads were filled with anthrax, botulinum toxin, and aflatoxin; they were deployed to four locations by early January 1991. Authority to launch chemical and biological warheads was said by Iraq to have been predelegated in the event that Baghdad was hit by nuclear weapons in the Gulf War. It was also clear that Iraq had an indigenous missile development program that was involved in designing longer-range missile systems capable of delivering chemical or biological warheads to ranges of 3,000 km.

Trials with 122-millimeter (mm) artillery rockets were reported to have been carried out successfully, although no weaponization in 122-mm rockets has been disclosed. Trials had been carried out with spray tanks but were reported as having been considered a failure, although three additional spray tanks were reported to have been produced and stored. Iraq's biological warfare facilities included a research unit at Salman Pak, and a major production facility at Al-Hakam (Zilinskas, 1997).

Accuracy of the assessment. The assessment made at the outset of the Gulf conflict by members of the coalition—that Iraq had biological weapons comprising anthrax, botulinum toxin, and plague in delivery systems ranging from simple aircraft bombs and artillery rockets to surface-to-surface missiles, including Scud short-range ballistic missiles—was broadly correct. However, there were inaccuracies with respect to some details. For example, plague as an agent and the deployment of artillery rockets have yet to be disclosed to UNSCOM, and aflatoxin and wheat cover smut fungus appear not to have been identified in the coalition assessments. Insofar as facilities are concerned, Salman Pak was known and attacked, but Al-Hakam was not. The Baghdad "baby milk factory," which was attacked, has subsequently been found to have had some connections with the Technical Research Center (TRC), which was responsible for much of the Iraqi BW program.

Russia

In 1992, President Boris Yeltsin admitted that the former Soviet Union had continued an offensive biological weapons program from 1972 until 1992 (Leitenberg, 1996a). This section consists of three parts: first, the assessment of the biological threat from the former Soviet Union/Russia in 1992; second, the actual threat as disclosed by Russia; and third, in view of what is now known about the biological capabilities of the former Soviet Union/Russia, the accuracy of the assessment. This analysis is complicated by the paucity of unclassified assessments prior to 1992 and the uncertainty that the former Soviet/Russian BW program has been fully disclosed.

Biological threat assessment. In June 1985 the Chemical Warfare Review Commission said that the "exact scope and nature of the Soviet threat is unclear" (Chemical Warfare Review Commission, 1985: 69), and that "at this time, the Department of Defense does not have an adequate grasp of the biological-warfare threat and has not been giving it sufficient attention. Both intelligence and research into this area, though improved after a virtual halt during the 1970s, are strikingly deficient. The Department should be devoting much more resources and talent to addressing the chemical and biological threats of the future as well as those of the present" (p. 71).

There are relatively few unclassified official assessments of the former Soviet Union's biological weapons capability. One of the earliest public statements arose from the outbreak of anthrax that occurred in Sverdlovsk in 1979. This was alleged by the West to have resulted from an accident at a suspect BW facility, although the Soviet Union stated that the outbreak had resulted from the illegal sale of contaminated meat on the black market. A 1986 U.S. Defense Intelligence Agency (DIA) report said that early in April 1979, an accidental release of anthrax occurred within a military facility in the southwestern outskirts of Sverdlovsk in which as much as 10 kg of dry anthrax spores were released, contaminating an area within a radius of at least 2–3 miles (Defense Intelligence Agency, 1986). Residents and workers within the contaminated area contracted pulmonary anthrax through inhalation, and a significant number of deaths occurred.

More than merely reporting on the Sverdlovsk anthrax epidemic, the 1986 DIA report assessed the Soviet biological warfare threat. It included what was called a "key judgment," which, after recalling the BWC and Geneva Protocol, stated:

> We believe that the Soviets have gone far beyond what is allowed by these treaties for the following reasons:
>
> • The size and scope of their efforts are not consistent with any reasonable standard of what could be justified on the basis of prophylactic, protective or peaceful purposes.
> • The Soviets continue to evaluate the military utility of biological and toxin weapons.
> • The Soviets are rapidly incorporating biotechnological developments into their offensive BW program to improve agent utility on the tactical battlefield. (Defense Intelligence Agency, 1986: v)

Somewhat stronger statements are made in the body of the DIA report, which says: "We have observed no reduction in Soviet BW offensive activity. We have concluded that the Soviets have and are developing and producing BW agents. They are continuing to test and evaluate delivery and dissemination systems for these agents" (p. 1). The report goes on to say: "In addition to anthrax, we believe the Soviets have developed tularemia, plague and cholera for BW purposes, as well as botulinum toxin, enterotoxin, and mycotoxins" (p. 2). This assessment is curiously silent on delivery means, with only the oblique comment that "even though high concentrations of anthrax are required to be delivered over a target population, the Soviets have no technical difficulties in achieving this" (p. 4). The DIA report also identified a test and evaluation facility on Vozrozhdeniye Island in the Aral Sea as a military BW R&D facility in Sverdlovsk.

The next year an assessment was provided in *Soviet Military Power 1987*, which said that the Soviet offensive BW program has been monitored by the United States for decades (U.S. Department of Defense, 1987). When the BWC entered into force in 1975, no reduction in the Soviet BW offensive activity was observed. Insofar as the Soviet biological agents are concerned, this report repeated the statement in the 1986 DIA report that "in addition to anthrax, we believe the Soviets have developed tularemia, plague and cholera for BW purposes, as well as botulinum toxin, enterotoxin, and mycotoxins" (p. 109). Very little information is provided on delivery means, other than to note that "an infectious agent grown in large numbers and then placed in a weapon/dissemination system becomes a BW weapon" (p. 109).

A book entitled *The Soviet Biochemical Threat to NATO*, which appeared in 1987, contains relatively little information on Soviet BW other than to record that the USSR has been actively interested in the subject since the early 1930s and then to note that strict security has characterized all the Soviet Union work in this field, so that little is known in the West about the Soviet BW apart from some generalized writing (Hemsley, 1987). The object of Soviet BW was said to be to reduce the enemy's ability to wage war, either directly, by attacking its armed forces or civil population, or indirectly, by attacking livestock or crops.

The Soviet Union also disclosed, in its report on confidence-building measures following the Second Review Conference of the BWC in 1986 (BWC, 1986b), five facilities under Ministry of Defense funding with containment units that specialize in permitted activities at Leningrad, Kirov, Sverdlovsk, Zagorsk, and Aralsk (the latter was declared to be a scientific testing field laboratory) (Geissler, 1990b).

In 1993, a U.S. House of Representatives report, after mentioning Soviet interest in anthrax, said: "U.S. authorities have maintained that the Soviet biological weapons program included the development of tularemia, plague, Q-fever, and cholera, as well as botulinum toxin, enterotoxin and mycotoxin" (U.S. Congress, 1993b: 3). No statement was made about delivery means, however.

Biological weapons capability of the former Soviet Union/Russia. In April 1992, President Yeltsin acknowledged that the former Soviet Union had continued an offensive BW program and signed a decree stating: "The development and implementation of biological programs in breach of the BWC is not permitted on the territory of the Russian Federation. The Committee for Issues relating to the Convention of Chemical and Biological Weapons shall, within one month, introduce proposals aimed at strengthening measures with regard to openness and confidence-building and at extending international cooperation under the BWC" (Yeltsin, 1992: 1).

In September 1992 a joint U.S./UK statement on biological weapons was issued in which "the Russian Government stated that it had taken the following steps to resolve compliance concerns" (U.S. Department of State, 1992: 2). These included the following:

> B. Confirmed the termination of offensive research, the dismantlement of experimental technological lines for the production of biological agents, and the closure of the biological weapons testing facility.
> C. Cut the number of personnel involved in military biological programs by fifty percent.
> D. Reduced military biological research funding by thirty percent. . . .
> F. Submitted the declaration to the United Nations under the terms of the Confidence Building Measures agreed at the Third Review Conference of the Convention in 1991.

The trilateral statement went on to say that, as a result of these exchanges, Russia has agreed to the following steps: "The provision, on request, of information about the dismantlement accomplished to date. The provision of further clarification of information provided for in Form F of its UN declaration" (p. 2).

The Russian declaration in 1992 regarding confidence-building measures (which requires only a declaration of past offensive and defensive *research and development* programs from January 1, 1946, onward [BWC, 1992]) stated that an offensive research and development program had continued from 1946 until March 1992 and that work had been carried out on the following agents: anthrax, tularemia, brucellosis, plague, botulism, VEE, typhus, and Q-fever. Relatively little information was provided about delivery means, although a statement was made that "military-technical evaluation was carried out of experimental samples of biological formulations loaded into prototypes (mock-ups) of biological munitions and spraying systems." Form F of the declaration also mentioned that as "the USSR lagged behind in the field of molecular biology of genetics and genetic engineering, the Government of the USSR, at the beginning of the 1970s, took the decision to accelerate the development of these branches of biological science and to utilize their achievements in the national economy." The facilities mentioned were Sverdlovsk, Kirov, and Zagorsk, with Vozrozhdeniye Island in the Aral Sea as an experimental base where military-technical evaluation was carried out. Mention was also made of Kol'tsovo, Obolensk, Chekhov, and Leningrad, where research on dangerous pathogens was planned.

There has been little official public comment on progress following the joint statement, although some indications can be gleaned from the annual reports of ACDA to the U.S. Congress. The January 19, 1993, report says, "The United States has determined that the Russian offensive BW program, inherited from the Soviet Union, violated the Biological Weapons Convention through at least March 1992. The Soviet offensive BW program was massive and included production, weaponization and stockpiling. The status of the program since that time remains unclear" (ACDA, 1993: 5). The ACDA also says that the declaration made by Russia under the confidence-building measures was regarded as inadequate. Three years later, the July 26, 1996, report stated: "The Russian Federation's 1993, 1994, and 1995 BWC data declarations contained no new information and its 1992 declaration was incomplete and misleading in certain areas" (ACDA, 1996b: 6).

The Russian declarations have not addressed the outbreak of anthrax at Sverdlovsk in 1979; indeed, as late as March 1997, the Russian delegation at the Ad Hoc Group negotiations in Geneva repeated the black market meat explanation. Such an explanation is even less credible now following the study of publicly available information published in 1994 (Meselson et al., 1994). Matthew Meselson's analysis was able to demonstrate that almost all the victims suffered from inhalation anthrax (not ingestion or percutaneous anthrax). Furthermore, the study showed that all had lived or worked in a narrow zone extending some 4 km to the southwest of a military facility in Sverdlovsk, that livestock had died of anthrax at the same time in villages located along the extended axis of this same zone out to a distance of 50 km, and that the wind had been in this same direction during most of the day of April 2, 1979, which was some two to three days before the first cases of human and animal anthrax appeared. As Meselson concludes, the narrow zone of human and animal anthrax cases extending downwind from the military microbiological facility in Sverdlovsk shows that the outbreak resulted from an aerosol that originated there.

Accuracy of the assessment. The assessments made by the United States, that the Soviet Union had biological weapons based on anthrax, tularemia, plague, Q-fever, and cholera, as well as botulinum toxin, enterotoxin, and mycotoxin, were broadly correct, although brucellosis, VEE, and typhus were not included in the U.S. published assessments. The situation with respect to genetically modified agents is unclear. Other information suggests that the Soviet Union program also included genetically modified agents, with genetically engineered plague and tularemia being identified (Adams, 1994; Barry, 1993). However, neither the assessments prior to 1992 nor the Russian statements since then have addressed this aspect. As to facilities, the indications are that the assessment made prior to 1992 has been broadly confirmed by the subsequent Russian declarations, although the precise role of the various facilities in the past program has yet to be disclosed.

As with Iraq, it has become apparent that the former Soviet Union's BW program was broadly similar to that which had been assessed in the West prior to the Russian admissions. It is also clear with respect to both Iraq and Russia that the agents around which their programs were formulated were the traditional BW agents. In both cases, however, there were indications of different agents—aflatoxin in Iraq and genetically manipulated strains of plague and tularemia in the Russian program—confirming the necessity of being aware that new or modified agents may be considered by a would-be proliferator in addition to the traditional ones.

Aum Shinrikyo

In March 1995, simultaneous attacks were mounted in the Tokyo subway system, in which members of the Aum Shinrikyo sect placed some eleven small containers of the nerve gas sarin on baggage racks or on the floor of subway trains and then punctured these containers to release the sarin (U.S. Senate, 1995). Subsequent reports made it clear that Aum Shinrikyo had also been working on developing biological weapons and had been close to completing this by March 1995 (Kaplan and Marshall, 1996). This section consists of three parts: first, the assessment of the Aum Shinrikyo biological threat prior to March 1995; second, the sects' actual biological capability; and third, the accuracy of the assessment.

Biological threat assessment. This case study is particularly interesting because there was minimal assessment of the capability of the Aum Shinrikyo cult prior to the attacks in the Tokyo subway system on March 20, 1995, even though the cult had used sarin almost nine months before on June 27, 1994, at Matsumoto when seven died. The minimal assessment can be traced to World War II and the U.S. military occupation government that took control of Japan in 1945 and was charged with transforming Japan into a democratic nation (Brackett, 1996). Prior to that war, new religions in Japan were legitimate only if the government said they were; a "religious police" acted aggressively to force new sects to disband. It was therefore hardly surprising that the United States ensured that the postwar Japanese constitution contained strong, unambiguous guarantees of religious freedom. These were further strengthened by the passing of the Religious Corporation Law in 1951, which gave religious organizations unusually strong protection against state intrusion into their affairs. Because of this historical context, police inquiries into the Aum sect were minimal prior to the Tokyo subway attack.

It is reported that U.S. intelligence officers in Tokyo noted the initial news reports about Matsumoto in the Japanese media and, after a brief period of interest because sarin nerve agent had been used, apparently classified the incident as a domestic Japanese issue. Instead of actively pursuing the case, they decided to wait for the Japanese authorities to tell them more (Brackett, 1996). Nothing more had happened before the March 1995 subway attack. David Brackett indicates that U.S. intelligence was not monitoring the continuing interest in the Japanese news media in the Matsumoto incident. This lack of interest is all the more surprising given the visit made by Kyle Olson of the Chemical and Biological Arms Control Institute, Alexandria, Virginia, who visited Matsumoto in December 1994 and concluded that the incident some six months earlier had been a field test by a terrorist group; his January 1995 report pointed out the vulnerability of the Tokyo subway system (Olson, 1994).

Aum Shinrikyo biological weapons capability. Following the March 1995 subway attack, there has been an extensive interest in the activities and aspirations of the Aum Shinrikyo sect (Kaplan and Marshall, 1996). Kaplan and Marshall reported that in April 1990, the sect had a microbiological facility in which *Clostridium botulinum* was being cultured in order to produce botulinum toxin, which had apparently been selected as the first weapon of choice for the sect. In addition, the sect had developed a spraying device that was fitted to a vehicle, and in April 1990, the cult drove through the area surrounding the Japanese parliament, the Diet, disseminating botulinum toxin. No casualties were reported. Three years later in June 1993, a second attempt was made to spray botulinum toxin in central Tokyo, using a vehicle-mounted spray device, on the occasion of the wedding of the crown prince. Once again, no casualties occurred. A third attempt, this time using anthrax, took place in late June 1993; it is reported that small birds died, plants wilted, animals grew sick, and neighbors lost their appetite—none of which sounds like symptoms of anthrax. The sect also obtained cultures of Q-fever. Further attempts to disseminate botulinum toxin were reportedly carried out in the Tokyo subway in March 1995 using briefcase dispensers, some five days before the sarin attack; again, no casualties resulted, reportedly because a dissident member of the sect had not filled the dispensers with the toxin. The Aum Shinrikyo sect appears to have had botulinum toxin, anthrax, and Q-fever available as biological weapon agents and have attempted to use vehicle-based and portable dissemination devices.

Accuracy of the assessment. There was no assessment of the biological threat from the Aum Shinrikyo sect, either in Japan or internationally. The reasons for this appear to stem primarily from the strict protection of religious sects in Japan; the sect was not carrying out illegal activities in its pursuit of chemical and biological weapons since Japan had not passed legislation implementing the BWC and making it a criminal offense for any person to work on biological weapons. International assessment had not been made, presumably because no information about the threat was being obtained from Japanese intelligence sources, and there was no incentive to mount an intelligence operation in a friendly country. Because Aum Shinrikyo was not identified as a terrorist organization, its activities were not being monitored. Aum purchased most of its dual-use equipment from indigenous sources. When it tried to procure key equipment abroad, its efforts were thwarted. Although a well-coordinated international intelligence effort could have discovered these attempts at purchasing key equipment, it would have necessitated much greater cooperation and ability to discern a pattern of suspicious procurement than is currently available. The major lesson is that intelligence agencies are not able to assess capabilities in terrorist groups unless they are recognized as such and have been subjected to surveillance over time or, ideally, penetrated.

82 DEFENSE AND PROPHYLAXIS

THE LIMITATIONS OF BIOLOGICAL THREAT ASSESSMENT

The limitations of biological threat assessment arise primarily from the difficulties of obtaining accurate intelligence about a potential aggressor's capabilities and intentions. Because pathogens and toxins occur in nature and biological equipment is consequently required to modify them for any purpose, it is difficult to distinguish prohibited from legitimate activities. For this reason biological threat assessment is dependent upon the creation of a web of information drawn from all available sources; such information needs to be evaluated so that discrepancies can be identified and their significance determined. Another important limitation of biological threat assessment is the risk that the assessor will evaluate the available information against the standards of the assessing country and thereby arrive at an erroneous conclusion.

How can biological threat assessment be improved? Additional attention can be given to monitoring the microbiological and biotechnological activities and standards in the country being assessed, so that a reliable baseline is available to the assessors against which to evaluate the significance of any information received from any source. The establishment of such a baseline, which needs to be continuously updated, will help to ensure that any biological threat assessments are as sound as possible. Another important element that needs to be improved is the capability to assess whether an outbreak of disease has resulted from the deliberate use of a biological weapon, from an accidental release from a laboratory or facility, or from a natural occurrence. A number of papers on the investigation of outbreaks have been prepared by South Africa for the Ad Hoc Group meetings in Geneva, and they indicate some of the factors to be addressed (South Africa, 1995a, 1995b, 1996a, 1996b, 1996c).

FUTURE DEVELOPMENTS

The introduction to this chapter explained why governments must possess the capability to assess biological threats emanating from abroad. There is an increasing international awareness of the importance of protecting the environment and a growing realization that states have a responsibility to safeguard their environmental resources for their future economic well-being. Likewise, maintaining the health of the population, of animals, and of crops is increasingly recognized as important for trade and prosperity. And as the world recognizes that the breakdown of national and international security carries immense socioeconomic penalties, the need to take steps to strengthen security by reducing the risk that BW might be used, either by an adversary state or by terrorists, becomes more pressing.

All of this underlines the importance of biological threat assessment, both civil and military. There are signs that some intelligence agencies are taking on a wider role—thus in a February 1996 worldwide threat assessment briefing, the director of the Central Intelligence Agency spoke not only about the proliferation of biological weapons as weapons of mass destruction in the hands of rogue states but also about the possibility that terrorists would use weapons of mass destruction and about "the growing threat of environmental degradation" (Deutch, 1996: 2). With respect to the latter, he noted that "a deteriorating environment can not only affect the political and economic stability of nations, it can also pose global threats to the well-being of mankind" and went on to say that "intelligence has an important role to play in our efforts to deal with these threats" (p. 21).

Such a governmentwide involvement is laudable because there is a vital need to ensure that biological threat assessment is coordinated across agencies. In many countries there is a strong inclination, often arising from historical antipathies against defense-related work, to keep such activities separate so that health, food and agriculture, and defense analysts function independently. However, biological threat assessment is becoming ever more important in enabling a state to assess whether its security is at risk from disease. There is a clear need to maintain a coordinated group of experts who are aware of the characteristics of diseases in humans, animals, and plants and are able to monitor developments around the world regarding health and security, so that timely advice can be provided to their governments on how to protect the resources of their countries from the risks of disease.

4

Detecting
Biological Warfare Agents

STEPHEN S. MORSE

In this chapter I aim to provide an overview of the main analytic approaches now being used to detect biological threat agents, with an emphasis on principles for the applications most widely employed by the U.S. armed forces. Efficacious biological detection capabilities are especially required when meeting the challenges of three situations: battlefield conditions, biological arms control, and terrorist attacks.

Although each situation presents unique technical requirements for biological detection systems, all systems are based on one or more of the methodologies now being used in laboratories and the field. Thus, the chapter will describe and discuss classical and molecular detection methodologies and then analyze practical considerations for biological detection systems employed in activities related to biological defense or biological arms control. The chapter concludes with a discussion of the limitations of current biological detection methodologies and the steps that are being, or ought to be, taken to overcome them.

CURRENT METHODOLOGIES

Current biological detection methodologies can be placed into five broad classes: microscopy; classical biological assay, such as culturing an agent or testing its effects on cells or animals; immunoassay, that is, detecting the binding of antigen to an antibody; nucleic acid (genetic) analysis, i.e., identifying gene sequences characteristic of organisms of interest; and physical and chemical methods.

Microscopy

Light microscopy, of course, is a well-known, widely practiced traditional method for identifying microorganisms. Simple staining techniques, such as Gram staining, can be employed on a large variety of samples to detect, partially identify, and roughly quantify most common bacteria and fungi in the sample within minutes. However, some bacterial species do not take up commonly employed stains, and observed morphology is rarely sufficient for full identification. For example, bacterial spores can be identified under the microscope (with the aid of special stains), but anthrax cannot readily be distinguished from other *Bacillus* species. Therefore, all samples must be further characterized for full identification. Sensitivity of microscopy is also relatively low.

Electron microscopy, which offers greater magnification than light microscopy, can be very useful in detecting viruses in samples but requires very expensive instruments, careful sample preparation, and the service of highly trained microscopists. In most cases, after preservation in a suitable fixative, the samples are treated with special stains, often metallic salts or vaporized metals, to provide sufficient contrast to visualize the desired structures. The sample is then sliced into very thin sections (about 10 micrometers or less to allow the electron beam to penetrate the sample) for examination. The last two steps in particular require specialized equipment, and the entire process of sample preparation generally takes at least a full day or more, with additional time needed to examine the samples. Because sample preparation and examination are critical and often tedious steps, it is difficult to test large numbers of samples. Existing equipment is also heavy and not easily transported. For these reasons, electron microscopes are found only in well-equipped and well-supported laboratories. The sensitivity of electron microscopy also is fairly low; it is generally estimated that a sample must contain at least 10,000 viral particles for reliable visual detection. Miniaturized electron microscopes may well appear in the future, making the equipment more widely available, but power requirements, sample preparation, and the need for expert operators will likely remain as issues.

In the laboratory, electron microscopy has proved immensely valuable as an investigative tool. A number of viruses, including Marburg and Ebola, were first identified and originally classified by electron microscopy. The morphologic information provided by electron microscopy (approximate size and shape of the virus and whether the virus is enclosed in a membrane like envelope) has classically been one of the key criteria used in viral taxonomy, and electron microscopy is one of the few methods available for narrowing down the choices when dealing with the unknown (Richman, 1993). Morphology is usually not sufficient for definitive identification, providing at best identification to the level of virus family (in some cases, to the subfamily level), although even this can at times be useful. For example, when Marburg and Ebola were first described, the morphology of these viruses was distinctive enough to eventually warrant the designation of a new viral family for them, the filoviruses, after their threadlike appearance.

Classical Biological Assay

The classical methods for identifying agents are based on biological criteria (reviewed in Murray et al., 1999; for environmental applications, see Hurst et al., 1996). Culturing putative biological warfare (BW) agents requires specialized containment facilities and specially qualified personnel, available in only a handful of laboratories. The approaches differ for bacteria and viruses. Classically, bacteria are grown in vitro on suitable media and specifically identified by their ability to use certain nutrients. Viruses are propagated in suitable cell cultures and identified by their cytopathogenic effect (damage induced in the cells as the virus replicates) (Murray et al., 1999; Richman, 1993). Additional confirmation of identity, for all classes of organisms, can be obtained by other assays (immunoassay, genetic testing, etc.) if necessary. For unknown or variant agents, such attributes as virulence or cytopathogenic effect in specific cell cultures or in animal models can be tested (albeit sometimes with difficulty). These methods remain the "gold standard" (after all, we are usually interested in the biological characteristics of the agents, including their ability to cause disease) but are slow, cumbersome, time consuming, and labor-intensive and require specialized expertise and reagents. Even the best current automated systems for bacterial identification require at least a half-day to provide tentative results; more often takes twenty-four to forty-eight hours to culture most common bacterial pathogens and an additional twenty-four hours to perform the definitive tests. The cell culturing of viruses will generally take several days to a week or more. Although promising new technologies for biological assay using miniaturized biological systems, such as cell-based detectors adhered to a microchip (sometimes dubbed "the canary on a chip"), are being developed, these efforts are still in their infancy (Matsuzawa et al., 1993).

Immunoassay

Probably the identification method most widely used at present for BW agents is immunoassay, which utilizes the formidable recognition abilities of the immune system. The introduction of a foreign substance into the body usually triggers the immune system to produce proteins, called antibodies, which can react with specific portions of the eliciting foreign substance, or antigen. The portion of an antigen recognized by any one particular antibody molecule is called an epitope.

Antibodies produced from the serum of hyperimmunized animals contain a mixture of different specificities. In addition, the supply is limited. To overcome these limitations, antibodies can also be produced in cell culture using hybridomas, made by fusing an antibody-producing cell from an immunized animal with an immortalized cell that allows the hybridoma to grow indefinitely in culture, and selecting for those hybridomas that produce antibodies reacting with the antigen of interest. Each hybridoma makes a monoclonal antibody, that is, an antibody of a single specificity (recognizing a single epitope). Unlike conventional antibodies, the product is extremely consistent, and there is no limit to the quantity that can be produced. The specificity of monoclonal antibodies, although often advantageous, can also cause a failure to detect some strains of an agent, which may lack the particular epitope recognized by the given antibody. The usual remedy is to produce a mixture, or cocktail, of monoclonal antibodies that will provide appropriate coverage. Recently, there have been a number of approaches using genetic engineering technology to develop other alternatives to conventional antibodies (Barbas and Burton, 1996; Dunn, 1996).

An antigenic analysis can be devised for virtually any biological product, although proteins (either protein components of agents or protein toxins; for toxins, see also Tucker, 1994) are the usual targets. A number of different formats have been developed for detecting antigens (reviewed in Rose et al., 1997); common formats include antigen capture enzyme immunoassay (EIA) or enzyme-linked immunosorbent assay (ELISA), and agglutination tests. An example of an antigen capture test is the commercial kit for detecting HIV-1 core antigen (p24) in clinical samples. In this assay, wells on a multiwell plate or other suitable surface are precoated with antibodies to the HIV p24 protein. When the sample is added, any p24 present in the sample is bound by the precoated antibody, hence the term "antigen capture." After washing, the bound antigen is then detected using a second antibody to p24, tagged with a suitable label (such as a fluorescent dye or, for EIA, an enzyme that will produce a colored product easily detectable in an ELISA reader, which is essentially an automated spectrophotometer). Commercial p24 kits generally provide sensitivity to 10–20 picograms per milliliter (ml) (roughly 10^{12} molecules) with excellent specificity, but it is likely that detection down to several thousand molecules or better could be achieved using more sensitive readout methods.

Another common test, particle agglutination, is used in the home pregnancy test kits available over-the-counter in most pharmacies. In this test, the antibody is attached to particles such as latex or gold and deployed on a slide or card. The rapid test cards, sometimes called "tickets," developed by James Burans and colleagues at the U.S. Naval Medical Research Center (NMRC) for a number of BW agents and among the most widely utilized current methods for agent testing, are based on a variation of this principle. When the sample is added, presence of the antigen in the sample causes clumping, or agglutination, of the antibody-bound particles, with development of a visible precipitate. Sensitivity is generally somewhat lower than for enzyme-linked or other amplified methods, but the reaction is rapid and easy to perform.

The same general principles can be applied to develop assays for other types of biologically significant binding events, such as detecting a biologically active molecule (e.g., a toxin or hormone) by recording its attachment to a specific receptor or even using synthetic molecules optimized for binding.

In all assays, ability to distinguish the signal (in the case of binding assays, specific binding) from the background noise is a key limiting factor. As more sensitive detectors are developed, it remains critical to minimize nonspecific binding in order to prevent false positives and ensure reliable results. An understanding of how to select suitable targets and of the biological principles underlying the binding reaction, critical now, will be even more important in the future. Computerized recognition algorithms to extract the features of significance and comprehensive databases of appropriate biological signatures will also be valuable in these applications.

Nucleic Acid Analysis

Nucleic acids are essential components of virtually all live agents. For most of these, DNA serves as the genetic material (with the major exception of a number of important viruses that contain RNA as their genetic material). Each organism possesses genetic sequences characteristic of that organism and responsible for its individuality.

In principle, any genetic sequence can be detected (Davis, Kuehl, and Battey, 1994; Ausubel et al., 1994; Sambrook, Fritsch, and Maniatis, 1989). When there is sufficient sample, the DNA or RNA can be characterized directly by the standard methods described below, but, in practice, polymerase chain reaction (PCR) is almost always performed to amplify the sequences of interest before further analysis. PCR is by far the most widely used approach to amplify the target nucleic acid, although alternative amplification strategies have been described. PCR and similar amplification methods produce many copies of the sequence of interest—the target sequence—if that sequence is present.

Instead of making many copies of the target, as PCR does, an alternative strategy is to increase the detection of low levels of initial target molecules. Some ingenious methods have been developed to do this. The branched DNA assay, for example, uses synthetic DNA probes that bind to the target DNA sequence and, because of their artificially branched structure, have multiple points for attaching labels, giving a larger and more readily detectable signal when the probe binds to the target DNA sequence. Another example is the Qß replicase system (Kramer and Lizardi, 1989). Qß is a virus that infects bacteria (phage). It contains an RNA genome, which it copies by its own RNA copying enzyme, Qß replicase. The enzyme recognizes certain unique features in the Qß viral RNA; it will copy, with equally great efficiency, any RNA containing these features. Nucleic acid probes can thus be constructed containing this recognition site attached to a probe for the target sequence one wishes to detect. If the bound probe can be separated, or the probe constructed to generate the functional Qß recognition site only when it binds, and Qß replicase is added, the enzyme will copy over the probe, producing many copies that may be easily detected. Because of the large multiplier effect that is possible with Qß replicase, the system must be carefully designed to ensure that only the bound probe will react.

However, for most samples in which the desired DNA is likely to be present only at low concentration, as is usually the case, amplification of the target DNA is usually the first step, most frequently by PCR (Mullis and Faloona, 1987; Saiki et al., 1988). A variety of PCR methods and applications have been described (Innis, Gelfand, and Sninsky, 1995). PCR can readily detect 100 copies (or fewer) of a gene (sometimes even one copy can be detected). A recently described PCR system for *Bacillus anthracis* detects as few as two spores (Carl et al., 1992). A number of reports indicate that even heat-sterilized or damaged samples can be amplified, although probably with reduced sensitivity in most cases. For example, *Mycobacterium tuberculosis* (the agent that causes tuberculosis) could be detected successfully in autoclaved sputum samples (Barry and Gannon, 1991). PCR is suitable only for DNA, but RNA (such as viral genomes) can be amplified by first using the enzyme reverse transcriptase to produce a DNA copy (called "complementary DNA," or cDNA), which then can be amplified.

The PCR reaction is initiated by adding to the sample short synthetic DNA sequences (primers), designed to be complementary to (and hence able to bind to) a known target sequence on the DNA to be detected. Specific PCR primers to allow the amplification of any desired nucleic acid sequence can be prepared. Generally, a pair of primers, attaching to opposite strands of the DNA double helix at positions several hundred bases apart, are used. During the reaction, the DNA between the two primers is copied as part of the amplified product. Because performing PCR requires only enough sequence information to prepare suitable primers, which are typically about twenty bases long, PCR has become a powerful approach for identifying unknown or variant organisms for which some limited sequence data may be available. The DNA produced in the reaction can then be further characterized (by sequencing, for example) to provide detailed information about the organism and allow comparisons with known agents.

Specificity of PCR is determined by the specificity of the primers and by key reaction conditions, such as temperature. Depending on gene sequence data available and other factors, in many cases specificity can be tailored to the desired level. By choosing highly specific primers and fairly stringent reaction conditions, detection can be limited to a specific organism. Alternatively, appropriately designed PCR systems can be used to detect families of pathogens by using primers to conserved regions (stretches of DNA that differ very little between different organisms in a given class). For bacteria, broad PCR systems have been described based on ribosomal RNA gene homologies (reviewed in Relman and Persing, 1996). As an example of tailoring specificity, in addition to PCR systems that will detect all retroviruses, systems have been described that will detect only viruses belonging to the lentivirus subfamily (such as HIV and its relatives) while generally excluding retroviruses belonging to other subfamilies (Gelman et al., 1992).

After amplification, the products can be analyzed or detected by any of the standard methods used to characterize nucleic acids (for methods, see Davis, Kuehl, and Battey, 1994; Ausubel et al., 1994; Sambrook, Fritsch, and Maniatis, 1989). One commercial system directly detects a fluorescent label that is incorporated as the PCR product is made (saving several hours of additional analysis), but most situations will require further characterization of the product in order to confirm its identity and rule out artifacts, especially in systems designed to detect multiple agents in a single assay. Amplified products are usually separated by size using electrophoresis (movement in an electric field) and confirmed by hybridization with a labeled probe of known sequence or, most definitively, by determining the sequence of the DNA product (sequencing). The DNA sequences can then be compared with the expected sequences in a databank, and any new variants identified can be added for future reference. Variations in portions of a sequence can often be valuable as unique identifiers for differentiating strains of a biological agent. Because sequencing can be laborious, there are also a variety of "rapid" hybridization-based methods that can provide genetic "fingerprints" to rapidly confirm identification (reviewed in Grompe, 1993).

Another method, restriction fragment length polymorphism (RFLP) analysis, can offer a quick check for agents that have been well characterized and are available in sufficient quantities. In RFLP analysis (the variation using amplified DNA, such as a PCR product, as a starting material is often called amplified fragment length polymorphism [AFLP]), selected restriction enzymes (which cleave at particular DNA sequences) are used to cut the DNA of interest to give a pattern of specific size fragments that are detectable visually after gel electrophoresis. Changes (such as mutations) that change a restriction site will result in an altered pattern. These analyses are, of course, not applicable to toxins (in which the gene coding for the toxin is not usually part of the sample), although they may be applicable to DNA clones used as expression vectors to manufacture the toxin. RFLP also usually cannot be used for RNA (it is possible to make the corresponding cDNA and test it, but this can lead to errors).

PCR has also been used to increase the sensitivity of detection by immunoassay ("immuno-PCR"). This novel method exploits the exquisite sensitivity of PCR for detecting a given DNA sequence (Sano, Smith, and Cantor, 1992). In this method, a synthetic DNA sequence is used as the label in an EIA reaction, in place of the usual enzyme tag, as a sort of molecular barcode. The DNA tag is then detected by PCR, increasing the potential sensitivity of the immunoassay to about 500 copies or less.

Physical and Chemical Analysis

Examples of physical methods are high-performance liquid chromatography (HPLC), mass spectrometry (MS), gas chromatography/mass spectrometry (GC/MS), and infrared spectroscopy. Physical methods are most suitable for agents not easily assayed by immunoassay or genetic methods, including many toxins, and can also be useful for additional characterization (when required) of agents detected by other assays. Most of these methods have the disadvantage of requiring specialized, often bulky, equipment and expert technicians.

Mass spectrometry has long been a mainstay for chemical characterization, including identification of chemical warfare agents. It is rapid, and the analysis itself generally can be done in a few minutes. More detailed description of the equipment and underlying principles can be found in a variety of references (see, for example, Bryden et al., 1995). Briefly, MS depends on physically fragmenting the molecule of interest into electrically charged ions, each with a characteristic mass, that are then introduced into the instrument in the gas phase. For each ion, the distance the ion moves in an electric field (or, equivalently, for the "time of flight" mass spectrometer, the time it takes for an ion to move a specific distance) is proportional to its mass, and this is what the instrument very precisely determines to accurately identify the mass of each ion. Under suitable conditions, a given compound will give a characteristic "signature," or distribution of ions of specific sizes, that allows the identification of the compound by comparison with known signatures that have been determined experimentally.

MS has long been used for characterizing relatively small molecules, but until the last few years, it was not feasible for larger molecules such as proteins and DNA. Several obstacles needed to be overcome. For example, sample preparation is critical. Until recently, large molecules, such as proteins and nucleic acids, were extremely difficult to ionize or could not be ionized reproducibly to give interpretable signatures. This has changed with the development of new methods for producing ions from samples, such as electrospray ionization and matrix-assisted laser desorption ionization (MALDI). In MALDI, the sample is deposited onto, or mixed with, a suitable organic material or solid organic substrate; light energy from a laser at an appropriate wavelength causes the ion to be formed from the sample and liberated from the matrix ("desorbed"). The development of MALDI has made it possible at last to analyze DNA by mass spectrometry (Köster et al., 1996). It is now possible to sequence stretches of DNA up to almost 100 bases long, and it is likely that much longer sequences will be achievable in the near future. However, sample preparation is still often as much art as science, and the best MALDI material for some types of compounds has generally been found by trial and error.

Identification of suitable signatures will also be essential. Most biological and environmental samples are complex mixtures, making it necessary to sort out the desired signature from the background noise. The signatures of biological agents are themselves likely to be complex; if whole organisms are used, some of the compounds detected may vary with environmental or growth conditions. Recent work has focused on finding agent components that could be used to identify potential signatures and some work on ways to prepare them for analysis (Bryden et al., 1995; Fenselau, 1994). Computer tools for analyzing and recognizing patterns may help to identify the salient signals and sort them out from the background noise. This will require a good database of signatures from known sources in addition to the computational tools.

"Peptide fingerprinting," using enzymatic digestion or chemical cleavage (e.g., with cyanogen bromide) to give specific fragments, is a well-established method of protein characterization. The products are usually identified by chromatography, although any suitable method of analysis can be used. Using an authentic sample as the standard is helpful. However, a disadvantage to peptide fingerprinting is that it is difficult to unequivocally identify any given fragment (rather like RFLP). Automated peptide sequence analysis (using stepwise chemical degradation in an integrated automated system) is also available. In addition to equipment requirements, these methods are generally time-consuming and require special expertise and relatively large quantities of the product, although smaller quantities can be used if the sample is pure.

PRACTICAL CONSIDERATIONS

A biological detection system should provide rapid, accurate detection and identification of BW agents. (Strictly speaking, these two terms are not quite interchangeable, the term "identification" implying a greater degree of characterization of the entity detected, but in practice most detection methods are systems that work by performing some degree of identification.) However, beyond this general profile, a system's intended use will determine which of a variety of other factors become important. Thus, in the analysis of samples collected during inspections carried out to address compliance concerns relevant to the Convention on the Prohibition of the Development, Production and Stockpiling of Bacteriological (Biological) and Toxin Weapons, and on Their Destruction (BWC), specificity may well be the most crucial parameter. Further, ease of use is less critical if samples will be tested in a laboratory rather than in the field. Under battlefield conditions, it would be essential for armies to be able to deploy a rugged system that provides immediate results with a low false alarm rate. The nature of potentially cross-reacting materials that could give false positives or that could interfere with the test will also be somewhat different depending on the nature of the sample and its source (e.g., whether environmental, food, or clinical). Following is a discussion of some of the practical considerations related to employing biological detection systems in the battlefield, as an adjunctive measure in biological arms control, and to meet the threat of biological terrorism.

Detection of BW Agents in the Battlefield

In the traditional scenario of BW attack, the agents are delivered as aerosols—the lethal "fluffy cloud." Concern has therefore usually focused on environmental detection, particularly of aerosolized agents. In addition to the usual desiderata for most systems that will be used under field conditions (rugged, easy to use by persons with minimal training, high sensitivity to detect target agents at low concentration, and high specificity to identify accurately with few false positives), there are a number of specific requirements for an ideal system.

Time is of the essence. The primary goal of battlefield detection is to provide sufficient warning of an attack to allow appropriate protective actions to be taken. Because a BW attack can come at any time, this usually translates into the requirement for detectors that can operate automatically and unattended and that give results in near real time. The analogy with a smoke detector is often made, and a similar immediacy of detector response is essential. In the classical fluffy cloud attack scenario, the concentration of organisms is likely to be fairly high, and therefore sensitivity may be less critical than specific and reliable detection that minimizes the false alarm rate. False alarms are an issue because troops will usually have to respond to an alarm by donning protective suits and masks, which can seriously degrade performance and generally cannot be worn for extended periods (in some situations, collective protection, such as shelters, may be available; but in either case, all normal activity is interrupted). For the same reason, the capability to give an "all clear" signal, indicating when it is safe to remove the protective gear, is important. This requires an ability to distinguish pathogens from harmless organisms (for example, using as assay targets virulence factors or pathogen specific products) and to differentiate biologically active from nonviable organisms (by detecting products that rapidly degrade after the pathogen dies, for example).

At present, several core assay technologies have been utilized, but immunoassays, with a variety of possible detector formats for read-out, remain preeminent. Because of their speed, portability, and ease of use, particle agglutination immunoassays, such as the NMRI test kits, have been widely employed in recent years. Perhaps partly because of the time required and despite its great potential, there has been less emphasis on PCR or other target amplification procedures. PCR is very powerful, so the situation may change as new systems reduce the time to carry out the PCR steps to a few minutes (Belgrader et al., 1999), but a more immediate response is still desirable. Some technologies now on the horizon (see conclusion to this chapter), such as array-based devices and miniaturized mass spectrometry for biological applications, may hold particular promise for the rapid detection, identification, and monitoring of pathogenic bacteria and viruses.

Sample collection and preparation (in general, a major limiting factor in all the applications we will be considering) become especially troublesome in open-air environments. Efficient, high-throughput aerosol sampling is necessary, but current equipment is fairly bulky and requires considerable power to operate. Because most instruments for biological analysis require liquid samples, material sampled from air must usually be transferred into a suitable liquid medium for testing (mass spectrometry is an exception, but here, too, the samples must be transferred to a suitable carrier substrate). Finally, open-air environments usually have high particulate counts, often including other particles of biological origin, so that the lethal cloud of pathogens must be distinguished from the background of similar harmless particles, reducing the usefulness of simple analytic devices such as particle counters as stand-alone detectors.

Given these difficulties and pending the maturation of new technologies to the point where they can be used routinely for unattended detection, the only available current solution, as a stopgap, is essentially to bring the laboratory onto the battlefield. The present real-world system for aerosol detection on the battlefield is the biological integrated detection system (BIDS), essentially a mobile laboratory (including a suite of instruments and reagents, and technical personnel) in a truck (Humvee). A 15-kilowatt generator carried in an attached trailer provides the necessary operating power. Air-sampling equipment built into the top of the vehicle constantly collects large volumes of air from the surrounding environment; the intake air goes to a particle analyzer, which is activated if it detects high levels of particulates. Suspect biological particles are routed to a collection device for further analysis, and the collected material is then tested by technicians using a variety of instruments, including a flow cytometer to determine whether the particles react with some general biological stains and individual immunoassays for the major suspected agents.

The classic fluffy cloud is only one of several possible BW exposure scenarios. For other possible routes of exposure, core technologies and considerations for detecting agents in food or water (including natural pathogens indigenous to an area) are similar to those already discussed. Again, sampling and sample preparation are among the paramount issues because many of the samples are complex and are likely to have high backgrounds of interfering substances, such as irrelevant proteins, particulates, and nonpathogenic organisms.

Finally, because an attack may well occur in locations where no detectors are present to provide warning, the first indication of an attack may quite possibly be sick personnel, perhaps presenting with a flulike illness (even with good advance warning of an attack, there will likely be individuals who for various reasons could have been at risk of exposure or who report malaise and will need to be evaluated). There will therefore be an essential need for a rapid and sensitive medical diagnostic device (or devices) to determine the cause and to differentiate the possible BW attack from the myriad of other infections, both common and unusual, that may begin with similar signs and symptoms (some of which may require medical attention but would be handled differently from an actual BW attack). Thus, immediate medical diagnostics will be required to evaluate exposure, to identify which individuals have and have not been exposed, and to guide appropriate treatment, control, and response in real time. Such instruments do not currently exist.

Detection of BW Agents for Arms Control

In recent years, a number of additional measures have been suggested to help provide assurances of compliance with the BWC. Any system will undoubtedly have to involve a variety of complementary measures, including declarations of agents and facilities. The exact details are still under discussion, but it is likely that treaty measures will include the filing of declarations by BWC state parties and a system of visits to some facilities by an international inspectorate. For the purpose of treaty inspections, where the results may have great political sensitivity, paramount considerations will include developing well-standardized and reliable methods that guarantee the integrity of the samples and data and that encourage confidence in the fairness of the process and the accuracy of the results. This presents a somewhat different challenge from the battlefield setting, which requires immediate and comprehensive detection of agents in the environment. Because some of the locations to be inspected, especially in industrialized countries, may be fermentation plants associated with pharmaceutical or biotechnology industries, protection of proprietary information will also be essential. Real-time detection, although always useful, will not be essential. Although a fairly extensive panel of tests will be required, the agents to be detected may be somewhat more limited in scope than in the other applications, in part determined by the declarations of the state parties and by any additional information that may be available to the inspectors.

During a site visit, a variety of environmental and process samples would be collected, from equipment, surfaces, and possibly soil and effluents near the facility. Some vials containing stocks of agents or products may also be tested to verify the identity of their contents or to test for possible undeclared agents. In comparison with the battlefield setting, greater sensitivity will be required because any agents of interest, if present, will probably be at low concentrations in the samples from equipment and surfaces. Whether the samples will be tested on-site or sent to an off-site lab may also affect the choice of technology. For on-site testing, the inspectors will need to bring all the necessary equipment and reagents with them; they will also have limited time to carry out the sampling and testing. A battery of validated tests that could be completed within approximately a day or less on-site, using relatively portable equipment, would work best. Such tests would generally be relatively simple to perform, such as antigen capture particle agglutination immunoassays, some well-characterized PCR applications, and perhaps HPLC or mass spectrometry. One important role for very rapid and sensitive on-site testing methods would be to allow immediate screening of samples at the time of collection in order to help guide sample collection efforts. Samples with unexpected results could then be subjected to more extensive characterization in a reference laboratory. In any case, all operations in sampling, sample handling, transport, and analysis will have to be carried out in such a way as to preclude contamination, guarantee a traceable and secure chain of custody, and where appropriate, ensure security of proprietary samples or data.

Given the constraints, well-established existing laboratory-based technologies, such as standard immunoassays and PCR, rather than the most advanced technologies, are likely to be the mainstay, at least initially (Titball and Pearson, 1993). More advanced technologies (such as array-based assays, which are discussed in the conclusion to this chapter), which will be useful for rapid on-site and field screening as well as in the laboratory, should of course be adopted and incorporated as they become established and validated in other applications.

There may also be special circumstances in which the international community would call for more detailed or intrusive inspections. An example is the United Nations Special Commission (UNSCOM), which was set up to determine the extent of Iraqi programs on weapons of mass destruction and to monitor Iraq's compliance with Security Council resolutions calling for the elimination of these programs. A number of nuclear, chemical, and biological inspection visits (many in combined missions) have been carried out under guidelines that allow extensive investigation and intrusive inspection of identified facilities. For example, UNSCOM mission number 145/BW 35 succeeded in collecting 350 samples at three locations in Iraq, including the Al-Hakam facility prior to its scheduled destruction in 1996. Wipe samples were taken from the surfaces of fermentors, aerosol generators, and other process and laboratory equipment at each of the facilities, as well as liquid samples from some stock vials, and tested for several agents using the NMRI immunoassay devices, culture, and PCR. Limited analysis was done in country, and most of the analysis on the samples collected at the Iraqi facilities was done in U.S. laboratories. Of the 350 samples collected and tested, one was reported positive by immunoassay, and fourteen were positive by PCR, reportedly for at least two different agents. No system yet devised has been able to guarantee the full identification of BW facilities and activities that a country is determined to conceal, and indeed much remains obscure about Iraqi intentions and activities. Nevertheless, the UNSCOM missions have brought a remarkable amount of information to light. Although such intrusiveness will rarely, if ever, be possible under normal circumstances, the fact that significant information could be unearthed is highly instructive and indicative of what is possible.

A final example is the investigation of alleged use under the BWC (Wheelis, 1991, and Chapter 5 in this volume). An inspection team investigating alleged use or alleged release of undeclared agents will need to distinguish this possibility from a natural outbreak of disease, and many of the procedures will generally be similar to those used for the epidemiological investigation of natural outbreaks. Unlike the case of natural outbreaks, where the cause may not be apparent before the field investigations begin and a wide variety of agents may have to be considered, inspectors investigating BW allegations may at least have some indications beforehand of which agents to concentrate on. Attempting to infer putative source of exposure and path of dissemination will require testing to identify the distribution of the outbreak and epidemiological and geographic modeling software to track its spread (for an example, see Meselson et al., 1994). Many of the needs will be the same both to field investigations and to public health practice (Morse, 1992, 1996). "Molecular epidemiology," molecular characterization of the agent with identification of distinctive molecular markers that can help to track the spread of the agent and possibly indicate the presence of strain specific markers that may give a clue to its origin, will be a valuable tool (Myers, McInnes, and Myers, 1993; Ou et al., 1992). As in the case of facility inspections, this work will require the collection, processing, testing, and transport of samples in an appropriate manner. In addition to environmental samples from the affected area, pathologic samples (such as blood, tissues, or affected agricultural products) may also be collected. As in facility inspections, extensive sampling will be required, and identifying where to take samples will be of considerable importance. Rapid diagnostic instruments that could allow preliminary screening of clinical or pathologic samples would be useful to help guide this process.

Detection and Biological Terrorism

With terrorist activities, we confront again many of the issues we have already considered. Because terrorists could strike anywhere and at any time, it is quite possible that there will be little or no advance warning (Carus, 1998b). The first indication of possible attack may be a suspicious package or even just some sick people, perhaps coupled with a claim of responsibility by some group (Henderson, 1999). It will then be necessary to identify and verify the cause, both to guide appropriate action and to differentiate an actual attack from a hoax, which can itself cause serious disruption in a city's normal activities.

Thus, the detection needs can be seen, approximately, as a combination of the two situations already discussed. First responders on the scene of a terrorist attack will need to be properly equipped and aware of the specific dangers they are facing, lest they themselves join the first victims. As in the battlefield situation, first responders, medical personnel, and emergency management workers will require rapid environmental detection to determine what threats they are dealing with, identify contaminated environmental areas, verify the progress of decontamination, and indicate when it might be safe to reopen an area. Because the nature of the threat may not be immediately apparent, simultaneous (or at least parallel) detection of both BW and chemical warfare (CW) agents would be desirable. At present, there is no single technology that adequately meets this need. Some technologies on the horizon (see conclusion to this chapter), including possibly mass spectrometry (already widely used for chemical agent identification) and array-based systems that include appropriate chemical agent probes or detectors, may solve this problem. But it is likely that, for some time to come, two or more different types of detectors will be required in parallel to cover both BW and CW agents.

In addition, as already discussed in the battlefield context, there will be a need for rapid medical diagnostics to identify those who have been exposed and to determine appropriate treatment and control measures. This need will be especially acute if, as is entirely likely, the first sign of an attack is just several sick individuals. It should be emphasized again, however, that there is currently no device for such immediate medical diagnostics.

Finally, the area of a terrorist attack is a crime scene, and law enforcement agencies will require suitable evidence. The evidence will be essential to help reconstruct the events, to identify suspects, to use at trial after suspects are apprehended, and to help to establish how the perpetrators obtained the agent. Both traditional physical evidence and biological evidence will be important. The collection and molecular characterization of the biological evidence will be similar to the process of investigating alleged use. Guaranteeing the integrity of the samples and maintaining a clear chain of custody will again be essential. For legal reasons and to ensure quality control, it is likely that most of the analyses will be carried out in a specialized laboratory setting.

CONCLUSION

At present, the methods for BW detection and identification and the types of molecules detected are generally common to all the applications, and the major differences are often choices of format rather than technological strategy. Immunoassay and, more recently, genetic detection, often with PCR as the first step, are the basis for virtually all the existing systems. Each of the methodologies described in the foregoing sections has certain attributes and, inevitably, certain disadvantages. Immunoassay, for example, has a long and proven track record, but the reagents are biological products available in limited quantities, and each batch requires careful standardization to give optimal results and minimize nonspecific binding.

It is also clear that there are workable approaches for identifying known agents in the laboratory, but we are still a long way from having truly portable multiagent detectors for the field. Many of the unfulfilled immediate needs have already been identified, for example, the difficulty of integrating sampling and sample preparation into the system, the need for rapid response and high sensitivity, the desirability of unattended operation, ruggedness for use in the field, and so on. In addition, both in the laboratory and in the field, we require broader capabilities for diagnosing exposure and for identifying the unexpected than we currently possess. These shortcomings in detection and identification are widely recognized as a major limitation in BW defense capabilities. In the past few years, the Defense Advanced Research Projects Agency (DARPA) in the Department of Defense, which is charged with the mission of developing new and innovative technologies for critical national needs, has initiated several new programs in the area of BW defense. Among other projects, to date DARPA has helped to support the development and biological application of miniaturized mass spectrometers and several other technologies and currently has programs in real-time sensing and environmental detection (begun a few years ago) and a new program in advanced diagnostics (to identify BW exposure or infection in the body and to identify cause, as rapidly as possible, preferably before signs and symptoms have appeared), as well as in therapeutic strategies.

A number of promising new technologies are now becoming feasible and promise greater power. I will mention two, biological MS and array-based applications. Applications of MS for identification of bacteria (Bryden et al., 1995; Claydon et al., 1996; Fenselau, 1994) and for DNA sequencing (Köster et al., 1996; Smith, 1996) have recently been developed and indicate the possibilities for extending the utility of MS in the near future. In addition to advances in applying MS to biological samples, the past few years have seen considerable progress in miniaturizing the equipment and making it more rugged and easier to use (Bryden et al., 1995). Finally, because biological signatures can be inherently complex and noisy, the development of computer databases for agent signatures and of better ways to identify signatures in the presence of a "noisy" background remain important areas for development.

The ability to identify a large number of agents at once in a single rapid and sensitive assay is a key consideration. The extension of broadly "generic" methods, such as mass spectrometry, is one promising approach. A recent major breakthrough has been the development of array-based methods in micro-formats (Abramowitz, 1996; Cheng et al., 1996; Kozal et al., 1996). As in conventional assays, the probes are immobilized on a surface, and binding of the target is detected. Unlike the conventional assays, large arrays consisting of many thousands or potentially even millions of independent binding probes can be placed on small microchips or similar surfaces, allowing a large number of agents to be detected simultaneously. Electrical fields can also be used to move analytes on the chip. Electrophoresis and many of the laboratory techniques described above (including PCR) can also be carried out on microchips ("microchip laboratories"), with great advantages in rapidity and ease of use (Abramowitz,

1996; Cheng et al., 1996). Limitations in sample preparation remain to be overcome, but using array-based methods appears technically feasible within the next several years, and the industrial development of this technology is currently an area of rapid growth.

In parallel developments, a number of devices have recently been described to detect the binding event with greater sensitivity (for some examples, see Hutchinson, 1995; Morgan, Newman, and Price, 1996; Rabbany, Donner, and Ligler, 1994; Baselt et al., 1997; Cornell et al., 1997; Turner et al., 1997). Some can detect a very small number of bound target molecules (in some cases, down to a few hundred or less). Several of these technologies have been commercialized for research use but are not yet suitable for deployment in the field, where ruggedness and stability under unpredictable environmental conditions are required.

In the foreseeable future, synergistic combinations of these technologies could be used in arrays to give exquisitely sensitive multiagent readouts in handheld devices. Deploying such arrays on flexible substrates could lead to wearable diagnostics, and the great sensitivity of these approaches offers the prospect of noninvasive diagnostics using biomarkers in sweat or exhaled breath.

The major challenge—as well as the real breakthrough potential—remains in developing the biological insights and integrating them into engineered systems. In the case of immunoassay, for example, biotechnology has succeeded in overcoming some of the limitations of producing reagents in quantity but has not yet found a way around the need for extensive empirical selection of binding reagents used in immunoassay. Although we are coming closer, with structural biology and combinatorial chemistry, we have still not learned how to effectively mimic or reproduce nature's ability to generate diversity of binding sites and exquisite sensitivity and specificity. Although it is possible to optimize for binding affinity and specificity by empirical selection, the theoretical basis of most binding reactions is still imperfectly understood, and it is not yet possible to tailor binding sites to provide the most desirable properties or new capabilities. Sequences for nucleic acid hybridization can be more readily predicted, but identifying suitable targets remains a nontrivial task. For bacteria, such important targets as virulence factors (the ability to produce certain toxins, for example) are usually relatively well conserved and are essential to the biological property that enables a serious pathogen, such as a BW agent, to cause disease. With viruses, identification of critical targets has been still more difficult. It is possible to identify antigens or genetic sequences that will allow the identification of a given known virus or even groups of viruses, but generic approaches to identify the viral equivalents of "virulence factors" still do not exist. The critical deficiency is in the biological end, in the insights needed to identify the appropriate biological markers and the ability to test them. In addition to the pathogen markers that have been employed to date, it would be interesting to consider host biomarkers of disease and other targets that have not been extensively explored.

Therefore, overcoming present limitations and providing the detection and diagnostic systems to meet the pressing needs of BW defense will require imaginative biological thinking in an integrated multidisciplinary effort. Engineering alone, with traditional biology grafted on, cannot solve these problems. There is need for integral partnerships of biologists with the other scientific disciplines and engineering, as well as a key role for industry.

We have only begun to exploit the possibilities for detection and diagnostics. PCR was a biological insight that revolutionized our capabilities. We cannot predict the next PCR, but multidisciplinary insights, rooted in biology, will be required to get there. We can expect excitement ahead as we learn to harness the power of biology to solve these important biological problems.

NOTE

This chapter has been "approved for public release, distribution unlimited" by the U.S. Department of Defense. The views expressed in this chapter are the views of the author and do not reflect the official policy or position of the Department of Defense or the U.S. government.

I am supported by the Milford D. Gerton Memorial Fund. I thank Mildred Donlon of the Defense Advanced Research Projects Agency (DARPA) for discussion and references on technologies relevant to her program at DARPA.

5

Investigation of Suspicious Outbreaks of Disease

MARK L. WHEELIS

Although the tactical, strategic, or political purposes behind a decision to use biological weapons could be complex and varied, the aim of biological warfare (BW) is simple: to cause disease among enemy troops, civilians, plants, or animals. Of course, outbreaks of disease are commonplace natural events as well and usually occur with increased frequency and severity during times of conflict. Thus there may be a substantial potential for ambiguity about the origin—natural or deliberate—of any particular outbreak. This situation has serious implications for the two international treaties that aim to prevent BW, the Convention on the Prohibition of the Development, Production and Stockpiling of Bacteriological (Biological) and Toxin Weapons, and on Their Destruction (BWC)[1] and the Geneva Protocol (GP),[2] because it invites a climate of destabilizing suspicion and distrust and could fuel proliferation by suggesting that a biological attack may be plausibly deniable. There is thus a substantial incentive for BWC state parties to these treaties to take steps to reduce the ambiguity associated with outbreaks of disease. In this chapter I analyze the extent to which this is possible and summarize current efforts to implement measures to do so.

DISEASE OUTBREAKS AND THE BWC

The ambiguity about the etiology of disease outbreaks may provoke suspicions among disease victims that they have been the target of a biological attack, particularly if the outbreak occurs at a time of heightened tensions or if there are features that appear unnatural. Alternatively, it may suggest to outsiders an accidental escape from a facility engaged in covert biologi-

cal weapons development or production, particularly if it appears to origi-
nate near a military or government facility. Such suspicions call into question the effectiveness of the BWC and the GP and erode their moral authority to the detriment of all nations.

The importance to the BWC of openness about disease outbreaks was
recognized by the Second Review Conference in 1986, which established
several confidence-building measures (CBMs) that aimed to "prevent or
reduce the occurrence of ambiguities, doubts and suspicions, and in order
to improve international co-operation in the field of peaceful bacteriological (biological) activities." Included among these was the obligation to
"exchange . . . information on all outbreaks of infectious diseases and similar occurrences caused by toxins that seem to deviate from the normal pattern as regards type, development, place, or time of occurrence" (BWC,
1986b: 6). The adoption of this particular CBM certainly received a stimulus from the then unresolved suspicions surrounding an outbreak of anthrax
in Sverdlovsk, USSR, in 1979. Accusations (later confirmed) that it resulted from the release of an aerosol of anthrax spores from a Soviet military
microbiology facility had complicated the First Review Conference (held in
1980) and were still being discussed at the Second Review Conference in
1986 (Sims, 1988). Certainly this is the kind of suspicion that the inclusion
of a CBM focusing on outbreaks would be expected to help reduce, since in
such a case the provided information would be expected to increase confidence that a suspect outbreak was, in fact, natural. Of course, the fact that
the information would be provided entirely by the suspect party would
decrease its credibility, and thus even when effectively implemented, this
CBM is unlikely to be capable of reducing serious suspicions very far.

Similarly, when a state party experiencing an outbreak of disease suspects that it has been the target of biological attack, it would have a substantial incentive, beyond the political obligation under the CBM, to com-
pile and publicize information about the outbreak. In this case, the result
would likely be increased suspicion because the provided information,
originating as it would from the accusing party, could be expected to reinforce suspicions of the hostile origin of the outbreak. Thus, in neither case
would the operation of this CBM be expected to be very effective in reducing suspicions about a questionable outbreak.

Clearly, this CBM cannot be relied on as a mechanism for effectively
clarifying suspect outbreaks. Instead, the principal benefit of its implementation would be enhanced understanding of global patterns of disease that
would result from better information about unusual but fully natural outbreaks. This enhanced understanding of disease ecology (i.e., the background of natural disease occurrence against which all suspect outbreaks
must be evaluated) would eventually be expected to sharpen the criteria by
which disease outbreaks would be considered suspect.

As it happens, however, the operation of this CBM has been disappointing. Few state parties have observed their political obligations to submit annual reports, and when they have, information contained in many of the reports is too sketchy and incomplete to be useful to determine compliance to the BWC (Hunger, 1996; Woodall and Geissler, 1990). No report has been filed concerning an outbreak publicly identified as potentially the result of hostile action or prohibited activity; the functioning of the CBM under these conditions thus cannot be assessed. However, as discussed above, there are reasons to be pessimistic about its effectiveness.

Even the potential utility of this CBM as a mechanism for enhancing knowledge of global patterns of disease has probably been substantially superseded by developments since the Second Review Conference. Attention paid to the global disease situation has greatly increased, driven largely by concern over emerging diseases. Global initiatives by national health authorities, international organizations, and the private sector have dramatically raised the profile of global epidemiology (e.g., Centers for Disease Control and Prevention, 1996; WHO, 1996b; Morse et al., 1996). Electronic bulletin boards, most notably ProMED Mail (Woodall, 1998), are revolutionizing the flow of epidemiological information by reducing the delay in dissemination from weeks or months (if ever) to hours or days and by providing a direct channel for information from medical, veterinary, and agricultural professionals, unfiltered by government agencies.

The potential ambiguity about the origins of outbreaks of disease poses another danger to the BWC: it may actually increase the probability that a few rogue countries will elect to develop or use biological weapons. The high background level of natural disease may be taken to indicate that it is possible to design a biological attack to mimic a natural outbreak and thereby have it remain undetected. This consideration may invite covert biological weapons proliferation and use.

Of course, many different scenarios for biological weapons use may be imagined, and the risk of covert use is different for different types of situation. Military scenarios often envisage the dissemination of substantial quantities of antihuman agent in aerosol form, typically a noncommunicable disease agent (i.e., one that is only poorly transmissible among people) to minimize uncontrollable epidemic spread. Disease resulting from such an incident would be unlikely to be misinterpreted as natural. Similarly, a terrorist attack with biological weapons would be unlikely to be misinterpreted as a natural event, especially because of the psychological value of advertising the attack. However, attacks designed to instigate epidemic spread from a point source would be more likely to be so misinterpreted, and hence this approach might be tempting to nations so long as distinction between natural and deliberately instigated outbreaks is difficult. Such attacks might be more likely to target crop plants or domestic animals than humans, to take place outside of declared hostilities between nation states, to involve very little in the way of specialized facilities or munitions, and to use small quantities of agent disseminated in a very small area. Since a successful covert attack would employ natural processes to spread disease from the point of attack, it could very easily be mistaken for a natural outbreak.

Clearly, what is needed is a mechanism whereby natural and unnatural outbreaks could be distinguished from one another. The availability of such a mechanism would discourage nations from believing that they could successfully conceal the use of biological weapons, and its use would help to address suspicions about disease outbreaks. This mechanism would function as a strong deterrent to the covert use of bioweapons, since such use would be expected to become known to the international community, with potentially serious political or economic consequences. It would thus strengthen the international norms and agreements against the use of biological weapons and would reduce further the incentive for their possession.

DIFFERENCES BETWEEN NATURAL AND UNNATURAL OUTBREAKS

How, then, can natural outbreaks be distinguished from "unnatural" ones (i.e., outbreaks initiated by human action)? The differences could be subtle and few in number. They could even be altogether absent, if a cunning aggressor went to considerable trouble to conceal its involvement in the episode. For instance, in some cases it might be possible to initiate an epidemic by introducing a naturally infected host into the target area and relying on fully natural processes to start an epidemic. In such a case, the epidemic would be unnatural only in the intent behind the travel or transport of the infected host, thus precluding the possibility of its being identified as unnatural by any technical means. Such a strategy appears to have been used in the 1950s by land speculators collaborating with Indian Protection Service agents against the indigenous peoples of the Mato Grosso in Brazil in a genocidal effort to displace the natives and release their land for auction (Davis, 1977).

However, the Brazilian case is certainly anomalous. The intended victims were unusually susceptible to the diseases employed,[3] they lived in small tribal groups within which there was very close physical contact, and they had limited access to medical care. The success of BW efforts in Brazil is best seen as the last sordid incident in a long history of dismal experience of Native Americans with imported Eurasian diseases (Wheelis, 1999), rather than as a model for contemporary, covert biological attack.

In the absence of factors such as were found in Brazil, there are substantial practical difficulties in the initiation of an epidemic by the dispatch of infected hosts to a target population. For example, in many diseases the period of greatest infectiousness often precedes the onset of symptoms, and infectivity may decline sharply thereafter. Infected hosts may be debilitated and tolerate travel poorly, and they may be recognizably ill on arrival. Such problems make it difficult to select appropriate hosts for travel and may lead to their recognition as a threat by the target population.

Furthermore, the initiation of an epidemic from a single host or a few infected hosts is a haphazard matter. Natural methods of spread from an isolated case are insufficient to guarantee an epidemic, even if the population is quite generally susceptible; in any epidemic, many infected hosts will be epidemiological dead-ends, not passing the disease on to others; or if they do, their contacts may not. Thus even in a susceptible population, epidemic spread may require repeated introductions. This would, in turn, increase the possibility that the target nation would detect the attack. These considerations suggest that a biological aggressor would be likely to use more reliable but less natural means of deliberately introducing disease agents among targeted populations.

The strains of infectious agent used might also differ from those expected in natural outbreaks, especially if an aggressor used a previously isolated strain of agent as a biological weapon. It would be a great temptation to use an agent already isolated and cultured, with proven virulence and well-studied properties. However, as a consequence of divergent evolution, such agents would be expected to differ in subtle (but now readily detectable) genetic ways from ones encountered naturally in the present time.

All organisms continually accumulate changes in their DNA as a result of mutation. Many of these mutations are selectively neutral, and, as a consequence of genetic drift, they become fixed into the genome of a population or, alternatively, are lost. Other genetic changes may become much more rapidly fixed in a population if they confer a selective advantage, or if they are located close to one that does. Thus over time, different populations of the same species become genetically distinct. These differences can be detected easily by molecular techniques that are now routine in thousands of laboratories around the world: polymerase chain reaction (PCR), restriction fragment length polymorphisms (RFLPs), nucleic acid sequencing, and so on (Hurst and Rao, 1993).

Thus there are two principal ways in which a deliberately instigated epidemic of human, plant, or animal disease may differ from a natural one. The outbreak might have unusual epidemiological characteristics at its very beginning as a result of unnatural means of introduction. Or, it might be caused by an agent that is genetically distinct from its contemporaries, showing closer relationship to agents identified as having caused past outbreaks than to its contemporary cousins. The foregoing considerations suggest that a thorough study of the early period of a suspicious outbreak and a detailed molecular analysis of its etiologic agent may provide sufficient evidence to determine whether the outbreak is natural or not.

EPIDEMIOLOGICAL ANALYSIS

One of the central goals of epidemiological study of a disease outbreak is to clarify its origin (Brès, 1986; Gregg, 1985), which can be reconstructed by a careful analysis of two principal types of evidence: interviews of people involved and the collection of biological samples that might provide evidence of the presence of an etiologic agent, or recent exposure to one.

The first step in any epidemiological investigation is to define the disease being investigated. This is often a trivial matter if the disease is well known and easily diagnosed. However, if the symptoms are not definitive or the agent novel, initial investigations are based on a "case definition" that is constructed quite broadly so as to include all likely cases. This case definition allows investigators to decide which patients evidencing illness are to be tentatively considered as part of the outbreak and which are to be excluded as coexisting cases of some other disease. As the investigation proceeds and more is learned about the disease, the definition typically is refined, becoming progressively more precise and less inclusive. When this happens, earlier cases are reanalyzed and retrospectively discarded if they do not fit the refined definition.

Once the symptoms of the disease of interest are defined, an attempt is made to locate each confirmed early case and determine precisely its physical location and time of onset of symptoms. Any movements of the infected hosts in the period of time during which the disease would have been incubating also have to be reconstructed. The locations and histories of each of these early cases can then be compared in an effort to determine any common exposures. If similarities are identified (for instance, presence at a common location or consumption of a particular food or drink), environmental samples may be taken from the implicated location or material to attempt to identify the presence of an infectious agent or a toxin. Samples may also be taken from healthy organisms exposed to the hypothetical source, to determine if any of them show evidence of current or past subclinical infection (a common phenomenon). If animal reservoirs or vectors are implicated, these too are sampled.

In parallel with epidemiological surveys, laboratory attempts are made to identify and, if possible, isolate and culture the etiological agent. If a toxin is suspected, tissues from victims and environmental samples are chemically analyzed for the presence of suspect compounds. If an infectious agent is suspected, several approaches are usually taken: microscopy of infected tissue, use of diagnostic reagents and probes, serological tests to determine if there has been recent exposure, and attempts to culture the agent from infected tissue and from environmental samples.

Once the agent is isolated, it is identified by routine physiological and immunological tests. It can also be analyzed by techniques that allow quantitation of the similarity of its DNA sequences (or RNA sequences, in the case of RNA viruses) to other isolates of the same species. The result is a measure of the agent's similarity to all other members of the same species that have been similarly characterized. This matrix of similarities can then be used to reconstruct the probable relationships among the different isolates, using any of several different computer algorithms. Since different populations of the agent may have different sequences, such phylogenetic information may point to the geographical source of the agent.

Even without isolation and culture, the presence of an agent may be demonstrable by the use of specific DNA probes, or by PCR, an amplification technique that extends the sensitivity of diagnostic techniques by orders of magnitude.[4] Not only does PCR allow agent detection and identification, but it also generates sufficient product for sequencing, thus allowing phylogeny reconstruction without isolation or culture.

EPIDEMIOLOGICAL ANALYSIS OF SUSPECT OUTBREAKS

How likely is it that a carefully conducted epidemiological analysis will discover an instance of covert biological attack or the escape of BW agents from a facility performing prohibited work? This question is impossible to assess with certainty because it is so dependent on the nature of the event and on conditions under which the investigation takes place. However, the extraordinary success of epidemiological investigations in reconstructing the course of recent outbreaks, including a number caused by novel agents, gives considerable grounds for optimism. Nearly all well-studied past outbreaks, no matter how complex or challenging, have yielded sufficient information to allow a comprehensive reconstruction of their natural origin and ecology. Unnatural events investigated with the same techniques and intensity would be unlikely to survive the attention without a considerable residue of suspicion remaining, even if proof of their unnatural origin was elusive. Three examples are particularly apt.

The 1976 outbreak of Legionnaires' disease in Philadelphia was sudden, highly localized, novel, affected a group of ex-soldiers, and was not transmissible among people.[5] It was initially suspected of being a result of deliberate attack, perhaps with a chemical or toxin agent. The U.S. Centers for Disease Control and Prevention mounted an intensive investigation, and within a year the etiologic agent had been isolated and characterized, diagnostic reagents developed for its routine detection, and several previous undiagnosed outbreaks were retrospectively identified; a general understanding of the ecology came soon thereafter (Fraser, 1980; Fraser et al., 1977; McDade et al., 1977). These findings developed a detailed and coherent story of the etiology of the outbreak, including placing it into a context of other previously unsuspected outbreaks, demonstrating conclusively that it was natural, and disproving the initial suspicions.

Similarly, the 1993 outbreak of Hantavirus pulmonary syndrome in the southwestern United States initially appeared quite suspicious. It was a novel disease affecting primarily young healthy adults, it had unusually high lethality, it was not transmissible person-to-person, and the first recognized outbreak consisted of sporadic cases in the vicinity of the U.S. National Laboratories at Los Alamos and Sandia (where classified weapons research is conducted). There was explicit speculation in the local press that the outbreak was caused by an escaped BW agent. However, within months the novel agent was identified, its natural ecology elucidated, and the causative factors underlying the outbreak determined (Ksiazek et al., 1995; Nichol et al., 1993; Schmaljohn et al., 1995). As with Legionnaires' disease, the development of sensitive and highly discriminatory diagnostic reagents allowed the retrospective identification of earlier, misdiagnosed cases.

In striking contrast is the ultimate elucidation of the origin of the anthrax outbreak in Sverdlovsk in 1979. For years the Soviet Union denied U.S. charges that the epidemic resulted from an escape of aerosolized anthrax spores from a military microbiology facility. However, when independent scientists were finally allowed site access in 1992 (after momentous political changes that caused the demise of the Soviet Union and the creation of the Russian Federation), a convincing epidemiological case was made supporting the bioweapons escape scenario (Meselson et al., 1994). The epidemiological findings were confirmed by results of necropsies performed on numerous victims evidencing that a large fraction of the deaths were due to inhalation of anthrax (Abramova et al., 1993) and by PCR results demonstrating mixed infection of victims by several strains of *Bacillus anthracis* simultaneously (not likely to be natural, but plausible in a biological weapon, which might combine several strains) (Jackson et al., 1998). These compelling conclusions were only possible retrospectively because physicians had retained autopsy material and because meticulous contemporary records had been kept (of patient jobs, residences, hospitalization, etc; of animal anthrax cases by date; and of meteorological conditions). All of this information, and more, would be expected to be available to investigators studying an ongoing outbreak. It is worth noting, however, that the conditions of this outbreak were dramatically unnatural and left a highly distinctive signature.

These examples, and countless more from routine investigation of the hundreds of outbreaks of human, animal, and plant diseases that occur each year, give substantial reason to believe that careful investigation, with full access to records and witnesses, conducted in a timely fashion would illuminate the origin of nearly all suspicious outbreaks. Furthermore, the technology of diagnostic reagents has improved dramatically in the last decade, with great and continuing improvement in sensitivity and precision.

However, there are certainly cases in which epidemiological investigation does not provide enough information to fully understand a particular outbreak. For example, despite several highly publicized and intensively studied outbreaks, the ecology of Ebola virus remains a mystery. If any of these outbreaks had been suspected of having been deliberately instigated, the suspicions would remain unresolved, perhaps exacerbated, despite the intensive study. This is atypical, however, and Ebola probably will not remain a mystery for long.

It is, of course, not necessary that a process be foolproof in order to function as a reliable deterrent to covert weapons use. So long as the possibility of being revealed as a biological aggressor is significant, even if it falls well short of certainty, the deterrent effect would be substantial.

EPIDEMIOLOGICAL INVESTIGATION AND THE BWC

The potential of careful epidemiological and laboratory study to determine the probable geographic origin of the pathogen and its means of natural introduction has suggested to several authors that an effective deterrent to covert bioweapon use would be a coherent system of global epidemiological surveillance that would subject all major outbreaks of disease to intensive study (Wheelis, 1992; Zilinskas, 1992a). Such a system would not only deter bioweapon use and increase confidence in the BWC and GP, but it would also have huge benefits to global public health (and to agriculture and veterinary health as well, if plant and animal disease were also covered). Indeed, it is these benefits to public health and well-being that would provide the most compelling justification for such a large undertaking.

However, despite the substantial benefits, it seems clear that the implementation of such an ambitious program of routine global epidemiological surveillance of plant, animal, and human diseases is well beyond the resources and attention that most of the world's governments are currently willing to commit to such an effort. Instead, it probably will come about gradually, by aggregation of a series of steps, each one improving local or regional epidemiology by a small increment. The determining forces are likely to be local public health needs, global concern over emerging diseases, the explosive development of international communications and data links on the Internet, and the accelerating development of rapid, sensitive, and precise diagnostic tools.

Until that time when all outbreaks will engage some measure of careful epidemiological study, bioweapon control will have to depend on more ad hoc arrangements for the investigation of outbreaks that are suspicious. Such outbreaks might have peculiar features that encourage speculation that they are the result of bioweapon use or escape of BW agents, or they might occur in a political context in which there are reasonable grounds for suspicion, or intelligence sources might suggest an unnatural etiology. The amount of evidence necessary to characterize an outbreak as "suspicious" and the authority to make that determination will obviously be contentious issues. However, there is little disagreement among epidemiologists, security experts, and diplomats that investigation of most unusual outbreaks should be routine, whether conducted by national or international public health organizations. Decades of experience indicate that the overwhelming majority of unusual events are fully natural. Only in the presence of positive evidence of possible unnatural etiology would an outbreak be considered suspicious, and these investigations become a treaty compliance issue.

There are many problems with ad hoc investigations: they can be crippled by lack of unanimity among nations about the need to investigate a particular outbreak; the necessity to arrange all aspects of the investigation on an ad hoc basis can consume time during which important evidence may disappear; the funding mechanism may be difficult to negotiate; and nations with something to conceal can dispute the right of access for investigations.[6]

However, recent efforts by parties to the BWC to explore the feasibility of a verification regime for the convention offer an opportunity to formalize a system of epidemiological investigation of suspect outbreaks, in a way that might avoid the crippling difficulties of dealing anew in an ad hoc fashion with each suspicious outbreak yet does not carry the impossibly ambitious requirements for funding and continuous international cooperation that routine surveillance entails.

INVESTIGATION OF SUSPICIOUS OUTBREAKS IN THE CONTEXT OF A VERIFICATION PROTOCOL TO THE BWC

For several years, BWC state parties have been investigating the possibility of a negotiated protocol to the convention that would incorporate some legally binding verification measures. In 1994 a Special Conference of States Parties to the BWC created an Ad Hoc Group to bring forward such a proposal (BWC, 1994a). The Ad Hoc Group is expected to report to a Special Conference of States Parties or to the next Review Conference in 2001.

Investigation of suspect outbreaks is among the measures the Special Conference expected the Ad Hoc Group to consider. The conference recognized that a "coherent regime to enhance the effectiveness of and improve compliance with the Convention . . . to be included, as appropriate, in a legally binding instrument" would include "measures for the investigation of alleged use" (BWC, 1994a, para. 35–36). The rationale for including such measures was not specified; however, two compelling ones can be adduced. First, although use is not specifically prohibited by the BWC, the preamble is very clear that preventing use is in fact the major goal of the convention: "The States Parties to this Convention . . . determined, for the sake of all mankind, to exclude completely the possibility of bacteriological (biological) agents and toxins *being used* as weapons . . . have agreed as follows" (emphasis added). Allegations of use are in fact allegations of an egregious violation of the most fundamental purpose of the convention.

Second, any use whatsoever of biological or toxin agents as weapons is prima facie evidence, of the strongest kind, that a stock of agent was held in excess of that devoted to peaceful purposes, thereby proving antecedent violation of Article I of the convention. This has been affirmed explicitly by the state parties at the Fourth Review Conference: "under all circumstances the use of bacteriological (biological) and toxin weapons is effectively prohibited by the Convention" (BWC, 1996d, pt. 2, para. 7).

The proposal to include investigation of possible use as one of the verification measures for a protocol to the BWC has generated considerable interest among its state parties. Many analytical papers have been submitted by them to the Ad Hoc Group, and the Federation of American Scientists (1996b) has contributed a detailed proposal for an investigatory mechanism. The Ad Hoc Group has made considerable progress in identifying issues and solving problems, to the point at which a "rolling" text of an agreement has been drafted (BWC, 1998a). It thus seems that if a legally binding protocol to the BWC is successfully negotiated, some form of systematic epidemiological investigation of possible instances of biological weapons use or escape has a good chance of being a part of it. Such a system would ensure that at least suspicious outbreaks could be thoroughly investigated, which would not only address the specific suspicions but would also contribute to the continuously growing knowledge of disease ecology, which is itself one of the best defenses against covert use.

CONCLUSION

Sophisticated epidemiological investigation of the early events in outbreaks of disease or intoxication has been the norm in the developed world for decades, where resources permitted. However, the ability to reconstruct the geographical and evolutionary history of various strains of pathogens is a recent development, resting on the "new biology" of PCR, restriction enzymes, gene cloning, sequencing, and phylogeny reconstruction computer programs. Thus, for the first time epidemiologists can trace epidemics past the primary case and back into recent evolutionary history. The application of these techniques will soon make it very difficult to mount an undetectable biological attack. In this way, covert BW will be very powerfully restrained.

Of course, detection could be avoided by an aggressor willing to go to considerable lengths to conceal its activities. This would require, at a minimum, that the aggressor isolates the etiologic agent from within its natural range shortly before use and then introduces it into the target population by means that mimic a natural introduction. However, complications inevitably would attend these steps, complications that would reduce the chances of success and that would increase the vulnerability of the aggressor to detection by nontechnical means, such as intelligence or defection of personnel. A system of epidemiological study of suspect outbreaks, while not making successful covert biological attack impossible, would thus make it more risky and consequently less likely.

The key issue is whether suspect outbreaks can be investigated in a timely, politically credible fashion. This will require some system of multilateral investigatory teams with rights of access to affected sites and with backup from sophisticated diagnostic laboratories. These arrangements must be negotiated and funded in advance of use, in order to avoid nearly inevitable and potentially crippling delays in mounting an investigation.

There is currently active interest on the part of BWC state parties in a legally binding protocol to the BWC, which would incorporate measures for the investigation of suspicious outbreaks under multilateral supervision. This would do much to reduce suspicions, enhance confidence in the BWC and GP, and deter covert biological weapons use. Of course, it is much easier to agree on the desirability of such weapons control measures than on their detailed provisions, and there is great danger that the difficulties of negotiating these details will derail the negotiations. It would be a great disappointment, and possibly a tragedy, if this opportunity were let slip. All suitable influence on governments involved in the negotiations should be exerted to keep their focus on the goal and to encourage compromise where necessary to achieve it.

NOTES

Mark Wheelis can be contacted through the Section of Microbiology, University of California, Davis, CA 95616; 530-752-0562; mlwheelis@ucdavis.edu.

1. Opened for signature at Washington, London, and Moscow April 10, 1972; entered into force March 26, 1975. The treaty prohibits the development, production, stockpiling, acquiring, or transfer of biological or toxin agents or delivery devices in "types and in quantities that have no justification for protective, prophylactive, or other peaceful purposes."

2. *Protocol Prohibiting the Use in War of Asphyxiating, Poisonous or Other Gases, and of Bacteriological Methods of Warfare,* opened for signature at Geneva June 17, 1925; entered into force February 8, 1928. This treaty prohibits the use in wartime of chemical or biological weapons.

3. Claimed to have been influenza, measles, tuberculosis, and smallpox.

4. See Stephen Morse, Chapter 4 of this volume.

5. A desirable property for a military biological agent, to minimize uncontrollable spread from the site of use.

6. However, the UN Secretary-General has clearly been empowered to mount such investigations by several resolutions of the General Assembly, most notably 42/37 C of November 30, 1987, and 43/74 A of December 7, 1988.

6

Biological Warfare Defense

STANLEY L. WIENER

Although the United States continues to update the preparedness of its armed forces to counter offensive biological warfare (BW), significant gaps remain in the nation's BW defenses. Toxins and infectious agents delivered as aerosols under favorable meteorological conditions have the potential to cause large-scale morbidity and mortality among affected persons, as well as widespread fear among soldiers and civilians outside the immediate theater of operations who may be threatened by similar attacks. U.S. forces will remain inadequately prepared and vulnerable to biological attack until the full spectrum of available defenses is fully implemented.

In this chapter, I analyze BW defenses in detail. I provide both a description of the response measures available to military and civil defense planners and an evaluation of the combinations of defensive measures that are appropriate under various conditions. In the course of the discussion, I consider the level of preparedness of the United States in each of the circumstances reviewed and make recommendations for improving the nation's BW defense capability. Finally, in an extensive technical appendix, I offer medical analyses of the diseases and syndromes that may be caused by known BW agents, including suggested diagnostic measures and treatment protocols.

COMPONENTS OF AN INTEGRATED BW DEFENSE PROGRAM

BW defenses fall into three broad categories: (1) physical barriers, such as masks or other protective gear; (2) medical treatments, including both pre- and postexposure responses; and (3) military options, from preemptive tactical strikes against enemy BW emplacements to strategic deterrence based on the threat of massive retaliation.

Physical Barriers

A BW attack most probably would be carried out through the delivery of a toxin or infectious agent in the form of an aerosol cloud. For such an attack to induce symptoms in the target population, particles of the bioactive agent in the 1- to 5-micron range must reach the lower airway and, in some cases, the conjunctivae of the victims. The most effective preventative measure when faced with the possibility of such an attack is the use of masks or respirators. During periods of BW threat, prolonged and continuous use of respirators is required. BW defense protocols suggest allowing no more than 20 percent of threatened personnel to remove their masks at any one time to eat and drink, and then only for brief periods. In this way, if an attack comes, casualties will be minimized.

Presently, the United States provides the M40A1 mask to its soldiers, but the utility of this device is limited by the fact that it cannot be worn comfortably for more than a few hours at a time. A new, lightweight, high-efficiency particulate air (HEPA) filter mask that could be worn continuously for twelve- to twenty-four-hour periods is under development.

For maximum comfort and effectiveness, a mask should weigh no more than 6 ounces, have a full face-piece to provide eye protection while maintaining an adequate range of vision, have small respiratory dead space and require low inspiratory pressure to ensure ease of breathing, and have three layers of HEPA filter material capable of excluding particles larger than 0.3 microns with greater than 99.9 percent efficiency.

Recent studies have demonstrated the efficacy of such lightweight filter systems (Franz, 1997). In these experiments, mice exposed to an aerosol of ricin or saxitoxin had a 100 percent mortality rate, whereas mice exposed to the same agent but with a double layer of T-shirt or cravat material taped across their mouths and noses sustained no deaths. Such dramatic results add impetus to the effort to develop and deploy the proposed lightweight BW respirator mentioned above.

Although soldiers in the field need respirators for protection, personnel working indoors (e.g., in command and control centers, military vehicles, or hospitals) can be protected by air purification systems that provide filtered air within the interior spaces. Such collective protection allows a shirtsleeve environment without the need for masks or other special clothing.

Medical Treatments Prior to Exposure

Proactive medical measures that can be taken in the event of a BW attack include administering vaccines and providing prophylactic antibiotics.

Unfortunately, at present neither treatment provides an ideal solution to the problem of protecting military forces. Highly effective vaccines exist for anthrax and botulism, but only a minority of U.S. military personnel has been inoculated; vaccines being developed against other BW agents are not yet ready for field use. Prophylactic antibiotics are expensive, require replacement at their expiration date, cause side effects, and can be rendered useless if agents resistant to antibiotics are used in an attack. For these reasons, the best pre-exposure prophylactic measure is the use of physical barriers to prevent the inspiration of aerosolized BW agents.

Medical Treatments After Exposure

Reactive medical responses taken after forces have been exposed to BW attack will be palliative at best, directed at saving lives and limiting permanent sequelae. Accurate diagnosis and appropriate management of an epidemic caused by biological weapons is a three-step process: (1) determining with certainty that the epidemic is BW-induced rather than a natural occurrence; (2) identifying the agent causing the symptoms; and (3) providing treatment. Below, I examine each step in detail and consider some of the difficulties likely to result from the unknowns associated with modern BW.

Determining the etiology of the disease. It is essential to distinguish outbreaks triggered by biological weapons from those with natural causes. In the past, epidemics induced by previously unknown natural agents (e.g., Hantavirus pulmonary syndrome and *Legionella pneumophila* bacteria) were initially suspected of being caused by BW attack. Such confusion can delay proper treatment. Use of the following clinical and empirical criteria can help response teams ascertain that the epidemic is the result of a biological weapon.

- A large number of nontraumatic casualties occur over an interval of one to four days, indicating a possible point-source outbreak
- A very high attack rate for the specific agent involved is measured, indicating a large dose inhaled or the higher virulence of a weaponized agent
- A high proportion of cases is very severe or fatal, also indicating a large dose inhaled or the increased virulence of a weaponized agent
- A higher rate of pulmonary involvement is found than would normally be expected, indicating the likelihood that the aerosol cloud typical of a BW attack was the causative agent (in natural outbreaks, most cases of anthrax are cutaneous rather than of the inhalation variety, most cases of plague are bubonic rather than

pneumonic, and most cases of tularemia are ulcero-glandular rather than pneumonic)
- Most cases are found in localized zones matching wind movements, indicating the point-source origin and wind-borne dispersal pattern characteristic of an outbreak caused by a BW aerosol cloud (in the affected zones, the frequency of cases will be inversely proportional to the downwind distance from the area where the outbreak is most heavily concentrated)
- Two or more unusual infections are found occurring together in large numbers of patients, indicating the likelihood of weaponized agents (e.g., ricin lung damage and inhalation anthrax seen in the same patients)
- The epidemic agents are previously unknown in the geographic area (e.g., pulmonary tularemia, smallpox, or ricin poisoning in Paris)
- Decreased or zero symptoms are found in those working in interior spaces with filtered air, such as command and control centers, combat vehicles, or hospitals
- Bomb fragments or intact rocket payloads containing liquid or powdered BW agents are found after a missile attack
- An admission or claim of BW use by a nation-state or terrorist group is made (such claims are commonly unfounded but still require careful evaluation, especially if symptoms are observed in the threatened population)

Identifying the causative agent. The second step in managing a BW-induced epidemic and determining appropriate treatment is to identify the toxins or infectious agents used in the attack. The clinical algorithms supplied in the appendix to this chapter can be used to make tentative identification of the most likely agents responsible for the casualties (see Wiener and Barrett, 1986: 511–515).

As illustrated in the algorithms, toxins behave like chemical agents, usually producing casualties in exposed individuals within a short period of time after an attack (e.g., chemicals such as nerve agents, Lewisite, phosgene oxime, and cyanide cause symptoms within thirty minutes, and some mustard gases and phosgene gas produce effects within two to eight hours). Toxin-related cases may become symptomatic within minutes (e.g., in the case of exposure to saxitoxin or T2 mycotoxins) or hours (e.g., if botulinum toxin, ricin, or staphylococcal enterotoxin B is used). If multiple attacks occur with weapons using the same chemical or toxin agents as payloads, cases may appear over longer time periods with multiple distinct incidence peaks that are separated by minutes to a few hours.

In contrast, aerosolized infectious microorganisms capable of proliferating in the host can cause symptoms that begin several days to several weeks after exposure. Unless there are multiple attacks with the same agent, the majority of cases will appear over a one- to four-day period with a single major incidence peak. The expected incubation periods are approximations based on the most likely time intervals between exposure and onset of symptoms, but variations are possible. In some circumstances, for example, victims who inhale botulinum toxin may not show the effects for up to four or five days; individuals exposed to a bacterial (e.g., anthrax) or viral infection may remain asymptomatic for up to four weeks.

To ensure accurate diagnosis, a careful and complete medical history of the outbreak must be obtained, and fifty or more casualties must be subjected to thorough physical examinations in order to determine the commonest signs associated with the illness. With this information in hand, the list of possible causative agents can be narrowed to four or five through the use of the diagnostic algorithms outlined in the appendix. Laboratory tests such as antigen capture techniques, cultures, and microscopy can then rapidly confirm the presence or absence of the suspected agents.

Over the last ten years, those responsible for BW defense have been able to focus on a more narrow range of agents than the broad list of potential threats that existed in the early 1980s. Two factors account for this improvement: (1) more complete intelligence as to the types of BW agents likely to be encountered is now available; and (2) as a result of continuing research on the effects of aerosols on primates and other animals, epidemiologists now have a better understanding of which BW agents pose a real threat.

Providing effective treatment. Medical personnel must begin emergency treatment as soon as symptoms are detected. Once a BW attack has been confirmed and the causative agents identified, targeted treatment to save lives and minimize permanent damage can be instituted. As discussed in greater detail later, managing the response to a successful BW attack may be a logistical nightmare as panic sets in and field hospitals are overwhelmed by large numbers of casualties.

Triage, or sorting, is used when resources are in short supply and medical personnel cannot attend to every patient. As with injuries caused by conventional weapons, battlefield casualties resulting from BW must be triaged according to the patients' conditions and prognoses. Care is provided first to those with the greatest need who have a reasonable chance of survival and not to the sickest, as would be the case when resources are unlimited. Categories typically include "expectant" (those mortally injured), "immediate" (those who require immediate attention and have a reasonable chance of survival), "delayed" (those whose treatment can be deferred because their illness is less severe), and "minimal" (those with only a minor illness).

In a successful BW attack, the number of cases falling into each category will depend on the concentration of the aerosol and the agent used. To give examples at the two extremes, the use of anthrax spores or botulinum toxin against an immunologically unprotected group will result in a large number of "expectant" cases, whereas in an attack against fully immunized troops, the majority of casualties will fall into the "minimal" category.

As medical personnel identify the "immediate" cases through triage, these patients can receive priority treatment. This may include administration of intravenous fluids and supplemental oxygen, correction of electrolyte/acid-base abnormalities, and respiratory and circulatory support. If the identified BW agent is susceptible to pharmaceutical treatment, antibacterial or antiviral drugs can be administered as indicated in the algorithms. For example, if plague pneumonia is diagnosed and found to be sensitive to the antibiotic ciprofloxacin, treatment with this drug can be started immediately. However, if lung damage is due to ricin, there is no effective drug therapy.

If the agent has not been isolated, it is possible to start small groups of ten to twenty patients on different antibiotic or antiviral drugs and observe their responses. It was through such trial-and-error emergency medical action that erythromycin was identified as an effective drug for the treatment of *Legionella pneumophila* infection during the Philadelphia outbreak in 1979. If an effective medication is identified, others with similar symptoms can be placed on that drug.

Until it is determined that no communicable agents are involved, quarantine precautions should be observed. Communicability should be assumed and barrier use initiated until the agents are accurately identified. The lightweight mask described previously that is being developed for protection against a BW aerosol attack could also be used by medical personnel to protect themselves from aerosols of communicable agents generated by patients. If the agents are highly transmissible, it may be necessary to dispose of the dead in on-site crematoria, in deep burial trenches, or, if logistically feasible, through return to the United States in sealed plastic body bags treated with disinfectants for closed casket services and burial.

Limitations and unknowns. We have no experience with a successful BW aerosol attack in the era of modern warfare that we can use to judge the effectiveness of various medical responses. However, a personal experience in 1979 gives some insight into the havoc that an aerosol cloud of microorganisms can cause. As a medical reserve officer and infectious disease specialist, I was asked by my commander to take charge of the response to an outbreak of an unknown febrile disease that had suddenly appeared among military-age men and women who had been traveling from the southwestern to the northeastern United States by wagon train for a period of seven weeks.

Approximately 80 of 100 individuals became ill over a two-day period. Most cases presented high fever, rigors, sweats, a nonproductive cough, myalgia, chest pain, and headache. Liver tenderness, wheezes and crackles, meningismus, and dyspnea also occurred in some patients. There was a spectrum from moderate to severe illness. Chest radiographs generally showed miliary nodules, subsegmental infiltrates, hilar lymph node enlargement, or a combination of these abnormalities, but in some cases the chest radiographs were completely normal. Sputum and blood cultures were not helpful in establishing a diagnosis. The cause of the epidemic was unknown.

In order to contain the outbreak, all the victims were placed in strict isolation, and barrier precautions were used. On the third day after onset, there were no more new cases among the wagon train party. Viral cultures were initially found to be positive, but one day after this finding we determined that the results were falsely positive for a new viral agent. Our clinical diagnosis was acute pulmonary histoplasmosis, a noncommunicable disease. However, this diagnosis was not confirmed by antibody studies for five weeks.

The small hospital caring for these patients was overwhelmed. Whole wards had to be used for isolation and therefore closed to other patients. Masks, gowns, and gloves were in short supply. Some of the nurses and laboratory personnel felt ill and thought they were coming down with this unknown "plague." However, we examined them and found they were afebrile and had normal chest radiographs.

Epidemiologic investigation later revealed that the wagon train had camped in a field outside Chattanooga, Tennessee, one week prior to the outbreak. The soil in this field was rich in histoplasma spores, since it had been the site of a grove of trees that had served as a blackbird roost before being cleared two years before. The epidemic arose from an invisible aerosol created by the wagon wheels as they entered and left the field seven days before the outbreak. No one in the traveling party recalled seeing clouds of dust at the encampment.

The difficulties in diagnosing and managing this outbreak give some idea as to the larger problems likely to occur after a full-scale aerosol attack involving one or more BW agents. In a military attack, the casualties might number in the thousands or tens of thousands. Supplies of beds, linens, intravenous line equipment, sterile fluids, antivirals, monoclonal antibodies, antitoxins, and antibiotics will rapidly become exhausted. There will be too few gowns, masks, and gloves to maintain strict barrier precautions. If the attacker uses contagious agents, such as *Yersinia pestis, Chlamydia pneumoniae,* smallpox virus, Ebola hemorrhagic fever virus, Marburg hemorrhagic fever virus, or Crimean hemorrhagic fever virus, the disease could spread rapidly within the community as a result of quarantine procedures breaking down due to a lack of supplies.

As in the case study described above, isolation, identification, and evaluation of the causative agent are likely to be time-consuming. Casualty rates will increase as epidemiologists rush to determine the susceptibility of the toxin or infectious agent to available drugs. Medical countermeasures designed to save lives and prevent permanent sequelae may be thwarted by resistant agents, inadequate supplies of specific pharmaceuticals, lack of means for parenteral administration, or exposure to BW agents for which there is no effective therapy.

As these observations demonstrate, in order for medical treatment to be an effective component of an integrated BW defense, medical personnel in the field will require adequate facilities and supplies, and support staff will need the logistical capability to evacuate large numbers of casualties. At present, neither of these conditions can be met. If U.S. forces were to sustain a BW attack in the near future, it is almost certain that mortality rates would be very high and medical facilities would be quickly overwhelmed.

Military Options

Strategic and tactical military actions are an important part of BW defense planning. First, field commanders can target and destroy enemy BW emplacements and materiel that threaten U.S. troops. However, the effectiveness of this type of preemptive response may be compromised if the enemy "hardens" its facilities (e.g., by placing them inside a mountain) or if inadequate intelligence fails to warn of an impeding attack.

Second, the United States can use the deterrent effect of the threat of massive retaliation in the case of a BW attack against its forces. Although the United States has no BW capability, it maintains a potent arsenal of strategic weapons, including nuclear arms, that can be used to retaliate in extreme circumstances. It is important to remember that the threat of retaliation may be effective if the enemy is a nation but will be less so in the case of a terrorist group or if the attacker cannot be identified.

Intelligence is a crucial component of BW defense. Field commanders need accurate information to target enemy BW emplacements. Those responsible for BW preparedness among U.S. forces need to know the enemy's biological warfare capability, the agents at its disposal, and the likelihood that the enemy will actually use BW in the theater of war. Strategic planners need to know the opponent's war plan and mind-set to determine the best way to deter BW attacks. Of course, more specific intelligence during a period of hostilities can provide medical defense authorities with the information necessary to decide when to prescribe prophylactic medications, such as vaccines or antibiotics, and when to issue "mask on" and "mask off" orders to soldiers in the field.

The various means of gathering intelligence must be integrated to ensure the most accurate information. Human intelligence (HUMINT) is particularly important in determining the type of BW agents available to the enemy and the likelihood that threatened retaliation will serve as an effective deterrent. Measurement and signal intelligence (MASINT) and imaging intelligence (IMAGINT) can provide warnings of enemy preparations to launch missiles with possible BW payloads or of actual launches of such missiles. MASINT and IMAGINT can also be used to gather information about BW production and storage sites and BW delivery vehicles (including location, number, type, range, payload size, susceptibility to antimissile defenses, etc.).

Since aerosol clouds are only effective in certain weather conditions, timely and precise meteorological forecasts are also a necessary part of BW defense preparedness. BW aerosols, like natural airborne pathogens, are tasteless, odorless, and invisible; and specific detection devices for biological aerosols, like the pulse laser system, are still in the development stage and are not yet in place for field use. Therefore, access to military intelligence, including accurate weather forecasts, is the only way commanders can determine when an attack is likely under way, thereby indicating that they should call into play the other components of BW defense.

Development and deployment of battlefield-ready BW agent detection systems would be a significant addition to BW defense. To be effective, these systems should have the capability for both early detection of aerosol clouds and rapid analysis and identification of agents making up the cloud once it is detected. At present none of the air monitoring, cloud detection, or biological integrated detection systems (BIDS) are operational and ready for wide area field surveillance. At this time the first warning of exposure to a biological weapon is likely to come from the onset of symptoms in "sentinel" cases, which may occur anywhere from minutes to days after an attack. In this situation, if exposure occurs when affected personnel are not protected by respirators, and if the causative agents are resistant to therapeutic interventions, the value of pre-illness detection and identification is limited and will not favorably affect the casualty rate (Wiener, 1996).

CIRCUMSTANCES IN WHICH
BW DEFENSES ARE CALLED INTO PLAY

BW defense planners can employ the measures discussed above—physical barriers, medical treatments, and military options—in various combinations depending on the state of affairs in the theater of operations. Two general scenarios are possible, each calling for a different combination of defensive actions: (1) a BW attack is threatened but has not yet been launched; or (2) an attack has occurred, personnel have been exposed to BW agents, and symptoms have begun to manifest themselves, either on a small scale in a few "sentinel" cases or on a large scale, resulting in numerous casualties.

In the first case, in which a BW attack is possible but has not yet occurred, the best defensive posture will include a combination of strategies. First, prophylactic vaccines and antibiotics can be administered in advance to personnel likely to be at risk. Second, when an attack is imminent, "mask on" orders can be issued to reduce the opportunities for exposure. Third, all facets of intelligence capability can be mustered to give maximum possible warning prior to a BW assault. In particular, defense planners will need to be on the alert for suspicious enemy aircraft or missile activity that occurs when meteorological conditions favor the success of a BW aerosol attack. Dangerous periods requiring heightened readiness include the early morning hours before sunrise (since sunlight hastens agent degradation), during temperature inversions (which keeps the toxin or infectious particles at ground level), and when wind velocities are between 3 and 7 miles per hour (when the aerosol will be dispersed within the target population without wind rapidly diluting its effectiveness).

In the second case, in which a successful BW attack has already been sustained, commanders must combine medical and military responses. Unaffected units can be moved to a higher state of readiness to counter similar BW assaults that may follow, and medical response teams can begin to treat exposed personnel. Large-scale logistical efforts will have to be undertaken to manage the overwhelming influx of casualties that will follow, and high rates of mortality may be unavoidable. In this situation, persons in authority at the highest levels, including the president, the cabinet, national security advisers, and the Joint Chiefs of Staff, will have to consider retaliation against the BW aggressor. The responses available may run the gamut from sanctions to a massive attack with conventional or thermonuclear weapons.

CONCLUSION

At present, all armies and civilian populations throughout the world are vulnerable to a BW attack, and it may be impossible to ensure complete protection against the effects of a biological warfare agent. In particular, U.S. military and civil defense planners must consider the following strategies that BW aggressors may employ to overcome defenses: the use of very large aerosol doses of agents that can circumvent immune defenses; the use of agents unknown or unfamiliar to the United States; the use of organisms resistant to stockpiled antibiotics; the use of frequent, sustained attacks or attack periods that cannot be predicted from meteorological information; the use of organisms modified by genetic engineering to enhance their resistance or virulence; the use of a combination of agents with each attack; the use of direct delivery within the perimeter of U.S. emplacements by human infiltrators; and the use of agents that damage or block mask filters and seals prior to the actual attack with toxins or infectious agents.

The problems faced by BW defense planners are compounded by the fact that important components of U.S. biological warfare defense strategy remain under development. Defense measures not yet ready for field deployment include lightweight masks that can be worn comfortably for extended periods; pre- and postexposure medications effective against agents for which there is presently no treatment; and battlefield-ready early warning systems capable of rapid detection and analysis of BW agents. As a result, an aerosol attack on U.S. forces in the near future is likely to produce massive casualties, including large numbers of fatalities.

The best chance for minimizing the likelihood of sustaining such catastrophic losses lies with appropriate use of proactive, preventative measures. It is far better to prevent casualties than to try to reduce suffering and minimize deaths after the fact. The pre-exposure measures that should be emphasized to maximize the effectiveness of an integrated BW defense strategy include immunization against the disease agents likely to be encountered; airway and conjunctival protection with a comfortable, lightweight mask that can be worn for long periods of time; preemptive destruction of enemy production, storage, and delivery systems; and the credible threat of massive, overwhelming retaliation against any BW aggressor.

*   *   *

APPENDIX

For each BW threat agent, the diseases and syndromes that may be induced, either through inhalation or cutaneous deposition, will be examined. The discussion includes clinical aspects, diagnostic methods, and possible treatments or prophylactic actions. At the earliest stage of an outbreak of illness it can be difficult to differentiate between symptoms caused by pathogens, toxins, or chemical warfare agents. Differential diagnosis strategies are presented in graphical form in the algorithms on pp. 141–145.

RESPIRATORY SYNDROME AGENTS

Proliferating Microorganisms

1. Inhalation anthrax. Infection produced by inhalation of a *Bacillus anthracis* aerosol usually begins to produce symptoms within one to six days. Fever, myalgia, malaise, fatigue, headache, and other nonspecific complaints are the initial symptoms. Attention may be directed to the chest by a nonproductive cough and mild anterior chest pain. Fever and other symptoms may remit for a brief period, to be followed by severe dyspnea, stridor, more chest discomfort, a nonproductive cough, diaphoresis, prostration, hypotension, and in some cases, nuchal rigidity and coma. These symptoms become more severe over a period of twenty-four to forty-eight hours and lead to death. Physical examination reveals an extremely ill febrile, tachypneic, and hypotensive patient with stridor, nuchal rigidity, tachycardia, diaphoresis, delirium, and/or coma. Chest radiographs usually show a widened mediastinum due to lymph node enlargement and hilar adenopathy. Pleural effusions may occur, but pneumonic infiltrates are uncommon.

In the terminal phase or early in the septic phase of the illness, Wright- and Gram-stained smears of peripheral blood may demonstrate gram-positive boxcar-shaped bacilli. Tissue imprints at autopsy may show similar organisms. Blood agar cultures of tissue swabs and blood cultures grow rapidly. A direct fluorescent antibody stain will identify *B. anthracis* in tissue sections or smears. An enzyme-linked immunosorbent assay (ELISA) antigen capture test exists as part of the BIDS system described above. Experimental inhalation anthrax in the rhesus monkey produced hemorrhages and edema in mesenteric (54 percent) and tracheobronchial (46 percent) lymph nodes, meninges (38 percent), and lungs (31 percent). Histopathologic changes included suppurative meningitis, pulmonary hemorrhages (31 percent), and pneumonia in only 15 percent (Fritz et al.,

1995). Autopsy studies of forty-two human victims of the 1979 Sverdlovsk epidemic of inhalation anthrax (Meselson et al., 1994) revealed hemorrhage, edema, necrosis of intrathoracic lymph nodes, and a severe hemorrhagic mediastinitis. A focal, hemorrhagic, necrotizing pneumonia located at a possible portal of bacterial entry was frequently present. Large pleural effusions, mediastinal edema, submucosal hemorrhagic lesions, and hemorrhagic meningitis were common (Abramova et al., 1993).

The estimated ID_{50} for humans is 8,000–10,000 spores. Inhalation anthrax is nearly 100 percent fatal, despite treatment with high doses of intravenous penicillin. Rare case reports of survival after penicillin therapy of this disease have appeared (Winter and Pfisterer, 1991). Penicillin is the drug of choice, unless resistant strains are used. Ciprofloxacin may be effective during the first day of illness. It was provided as a prophylactic agent in the Gulf War. The Michigan Department of Public Health–Protective Agent (MDPH-PA) vaccine was effective in primates against 500 aerosol lethal doses of anthrax spores for up to two years (Wiener, 1996).

2. Pneumonic plague. Inhalation of an aerosol of *Yersinia pestis* can lead to a severe, acute pneumonia and bacteremia. Symptoms include high fever, rigors, cough, hemoptysis, and dyspnea. Purulent sputum containing bipolar gram-negative bacilli and neutrophils is commonly present. Severe cases may progress to septic shock and death in twenty-four hours. Physical examination reveals fever, tachycardia, tachypnea, and signs of consolidation in one or more pulmonary regions. Chest radiographs reveal patchy (subsegmental), segmental, or lobar consolidation and hilar/mediastinal adenopathy.

Sputum cultures grow on blood or McConkey agar. Large numbers of bipolar bacteria can be seen on a Wright stain of peripheral blood collected from patients with septicemia. Other methods of rapid diagnosis include ELISA tests for *Y. pestis* F1 antigen (Shepherd et al., 1986); a direct fluorescent antibody test; a fiber-optic biosensor that detects *Y. pestis* antigen-antibody complexes (Cao et al., 1995); and polymerase chain reaction (PCR) to detect whole antigen and bacteria (Hinnebusch and Schwan, 1993).

Ciprofloxacin can be used for prophylaxis or early therapy, but strains resistant to this drug have been reported from the former Soviet Union. Treatment of sensitive strains with intramuscular streptomycin or oral tetracycline reduces mortality, but strains resistant to this therapy can be used in a BW attack. The current licensed plague whole cell vaccine does not protect against plague pneumonia, but new vaccines under development may.

3. Pulmonary tularemia. A nonspecific febrile disease with a nonproductive cough occurs after aerosol infection with *Francisella tularensis*. Severe cases may have dyspnea, cyanosis, and pleuritic chest pain.

Examination may reveal fever, tachycardia, tachypnea, and signs of segmental or lobar consolidation with crackles over areas of percussion dullness. Chest radiographs may show subsegmental or segmental infiltrates or lobar consolidation and hilar adenopathy.

Gram or a direct fluorescent antibody stain may identify the organism in sputum. An ELISA utilizing monoclonal antibodies against *F. tularensis* lipopolysaccharide has been developed and used for antigen capture in clinical samples and tissue (Fulop et al., 1991); a rapid detection kit based on PCR directed at the FopA gene can detect *F. tularensis* in blood and tissue samples (Fulop, Leslie, and Titball, 1996); and immunoelectron microscopy (IEM) has been used to confirm presumptive *F. tularensis* isolates (Geisbert, Jahrling, and Ezzell, 1993).

Penicillin has no effect on either plague or tularemia pneumonia, and they are referred to as penicillin-resistant pneumonias, along with Q-fever and some gram-negative bacterial pneumonias. Ciprofloxacin may be used as a prophylactic drug, as it was in the Gulf War. Intramuscular streptomycin and oral tetracycline are effective against most non-BW clinical isolates. Strains used in a BW attack may be selected for use because they are drug resistant. Inhalation of fewer than ten bacteria may produce illness.

4. Q-fever. Exposure to an aerosol of *Coxiella burnetii* will cause pneumonia in a high percentage of the exposed force. Only one organism is necessary to cause illness. A generalized febrile illness with severe headache (i.e., an important clue to diagnosis), chills, diaphoresis, myalgia, nausea and vomiting, and diarrhea are the more frequent nonspecific flulike symptoms that characterize this illness. Respiratory symptoms include a nonproductive dry cough and pleuritic chest pain. Physical examination may be negative or reveal crackles in the atypical pneumonia syndrome or demonstrate dullness to percussion, bronchial breath sounds, and egophony in localized areas or in a lobar distribution in the rapidly progressive pneumonia syndrome that may be associated with this agent. Chest radiographs may show patchy pleural-based or less peripheral subsegmental and segmental infiltrates or lobar opacification. Multiple rounded opacities, hilar adenopathy, and areas of atelectasis may occur (Marrie, 1990). Less common manifestations of Q-fever include granulomatous hepatitis, culture negative endocarditis, and neurological syndromes such as aseptic meningitis/encephalitis and a slowly progressive myelopathy.

Rapid diagnosis prior to a serum antibody response can be obtained by using PCR (i.e., to amplify *Coxiella* DNA in clinical samples) and restriction analysis (e.g., restriction enzyme digestion and dot blot hybridization) (Stein and Raoult, 1992). Both serological tests for antibody and leukocyte culture (viral cultures and shell vial method) require a longer period to identify *C. burnetii* (Gil-Grande et al., 1995).

A formalin inactivated whole cell vaccine provides 95 percent protec-

BIOLOGICAL WARFARE DEFENSE

tion against aerosol exposure after a single dose. Tetracycline is an effective prophylactic and therapeutic agent. In vitro studies suggest that ciprofloxacin and other quinolones would also be effective for prophylaxis and therapy. An atypical pneumonia syndrome can be caused by mycoplasma pneumonia, *Chlamydia pneumoniae* or *C. psittaci, Legionella* species, influenza virus, and adenovirus, but in 1997 these were not considered to be BW threat agents because of low attack rates of severe disease, nonlethality of most infections, and difficulties in the production and stability of some of these agents. Rapidly progressive pneumonia can also be caused by common community-acquired pathogens such as penicillin-resistant *Streptococcus pneumoniae, Klebsiella pneumoniae, Legionella* species, and *Neisseria meningitides.*

5. *Pulmonary histoplasmosis.* Exposure to an aerosol cloud of *Histoplasma capsulatum* spores will cause a disabling but seldom lethal flulike illness, five to seven days later. Symptoms include fever; chills; rigors; sweating; prostration; arthralgia; myalgia involving the chest wall, neck, back, and extremities; a dry cough; and a substernal sharp pain associated with coughing. Neck pain and stiffness and headache may suggest meningitis. Physical examination reveals fever, rigors, postural hypotension in some cases, scattered wheezes, crackles, nuchal stiffness in up to 10 percent of cases, and liver tenderness without hepatomegaly or abnormal liver function tests. Chest radiographs may show patchy infiltrates or miliary lesions in all lung areas or normal lungs associated in the majority of cases with hilar adenopathy.

Diagnosis may be rapidly confirmed by stain and culture of sputum or broncho-alveolar lavage fluid and histologic study of lung tissue obtained at bronchoscopy. An antigen detection test on urine may be positive in up to 39 percent of patients with acute pulmonary histoplasmosis. Patients with severe pulmonary involvement are more likely to be antigen positive. Since many cases will be available for testing in a successful BW attack, a sensitivity of 39 percent is adequate for diagnosis of the epidemic (Williams et al., 1994). Serologic diagnosis using an ELISA and/or Complement fixation test may require three or more weeks until antibodies can be detected.

Therapy with itraconazole or fluconazole may be effective; amphotericin B can be used for severe cases.

Aerosolized Toxins

1. *Staphylococcal enterotoxin B (SEB).* Symptoms begin from three to as long as twelve hours after exposure. After a single exposure, most cases will have presented within twenty-four hours. There is an abrupt onset of fever, chills, myalgia, dry cough, dyspnea, and retro-sternal pain. Nausea, vomiting, and diarrhea may occur. Severe cases may develop shock and

die. Chest exam may reveal tachypnea, wheezing, or crackles due to alveolar edema. Chest radiographs may show areas of patchy infiltration and, in severe cases, bilateral pulmonary edema with a normal-sized heart. The illness may be fatal but is more likely to be incapacitating for one to four weeks.

Toxins can be detected shortly after exposure in serum and for more prolonged periods by antigen capture tests such as ELISA and an enzyme-linked immunofiltration assay (ELIFA). The latter was less sensitive but was easy to perform, fast, and simple. The avidin-biotin amplification system makes these antigen detection tests highly sensitive (Dupont et al., 1990; Adesiyun et al., 1992).

There was no specific therapy available in 1996. Passive immunotherapy reduces mortality if given within eight hours of exposure, but such antibodies are not available for clinical use. Vaccines against SEB are under development but not available for preventive use in humans.

2. Ricin. After aerosol exposure, there is a latent period of four to eight hours before fever, dyspnea, nonproductive cough, myalgia, and profuse diaphoresis occur. Based on an experimental model of ricin inhalation, death occurs in two to three days. Severe bronchial and alveolar edema occurs, and necrosis of bronchial epithelium is prominent. Chest radiographs may show diffuse pulmonary edema with a normal heart size (e.g., acute respiratory distress syndrome [ARDS]) or diffuse or focal segmental or lobar infiltrates in both lungs. Experimental ricin inhalation using rhesus monkeys results in multifocal to confluent fibrinopurulent pneumonia, airway inflammation and necrosis, and diffuse alveolar edema at thirty-six to forty-eight hours. Similar lesions occur in a rat model (Wilhelmsen and Pitt, 1996). Time to death is aerosol-dose dependent and varies between thirty-six and seventy-two hours. Examination reveals tachypnea, fever, tachycardia, diffuse wheezing, and crackles.

A sensitive and specific ELISA has been developed to detect ricin in clinical samples. Colorimetric and highly sensitive chemiluminescence methods are used to complete the assay that can detect 0.1 to 1 ng/ml in urine or serum (Poli et al., 1994).

There is no specific therapy. In a mouse model, a monoclonal and a goat polyclonal antibody to ricin neutralized this toxin in vivo, resulting in increased survival (Lemley, Amanatides, and Wright, 1994). Mice can be actively immunized against a ricin aerosol challenge using ricin and Freund's or Ribi adjuvant (Hewetson et al., 1993). A vaccine to protect human subjects is not available for field use. In a mouse model, minimal coverage (e.g., two layers of T-shirt material) of the nose and mouth during a ricin aerosol has been highly protective.

3. T2 mycotoxins. Skin exposure to an aerosol of T2 causes redness, burning pain, tenderness, and blister formation within minutes. Skin gan-

BIOLOGICAL WARFARE DEFENSE

grene with sloughing may occur in severe cases. Nasal pain, itching, sneezing, epistaxis, associated dyspnea, wheezing, and cough follow inhalation. Nausea, vomiting, abdominal pain, and bloody diarrhea follow gastrointestinal exposure. Visual blurring, conjunctivitis, and lacrimation follow eye exposure. T2 toxicity should be considered when there is immediate skin discomfort, a respiratory syndrome, or a bloody diarrhea syndrome.

Gas liquid chromatography–mass spectrometry can confirm the presence of these toxins with high sensitivity and specificity. There is no specific prophylactic approach other than physical protection and skin decontamination and no specific therapy (*Medical Management of Biological Casualties Handbook,* 1996).

Chemical Warfare Agents

1. Phosgene. This agent may appear as a white or colorless cloud with an odor of sweet, newly mown hay. The initial symptoms include lacrimation and burning discomfort in the eyes, mouth, and throat, nonproductive cough, and substernal pain and/or pressure after a latent period of three to twenty-four hours (latency is inversely related to the inhaled dose and the victims' physical activity after exposure). Initial symptoms of severe pulmonary damage include dyspnea, cough, and cyanosis. Examination reveals tachypnea, tachycardia, and scattered or diffuse fine or coarse crackles. Radiographs show patchy or diffuse pulmonary edema. Exudation of protein-rich fluid into the alveoli results in severe hemoconcentration, hypovolemia, hypotension, and shock. Death is caused by hypoxemia and/or hypovolemia. Pneumonia may occur in survivors of ARDS produced by this agent. Therapy is supportive, and there is no specific antidote. There is no military detector for phosgene.

2. Nerve agents. Onset of symptoms occurs within one or two minutes of inhalation. Eye pain or a forehead ache, visual blurring, nausea, and vomiting are common early symptoms. Bilateral miosis and conjunctival injection are associated physical findings. Severe dyspnea, wheezing, and chest tightness are caused by bronchoconstriction and increased bronchial secretions. These effects are produced by excessive acetylcholine in the airways due to inactivation of acetylcholinesterase at bronchial cholinergic receptor sites. Respiratory arrest may occur secondary to peripheral impairment of respiratory function or effects on the brain. Nausea, vomiting, and diarrhea reflect excess cholinergic activity in the gastrointestinal tract. Rhinorrhea, lacrimation, and increased salivation may occur. Muscle twitching and fasciculation are frequent early symptoms, soon followed by weakness and flaccid paralysis. Seizures, respiratory arrest, and coma are signs of severe exposure. The rapid onset of an acute obstructive lung disorder–associated rhinorrhea, lacrimation, miosis, skeletal muscle twitching and weakness/paralysis, and/or seizures/unconsciousness suggest a diagnosis of nerve agent poisoning.

Nerve agents can be detected by using M8 or M9 paper and M8A1 and M8 alarm systems. Treatment includes use of atropine and 2-PAMCL. Pyridostigmine was used as a pretreatment to protect cholinesterase from nerve agent attack during the Gulf War.

3. Blister (vesicant) agents. Blister agents are chemicals that first damage the skin. Skin involvement begins with pruritus, burning pain, and erythema. All areas of the skin may be affected, but involvement of moist areas in the perineum, external genitalia, neck, axillae, and antecubital fossae is most frequent. Vesicles form and coalesce into large bullae filled with a straw-colored fluid. There is a latent period of two to six or more hours after exposure until skin symptoms begin. Some lesions resulting from severe exposure are characterized by a central area of skin necrosis surrounded by vesicles/bullae. Secondary bacterial infection of areas of ulceration or bulla collapse may occur. Vesicants include the mustard gases (i.e., distilled sulfur mustard), sulfur mustard and nitrogen mustards, Lewisite, and phosgene oxime. The mustards are the most important vesicants and are the group most likely to be used in a chemical attack.

Mustard "gas" actually is a yellow-to-brown oily liquid with a garlic, onion, or mustard odor. Airway involvement at lower doses causes burning or aching discomfort in the nose, sinuses, and throat. More severe exposures cause hoarseness, productive cough, dyspnea, and pulmonary edema/hemorrhage in focal areas. ARDS is rare. Airway necrosis may result in pseudomembrane formation that may cause local airway obstruction. Denuded bronchial epithelium may be extensive and predisposes the victim to bacterial colonization and rapid proliferation, resulting in diffuse pneumonitis. Bone marrow suppression with granulocytopenia further impairs host resistance, resulting in a rapidly progressive and often lethal outcome. Respiratory symptoms begin two to thirty-six hours after exposure and include a nonproductive refractory cough, dyspnea, chest tightness, and sharp, transient substernal chest discomfort intensified by breathing and/or coughing. Auscultation reveals widespread or localized wheezes and crackles. Eye involvement by mustard vapor causes itching, burning, photophobia, and injection of the conjunctivae. Blepharospasm (spasm of the eyelids) and severe edema of the eyelids results in eye closure and functional loss of vision. Iritis and corneal edema and ulceration may occur in severe cases.

Mustards can be detected by the M256A1 and M8 alarms and by M8 and M9 paper. Lewisite causes immediate irritative symptoms in contrast to the mustards. Phosgene oxime is an urticant and/or corrosive, has a bad odor, and causes immediate skin and eye irritation. It should not be confused with phosgene. Immediate decontamination with copious amounts of water, hypochlorite, the M258A1 kit, and the M291 kit provides the only hope of minimizing mustard-related damage. Discarding contaminated clothing and showering will prevent secondary vaporization and respiratory and eye damage during transport (*Medical Management of Chemical Casualties Handbook,* 1993).

DIARRHEAL AGENTS

1. Viral hemorrhagic fever agents. These viral agents may be transmitted by aerosol. Similar symptoms occur with Ebola and Marburg virus infections (Johnson, 1990). Initially there are flulike complaints such as fever, headache, myalgia, sore throat, cough, dysphagia, vomiting, chest and/or abdominal pain, prostration, and diarrhea. Within three to five days after onset, hemorrhagic symptoms begin. These may include hemorrhagic conjunctivitis, bleeding gums, and oral and lip ulceration, hematemesis, melena, hematuria, epistaxis, and vaginal bleeding. Physical signs include conjunctivitis, pharyngitis, cervical lymphadenopathy, petechiae and ecchymoses, a maculopapular rash, and abdominal tenderness and prostration. The rash may become hemorrhagic. Evidence of hepatocellular damage, marrow depression (e.g., thrombocytopenia and leukopenia), proteinuria, and coagulopathy may occur.

Diagnosis of Ebola virus infection can be rapidly confirmed by a sandwich enzyme immunosorbent assay using anti-Ebola antibodies for viral capture and detection (Ksiazek et al., 1992). Immunoelectron microscopy may also be used to detect Ebola particles in tissue or cultured cells (Geisbert and Jahrling, 1990). There is no medical prophylaxis or therapy. Universal precautions are required to prevent person-to-person spread since free virus particles may be present in the alveoli of the lung (Jahrling et al., 1996). Marburg virus is a filovirus morphologically indistinguishable from the Ebola virus. Rapid diagnosis of Marburg virus infection can be made by immunoelectron microscopy of cell culture samples or tissue (Johnson et al., 1996).

Congo-Crimean hemorrhagic fever virus can be spread by aerosol. The disease begins with a severe flulike illness similar to that described for Ebola/Marburg above. Symptoms include headache, fever, diarrhea, vomiting, sore throat, and chest and abdominal pain. The incubation period may be as short as two days. Hemorrhagic manifestations begin on days three to six and include epistaxis, petechial rash, hematemesis, and melena. Abnormal liver function with jaundice in severe cases and coagulopathy may occur. Renal failure occurs with severe disease and hypotension. Leukopenia and thrombocytopenia are frequent findings.

The virus can be isolated in cell culture or by mouse inoculation. Rapid

antigen detection in human sera can be accomplished with an antigen capture ELISA (Saluzzo and Guenno, 1987). A nested reverse transcriptase
polymerase chain reaction (RT-PCR) can detect virus in serum without use
of cell culture (Schwarz et al., 1996). Ribavirin may have antiviral activity
against this agent.

Lassa fever virus is also transmissible by aerosol. It also causes a nonspecific flulike illness with diarrhea, myalgia, arthralgia, fever, diaphoresis,
generalized aching, and exudative tonsillitis. Facial and neck edema, flush-
ing, and bleeding in the skin, mouth, bowel, and urinary tract and from the
nose begin by day six. A maculopapular and petechial rash may occur.
Severe cases may develop ARDS, encephalopathy, severe bleeding, and
shock. There may be evidence of hepatocellular damage, but jaundice is
uncommon. Leukocyte and platelet counts remain normal or only slightly
depressed. PCR or virus isolation can be used to confirm the diagnosis.
Ribavirin has activity against Lassa fever virus if used within the first
week. The diarrhea occurring with these agents is usually positive for
occult blood after days three to five and may be grossly bloody.

2. *Bacterial agents.* *Shigella* species and Shiga-like toxin-producing
Escherichia coli (SLTEC) could be used to contaminate water and food
supplies. They would not be used as aerosol agents but would require clandestine activity by enemy forces to be effective. *Shigella* species cause
fever, chills, myalgia, vomiting, crampy abdominal pain, and diarrhea.
Stools are initially watery, brown/yellow and voluminous and then become
smaller and mucoid with shreds of blood or grossly bloody. Increased fecal
frequency, urgency, and tenesmus occur. Fever as high as 106 degrees F,
lower abdominal tenderness, blood-streaked or bloody stool, rectal tenderness, and hyperactive bowel sounds are common examination findings.
Less than ten organisms may cause illness. SLTEC causes a similar illness,
and *E. coli* O157:H7 and O104:H21 have recently been isolated from outbreaks (MMWR, March 1996; July 1995). Incubation periods are one to
three days, and culture for these strains is required for definitive diagnosis.
Quinolones are effective against these dysentery-producing agents
(DuPont, 1990; MMWR, June 1995).

DISORDERS PRODUCED BY RASH AGENTS

1. Hemorrhagic fever agents such as Ebola virus, Marburg virus,
Congo-Crimean hemorrhagic fever, and Lassa virus cause skin pallor,
edema, and maculopapular rashes that may become petechial. The illnesses
produced by these agents are described above.

2. Variola. Smallpox begins with fever, chills, headache, malaise, prostration, back pain, myalgia, acute chest or abdominal pain, and nausea and vomiting. Fulminant cases develop oral submucosal hemorrhages as well as blood-filled bullae within two days after onset. Within three days, a generalized maculopapular rash develops. There may be diffuse erythema of the face and dorsum of the hands. Petechial bleeding into maculopapular lesions or erythematous skin occurs. Redness and petechial bleeding in the bathing trunks region is characteristic of fulminant smallpox. Hemoptysis, hematemesis, epistaxis, oral bleeding, melena, and vaginal bleeding are often present. Fulminant variola is usually fatal. It can be confused with a viral hemorrhagic fever.

Variola virus can be detected by electron microscopy, immunoelectron microscopy, and routine histopathologic study of lesion biopsies. Specific diagnosis may require chick embryo culture. Malignant variola also presents with systemic symptoms and a macular/petechial rash on the upper trunk, neck, and face. Vesicles and papules are palpable in the area of the eruption. Similar lesions and petechiae occur in the mouth. The maculopapular rash spreads to the extremities. By day ten, skin lesions have evolved into vesicles. Typical cases of variola cause systemic symptoms and maculopapules that evolve into vesicles and pearl-like pustules in a centrifugal pattern.

HEMORRHAGIC AGENTS

These include the hemorrhagic fever agents and fulminant or malignant variola described above.

MENINGITIC/ENCEPHALITIC AGENTS

Venezuelan equine encephalitis (VEE) is caused by an alphavirus that can be spread by aerosol dissemination. The incubation period varies between one and five days. Influenzalike symptoms are common and include fever, rigors, headache, malaise, low back and leg aching, nausea, vomiting, diarrhea, lethargy, sleepiness, sore throat, and leukopenia. Neurologic symptoms occur in less than 4 percent of cases and only rarely in adults. Meningismus, paralysis, confusion, coma, and convulsions occur in children, and the fatality rate in this group may reach 20 percent. Viral isolation from serum and antigen capture immunoassay can provide diagnostic confirmation.

An ELISA for detection of IgM anti-VEE antibody has been developed (Rosato, Macasaet, and Jahrling, 1988). There is no specific therapy available. VEE virus is a disabling and seldom lethal agent (MMWR, October 1995).

PARALYTIC AGENTS

1. Clostridium (botulinum toxins). Aerosolized botulinum toxin causes a clinical illness like that resulting from ingestion of contaminated food. Onset is usually within ten to twenty hours after exposure but may be up to four or five days, an exception to the usual time course of toxin related illness. Weakness, dizziness, and fatigue are early complaints. A dry mouth, tongue, and throat result from inhibition of salivation. Sore throat resulting from throat dryness is a common complaint. Nausea, vomiting, diarrhea, or constipation and abdominal pain may occur. Abdominal distension with obstipation and urinary retention may soon follow. Diplopia, blurred vision, photophobia, ptosis, dysarthria, dysphonia, and dysphagia are common early symptoms. Descending flaccid paralysis soon develops, and the patient may lie helpless in bed, unable to move a limb or change position. Respiratory muscle weakness can cause dyspnea and hypoxemia and may progress rapidly to respiratory arrest. Common signs include shallow rapid respirations, ptosis, extraocular muscle palsies, and dilated, fixed pupils (Townes et al., 1996).

Botulinum toxin can be detected in patient serum in a mouse neutralization bioassay. ELISA and chemiluminescence immunosorbent assays (CLISA) for type A botulinum toxin are under development (Ligieza, Reiss, and Michalik, 1994) but are not available for field use. Antitoxin given as soon after exposure or onset as is possible may lessen disease severity. Vaccine to botulinum toxins A-E is protective against aerosol attack with these agents.

2. Nerve agent poisoning. This is described above. Muscle fasciculations, twitching, seizures, and coma accompany a flaccid paralysis. Cranial nerve involvement as in botulism does not occur, and cholinergic symptoms/signs such as lacrimation, salivation, wheezing, diarrhea, and miosis help differentiate this type of neurological toxicity from Botulinum toxin poisoning.

3. Cobra venom neurotoxin inhalation. To produce this disorder would require genetic engineering to create an altered bacterium that can express this toxin in vitro or in vivo. Symptoms of cobra venom neurotoxicity include lethargy, a generalized flaccid paralysis, ptosis, dysphagia, dysarthria, nausea, respiratory weakness, and coma. These findings may mimic botulism. Cobra toxin can be detected by an immunoassay of serum. Antitoxin administration may reduce the severity of the illness produced.

At present there is no weapon system that utilizes cobra venom toxins. It is mentioned as a potential weapon system of the future.

RAPID DEATH AGENTS

1. Cyanide. Inhalation of cyanide vapor may cause the rapid onset of hyperpnea, collapse, loss of consciousness, and seizures. Respiratory arrest and death may occur within minutes. Severe respiratory distress in noncyanotic individuals should suggest the diagnosis in a chemical warfare setting. Rapid death cannot usually be prevented. Cases with a slower onset can be improved or salvaged by administering sodium nitrite and sodium thiosulfate intravenously. Cyanide can be detected by the M256A1 ticket and by detecting an odor of bitter almonds in the air and/or victim's breath (*Medical Management of Chemical Casualties Handbook,* 1993).

2. Saxitoxin. This rapidly acting toxin blocks sodium channels in nerve and muscle tissue, causing flaccid paralysis by interfering with depolarization. Initial symptoms include generalized numbness and paresthesia, incoordination, and lightheadedness. Headache, weakness, and confusion soon follow. Weakness progresses to flaccid paralysis, resulting in respiratory insufficiency and arrest. This agent is not likely to be used for broad area coverage but more likely against small tactical targets.

Saxitoxin can be detected in rat urine after parenteral administration of a sublethal dose. Saxitoxin can be isolated from urine by an ion-exchange procedure and identified and measured by a precolumn-oxidation-HPLC method, coupled with fluorescence for detection. Final identification can be obtained by electrospray ionization mass spectrometry (Stafford and Hines, 1995). Enzyme-linked immunofiltration tests for saxitoxin in tissue are under development (Usleber et al., 1995).

COMMUNICABLE BW AGENTS

The threat agents most likely to cause person-to-person spread include the hemorrhagic fever agents, variola, and plague pneumonia. Autopsy of an anthrax victim poses some risk as well. Universal barrier precautions are required to prevent secondary spread. Disposal of those dead of highly contagious agents can be done by cremation or deep burial with liberal use of disinfectants. Blankets and linens may require burning, steam disinfection, boiling, or soaking in 3 percent Lysol. Use of sealed thick polythene body bags with a vent to allow release of gases from the decomposing body is a possible way to return bodies to their families for burial. The exterior of the bag must be treated with disinfectants before shipment home for burial. These methods were used during major smallpox epidemics in the past.

ALGORITHMS

An attack in which biological, chemical, or toxin weapons are used will, if successful, cause a large number of casualties. The spectrum of symptoms exhibited by victims will be wide with many severe or fulminant cases, a smaller number of typical textbook cases, and a group of mildly or barely symptomatic patients. If a biological attack takes place, incubation periods will be shortened relative to naturally occurring diseases and the mortality rate will be higher. If multiple agents are used in an attack, clinical findings will be complex and represent a mixture of symptoms, signs, and laboratory and radiological findings that are the sum effects of two or more toxic and/or proliferating agents. However, the clinician may actually be helped diagnostically by the wide spectrum of disease and the occurrence of classical cases and clinical diagnosis may be easier than in a single case. Findings from autopsies, laboratory tests, and radiographs will accelerate the making of one or more diagnoses.

The algorithm in Figure 6.1 uses the time span during which most cases present themselves to separate chemical/toxin-related disease from illness induced by proliferating agents. A clustering of most cases within a period of minutes up to 24 hours is suggestive of a chemical or toxin being the responsible agent. However, were multiple attacks to be carried out over a 48-hour period, a more confusing situation may result.

The algorithm in Figure 6.2 differentiates possible chemicals and toxins from each other on the basis of clinical findings in the majority of victims. Thus, if a substantial number of patients die quickly (Question 1), a rapid death agent—such as a nerve agent, cyanide gas, or palytoxin and saxitoxin—probably is responsible, killing by causing cardiopulmonary arrest. If most patients survive for longer than an hour, the clinician looks for fever (Question 2). If there is fever accompanied by rash (Question 3), then T2 is the likely responsible agent; if fever without rash, then ricin or SEB are more likely. High lethality with liver and renal toxicity (Question 4) points toward ricin, while lower lethality and predominantly pulmonary symptoms are characteristic of SEB poisoning.

Returning to Question 2, if there is no fever, the clinician looks for paralysis (Question 5). The presence of paralysis suggests botulinum toxin or a nerve agent. Cholinergic symptoms (Question 6) with visual loss, diarrhea, sweating, salivation, coughing, wheezing, muscle twitching, and seizures or coma point toward a nerve agent, while flaccid, quiet paralysis with bulbar symptoms such as double vision, impaired speech, and swallowing indicate botulism. If there is no paralysis (Question 5), the clinician looks for severe respiratory symptoms, high white blood cell count, and higher than normal hematocrit (Question 7). The presence of these symptoms and signs indicate phosgene as the causative agent. A smell resembling new mown hay during the attack also suggests phosgene. If the answer to Question 7 is "no," and patients exhibit blisters, skin pain with redness, and some eye and lung symptoms (Question 8), the indication is that mustard gas was responsible. Confirmatory laboratory tests are suggested under the name of the possible causative agents.

The algorithm in Figure 6.3 differentiates between proliferating bacterial and viral agents that are most likely to be used by enemy military forces or terrorists. Question 1 seeks to separate acute but more slowly developing diseases from each other on the basis of the most common and, often, most severe presenting symptoms. Diarrheal illness is differentiated on the presence or absence of blood in the stool, which can be done by observation or testing for occult blood (Question 2). Stools passed by patients affected by one of the bacterial species causing dysentery (*Escherichia coli* O157:H7, *Campylobacter* species, *Salmonella* species, or *Shigella* species) or Marburg/Ebola viruses contain blood, but stools produced by persons suffering from cholera do not.

Patients with respiratory symptoms are subjected to radiological examinations (Question 3). If these examinations demonstrate necrotizing pneumonia (Question 3E), it indicates that the causative agent is *Francisella tularensis* (tularemia), *Yersinia pestis* (plague), *Pseudomonas mallei* (glanders), or *Pseudomonas pseudomallei* (melioidosis). If the radiological studies show segmental or subsegmental pneumonias (Question 3D), these findings are nonspecific, having many causes. The acute respiratory distress syndrome (ARDS) (Question 3A) can occur with Hantavirus disease or secondary to severe sepsis or bacterial or viral pneumonia. The appearance of large hilar nodes (Question 3C) suggests anthrax, tularemia or, less likely, acute histoplasmosis (this is not considered a threat agent). Further, pneumonic infiltrates can occur with all of these agents. The presence of a wide mediastinum (Question 3B) is characteristic of anthrax and, occasionally, plague.

Returning to Question 1, meningeal symptoms, such as headache, photophobia, and retro-orbital pain, is indicative of encephalitis caused by Venezuelan equine encephalitis virus and other encephalitic viruses. If the victims present a rash, the clinician needs to identify the type of rash (Question 4). If the rash is pustular, the illness could be smallpox, melioidosis, or glanders, Maculopapular rashes are nonspecific and can occur early in smallpox and in Ebola/Marburg, Congo-Crimean, and Lassa hemorrhagic fevers. Ecchymotic rashes in epidemic form also suggest the presence of one of the hemorrhagic fevers.

Figure 6.1   Algorithm for Acute Illness

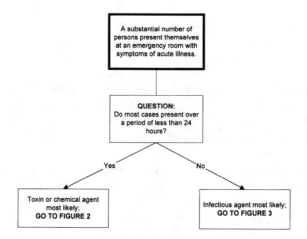

Figure 6.2   Algorithm for Toxins and Chemical Agents

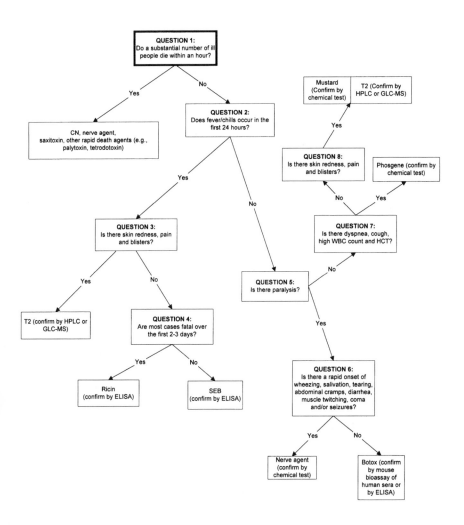

Figure 6.3   Algorithm for Infectious Agents

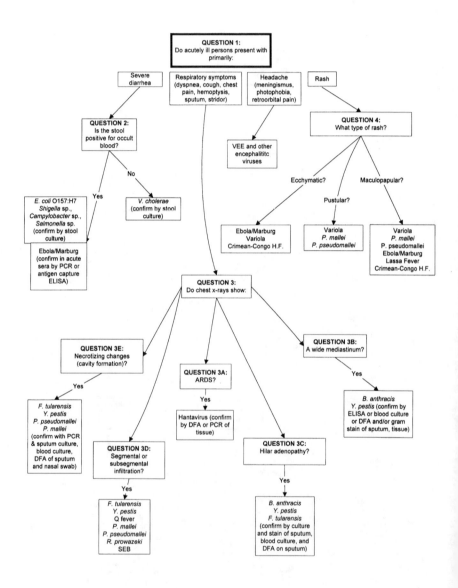

PART 3
International Control

7

Strengthening the International Arms Control Regime

MARIE I. CHEVRIER

Among the triad of weapons capable of mass destruction, nuclear and chemical weapons have attracted the bulk of political and academic attention.[1] Biological weapons arms control has been treated as a neglected stepchild, usually disparaged and shunted aside. Nations have questioned the efficacy of that regime yet have been loath to remedy its shortcomings. Some nations have alleged that other states possess clandestine biological weapons programs, yet only one nation, Cuba, has availed itself of existing international machinery to address such concerns. In the meantime, revelations of Iraq's, South Africa's, and the USSR's biological warfare (BW) programs, as well as the use of chemical and, allegedly, biological weapons by the terrorist sect Aum Shinrikyo, have increased public awareness of the potential of biological weapons to wreak havoc in our society.

The international community seeks to prevent nations and subnational entities from acquiring, deploying, and using biological weapons by creating a web of treaties and activities. Although casual observers may think of arms control only in terms of negotiated, signed, and ratified international treaties, the scope of arms control activities is much broader, encompassing "disarmament, negotiated constraints, nonproliferation, export controls, confidence- and security-building measures, unilateral declaratory defense policies, aspects of diplomacy, international law, defense conversion, and certain activities related to international peacekeeping" (Lehman, 1996).

The strength of any international regime "refers to the stringency with which rules regulate the behavior of countries" (Aggarwal, 1985: 20–21). How would the international community recognize a strong biological weapons arms control regime if it had one? First, the regime would be truly universal. Second, all parties would be in actual compliance with the rules, or, lacking perfect compliance, the greater the degree of compliance, the stronger the regime. Third, all parties would be convinced that grounds for confidence in other countries' compliance existed.[2] Fourth, mechanisms would exist within the regime to enable countries under suspicion of non-compliance to alleviate other countries' concerns and facilitate the gathering of evidence to confirm, support, retain, or reject suspicions of noncompliance. Fifth, a nondiscriminatory method for adjudicating compliance disputes would be available. Sixth, violators would face clear, straightforward penalties.

As will be seen, the biological arms control regime is stronger than it is usually given credit for when viewed with the proper breadth (i.e., the regime's treaties, formal and informal confidence-building measures [CBMs], and other national and international activities that support the principles and norms of the regime). Nevertheless, the regime has two important, interrelated weaknesses: (1) widespread questions regarding the compliance of ten or so countries with the treaty and concerns about biological weapons programs in a few countries that are not party to the treaty and (2) the lack of a framework within the regime by which it is possible to verify treaty compliance or resolve compliance concerns.

In this chapter, I describe and assess the existing biological arms control regime and propose means for strengthening it. Accordingly, the chapter has four sections: (1) an analysis of the strengths and weaknesses of the biological arms control regime, (2) a history of attempts to strengthen the regime by strengthening the Convention on the Prohibition of the Development, Production and Stockpiling of Bacteriological (Biological) and Toxin Weapons, and on Their Destruction (BWC), (3) a history of attempts to strengthen the regime outside the BWC, and (4) a concluding section wherein I propose ways to maintain the regime as a bulwark against the acquisition and use of biological weapons into the next century.

STRENGTHS AND WEAKNESSES OF
THE BIOLOGICAL WEAPONS ARMS CONTROL REGIME

Although an entire gamut of activities form the building blocks of arms control, the security purpose of arms control is achieved through explicit or implicit cooperation with other states (Rattray, 1996: 8). The unifying element, essential to defining an activity as arms control, is that its effect is to limit or diminish armaments or the means of warfare.[3]

The word "regime" also has special meaning in international relations parlance:

Regimes can be defined as sets of implicit or explicit principles, norms, rules and decision-making procedures around which actors' expectations converge in a given area of international relations. Principles are beliefs of fact, causation and rectitude. Norms are standards of behavior defined in terms of rights and obligations. Rules are specific prescriptions or proscriptions for action. Decision-making procedures are prevailing practices of making and implementing collective choice. (Krasner, 1983: 2)[4]

When applying the definitions of "arms control" and "regime" to the biological weapons arms control regime, it appears evident that the regime is comprehensive and contains many strong components.[5] The principles that there are no circumstances in which the deliberate spread of disease can be justified and that the use of disease as a weapon is always wrong underlie the regime.[6] The norm of nonuse of biological weapons flows from these principles and is incorporated in the obligations of two international agreements, the 1925 Geneva Protocol, which predates the BWC by fifty years, and the BWC. This norm has endured remarkably well; with very rare exceptions, nations and subnational groups have not used biological weapons as either a weapon of war or of terror. Complementing the Geneva Protocol prohibition against use, parties to the BWC agree to forgo the possession and acquisition of biological weapons, to destroy any existing weapons, and to refrain from assisting any other country in obtaining them. BWC treaty parties have also made it clear that the ban covers use in all circumstances.[7]

Other regime components reinforce its norms and principles: the United States' 1969 unilateral renunciation of BW; the formal information-exchange or CBMs adopted by the BWC Review Conferences in 1986 and 1991; the findings of the Verification Experts (VEREX) process;[8] the establishment of the Ad Hoc Group process to strengthen the convention;[9] activities to restrict exports of equipment and materials that could be used to make biological weapons; the trilateral process among Russia, the United Kingdom, and the United States to address long-standing problems with Soviet, and subsequently Russian, compliance with the BWC; and, arguably, the United Nations Special Commission's (UNSCOM's) investigation of Iraq's biological weapons activities.

The BWC sets forth its obligations in strong language. The parties are determined "to exclude completely the possibility of bacteriological (biological) agents and toxins being used as weapons." Article I outlaws the possession of *any quantity* of biological agents or toxins that has "no justification for prophylactic, protective or other peaceful purposes." Possession of even a very small quantity of biological agent or toxin attached to a dissemination device for clandestine delivery would be a violation of the treaty. In contrast, a vaccine production plant could possess a large quantity of agent or toxin that would be consistent with a peaceful purpose. Thus, the quantity of agent or toxin that countries possess is not the critical factor in the definition of what the BWC prohibits. The strong terms of the BWC accurately place the onus on a party to demonstrate its justification for possessing types and quantities of agents that others may regard as suspicious. Moreover, Article I's wide prohibitions have withstood the test of time. No party has withdrawn from the treaty, in force since 1975; indeed, many nations that were not original parties have acceded to the convention, including France and China.[10]

The norms and principles of the biological weapons regime extend throughout the world. The Geneva Protocol has 146 parties, and the BWC has 142 parties; eighteen additional countries originally signed the latter treaty but have not yet ratified it.[11] Although the regime is not completely universal, most of the countries that are not parties to the BWC are relatively small countries in Africa and several island nations in the Pacific or the Mediterranean. Outside that contingent, a number of the newly independent states of the former Soviet Union have not yet acceded to the BWC, nor have several significant states in the Middle East.

Just as other arms control regimes are criticized in some quarters for certain perceived weaknesses, so too is the biological weapons arms control regime: "If the principles, norms, rules, and decision-making procedures of a regime become less coherent, or if actual practice is increasingly inconsistent with principles, norms, rules, and procedures, then a regime has weakened" (Krasner, 1983: 5).

Although the principles, norms, and rules of the regime have endured well, three interrelated factors have lead to widespread concern that actual practice of nations is increasingly inconsistent with the rules. First, a number of countries are suspected of acquiring or demonstrating interest in acquiring biological weapons. Second, a great deal of uncertainty surrounds the question of whether some countries are in compliance with the convention. The relative ease of hiding a biological weapons program and the dual-use nature of biomedical equipment and biological agents and toxins—which are characteristics of the weapons and not weaknesses of the regime per se—contribute to the level of uncertainty. Third, the parties are limited in their ability to reduce compliance uncertainty because the BWC has no measures or procedures to promote, assess, and verify compliance with its provisions.

The Question of Compliance

A dozen countries, give or take a few, appear as the usual suspects when the issue of who might possess a biological weapons program is raised.[12] Unclassified U.S. sources of information regarding countries that may have, or may be interested in acquiring, biological weapons programs include reports of the U.S. Arms Control and Disarmament Agency (ACDA) and congressional testimony by the Central Intelligence Agency (CIA) officials. In its most recent annual report to Congress, ACDA discusses eight countries that it listed in previous years as states whose compliance with the BWC continues to be of concern: China, Egypt, Iran, Iraq, Libya, Russia, Syria, and Taiwan (ACDA, 1998). Earlier, CIA officials had testified to possible programs in Israel,[13] North Korea, and Cuba in addition to those mentioned in the ACDA report (U.S. Congress, 1993a). Other sources contain similar numbers of countries of concern (Pearson, 1993b: 150). Jane's Consultancy Services reports a more extensive list of countries that might have a connection to biological weapons activities (Reed, 1993), including eight countries in addition to those listed above: the South Asian countries of India and Pakistan; three former Soviet republics (Ukraine, Belarus, and Kazakhstan); and Jordan, Algeria, and South Africa.

A question arises, however, as to the significance that can be attached to the appearance of a country on some of these lists. The extent of noncompliance or the degree of suspicion regarding each country's putative program (or intentions to establish one) varies from an admitted or known program in Iraq and one that Russia admits occurred in the USSR to much scantier evidence of wrongdoing. The evidence against Taiwan, which appears in the ACDA report, is that it "has been upgrading its biotechnology capabilities by purchasing sophisticated biotechnology equipment from the United States, Switzerland and other countries." The ACDA report concludes: "The evidence indicating a BW program is not sufficient to determine if Taiwan is engaged in activities prohibited by the BWC" (ACDA, 1998: 94).[14] Similarly, the report from Jane's includes Algeria but says it has "no ambition evident"; about Jordan, the report states that it is "unlikely to seek [a] capability." Classified evidence may exist concerning these countries' interest in acquiring biological or toxin weapons; if so, the strength of the compliance concern cannot be evaluated by those who do not have access to classified documents (Dando, 1994: 180–181; Harris, 1990; Carus, 1991: 23–29).

Further analysis of the lists yields the following. Grave questions remain regarding the current and future status of the two known or admitted programs in the former USSR and Iraq (Leitenberg, 1996b: 3–16; Zilinskas, 1997a; Barton, 1998). In 1992, President Boris Yeltsin admitted that a program existed in the USSR in violation of the BWC and stated that he would terminate it. To that end he agreed to trilateral inspections with the United States and the United Kingdom. The trilateral process is secret; therefore, no public information is available to provide assurance to other treaty parties that Russia is fulfilling its obligations under the BWC. In addition, the process has thus far failed to demonstrate to its participants that Russia has terminated the program left over from the USSR.[15] Revelations of a defector from the Soviet BW program have cast further doubt on Russia's current compliance (Alibek, 1998a, 1998b, 1998c, 1999).

A challenging situation also persists in Iraq. Although the intelligence assessment existing before the Gulf War that Iraq possessed anthrax and botulinum toxin weapons has been confirmed by UNSCOM, Iraq has been able to successfully hide the full extent of its program. UNSCOM remains unconvinced that Iraq has destroyed all of its biological weapons program (UNSCOM, 1999a).[16] Indeed, Iraq's political leaders who sought to acquire biological weapons are still in power, the scientists and engineers that developed and produced biological weapons work much as before, and the biological infrastructure underpinning the BW program is still largely in place. Since Iraq has refused to allow UNSCOM inspectors to enter its territory, biological weapons are easier for Iraq to reacquire than either nuclear or chemical weapons.[17] The situations in both Russia and Iraq require continued scrutiny.

South Africa's program has, reportedly, been terminated,[18] which leaves serious concerns about possible programs in China, Egypt, Iran, Israel, Libya, and Syria.[19] Given that five of these six countries are in the political powder keg that is the Middle East, making progress on regional security problems might expedite the elimination of biological weapons in the area. Many nations in this region have called for a Middle East zone free of weapons of mass destruction, implicitly linking Israel's willingness (or lack thereof) to give up nuclear weapons to their own willingness to forgo chemical and biological weapons (Algeria et al., 1995: 242).[20] Regional security issues could also affect possible biological weapons programs in North and South Korea, China, Taiwan, India, and Pakistan.

The Problem of Uncertainty

The discussion of compliance with the BWC underscores a serious shortcoming of the regime; namely, the uncertainty associated with countries' compliance with the treaty. At present, it is difficult, at least theoretically, for one country to establish empirical grounds for confidence in another country's compliance with the rules. The level of uncertainty is due to two factors: (1) the purported ease with which a country could acquire and hide a biological weapons program (due to the dual-use nature and relatively small scale of much of the equipment needed to establish an offensive program), and (2) the absence of methods under the convention for countries to demonstrate their own compliance or to ascertain whether others are in compliance with the treaty.

Creating and sustaining grounds for confidence in all countries' compliance with the BWC is problematic because the judgment of whether a country is in compliance is not independent of the identity of the country in question. One country could remain suspicious or be confident of another country's compliance when presented with evidence, depending upon other, often unrelated, characteristics of the country. If a country is democratic, scrupulously compliant with other treaty obligations, not an aggressor in recent international conflicts, and cooperative with respect to inquiries, a relatively low standard of evidence is sufficient to convince most countries of its compliance. Alternatively, if a country is a closed society with a totalitarian or autocratic form of government, has been lax in its compliance with other agreements, has an aggressive reputation, and hinders or delays responses to inquiries regarding treaty compliance, a more stringent standard of proof is necessary to convince other nations of its compliance. The relationship between the country presenting evidence of compliance and the country making the judgment of compliance is also relevant. Pakistan, for example, would probably require considerably more evidence than Egypt to be convinced that India was acting in compliance.

Uncertainty of compliance is exacerbated by the difficulty of determining a country's intentions with regard to potential biological weapons agents or toxins that it may possess. In outlawing the development and possession of biological agents and toxins that have no justification for prophylactic, protective, or other peaceful purposes, the treaty acknowledges the dual-use nature of biological agents and toxins. No attempt has been made, nor is it possible, to define quantities of agents and toxins that have a justification for "protective, prophylactic or other peaceful purposes." Developing objective criteria for permitted (or prohibited) quantities of agents or toxins entails the risk of limiting the purposely broad and inclusive prohibitions, thereby weakening rather than strengthening the treaty.[21] The treaty is crystal clear regarding its ban on the possession of weapons, however. The phrase referring to intentions applies only to the possession of agents and toxins; weaponized agents or toxins are perforce forbidden.

The Absence of Cooperative
Measures to Verify Compliance

Article VI of the BWC purports to deal with questions of compliance, yet it has two glaring limitations: (1) the language obliquely refers to investigations of compliance but does not create an international organization with an inspectorate to conduct inspections or investigations; (2) the United Nations Security Council, which is the designated arbiter of compliance controversies in the BWC, is hampered by the ability of the permanent members to veto any action and the distaste that many members of the United Nations feel for the Security Council because of its undemocratic composition (South Centre, 1996: 147–149).

STRENGTHENING THE ARMS
CONTROL REGIME WITHIN THE BWC STRUCTURE

Each of the four Review Conferences of the BWC has recognized the limitations of the convention, and each has taken steps to buttress the convention within the political climate prevailing at the time. At the first, in 1980, the Swedish delegation led efforts to amend Articles V and VI of the BWC,[22] proposing that a consultative committee be established to conduct fact finding with on-site inspections (OSI).[23] The Soviet Union and its allies objected strenuously to the Swedish proposal on the grounds that the Review Conference was not the proper forum for amending the convention.[24] The delegates resolved the controversy by recognizing the right of any party to request a consultative meeting at the expert level under Article V of the treaty, which calls for consultations and cooperation on any problems that may arise in relation to the convention (BWC, 1980).[25]

The Second Review Conference, in 1986, once again took up the deficiencies of Article V.[26] Delegations decided that a consultative meeting will be called at the request of any party and agreed upon other details of such a meeting (BWC, 1986a).[27] The BWC state parties at the Second Review Conference agreed to exchange information annually in two areas: (1) research centers or laboratories that "meet very high national or international safety standards . . . or specialize in permitted biological activities directly related to the Convention" and (2) the outbreak of diseases "that seem to deviate from the normal pattern. . . ." They also agreed to encourage publication of research related to the convention and to promote "use of knowledge gained in this research" and "contacts between scientists" (BWC, 1986a: 6).

The Third Review Conference, held in 1991, clarified and added details to the information exchange established in 1986. Four information declarations were added, requiring (1) a description of all offensive and defensive BW programs that were in place on or after January 1, 1946; (2) declarations of ongoing research and development programs in biological and toxin weapons defense; (3) detailed information on all human vaccine production facilities; and (4) reports as to what BWC state parties have done to implement the BWC domestically.

Compliance with the politically binding declarations agreed to at the Second and Third Review Conferences has been disappointing. The majority of the treaty parties have not devoted the resources to meeting the requirements of the declarations (Geissler, 1990a; Hunger, 1996).[28] However, although the information exchange has done little to build confidence in treaty compliance, the endeavor has not been totally without merit. More than half of the treaty parties have made at least one such declaration. Additionally, the information contained in the declarations reveals something about the biotechnological capabilities of countries submitting declarations. Finally, some countries have disclosed details of past biological weapons programs that could be helpful in ascertaining ways to identify current or future programs.[29]

The Third Review Conference also reinforced the agreement of the Second Review Conference to call a consultative committee at the request of any party by elaborating many procedural details for such a meeting.[30] The most far-reaching action by the Third Review Conference was to initiate the VEREX process (BWC, 1991).

Momentum for a verification protocol for the BWC, which had been growing since the treaty was negotiated, had accelerated in the years leading up to the Third Review Conference. Advances in microbiology and biotechnology led some countries to fear that technological factors that once complicated the production of reliable biological or toxin weapons could be overcome more easily. As the perception of limited military utility for biological weapons began to change, treaty parties saw strengthening the convention as a more urgent task.[31] In addition, an intrusive protocol for the BWC appeared more politically feasible.[32]

Despite widespread support among BWC state parties for some type of on-site measures to verify compliance, other BWC state parties, including the United States, have maintained that the BWC is not verifiable (Moodie, 1993: 52).[33] To settle the issue, the Third Review Conference established a group of "Governmental Experts . . . to identify and examine potential verification measures from a scientific and technical standpoint" but not to commit to incorporating any measures into an addition to the treaty (BWC, 1991: 9). This group of experts—and the process that it undertook—became known by the acronym VEREX.[34]

The experts participating in VEREX examined and evaluated twenty-one off-site and on-site measures and concluded that some of the measures, especially when used in combination, would make the treaty a more effective instrument (BWC, 1993). In September 1994, delegates attending a Special Conference of the BWC to consider the findings of VEREX established a new Ad Hoc Group (AHG) to draft proposals for inclusion of some VEREX measures in a legally binding instrument to strengthen the effectiveness of the convention (BWC, 1994b). The AHG has held negotiating sessions several times a year since January 1995.

Under its mandate, the AHG had to consider four separate areas: (1) definitions of terms and objective criteria, (2) confidence-building and transparency measures, (3) measures to promote compliance, and (4) measures to implement Article X of the convention.[35] The work of the AHG was originally organized around these four areas under the guidance of "friends of the chair" but moved to a negotiating text, or "rolling" text, in July 1997. Many details of the instrument remain to be worked out, but its image is taking shape. Declarations of certain biological facilities and activities, challenge investigations of alleged use or other treaty violations, other on-site measures to clarify declaration discrepancies or deter violations, and other measures to strengthen Article III and implement Article X are likely to be among its components.[36]

Declarations

The VEREX process specified declarations, along with on-site inspections, as the measure that most commonly could be used in combination with other measures to verify compliance with the BWC (BWC, 1993). The purpose of declarations in the context of a legally binding protocol to the BWC, according to the VEREX summary report, would be to provide "a base line of information regarding all three areas of development, production and stockpiling" (BWC, 1993).[37] The purposes of declarations have been described in this way:

> Declarations help strengthen confidence in compliance with the Convention by increasing transparency and thus helping to avoid false suspicions of non-compliance. Declarations make evasion of obligations more difficult, and could thus have a deterrent effect. To be fully effective, declarations may have to be linked to *other measures*. Declarations should address relevant issues related to compliance with the Convention and implementation of the compliance regime. (BWC, 1996c: 31)[38]

Declarations that became part of a legally binding instrument would identify those facilities and activities of greatest relevance to the convention. Numerous details restricting or expanding the pool of facilities that must be declared are under debate, yet the following general categories of activities and facilities are in the rolling text of July 1998 (BWC, 1998a). The first obligation would be to declare information about past offensive BW programs and past and current defensive programs to protect against BW. Human and animal vaccine production facilities (and similar facilities to produce plant inoculants) constitute the second area for declaration. Third, facilities that have special equipment or design features to prevent the release of biological organisms (referred to as containment, biocontainment, or biosafety) would be declared. Various proposals are in the negotiating text to specify containment features or combine containment features with the possession of certain agents or toxins. Fourth, facilities (with a few exceptions) that work with or possess biological agents or toxins on an agreed-upon list would be declared.[39] Fifth, facilities that produce biological agents and that meet other specific criteria would be declared. In addition to the obligations to declare activities and facilities, an obligation to declare transfers of listed agents, toxins, and equipment and the appearance of disease outbreaks caused by certain agents is under consideration (BWC, 1998a).

Negotiators are weighing the pros and cons of specific declaration criteria. The task of the negotiators is to clarify in treaty language the specific activities and facilities that are of most relevance to the treaty without creating unnecessary burdens for BWC state parties; for example, by creating a deluge of declared facilities that would overwhelm the implementing organization. The number of declared facilities is likely to be approximately 2,500 worldwide.[40] The scope of declarations is relevant beyond the requirement to provide information since declared facilities are likely to be subject to some type of on-site visits by the organization that will implement the protocol.

On-Site Measures

The choices that the Ad Hoc Group negotiators make with respect to the types, frequency, and intrusiveness of on-site measures to be included in their proposals for a legally binding instrument will have a profound effect on the degree to which the BWC is strengthened. Although the negotiators within the Ad Hoc Group generally agree that on-site measures have an important role in strengthening the convention, they disagree on their applications.

The July 1998 rolling text contains descriptions of four different types of on-site visits (other than those made in response to a specific allegation of a treaty violation): (1) random visits, (2) clarification visits, (3) requested visits, and (4) voluntary confidence-building visits.[41] The four proposed types of visits differ on the procedure for initiating or launching the visit, the purpose of the visit, and how the visit would be conducted.

Random visits would be selected by the implementing organization, from among declared facilities only, on a modified random basis.[42] The purposes of proposed random visits are to confirm that the information submitted through declarations is accurate and consistent with the protocol requirements and to deter proliferators from using declared facilities to hide forbidden offensive programs. The same number of random visits would probably occur year after year, and states could accurately calculate the probability that any particular facility would be visited in any given year.

Clarification visits would arise if declaration information was unclear. Either BWC state parties or the organization would identify such problems with declarations, and the executive council of the organization might review the request for a visit. The purpose of clarification visits would be "to resolve any ambiguity, uncertainty, anomaly or omission in the declarations of a State Party and to promote accuracy and comprehensiveness in future declarations" (BWC, 1998b: 49). Clarification visits would most commonly be to declared facilities. In the case of an omission in a declaration—a facility that should have been declared but was not—the clarification visits could take place in a facility that was not declared. The number of clarification visits would likely decline over time as countries became more experienced with declaration requirements.

Requested visits would occur if a BWC state party invited or requested the organization visit a facility. The purposes of request visits would be to assist the state party in completing full and accurate declarations, to further cooperation and assistance among state parties, or to resolve a specific concern related to a declaration.

Voluntary confidence-building visits would be coordinated between or among BWC state parties. Their purpose would be to build confidence by developing transparency, communication, and regular contact among experts from different countries. Alternatively, a state party could request a confidence-building visit. In that case, state parties would submit a list of facilities for visits and could include undeclared as well as declared facilities. The visits would be conducted by experts nominated by state parties, not by permanent professional staff members of the implementing organization (BWC, 1998b: Annex G, 230–238).

The disagreements among countries concerning the appropriate role of on-site measures, particularly in the absence of suspicions of noncompliance, crosses traditional alliances and working groups. Neither the Western Group nor the nonaligned group is in full internal agreement on this issue. Within the Western Group, the United States and Japan oppose random on-site visits, but many members of the European Union, Canada, and Australia steadfastly support them. The United States supports clarification visits and has proposed many details for the visits.[43] Within the neutral and nonaligned countries, India, one of this group's traditional leaders, and Iran have taken a position similar to the United States, whereas Brazil supports random on-site measures. Russia and China also oppose them.

Countries supporting a broader role for on-site measures stress the importance of random visits to deter violations of the BWC. Although on-site measures are not the only instrument to discourage countries from attempting to acquire biological weapons, being subject to random visits of biological facilities is thought by many to be an essential ingredient in the mix of deterrent activities (Pearson and Dando, 1997; MacEachin, 1998). Supporters also emphasize the link between random visits and challenge investigations. Random visits, over time, would generate much useful information regarding the structure and practice of biological research and development in many countries. Supporters also point out that the BWC should not have a weaker compliance regime than the Chemical Weapons Convention (CWC) or the Nuclear Non-Proliferation Treaty, both of which subject their treaty parties to routine inspections of chemical or nuclear facilities. The lack of random visits could imply that it is less important to have a stringent regime to control biological weapons. Clarification visits are thought to be a less politically laden way to probe compliance concerns that do not reach the level of allegations of treaty violations, but they are also thought to have a weaker role than random visits in deterring noncompliance because a country could avoid clarification visits by being scrupulously careful in preparing declaration information. To the extent that a consultation between or among states preceded a clarification visit, the deterrent effect of a short-notice visit would be destroyed.

Opponents of random visits emphasize the possible loss of commercial proprietary information by biotechnology or pharmaceutical companies subjected to visits. The United States, which is a leader in the biotechnology and pharmaceutical industries, is reluctant to support random on-site inspections without full support from the industries to be affected. In the United States these industries are not united themselves on a position with respect to on-site inspections in a protocol.[44] Other countries may not be convinced that the benefits accruing from inspecting declared facilities outweigh the expense of doing so. Others may be opposed to foreign inspectors in their countries or territories in principle. Yet another argument is that states would never declare a facility engaged in clandestine, prohibited activity and, therefore, inspections of declared facilities would be a waste of time and money.

The controversy over on-site inspections is reminiscent of the long-standing issue of verification and the BWC. Since the Reagan administration, the official U.S. position is that compliance with the BWC cannot be verified. A tenet of the argument is that any country determined to make biological weapons could successfully conceal its program in relatively small, unremarkable facilities. Hence no process or means to gather information regarding a country's compliance would be sufficient to make a judgment that a country is in compliance with the BWC in the face of suspicions of noncompliance. Thus, the U.S. position regarding BWC verification focuses primarily, if not exclusively, on whether the process could reliably detect violations; in doing so it undervalues or disregards the other purposes of verification, particularly verification's role in deterring biological weapons acquisition.[45] The position of the Clinton administration differs somewhat from its predecessors. Rather than emphasizing the difficulties of detecting violations of the BWC, the president has expressed support for strengthening the treaty through the Ad Hoc Group process.

In addition to the disagreement over random inspections of declared facilities, negotiators do not agree on the procedures to launch on-site field or facility investigations of activities alleged to constitute a treaty violation. It is generally assumed that to prevent frivolous or retaliator requests, a council, composed of representatives of treaty parties, would filter requests. Some countries envision that on-site inspections would take place automatically after a country makes a request, unless the council denies the request. This principle, dubbed "red light," is the principle incorporated in the CWC.[46] Other countries support an alternative with subtle but significant differences. The "green light" principle supposes that a request for an on-site inspection would proceed only if the council gave its approval.

The "red light" and "green light" procedures would have different effects on both the party lodging an allegation and the party responsible for convincing the BWC council of the merits of its position. Under the red light procedure, the onus would be primarily on the accused country, which would need to convince the council members that the challenge was frivolous or motivated solely by politics. Under the green light procedure, the burden would rest more heavily on the country bringing the challenge to support the contention that its suspicions were realistic or based on valid information. Conceivably, an accusing country could face a dilemma under the green light procedure: it would either risk revealing sensitive sources of information from which the suspicions arose or face the prospect of international embarrassment if its challenge failed to gain sufficient support to proceed. The percentage of council members needed to deny or approve a request is a secondary disagreement. Council voting procedures more complicated than simple red or green light procedures are also possible.

Much greater agreement exists on the need and procedures for field and facility investigations of alleged use or other potential treaty violations. Although Russia submits that investigations of treaty violations should go through the UN Security Council (where it has veto power), it has no support for this position with other BWC member states. Russia has isolated itself on other issues as well.

Other contentious issues divide the participants in the AHG negotiations. Among them are the continued existence of export restrictions on BWC state parties after the implementation of the protocol; the extent and control of access to facilities; the size, structure, and powers of the organization that will implement the protocol; and ways to implement Article X of the treaty. Each of these issues will require resolution hand in hand with the issues previously discussed that bear most directly on the weaknesses of the regime.

While the AHG continued its work, the Fourth Review Conference of the BWC took place in Geneva in November 1996. Iran surprised the conference in the first week by proposing an amendment to Article I that would have specifically outlawed the use of biological or toxin weapons. The conference affirmed with clear and strong language in the Final Declaration that "the use under any circumstances, . . . of bacteriological (biological) and toxin weapons is effectively prohibited under Article I of the Convention" (BWC, 1996a: pt. 2, 1) and reaffirmed the prohibitions in Article I "never in any circumstances . . . in order to exclude completely and forever the possibility of their use" (BWC, 1996b: 2). The conference referred the question of amending the BWC to the depositary governments.[47]

The conference took several other actions that lent support to the AHG in completing its task. Without exception, every treaty party that spoke in the general debate spoke in support of the work of the AHG. The statements indicate that the parties to the BWC are committed, at least in their public stance, to strengthening the convention through the negotiations for a legally binding instrument.

STRENGTHENING THE REGIME OUTSIDE THE AD HOC GROUP

Initiatives to strengthen the biological arms control regime outside the mandate of the Ad Hoc Group must also be undertaken. Some actions to that effect can be taken up by states individually or collectively through the convention review process, whereas others can only be achieved outside the convention structure. Perhaps the best way to strengthen the BWC outside the Ad Hoc Group is to take such actions as necessary to secure universal adherence to the treaty, take political action against nations suspected of possessing BW programs, resolve compliance concerns using existing mechanisms, and impose sanctions on those who violate the BWC.

Although 142 countries are party to the BWC and another eighteen have signed but not ratified the treaty, it is not truly universal.[48] A number of strategies could be developed and followed to prod those countries that are not full participants in the regime either to accede to the convention or to ratify what they have already signed. High-level representatives of national governments that are BWC state parties could encourage those countries who have ratified or signed the 1993 CWC, but have not taken action on the BWC, to do so. Ten countries that have ratified or acceded to the CWC, which is of more recent origin than the BWC, are neither parties nor signatories to the BWC.[49] Seventeen countries that have signed the CWC but not yet ratified it are not BWC parties;[50] six others have ratified the CWC but have thus far only signed the BWC.[51] BWC state parties that have the closest diplomatic relations with these countries could dispatch representatives and urge the nonmembers to accede to the BWC as soon as possible. Adding thirty or more countries as parties to the BWC, with associated publicity regarding their commitment to forgo the possession of biological weapons, would greatly strengthen the norm upon which the regime is based. There seems to be little rationale for governments to become members of the intrusive and potentially expensive CWC while remaining outside the BWC.

In addition to trying to gain universal adherence to the BWC, nations can apply some of the treaty's provisions to stop the international proliferation of biological weapons. Graham Pearson (1993b) argues that biological weapons proliferation can be stopped through a "web of deterrence." Four elements form the strands of the web: (1) effective defenses against biological weapons, (2) a strengthened biological arms control regime, (3) export controls, and (4) an international commitment to respond to biological weapons proliferation and possible use. Engineering a coordinated response to the countries that are currently suspected of harboring biological weapons activities, the last strand in the web, has not yet occurred. States could employ a step-by-step approach, gradually applying more political and economic pressure to the suspect countries.

Articles V and VI of the BWC describe processes to resolve questions of compliance. Article V obligates parties to "consult one another and to cooperate in solving any problems which may arise." Article VI establishes the right of any party to lodge a complaint with the United Nations Security Council.[52] Although the obligation to call a consultative meeting at the request of any party has been in existence since the Second Review Conference in 1986, Cuba has been the only country to call for such a consultative meeting, which took place in 1997. A novel use of the right would be for a country whose BWC compliance is in question to request a consultation and cooperation with the questioning country or other, more neutral parties, in order to alleviate suspicions of noncompliance. Resolving lingering suspicions regarding compliance prior to entry into force of a compliance protocol might allow countries currently under suspicion to enter into the compliance agreement with a clean slate. Some might argue that this approach would have limited value; it is, after all, impossible to prove a negative. Nevertheless, if a country was sincerely willing to undergo inspection and cooperated with the inspectors, the endeavor might dispel compliance doubts in some cases.

The BWC has no provision for instituting sanctions for violating the provisions of the convention other than the means available to the United Nations Security Council.[53] The BWC state parties could make it clear to possible violators that national and collective measures will be taken in instances of noncompliance. Pearson (1993b: 160) has argued that the exact nature of the penalties that would be applied should be uncertain. The graduated list of possible sanctions, however, should be made public so that a country contemplating a clandestine program would know the range of possible sanctions but be uncertain which would be applied. BWC state parties could follow the example set in the CWC and formally set forth their commitment to respond to noncompliance with the BWC at the next Review Conference or as a component of the protocol. Agreeing that a violation of the BWC is a sufficiently important security matter to warrant an international response strengthens the norm against BW as well as the deterrence power of the treaty. It could increase confidence in compliance by recognizing that fewer countries are likely to take the risk of violating the treaty if painful consequences flow from discovery. It is the combination of the probability of discovery and the consequences that strengthens deterrence.[54]

The foregoing four approaches by no means exhaust the possibilities of strengthening the BWC outside the Ad Hoc Group process. Individual states can contribute to strengthening the convention in other ways as well. For example, Richard Falk and Susan Wright have called for openness with respect to defensive military programs (Falk and Wright, 1990: 341). Matthew Meselson and Julian Perry Robinson have stressed the importance of all countries making the domestic possession of biological weapons a crime, which would allow arrest and prosecution of subnational groups before they used biological weapons (Meselson and Perry Robinson, 1996). In this book, the use of defensive measures and intelligence are dealt with thoroughly Chapters 6 and 10.

Nongovernmental organizations (NGOs) can also make contributions to international biological arms control. The Stockholm International Peace Research Institute (SIPRI) has published extensively on biological weapons issues.[55] The University of Bradford Peace Studies Department has issued numerous briefs on issues relevant to the protocol negotiations.[56] The Federation of American Scientists (FAS) Working Group on Biological and Toxin Weapons Verification developed detailed proposals for a verification regime prior to the 1991 Review Conference and for a compliance regime in advance of the Special Conference in 1994 (FAS, 1990, 1994).[57] The FAS has also issued working papers on many topics, including the investigation of disease outbreaks and a proposed structure and budget for the BWC organization.[58] The Monterey Institute of International Studies sponsored a workshop on "The Utility of Sampling and Analysis for Compliance Monitoring of the Biological Weapons Convention" for industry, academic, and government participants and has published its proceedings (Tucker, 1997).[59] The Chemical and Biological Arms Control Institute publishes a newsletter containing opinion essays on strengthening the BWC and has sponsored other activities.[60] The Stimson Center has also issued a report on biological weapons proliferation.[61] The Harvard-Sussex Program on Chemical and Biological Warfare Armament and Arms Limitation publishes a quarterly journal that includes a chronology of events.[62] The

Pugwash Conference on Science and World Affairs has held workshops on strengthening the BWC (Kaplan, 1999), and its council issued a statement to the Fourth Review Conference of the BWC stressing its views on a number of issues of concern. These and other efforts have attracted considerable comment and debate. Aside from the substantive merits or problems of any particular recommendations for strengthening the biological weapons arms control regime, NGOs can develop proposals and engage in activities while subjecting them to international scrutiny that would be impossible for many countries to do because of political or policy implications. Those who disagree with the thrust of NGO positions can draft alternatives for public discussion and review.

Nations located in global hot spots, such as the Middle East, South Asia, and East Asia, generally are concerned with security matters that go far beyond the specific issue of biological weapons. Decisions that these countries make on individual arms control agreements appear to be, in most instances, secondary to overall national security and undertaken with an eye to increasing bargaining power with potential adversaries. Consequently, regional security and confidence-building measures that lower suspicions among longtime adversaries could open the way for countries in these geographical areas to commit to other, multinational agreements such as the BWC. Countries outside these sensitive regions can lend their good offices and impartial negotiating and mediating services to reach peaceful resolution of long-standing conflicts. Moreover, proposals such as a Middle East zone free of all weapons of mass destruction are worthy of international support and further refinement. As we have seen in the earlier discussion of compliance problems, a settlement in the Middle East is probably a necessary forerunner to some of the countries joining the BWC— although why this needs to be so is difficult to understand. Some Middle Eastern states have already demonstrated their willingness to be bound by the provisions of the BWC by signing it. Ratification, however, appears to await corresponding action in other states.[63]

CONCLUSION

The biological weapons arms control regime, consisting of formal treaties, confidence-building measures, export controls, and other activities, supports the long-held principle that the deliberate dissemination of disease-causing agents or toxins is repugnant to mankind. The 1925 Geneva Protocol (prohibiting use) and the BWC (prohibiting possession) are the complementary core of the biological arms control regime. A strong BWC anchors and supports the other regime components, whereas the weaknesses of the BWC undermine the entire regime structure. Thus, strengthening the BWC is imperative.

Fortunately, BWC state parties recognize the role of a strong treaty in upholding the norms and principles of the regime. The predominant international endeavor to address the weaknesses of the regime is the Ad Hoc Group process established by the parties to the BWC to strengthen the treaty. A legally binding instrument in the form of a protocol to the convention has been gathering support among the parties for many years. It is essential to a strong regime; it remains to be seen, however, whether the parties possess the political will to take hold of what is within their grasp.

Resolving disagreements about on-site measures to strengthen the BWC is one of the most arduous tasks facing the Ad Hoc Group. Biological weapons activities are relatively easy to hide, and violators would be unlikely to declare their own illicit programs. If the biological weapons organization cannot quickly and expeditiously arrange challenge investigations at declared or undeclared locations, the probability of detecting an illicit activity is reduced. Similarly, relatively frequent, short-notice, non-challenge visits would increase the probability and risk of detection, thereby increasing deterrence and strengthening grounds for confidence in the convention.

All sides appear to recognize trade-offs between regime intrusiveness and reducing the uncertainty of compliance. However, those who support random on-site measures and "red light" procedures seem to place greater significance on their deterrent value, especially on the average or possible proliferator. Those who oppose such measures are perhaps more wary of the power of random inspections to deter determined proliferators.

Countries that fear a loss of national security information and businesses that fear the loss of trade secrets or other commercial proprietary information through inspections could reduce the uncertainty associated with nonchallenge visits by taking part in trial visits on a national or bilateral basis, gaining experience with inspection procedures from the points of view of both inspectors and inspected.[64] Those that have participated in national trial inspections (United Kingdom, 1994), bilateral or multilateral trial inspections (Netherlands and Canada, 1993; Denmark et al., 1998), and UNSCOM inspections (Zilinskas, 1995; St.-Onge, 1995; Huxsoll, 1995; Mohr, 1995; Johnson-Winegar, 1995) have developed practical knowledge of how to conduct inspections and a feel for what can be achieved through on-site visits. Increasing the number of visits and involving additional countries would augment the practical knowledge needed to refine arguments about what can be achieved through on-site measures and enrich the discussion of how to conduct inspections.

Many contentious issues that are being discussed at the Ad Hoc

Group's deliberations may also be amenable to resolution. Resolution of the problems associated with a list of agents and toxins, a once contentious issue, now appears within reach. The key lies in a clear and precise statement of what the purpose of the list would be in a legally binding protocol.[65] Great progress has been made on the procedures for field and facility investigations of alleged use or other allegations of treaty violations. The Ad Hoc Group process going on at Geneva may soon come to a critical crossroads, however. Certain countries, some of which may be harboring secret biological weapons programs in violation of the convention, may seek to dilute the effectiveness of a future protocol. The protocol will add little value to the existing regime if proposals to visit declared facilities and inspect suspect facilities, whether or not they are declared, are rendered ineffective. At some point, those countries wanting to strengthen the regime will have to decide whether to develop proposals for a legally binding instrument that goes no further than a least common denominator approach. Alternatively, they may need to be prepared to apply increasing diplomatic and political pressure on those countries whose positions prevent consensus if there are a small number blocking agreement, or create inducements to secure their assent.

The BWC cannot and will not become a stronger impediment to the proliferation and use of biological weapons without a clear and strong commitment from most countries to do so. Being committed to a stronger BWC means that countries will have to recognize and accept the trade-offs between regime intrusiveness and reducing the uncertainty of compliance, that countries must spend the money to create an inspection organization that will be effective without being extravagant (Pearson and Dando, 1998; FAS, 1998), and that governments must engage companies in the biotechnology business to participate in devising a protocol to strengthen the regime. Through regular participation, industry could help to craft a protocol in which the chances of a frivolous challenge inspection are acceptably small, and concerns about the possible loss of commercial proprietary information should, accordingly, be minimized. Industry is also likely to come to recognize that increased trade opportunities should follow from increased transparency underpinned by the protocol.

The active participation of the United States is critical to achieving a sound protocol. Vinod K. Aggarwal (1985: 29–30), for instance, argues that the commitment of a single major power within an anarchic system is conducive to strong and stable international regimes. One tenet of his argument is that a single strong power or several powerful states will be willing to offer inducements to weaker states because the stability emanating from a strong regime is a benefit to the strong countries. The United States must continue to demonstrate its commitment to a strengthened BWC in spite of historical policy reservations regarding the question of whether the convention can be verified and to what particular standard.[66] It is not necessary that the United States take a leadership role on every issue. Quite the contrary, delegating responsibility for drafting proposals will stimulate ideas and enhance a broad sense of ownership of the end result. Yet the United States must be seen as a resolute supporter of the fundamental concept of a protocol that includes on-site measures, or the entire endeavor is likely to languish or fail.

Failure of the Ad Hoc Group to fulfill its mandate—to present a proposal for a legally binding instrument, including off-site and on-site measures evaluated by the VEREX process—would not leave the vitality of the BWC unchanged. Failure could create additional uncertainty about the strength of the BWC and send the wrong message: that the political will to strengthen the BWC did not exist, despite its long-recognized shortcomings.

Beyond the formal arms control structure, the members of the Australia Group[67] will contemplate the future of their organization. They will continue to assess whether there is an effective alternative to the group's procedures that can meet the political and legal obligations not to assist proliferation of such weapons absent the rancor that has developed regarding the group on the North-South axis. The challenge to the group and its antagonists is to devise a system that will restrict dual-use exports that might be put to a nefarious end while expediting legitimate trade in a nondiscriminatory fashion (Roberts, 1998). Multilateral trade controls coupled with an improved biological weapons arms control regime and increased transparency may well produce an alternative to the Australia Group that is acceptable to all sides in the current debate (Pearson, 1997).

Finally, the international community cannot afford to sit back and await developments. Scientific and technical innovations are likely to continue to heighten the potential for biological weapons use. A protocol to strengthen the BWC must be accompanied by sustained awareness of opportunities for international cooperation to confront the threat of biological weapons.

The end of the Cold War has spawned a political environment of cooperation that has led to remarkable achievements in multilateral arms control. In 1995, the parties to the Nuclear Non-Proliferation Treaty agreed to a permanent extension of that agreement, and the states participating in the Conference on Disarmament have concluded a Comprehensive Nuclear Test Ban Treaty. The Chemical Weapons Convention entered into force on April 29, 1997. With these tasks completed, the opportunity has arrived to carry out the tasks necessary to strengthen the biological member of the arms control family. For the first time in decades, the international community can give the regime concerted attention and reap the benefits of an international environment unconstrained by the Cold War. The conditions are in place to strengthen the regime to the extent that it can become a fully functioning participant in the campaign against weapons of mass destruction.

To conclude this chapter, I believe it is necessary to look beyond the development and implementation of a compliance protocol for the BWC; it is not too early to look at what steps need to be envisioned and planned now to ensure a vital biological weapons arms control regime well into the next century. In particular, four propositions merit more intensive research and comment by security analysts and those of us in academia who are concerned with international biological arms control.

First, international inspectorates in nuclear, chemical, and biological weapons regimes will have much to contribute to one another. Each has, or will have, experiences that may be instructive to the others in carrying out their tasks. The need for some type of coordination among the three regimes is evident. Developing and maintaining a productive association among the regimes would most likely increase the effectiveness of each.[68]

Second, intellectual and informational links should be forged between the BWC organization and national and international health agencies such as the World Health Organization, the International Office for Epizootics, the International Centre for Genetic Engineering and Biotechnology, and the U.S. Centers for Disease Control and Prevention. Clear working relationships between the BWC organization and these groups as well as others that may be established, such as an international vaccine production program or a program to control or monitor emerging diseases, could assist in the process of resolving suspicious activities or outbreaks of disease.[69] This task may be more difficult to accomplish than appears at first glance. Many of the health organizations suspect that their effectiveness in their primary mission, disease prevention and control, could be compromised by taking part in activities that are perceived as political. Any connections between these organizations may have to be indirect, sponsored by a neutral third party or organization, for example, and focus on topics of direct interest to all participants. The role of these organizations in the international surveillance of diseases and the benefits of providing timely information regarding disease outbreaks to one another is one such topic worthy of further exploration.

Third, proliferation patterns indicate that countries that try to acquire one type of weapon of mass destruction often explore the acquisition of others as well.[70] Given the apparent links between nuclear, chemical, and biological weapons proliferation, the international community needs to decide how to treat states that do not conform to international norms or flagrantly ignore them. The United Nations' response to Iraq—creating UNSCOM to oversee and confirm the destruction of Iraq's weapons—sets a new standard of international cooperation and behavior on three important levels: political, legal, and institutional. The organization of UNSCOM could be examined as a possible model that might be suitably modified to fit different circumstances for coordinated international action in response to egregious violation of international norms, including the possession or use of biological weapons. That is a complex question and beyond the scope of this chapter. Nevertheless, the international cooperation demonstrated by UNSCOM, despite its flaws, serves as a warning to countries and their leaders who refuse to conform to international norms of behavior that serious consequences could greet their egregious actions.

Fourth, rapid advances in biotechnology are likely to continue apace. Individual states and the international community must be ever vigilant concerning the potential effect of achievements in science and technology on the components of the biological arms control regime. Some discoveries may be beneficial, making the detection of agents or toxins easier or defenses against biological weapons less cumbersome. Others could accelerate a country's ability to develop, produce, or disperse biological weapons. The BWC parties have continued to reaffirm that all advances in microbiology, genetic engineering, and biotechnology are covered by the convention. Nevertheless, reviews of changes in science and technology that have an impact on the functioning of the BWC, which presently occur every five years at the time of Review Conferences, may be too infrequent. Yearly or biennial reports on the changes in science and technology that have an impact on the BWC may be necessary.

NOTES

1. I would like to thank Barbara Hatch Rosenberg, Graham Pearson, Gordon Vachon, Ken Ward and, above all, Raymond Zilinskas for their detailed reading and thoughtful comments on earlier drafts of this chapter. Moreover, I am indebted to the many diplomats and their staffs who shared their time and opinions with me.

2. Schelling distinguishes between having confidence in others' compliance with arms control measures and having grounds for confidence. He states the problem of confidence in treaty compliance in this way: "Facing a potentially hostile enemy, what one wants is not to *be* confident, but to be *as* confident as the true state of affairs justifies. What one wants is *grounds for confidence,* evidence that confidence is justified" (1984: 56; emphasis in the original). This subtle distinction puts the proper focus on the evidence for confidence rather than the judgment that a country is confident of another's compliance.

3. In contrast, Schelling and Halperin, in their classic study *Strategy and Arms Control,* define the unifying characteristic as "the recognition of the common interest, of the possibility of reciprocation and cooperation even between potential enemies with respect to their military establishments" and go on to suggest that limiting or diminishing arms is not a necessary feature (1961: 2).

4. As Krasner (1983: 2) notes, this definition is consistent with earlier definitions of regimes. It is also consistent with subsequent definitions. Bernauer, for example, accepts Krasner's definition and elaborates on it (1993: 51).

5. Bernauer (1993: 52–59) uses the word "fragmented" to describe the regime to control chemical weapons before the CWC was completed because it consisted of many parts, and the CWC was an attempt to compose a comprehensive regime. However, even a fragmented regime can be comprehensive; therefore, I prefer the word "integrated" to describe a regime with one principle instrument and well-coordinated auxiliary instruments.

6. This principle is clearly stated in the preamble to the BWC (1975): "Convinced that such use [that of biological agents or toxins as weapons] would be repugnant to the conscience of mankind."

7. See discussion of 1996 Fourth Review Conference herein, at the end of the second section of the chapter.

8. VEREX is an acronym for the Ad Hoc Group of Governmental Experts to Identify and Examine Potential Verification Measures from a Scientific and Technical Standpoint, which was established in 1991 by the Third Review Conference of BWC. Before VEREX disbanded in 1994, it had developed twenty-one verification measures, some of which undoubtedly will be applied by the future BWC compliance regime.

9. The Ad Hoc Group (AHG) was established in 1994 by the Special Conference assembled for the purpose of considering the findings of VEREX. As this is written in early 1999, the AHG continues its work to establish a BWC compliance regime.

10. When an international treaty is completed, government representatives sign it and return to their capitals for the treaty to be ratified. When the requisite number of nations have ratified, the treaty goes into effect. Thereafter, countries no longer sign and ratify but accede to the treaty. Significantly, when a state signs a treaty, it is committed to doing nothing contrary to the aims of the treaty. Countries who have either ratified or acceded are formally called States Parties.

11. An up-to-date list of all parties and signatories to the BWC is maintained on the website of the Swedish International Peace Research Institute at www.sipri.se/cbw/docs/bw-btwc-rat.html.

12. This section concerns compliance with the principles, norms, and rules of the BW arms control regime and not necessarily with the specific provisions of the BWC. Thus, states that are not parties to the BWC are still included in the discussion.

13. The CIA testimony concerned BW proliferation, not treaty compliance. Israel, who is not a party to the BWC, is thus mentioned as a country that may be interested in acquiring BW, but not as a country in violation of treaty obligations.

14. The report states the following relating to each country's compliance with the BWC: for China, "it is highly probable that it remains noncompliant with these obligations"; for Egypt: "it remains likely that the Egyptian capability to conduct BW continues to exist"; Iran "probably has produced BW agents and apparently has weaponized a small quantity of those agents"; Libya "has the expertise to produce small quantities of biological equipment for its BW program and . . . is seeking to move its research program into a program of weaponized BW agents"; in Russia, "some facilities . . . may be maintaining the capability to produce BW agents" and "the progress [toward achieving openness intended in the Joint Statement] has not resolved all U.S. concerns"; for Syria, "it is highly probable that Syria is developing an offensive BW capability"; and for Taiwan, "evidence indicating a BW program is

not sufficient to determine if Taiwan is engaged in activities prohibited by the BWC" (ACDA, 1998: 92–94).

15. The most recent ACDA compliance report states that "some facilities . . . may be maintaining the capability to produce biological warfare agents" and that the trilateral process "has not resolved all U.S. concerns" (1998: 92–93) .

16. See UN Security Council, 1998, pp. 55–77, or reports in the popular press.

17. Prior to 1991 Iraq had signed but had not ratified the BWC. Thus, although not a state party to the BWC, by signing the treaty Iraq undertook the commitment to do nothing contrary to the aims of the treaty, a commitment it obviously broke. Iraq ratified the BWC in 1991 and by its terms is now required to destroy its biological weapons.

18. See Leitenberg (1996b: 41–44) for a lengthy discussion of the South Africa program.

19. The 1998 ACDA compliance report contains serious concerns about all of these countries except Israel. Israel is neither a signatory nor a party to the BWC; consequently, it would not belong among a list of countries whose compliance with treaties was assessed. Nevertheless, CIA officials in 1993 testified before Congress that Israel has a possible BW program (U.S. Congress, 1993a).

20. Chapter 2 in this volume specifically addresses proliferation in the Middle East and regional CBMs.

21. See Chevrier (1995b: 210–211) for a more comprehensive explication of this problem.

22. BWC/CONF.I/C/SR.3, par. 2–4: March 12, 1980. Quoted in Sims (1988: 174–175).

23. BWC/CONF.I/C/SR.8, par. 41: March 17, 1980. Quoted in Sims (1988: 178–179).

24. BWC/CONF.I/SR.3 par. 27–30. Quoted in Sims (1988: 176).

25. The First Review Conference was also marked by the U.S. Department of State seeking an explanation for the anthrax outbreak in the Soviet city of Sverdlovsk and declaring its suspicions that the Soviets were not in compliance with the BWC. Commenting on the effect of the Sverdlovsk incident on the First Review Conference, Julian Perry Robinson made the following observations:

> The Sverdlovsk allegation very much affected the content of the Final Declaration on the thorny issue of the Consultative Committee. On the one hand it illustrated most graphically the need for some form of international verification procedure. On the other hand it suggested that the USSR would be the subject of the first complaint to be brought before the committee, and few states were happy to contemplate the political furor that would ensue, and the attendant threat to the BWC's continuation . . . [so it] paradoxically strengthened the position of the USSR. (Perry Robinson, 1980: 393)

26. See BWC (1986c) remarks of the representatives from the Federal Republic of Germany (SR 3, par. 26, p. 5), Norway (SR 4, par. 15 and 16, p. 5), Pakistan (par. 39, p. 10), New Zealand (SR 5, par. 6 and 7, pp. 2–3), Finland (par. 22, p. 5), Austria (par. 32, p. 7), and China (par. 44, p. 8).

27. This consultative meeting can engage technical experts, for example, and call for actions by the United Nations to clarify or resolve compliance issues. Note the subtle distinction between the right of a state party to request a consultative meeting and the obligation to call a meeting if a party requests one.

28. Several explanations can be offered to explain why parties have failed to submit declarations—among them that completing the declarations was more complicated than anticipated (Gerbrandy, 1996), and that few, if any, consequences emanate from inaction. Nevertheless, the sporadic compliance with declaration requirements is testimony that a large number of treaty parties have not taken their politically binding obligations under the treaty as seriously as had been anticipated. In contrast, Brazil, for instance, has argued that the paltry response to the information exchange is evidence of the difficulties of keeping track of relevant industries. Consequently, delays in submitted declarations and information gaps in declarations would not necessarily indicate deliberate disregard of a country's obligations. Rather, it might reflect an inability to perform the required duties; see Brazil (1994).

29. Five countries, Canada, France, Russia, the United Kingdom, and the United States, have declared past offensive biological research and development programs (Hunger, 1996: 84).

30. Specifically, it sets forth rules concerning the timeliness of a response to a request, discusses the role of the depositary governments, and establishes how costs for such a meeting would be met.

31. Julian Perry Robinson suggests that the perception of low military utility of biological weapons was a myth that was purposely spread to reduce international interest in the weapons. See Perry Robinson (1996).

32. Progress in the negotiations for a Chemical Weapons Convention suggested that nations seemed to be willing to accept a very intrusive verification procedure to control chemical weapons and, tellingly, a few toxins that, of course, are also covered under the BWC (Moodie, 1993: 52).

33. See Norway (1991), Canada (1991a), Sweden (1991), the Soviet Union (Vasiliev, 1991), Nigeria (1991), India (1991), Czechoslovakia (1991), Belgium (1991), Australia (1991), and the Netherlands (1991).

34. See Chevrier (1992), Rosenberg (1993), and Moodie (1993) for more in-depth analyses of the 1991 review conference.

35. Article X of the BWC establishes the obligation of states to facilitate their right to participate in "the fullest possible exchange of equipment, materials and scientific and technological information for the use of bacteriological (biological) agents and toxins for peaceful purposes." The language of the article is patterned after Article 4 in the Nuclear Non-Proliferation Treaty.

36. See Chevrier (1995b) for a more detailed analysis of the issues: lists of agents, verification, regime intrusiveness, objective criteria, and threshold quantities.

37. The Federation of American Scientists' Working Group on Biological and Toxin Weapons Verification argued that declarations, as part of a legally binding compliance protocol, "would mandate a critical degree of openness that would help to circumvent the difficulties of determining intentions or further defining prohibited activities" (FAS, 1995a). I am a member of the FAS group and was the principal author of this report.

38. This friend of the chair paper, the declaration, is "the results of discussions and exchange of views of those issues. . . . These papers are without prejudice to the positions of delegations on the issues under consideration in the Ad Hoc Group and do not imply agreement on the scope or content of the papers."

39. Because a large quantity of biological agents could be grown rather quickly from a very small seed stock, some favor possession of listed agents as the relevant criterion for declaration. Others think that mere possession of a listed biological agent is too broad a criterion for declaration purposes and prefer "working with" a listed agent to trigger a declaration.

40. That number is the estimate of the FAS. See FAS (1997), or go to the FAS Web site www.fas.com.

41. Requested visits are sometimes referred to in the protocol as voluntary visits. To distinguish these visits from voluntary confidence-building visits, I refer to them as requested visits.

42. A purely random selection would give all declared biological laboratories or facilities an equal probability of being selected for inspection. A weighted random selection is a type of random selection that would give certain laboratories—those that met some criterion, production capacity, for example—a higher probability of being selected. A laboratory with production capacity above a certain level, in this example, would be given a greater weight. Other modifications to a purely random selection process could set limits on the number of such inspections that any country would be subject to in a given time period.

43. See BWC, 1998c.

44. The Pharmaceutical Research and Manufacturers of America (PhRMA) officially opposes nonchallenge visits, but executives of some biotechnology firms do not. See Woollett (1998) and Monath and Gordon (1998).

45. There are four distinct yet interrelated purposes of verification. The first is security. Verification ensures that security interests are not undermined by violations of an agreement designed to restrain an arms race. Second, the process makes it easier to detect any violations. Third, verification provisions discourage or deter all parties from violating the treaty. Fourth, verification builds confidence, in a specific arms control agreement and in arms control generally, among the domestic public, between adversaries, and throughout the international community (ACDA, 1976, 1983; Gayler, 1986; Colby, 1983; Dyson, 1984; Einhorn, 1982).

46. In the CWC, the request goes forward unless two-thirds of the Executive Council deny the request.

47. See BWC (1996b), Annex I, Chairman's Summary, Agenda Item 13, for a lengthy discussion of the treatment by the conference of the Iranian proposal.

48. Taiwan is included among these countries even though it is no longer officially recognized as an independent state by the United Nations.

49. Algeria, Cameroon, Cook Islands, Guinea, Mauritania, Moldova, Monaco, Namibia, Tajikistan, and Trinidad and Tobago.

50. Azerbaijan, Central African Republic, Chad, Gabon, Haiti, Holy See, Israel, Kyrgyzstan, Liberia, Madagascar, Marshall Islands, Nauru, Saint Vincent and the Grenadines, Samoa, Tanzania, United Arab Emirates, and Zambia.

51. Burundi, Cote d'Ivoire, Guyana, Mali, Morocco, and Nepal. Members and signatories of the Chemical Weapons Convention were taken from the Web site of the Stimson Center, updated on September 15, 1998: www.stimson.org/cwc/signers.htm. Members and signatories of the BWC were taken from the SIPRI Web site: www.sipri.cbw/docs/bw-btwc-mainpage.html.

52. Some countries consider Articles V and VI to constitute a two-step process, whereby a complaint would be lodged with the UN Security Council only after consultations. Others point out that nothing in the language of Article VI requires a consultation to precede the UN Security Council complaint.

53. Suspicion of noncompliance makes it more likely that a country will find itself subject to Australia Group export controls and other, less tangible consequences such as negative publicity. However, no consequences within the treaty per se ensue.

54. Although the 1992 statement resulting from the UN Security Council summit goes in the right direction in "serving notice," the UN Security Council is often considered a last resort and brings with it its own procedural difficulties.

55. See the SIPRI Web site at www.sipri.se/cbw/cbw-mainpage.html.

56. The Web site of the Bradford project is www.brad.ac.uk/acac/sbtwc/.

57. See the FAS Web site at www.fas.org/bwc/index.html.

58. The author wishes to acknowledge that she contributed substantively to many of the FAS publications.

59. See the MIIS Web site at cns.miis.edu/html/cbwnp/.

60. The CBACI Web site is www.pressroom.com/~cbaci/.

61. The Stimson Center Web site is www.stimson.org.

62. The HSP Web site can be found at fas-www.harvard.edu:80/~hsp/.

63. See, in particular, Inbar (1996) on Israel's strategic thinking and Steinberg (1994) on security and confidence-building measures in the Middle East.

64. This is in contrast to uncertainty regarding compliance addressed in a previous section.

65. Vorobiev reports on the controversy regarding the use of lists in a compliance protocol yet states that the development of a list of forty-two human pathogens and criteria for including them on a list is a "remarkable achievement" (Vorobiev, 1996: 3).

66. See Chevrier (1990) for a discussion of the conceptual differences between the political judgment of verification and the activities of verification with respect to the BWC. The article also discusses the operational differences, or lack thereof, between adequate and effective verification.

67. The Australia Group is an informal group of thirty-one industrialized countries that are committed to preventing the proliferation of chemical and biological weapons. The countries participating in the group are suppliers and/or trans-shippers of chemicals, biological agents, and/or production equipment that could be used in chemical and/or biological weapons programs. Representatives of the group meet several times a year to exchange information on exports and imports of equipment and supplies deemed sensitive due to their possible applications in biological and chemical warfare programs.

68. The United Nations report, "Verification in All Its Aspects, Including the Role of the United Nations in the Field of Verification" (1995) grapples with many of these difficult issues.

69. See Chapter 5 in this volume.

70. See Carus (1991: 29) and Chevrier and Smithson (1996) for an examination of the connection between CW and BW proliferation. Iraq's programs to acquire weapons of mass destruction included nuclear weapons as well.

8

Industry and Arms Control

WILL D. CARPENTER AND MICHAEL MOODIE

A novel dimension of post–Cold War arms control is the extension of arms control obligations into new segments of society, particularly the industrial sector. This requirement exists because arms control efforts are now addressing problems for which key aspects are the dual use of materials and equipment: they have legitimate peaceful purposes, but they can also be used for the illicit pursuit of weapons of mass destruction. This dilemma is central to current biological arms control efforts. Because of the dual-use issue, an effective, technically valid, and verifiable biological arms control regime will only be achieved through the participation of industry in the preparation of the regime, especially regarding the coverage of the industrial activities that are certain to be one focus of the effort.

Fortunately, there is a precedent for examining the role of industry in the development of an arms control regime. Industry was deeply involved in the negotiations over the Chemical Weapons Convention (CWC) and played an important role in shaping the final form of that landmark arms control agreement. An examination of the role of industry in the CWC process yields valuable considerations for those industries that might be affected by current efforts to bolster the biological arms control regime.

INDUSTRY AND THE CWC

In 1978, a detached observer would not have been optimistic about the prospects for government and chemical industry cooperation on the Chemical Weapons Convention. The environment for the government-industry relationship at that point had been anything but good. The U.S.

177

Environmental Protection Agency (EPA) had been established in 1970 with a broad base of support, including that of the chemical industry. Environmental issues were hotly debated in Congress, the media, and the public. Environmental laws were being passed by Congress and implemented by the EPA at an accelerating rate. The debate over the laws and their implementation between industry and government became more and more intense.

The regulating agencies, especially EPA, and Congress did little to obtain and use industry inputs. For its part, industry would too often criticize EPA or congressional proposals without providing possible solutions as to how the government could reach its objectives. In general, industry did not take advantage of opportunities to create "win-win" solutions for both government and industry that would have provided the desired environmental changes in the way industry found most cost-effective.

In addition to the significant adversarial relationship, another very real problem was present in 1978, one that continues today. Trade associations and individual companies must expend considerable resources to participate in the legislative and regulatory processes that have a major impact on their very existence. Even more resources must be spent on compliance with laws and regulations in force. There is no enthusiasm for participating in an issue that appears to have little relevance to business and appears to be years away in its impact. Even recognizing the impact, the views of companies still are captured by the expression: "When you're waist deep in alligators, you forget you started out to drain the swamp." As a consequence, those people responsible for government relations spend resources, particularly "sweat equity," only on key issues of major importance. Those issues that fall into the "nice to do" category are not funded. In 1978, that was the category into which the CWC fell.

Despite this dismal atmosphere, those in industry were learning lessons in the government relations process, and in early 1979 those lessons began to be applied to the issue of chemical weapons. The first lesson is that issues must be identified very early, long before they receive attention from the Congress, the media, or the general public. This is done by utilizing a wide range of sources of information, correlating a collection of seemingly unrelated items, recognizing the significance of what is and is not happening in a given area, and projecting the importance of these assessments into the future. There are a number of significant benefits to correctly identifying a major issue as early as possible. The impact of the issue on an organization or industry can be determined in time to develop possible courses of action, create a strategy to control the impact of the event, and mobilize the resources needed to implement that strategy.

This elegant, orderly approach may not be as simple in actual practice, but it does describe the process used between 1979 and 1985 by the

Chemical Manufacturers Association (CMA). The CWC was projected to be a future major issue for the chemical industry for several reasons:

1. Government regulation of the chemical industry was widespread, intrusive, and took many forms—inspections, reporting, documentation, and preapproval of every type of activity. It was not difficult to see this type of activity being included in the CWC.
2. Progress toward international arms control agreements was accelerating. Chemical and biological weapons were included.
3. The Convention of the Prohibition of the Development, Production and Stockpiling of Bacteriological (Biological) and Toxin Weapons, and on Their Destruction (BWC) was already a reality, and concern about the lack of a verification provision had already been raised.
4. The initiation of a dialogue between CMA and the U.S. Arms Control and Disarmament Agency (ACDA) presented the chemical industry with a unique opportunity to take a proactive stance on the issue.

Second, industry must help government to determine its real objectives and what must be done to achieve them. The less informed the government is about an issue, the more likely its objectives and requirements will be poorly defined and not closely linked. This is also true of industry, and in the case of the CWC both parties suffered from this deficiency. The corollary of this principle is that industry must determine how to be a resource for the government in clarifying needs and objectives and meeting government needs once they are determined.

Industry had approximately five years to become informed about the CWC. A wide range of topics had to be addressed: What agencies were involved? What were the relationships among those agencies, especially their differences? What knowledge did the government employees involved have of the chemical industry? How did the process work, both internally and in international negotiations? Did Congress play a role?

The third lesson is the reciprocal of the second: What are the needs and objectives of industry? How can they be met and how can they be reconciled with those of government?

The industry that was potentially affected by the CWC was much larger than that represented by CMA. Efforts to establish a broader base were, however, largely unsuccessful. The international chemical industry was also a key factor. In 1978, U.S. participants had to find out what their foreign colleagues were doing with respect to the treaty. How wide a range of opinions and objectives existed in industry?

Fourth, multiple lines of communication are needed, and they must be consistent. In this case, industry had to communicate not only with ACDA (the lead agency with whom industry had not previously interacted), but with the Departments of Defense, Commerce, State, and Energy, as well as Congress. Other trade associations—both domestic and international—also had to be kept in the loop, as did some key nongovernmental organizations (NGOs). In fostering those communications, industry also recognized that it had to learn the "tribal language" of those individuals and organizations with which they were working. This is no small task, but it is key to acceptance and success. Internal communications are also a key to success, particularly keeping industry leaders informed of actions. The principle in this case is: no surprises.

These multiple lines of communication allowed industry to demonstrate that it is a resource, not a roadblock. It created the opportunity to teach a wide range of people about industry and, in turn, to learn about other organizations and positions involved with the issue at hand.

A Bit of History

On December 12, 1978, members of the Manufacturing Chemists Association (MCA), the predecessor to CMA, met with Ambassador Adrian Fisher of ACDA and others for a briefing on the status of the CWC negotiations. One of the specifics of the meeting was a request by Ambassador Fisher for input and assistance from the chemical industry trade association.

Robert Mikulak of ACDA and one of this chapter's authors (Will D. Carpenter) initiated a dialogue shortly after that meeting, and in mid-January 1979, Mikulak invited CMA to join ACDA at a workshop in Bonn, Germany, to be held in March of that year. These initial discussions took place almost exactly fourteen years before the signing of the CWC in Paris.

Several points should be made about the success of the cooperation of these two organizations during this decade and a half: First, there was a thread of continuity in the relationship, in that Carpenter and Mikulak worked together throughout the period. This continuity was perhaps the most important factor contributing to the success of the effort. Some of the benefits, perhaps obvious to most, were that (1) the institutional procedures, methods of operation, decisionmaking, and issues of both ACDA and CMA and those of the individuals involved were learned by their counterparts. Having this knowledge avoided delays, misunderstandings, and duplication of effort, and the ability to anticipate issues, problems, and needs was greatly enhanced; and that (2) with this continuity, the opportunity to find mutually acceptable solutions was also heightened. In the case of CMA, its representatives obtained an understanding of issues and government operations that they had previously lacked.

From the mid-1980s to the mid-1990s, the CMA effort consisted of several components. First, the CMA Chemical Warfare (CW) Committee met on a monthly basis. Attendance ranged from as few as five people to as many as twenty. Representatives from General Electric, Stauffer-ICI, DuPont, Ethyl, and Monsanto were among the long-term contributors. The monthly meetings usually comprised two parts. The first was a discussion of issues among industry representatives themselves; the second brought together those industry representatives and government officials to discuss issues of mutual interest. The ACDA representative usually gave industry an update on the progress of the negotiations as well as issues of importance in the internal U.S. policy discussions.

In order to secure maximum participation, invitations to these meetings were sent to every CMA member company as well as to other trade associations, together with a summary report of the current status of the negotiations. These invitations were not too successful. Only a limited number of companies responded, and from the trade associations, only the Pharmaceutical Manufacturers Association (now the Pharmaceutical Research and Manufacturers of America) and the Synthetic Organic Chemical Manufacturing Association regularly attended. On the government side, ACDA, the Department of Defense, and the Joint Chiefs of Staff were consistent participants. Others, such as the Commerce and State Departments and the Central Intelligence Agency, were infrequent participants.

Second, in addition to these monthly meetings, a number of other activities were very useful in enhancing the key government agencies' knowledge of the chemical industry. These activities included tours of industry facilities, including organophosphorus pesticide production facilities, very large multipurpose production sites, specialty facilities, thiodiglycol production sites, and others. These visits served as an introduction to the chemical industry. Later, trial inspections at industry sites were used to test the validity of the draft procedures being negotiated in Geneva.

Seminars on protection of intellectual property and security of facilities were also held for government officials. Other seminar subjects included marketing and distribution procedures, regulatory requirements, shipment and storage, formulations, and production storage. The seminars were open to any government official wishing to attend. In addition, CMA spent considerable time with government contractors and consultants to enable them to complete their assignments in support of the U.S. negotiating effort.

All of these efforts were carried out at no government expense. Industry did not request, nor did it receive, any reimbursement for these activities. One of the benefits of these activities was the creation of very comfortable communications among a number of industry and government representatives, resulting in very efficient exchanges of information. This, in turn, improved the quality of the inputs into the negotiating process.

During this period, ACDA initiated a process that also proved to be very useful in furthering industry's understanding of the convention and providing useful contributions. From the mid-1980s to the mid-1990s, industry representatives were invited to act as observers in the discussions on chemical weapons at the Conference on Disarmament in Geneva. Other countries also invited their respective industries to participate. Then CMA arranged for industry meetings with its counterparts from Canada, Japan, Australia, and Europe to work together on CWC issues. The schedule for CMA representatives in Geneva would be as follows:

- A meeting with U.S. diplomats to review issues, positions, problems, and objectives
- A meeting of Western chemical industry representatives to review positions, formulate strategy, and determine objectives
- A meeting of chemical industry representatives with Western Group government representatives
- A Conference on Disarmament meeting on CW with chemical industry representatives acting as observers
- Frequently, either before or after these sessions, the Pugwash Conferences on Science and World Affairs was held, which proved to be a valuable addition of still another forum on chemical weapons issues—this time with a scientific orientation—for chemical industry participation (see Kaplan, 1999; and Chapter 11 of this volume)

The net effect of these activities was to provide the Western chemical industry ample opportunity to have thorough discussions with their counterparts from other countries and with the diplomats directly involved in the negotiations, both from the United States and elsewhere. For the chemical industry, it was equally important that the observers in the negotiations viewed it in a positive light as a resource.

CMA representatives testified before Congress in support of the CWC on several occasions, both during the negotiations and after the treaty was signed by the United States and more than 130 other countries. With few exceptions, however, there was little interest in the Congress on this issue until the late summer of 1996; it was simply not high on the agenda of either the Congress or the Clinton administration. Once the CWC was signed, CMA actively participated in presentations sponsored by ACDA around the country to brief industry and others on the implications of the CWC. More than twenty meetings were held over the three-year period from early 1993 to early 1996.

A summary of CMA's efforts over an eighteen-year period of involvement with the Chemical Weapons Convention is one of significant contributions toward a treaty that is technically sound and acceptable to industry.

The CWC is intrusive enough to accomplish its purpose yet still sensitive to the need to protect trade secrets and other intellectual property. At the time of writing, it is still not determined whether these years of effort will result in an operational CWC. But it does represent an approach that can serve as a model for industry participants in national and international debates regarding other critical security questions, such as the future of the BWC.

IMPLICATIONS FOR INDUSTRY INVOLVEMENT IN BIOLOGICAL ARMS CONTROL

Participants in the biological arms control process hope that the contribution of the chemical industry to the Chemical Weapons Convention will serve as model for industry with interests at stake in the current effort to strengthen the BWC. Certainly, the pharmaceutical, biotechnology, and brewing, dairy, and baking industries that may be affected by the current arms control negotiations have motivations for involvement similar to those that inspired the active participation of the chemical industry in the CWC. They share the goal of preventing the use of such horrific weapons by rogue states or terrorists. Such industries in no way want to be associated with biological weapons. Nevertheless, industries have a number of interests that could be affected by the outcome of the negotiations that they want to protect, the most important of which is the confidentiality of critical proprietary business information. As with the chemical industry and the CWC, pharmaceutical, biotechnology, and other industries have a lot riding on the ability of the negotiators to draw an appropriate balance between global and national security interests and critical commercial and economic concerns. It is clear that in the case of the CWC, such a balance was only achieved with the help of industry. It will be the same in the case of biological arms control.

During the fifteen years between the entry into force of the BWC in 1975 and the early 1990s, the primary vehicle for biological arms control activity has been the Review Conferences held every five years. The first two of these conferences (in 1981 and 1986) seemed to treat the biological weapons challenge as an interesting theoretical possibility but not a real security problem. After the Gulf War, when the international community directly confronted the threat of the use of biological weapons, attitudes changed, and the arms control process accelerated. At the 1991 Third Review Conference that followed the Gulf War, the debate over the need for and viability of a verification regime for the BWC gave rise to the Verification Experts (VEREX) report (BWC, 1993). This report, in turn, prompted the creation of an Ad Hoc Group whose mandate is to negotiate a legally binding protocol to the BWC that will identify measures to bolster confidence in compliance with the convention, elaborate additional confidence-building measures if they are deemed necessary, and specify measures for facilitating the implementation of the BWC provisions relating to technical cooperation and assistance.

As these talks have proceeded, negotiators are beginning to discuss issues at a level of detail for which the expertise and perspective of industry could be crucially important. Industry input will be indispensable for the diplomats negotiating the protocol who must evaluate the feasibility and impact of the specific details regarding declarations and on-site activities that are currently being proposed. In some cases, estimates of the costs and benefits of certain declarations or on-site requirements will turn on highly technical issues that industry experts can help explain. Those experts can also identify the potential impact of certain measures on business activities. It is only when the negotiators are armed with all of the important information, including these critical technical and economic details, that they can make the decisions that best balance all the various international and national interests affected by any new biological arms control regime.

At least some government participants in the biological arms control process were initially disappointed with the involvement of the pharmaceutical, biotechnology, and other industries as these activities got under way following the Third Review Conference (1991). Only a small number of industry representatives—from a handful of companies and trade associations—followed the arms control process on a regular basis, and many of these industry participants did not hold senior corporate management positions (as was the case with the chemical industry representatives who worked on the CWC). Many companies were either not aware that an effort was underway in the arms control arena that could have an impact on their business, or they did not think what was happening was important. When contacted by analysts attempting to solicit industry views, for example, the Washington representative of one of the nation's leading biotechnology companies expressed surprise that his company's activity might in some way relate to the biological weapons problem. In another case, a corporate representative was highly resentful of being linked to biological weapons, implying that such inquiries impugned his company's good name and its contributions to advancing humankind. The fact that some of the materials with which their companies were working also could be used for biological weapons, that the processes they used could also facilitate the production of biological weapons, or that the research they were conducting might provide information that might also be valuable ultimately to a proliferator had never been recognized.

A skeptical industry attitude toward arms control is not new. The chemical industry also started from a position that the CWC was "a loser" for industry. It was only over time and with assertive leadership that the position of the chemical industry evolved to the very helpful posture it ultimately assumed. Something similar may be happening in the pharmaceutical, biotechnology, and other industries that have a stake in the current BWC protocol negotiations. Certainly, once the Ad Hoc Group negotiations began in 1995, industry began to become more active in elucidating its concerns.

On June 12, 1996, for example, Gerald Massinghoff, then president of the Pharmaceutical Research and Manufacturers of America (PhRMA), wrote to ACDA director John Holum expressing the support of his group for efforts to "reduce the risk of biological weapons proliferation" (PhRMA, 1996c). He went on to express their hope that they would be able to support "ratification of a BWC protocol with the same enthusiasm that we [PhRMA] and the Chemical Manufacturers Association (CMA) support the Chemical Weapons Convention" (PhRMA, 1996c). Massinghoff was restating a position taken by the PhRMA board expressing its support for "the international goals and objectives of the Biological Weapons Convention":

> Classical microbiology and the newly emerging biotechnologies have enabled, and will continue to enable, many new health care products to be developed. Their development should continue, while appropriate restrictions on the potential misuse of the technologies to create weapons is enforced in a manner which does not expose American industry to the loss of its legitimate competitive trade secrets and other confidential business information. (PhRMA, 1996a)

The PhRMA statement reflects a realistic assessment of the interests industry has at stake in the current arms control negotiations. On the one hand, industry shares the commitment to eliminate the threat of biological weapons. On the other, the specifics of the arms control regime that are being debated in Geneva give rise to a series of concerns regarding their impact on the position of U.S. companies in a highly competitive international market. In his letter to ACDA director Holum, Massinghoff underlined these concerns, noting that although there is a recognized need for compromise in any negotiation, "certain provisions should not be subject to compromise." He was apparently alluding to provisions to ensure that critical business information would not be made public and that, more generally, industry competitiveness would not be jeopardized.

INDUSTRY CONCERNS

Industry concerns regarding the negotiations relate to both the declarations and the on-site activities that are considered to be the core elements of measures to bolster confidence in compliance with the BWC. Declarations have become an important aspect of verification regimes, providing the baseline of information as well as regular updates that assist in assessing compliance of a state party with its treaty obligations. In the case of the BWC, negotiators must decide what factors will trigger the requirement to make declarations as well as what the content of those declarations will be.

A number of factors related to biological research and commercial activity have been proposed as the criteria that will require a facility to report on its activities. Those factors that could serve as such a declaration trigger include production capacity; work with specific biological agents or toxins; facilities with high "containment" levels; specialized equipment such as fermenters of a certain size; or certain kinds of activities or capabilities, such as aerosol test chambers. Negotiators must select which of these factors, either individually or in combination, will require a state party to the protocol to make a declaration. Each of these factors is likely to "capture" a different range of facilities, some of which may be of greater concern to the objectives of the BWC than others. Negotiators must focus on those factors that will increase the chances that declarations will be made regarding those facilities of greatest concern rather than facilities whose activities have little relevance to the BWC. From industry's perspective, this will be difficult in light of its argument that "there is no characteristic or combination of characteristics that can discriminate facilities that develop, manufacture, and store biological warfare agents from legitimate facilities" (PhRMA, 1996b).

Some U.S. industry representatives have expressed the concern—one shared by U.S. and other Western negotiators—that the factors that trigger declarations should not create a situation in which capacity related to microbiology, biotechnology, and related fields is equated with the degree of threat (i.e., the greater the capability, the greater the potential threat). Such a mentality would create a regime that, by virtue of the scale of the enterprises and the advanced nature of the work involved, concentrates on companies and commercial facilities in the United States and elsewhere in the West. These enterprises are obviously not of proliferation concern. The triggers for declarations must be carefully defined, therefore, to ensure that the focus of the verification effort is on those states and activities of genuine concern rather than on facilities and activities that are not.

With respect to the content of declarations, one issue that must still be decided by the negotiators is what level of detail will be required. Two schools of thought appear to exist in answering this question. One school argues that declarations should be simple, with only basic information provided, to ensure that confidential business and national security information unrelated to the BWC is protected. Not surprisingly, this appears to be the view that is favored by industry representatives who follow the negotiations. Another view, however, argues that if declarations are to be meaningful and provide those responsible for overseeing implementation of the new protocol with an adequate basis for assessment, more information is needed, not less. From an industry viewpoint, the more information that is provided, the greater the chances that critical proprietary business information will be revealed with potentially disastrous results.

In addition to declarations, the measures to enhance confidence in compliance under discussion in Geneva envision on-site activities at governmental and nongovernmental facilities, including commercial business enterprises. On-site activity has become a major feature of most of the newer arms control agreements. In the case of the CWC, for example, the treaty elaborates a system that includes both "routine" inspections at declared facilities, including business operations, as well as inspections "by request" or "challenge" inspections at any facility.

Some participants in the BWC protocol negotiations envision a similar system, arguing that it is the best way to reinforce deterrence of unwanted proliferation activity. Other participants, however, remain skeptical that routine inspections will serve much purpose, given the speed at which facilities can be cleaned up, the ease of destroying incriminating evidence, the costs of putting such an elaborate inspection system in place, and the risk that could be posed to confidential business information.

Industry has argued against routine, or informal, visits to declared commercial facilities. The majority of declared facilities will be in the West, especially in the United States, the global leader in pharmaceuticals and biotechnology. Because a system of "routine inspections" would likely make the number of visits proportional to capability, most inspections would likely be conducted in those countries, particularly the United States, that are not of proliferation concern. From a Western perspective, then, such a system of routine inspections would entail major financial outlays for little gain in meeting the real objectives of the treaty.

Industry has also argued that any such visit could blacken the reputation of a facility, since despite efforts to the contrary, doubts would be created about activity at that facility. As long as any doubt lingers, the facility would operate under a cloud. From an industry perspective, it is virtually impossible to "prove the negative," that is, to demonstrate conclusively that a facility is not engaged in activities prohibited by the BWC.

In addition to the nature of the inspection system that will be adopted, the process by which the decision will be made to conduct a "short notice" visit or "challenge inspection" has generated industry concerns. Industry has argued, for example, that such visits should only be conducted if there is substantive evidence of violation of Article I of the BWC, which states the basic prohibitions against developing and producing biological weapons. Industry also sees the potential need for visits if there is an unusual outbreak of disease, or if there is an allegation of BW use. Short of such evidence, it is implied, short notice visits on request should not be allowed.

In a related matter, industry argues that the decision to conduct a short notice visit should be governed by a "green light" process. In the case of the CWC, the decision system is based on a "red light" process; that is, that the inspection will go forward *unless* the Executive Council, the body empowered to oversee implementation of the convention, votes to stop a requested inspection. In the BWC case, industry contends that a majority of at least two-thirds of the international executive body should have to cast a vote of approval before an inspection team embarks on a visit. According to industry, this system will filter out frivolous or malicious requests for intrusive inspections that may have little to do with the biological weapons problem and more to do with industrial competition.

This position appears to be receiving at least some support among the negotiators. It does raise the issue, however, of the nature of the evidence that will be needed to convince the requisite number of nations to approve a short notice inspection. Given the speed with which inspectors must respond to allegations, drawn-out discussions about the quality of evidence will be counterproductive in meeting the objectives of the new protocol. Yet, past cases (e.g., Soviet offensive biological warfare activity at Sverdlovsk in the 1970s, construction of the Krasnoyarsk radar in violation of the Anti-Ballistic Missile Treaty, and North Korea's noncompliance with the Nuclear Non-Proliferation Treaty) indicate there is likely to be significant differences over evidence of noncompliance. For this reason, a more lenient standard than that required under the U.S. legal system for "probable cause" should be applied, although some details regarding the nature of a facility's activity, specialized equipment that may suggest illicit activity, or agents on which it might be working must be provided.

The utility and impact of specific activities during on-site visits are also of concern to industry. Negotiators are considering, for example, a range of activities that inspectors could undertake, including the following:

• Sampling and analysis involve the taking of samples from the production line, equipment, and adjacent surfaces and their subsequent analysis for organism or toxin identification. For the inspectors, samples could either demonstrate that products being developed and manufactured areas are as claimed or indicate illicit activity. However, analysis of samples from the production line could generate information that, if revealed to outsiders, would compromise confidential business information (CBI).

• Record review and auditing refer to the examination of production records as well as other business information (e.g., customer and supplier lists). This information will help inspectors to determine a pattern of activity at a particular site and to identify anomalies that might bear further scrutiny. Some of the information, however, might be critical to the competitiveness of a particular facility or company that would not want it reported.

• Examination of production processes entails the visual assessment of activity at a site, including the parameters or conditions under which production takes place. Again, this information will help inspectors to determine the validity of the claims made about the activity of a particular site. At the same time, however, some of the aspects of production processes are key factors determining the uniqueness of some highly competitive products.

• Identification of key equipment might provide some clues to inspectors of activity not consistent with statements regarding activity at a facility. From an industry perspective, however, knowing the key equipment that is involved in a particular situation might provide important clues to production secrets or other CBI.

• Interviews with facility personnel could be done by inspectors on either a formal basis or on the spur-of-the-moment with personnel who might be present while conducting other activities. On some occasions, information provided through interviews could fill in gaps (e.g., an employee who has worked at a facility for some time could provide background on past activities) or otherwise contribute to the picture that inspectors build up regarding a specific site. Industry worries, however, that interviews with untrained or unprepared personnel could lead to the inadvertent disclosure of important CBI.

Given its concern that critical proprietary business information could be revealed through any of these activities, industry insists that the "managed access" approach developed for the CWC be adopted in any of the measures included in the new BWC protocol. Managed access is a technique that allows the state party on whose territory the inspection is being conducted to deny inspectors' requests for information or for conducting certain activities. In the case of the CWC, however, there is some question as to who—the state party or the facility representative—has the final say on what information can ultimately be revealed. States parties have an obligation to ensure that confidential business information on any of their industrial facilities that may be inspected is protected. However, the state party also has the obligation to ensure that the inspection meets the objects and purposes of the CWC. In the event that a conflict arises out of the disposition of certain information, it is not clear in the CWC that industry would have the final say in determining whether proprietary information can or cannot be divulged to inspectors or whether inspectors can or cannot remove information from the site. In the case of the BWC, industry is now arguing that when there is a disagreement, it should be clear that neither the host government nor the inspection team has the authority to compel a facility to divulge information that it deems proprietary.

CONCLUSION

Industry has made important strides in organizing itself to engage in a process with the government negotiators of the new BWC protocol. An industry working group, for example, has been established under PhRMA's aegis, which also includes the Biotechnology Industry Organization (BIO), the Animal Health Institute, and the American Society for Microbiology (ASM) as members. This group has become much more active over the past two years, and it now meets at least quarterly with U.S. agency representatives involved in the negotiations. At the invitation of industry, members of the U.S. delegation to the Ad Hoc Group talks participated in a two-day tour of a major fermentation facility to see firsthand the reality of industry concerns and interests involved in the negotiations. Overall, industry's focus on issues involved in the BWC negotiations has intensified, which must be seen as a positive development.

Industry involvement in the BWC process and its interactions with government, however, are not without problems. In the case of industries affected by the BWC protocol negotiations, for example, PhRMA is clearly the first among equals, and BIO, the trade association representing U.S. biotechnology firms, is also a key player. In addition, however, depending on decisions made by the negotiators, the impact could be felt among several other industrial sectors as well, including brewers, the dairy industry, and the large industrial baking concerns, all of which use techniques and equipment—such as fermenters—similar to those for making biological weapons. These groups are currently not represented in the PhRMA-led industry working group, and they do not necessarily share the same interests as the pharmaceutical or biotechnology industries. Coordinating such a potentially large industrial community to ensure that the full range of their interests is reflected could be a very difficult job. Without such coordination, however, problems could arise down the line that currently have not been anticipated.

Another challenge for industrial coordination relates to its international dimension. In the case of the CWC, U.S. chemical industry representatives worked closely with colleagues from Europe, Japan, Australia, Brazil, and elsewhere to ensure that the global industrial perspective was shared with the negotiators. Such an international industrial effort has not yet emerged with respect to the BWC protocol negotiations. Although trade associations in Europe and Japan are aware of the negotiations and are evaluating their positions—Britain's Association of British Pharmaceutical Industries has been especially active—no mechanisms have yet been developed for bringing industry representatives from around the world together to share concerns about the negotiations, develop common understandings of the issues, and promote shared approaches to potential solutions. If industry input into the negotiations is to have maximum impact, industry must develop these mechanisms on the international level in the not-too-distant future.

Finally, U.S. industry and government representatives must still forge the relationship of trust that was so critical to the effective partnership on CWC issues. U.S. industry is still smarting over its experience when a major U.S. pharmaceutical producer was visited under provisions of a trilateral agreement between Russia, the United Kingdom, and the United States. According to an industry representative deeply involved in BWC-related efforts, that experience was very bad: "The company was unjustly accused, significant access to proprietary information was demanded, U.S. government assistance was dismal, and there was direct political pressure applied on the company to participate" (personal communication). These last two elements are especially telling. They suggest that industry is not yet convinced that U.S. negotiators are doing their best to protect industry interests while advancing the objectives of the treaty. Industry representatives have also expressed frustration at the slowness with which the government's interagency process has developed positions on issues of special interest to industry. Industry also appears to feel that it is not getting the full story or a straight explanation from U.S. government negotiators. From the negotiators' point of view, industry does not always demonstrate that it appreciates the full range of interests—with industry's view only one among them—that must be balanced in the complex negotiations that are under way.

Substantial progress in biological arms control without jeopardizing important commercial and economic interests will occur only if industry plays an appropriate role. The CWC ratification process in the United States underlined the reality that a successful outcome will be achieved only if the result of the negotiations has strong industry support. That support will be forthcoming only if industry engages with government representatives in a cooperative and productive partnership that secures both industry interests and national security objectives in a balanced way acceptable to both. Industry has pursued a significant effort to foster that engagement. An important foundation has been laid and a process initiated. Government and industry must now intensify their efforts to build the trust needed for effective partnership. If they do so, they will put themselves in a position to make a major contribution to global security and stability without endangering commercial and economic interests.

9

Prevention Through Counterproliferation

W. SETH CARUS

The U.S. Department of Defense (DOD) has adopted the term "counterproliferation" to encompass those activities that DOD undertakes to respond to adversaries armed with nuclear, chemical, or biological (NBC) weapons. Counterproliferation operations include counterforce capabilities (offensive operations to destroy NBC arsenals), active defenses (primarily defenses against ballistic and cruise missiles), and passive defenses (protective clothing and medical treatments). In this chapter I describe the origin of DOD's counterproliferation efforts, the responses of DOD to the concept, and the status of the programs adopted to develop the needed operational capabilities. I conclude with an assessment of the future of counterproliferation.

DEFINING COUNTERPROLIFERATION

The term "counterproliferation" was first used by DOD in late 1992 to describe both traditional nonproliferation activities intended to prevent proliferant countries from acquiring NBC capabilities and military capabilities specifically needed to fight adversaries armed with NBC weapons.[1] It was adopted to distinguish DOD's role in efforts to counter the proliferation of so-called weapons of mass destruction, including NBC weapons and associated missile delivery systems, and was accepted by the new defense team when the Clinton administration entered office in January 1993.[2]

The precise definition of counterproliferation and the differences between counterproliferation and nonproliferation have never been clearly delineated.[3] As currently used, counterproliferation has more of an organizational meaning than a functional one. According to official usage, counterproliferation encompasses DOD responsibilities "to prevent or counteract proliferation." One official report makes the following statement about the counterproliferation tasks assigned to DOD:

> [They] span the spectrum from military operations to diplomatic efforts and include: support for proliferation prevention and intelligence activities, deterring the use of NBC weapons, defending against NBC weapons, protecting against their effects, and maintaining a robust capability to find and destroy NBC weapon delivery forces and their supporting infrastructure with minimum collateral effects, should this become necessary. (CPRC, 1996)

This definition is unhelpful in distinguishing counterproliferation from the more traditional notion of nonproliferation, and it does not provide a clear guide to differentiating between the activities of DOD and other government agencies. The inability to clearly define counterproliferation appears to reflect some significant differences between the Department of State and other agencies, since both the Department of Energy (DOE) and the intelligence community (IC) are an integral part of the overall DOD approach to counterproliferation. DOD assigns a far higher importance to defense measures, including possible offensive options, than do many in the State Department. In addition, some State Department officials may view the DOD counterproliferation initiative as an effort to undermine the State Department's lead role in the nonproliferation arena.

THE ORIGINS OF COUNTERPROLIFERATION

The origins of counterproliferation date to the U.S. involvement in Desert Shield and Desert Storm, the operation names assigned by DOD, respectively, to the defense of Saudi Arabia following the Iraqi invasion of Kuwait on August 2, 1990, and to the subsequent attack on Iraq to liberate Kuwait starting on January 17, 1991. The decision by President George Bush in early August 1990 to send U.S. military forces to the Middle East resulted in a profound change in the priority assigned to threats of chemical and biological warfare (BW). The intelligence community warned that Iraq had developed an arsenal of BW agents, including both anthrax and botulinum toxin. Experience with Iraqi use of chemical weapons suggested that Saddam Hussein might use biological weapons as well. As a result, DOD focused considerable attention on the need to develop responses to the Iraqi BW threat (Cochran et al., 1993).

The response to the biological weapons threat took three forms. First, the Bush administration informed the Iraqis that any use of biological weapons would result in severe retaliatory responses by the United States. Although such messages were sent in various forms, the key episode was the meeting that took place between Secretary of State James Baker and Iraqi Foreign Minister Tariq Aziz on January 8, 1991. At that meeting, Baker brought with him a letter from President Bush to Iraq's president Saddam Hussein (Woodward, 1991). The letter included the following language:

> The United States will not tolerate the use of chemical or biological weapons, support for any kind of terrorist action, or the destruction of Kuwait's oil fields and installations. The American people would demand the strongest possible response. You and your country will pay a terrible price if you order unconscionable actions of this sort. (*New York Times*, 1991).

This language is consistent with the wording that Secretary Baker subsequently claims that he used in the discussions with Aziz. Baker also "purposely left the impression that use of chemical or biological agents by Iraq could invite tactical nuclear retaliation" (Baker, 1995b). Although Aziz read the Bush letter, he refused to take it with him. (Perhaps for this reason, a decision was made to release the text of the letter to the press. It was published in the *New York Times* on January 13, 1991.)

The second component of the response to Iraqi biological weapons was military preemption. Specifically, the war plans for attacking Iraq gave a high priority to known and suspected BW-related sites, including the biological research facility at Salman Pak and four adjacent refrigerated storage facilities that the intelligence community thought were used to store biological agents. Unfortunately, intelligence was scanty on Iraq's biological weapons program, but as more information was acquired the size of the target set grew. Between August 2, 1990, and January 17, 1991 (when the air war began), the intelligence community's estimate of the number of BW-related sites grew from two to nineteen (Cochran et al., 1993).

These plans led to a focused effort to destroy Iraqi BW infrastructure during the war. The United States Air Force mounted attacks on suspected Iraqi BW sites starting on the first day of the war. The effectiveness of these attacks, however, is open to question. According to one informed review, a retrospective analysis indicated that these air attacks were of questionable military value (Watts et al., 1993). It appeared likely that the Iraqis removed most items of value from the research and development sites and production facilities that were attacked, and there was no evidence that the bunkers targeted contained any biological munitions (Watts et al., 1993). These conclusions are consistent with the views of Ambassador Rolf Ekéus, chairman of the United Nations Special Commission (UNSCOM), which was given responsibility for dismantling Iraq's biological, chemical, and ballistic missile programs following the war (the International Atomic Energy Agency was tasked with demolishing the Iraqi nuclear program). UNSCOM investigations suggest that the air attacks inflicted limited damage on Iraq's BW program and had not materially affected its ability to deliver biological agents.

Finally, efforts were made to enhance biological defenses provided to U.S. forces deployed in the theater. Unfortunately, DOD had limited stocks of the anthrax and botulinum toxoid vaccines, insufficient to protect U.S. troops deployed to Saudi Arabia, much less those of allied countries or the civilian population of coalition allies in the region. Accordingly, a crash program was initiated to produce both vaccines for selected protection of some U.S. personnel, which is discussed in the following way in an official DOD account of the war:

> There were limited stockpiles of drugs and vaccines for biological defense before and during Operations Desert Shield and Desert Storm. The industrial base could not supply all the items needed. Long production lead times, and the legal and medical problems related to the use of these drugs delayed their fielding. (U.S. Department of Defense, 1992)

The inadequacies of the biodefense program in late 1990 are clear from a review of the efforts to immunize forces deployed to Saudi Arabia against anthrax and botulinum toxin, then thought to be the two main threat agents. The then existing anthrax vaccine required that six doses be given over an eighteen-month period to produce optimal antibody responses, which clearly was not possible in this context. In the final tally, it appears that about 150,000 troops were given at least one dose of the anthrax vaccine. It is believed that few received more than two doses. The recommended dosage schedule for the botulinum toxin vaccine is three doses over a one-year period. Only 8,000 personnel received at least one dose (IOM, 1996). Thus, of the more than 500,000 U.S. troops sent to the theater, fewer than one-third received any kind of protection. Although anthrax and botulinum toxin were long recognized as likely BW threat agents, DOD clearly lacked the assets needed to protect personnel likely to be subjected to attacks using those agents.

The lack of an efficacious vaccine in sufficient dosages was only one of many biodefense inadequacies exposed during the crisis. No adequate BW agent detectors were available. Thus, although gas masks issued to coalition forces provided excellent protection against both chemical and biological threat agents, there were no warning systems to alert troops of the need to don their masks.

Once the crisis ended, it became clear that DOD needed to take steps to rectify its biodefense problems. This is reflected in the official account of Desert Storm issued under the name of Secretary of Defense Dick Cheney.

It concluded that "BW defense should be emphasized more fully in DOD programs." Specific inadequacies identified detectors, vaccines, protective equipment, and medical treatments (U.S. Department of Defense, 1992: 1).

In the wake of the conflict, several DOD initiatives were begun to address some of the problems revealed by the Iraq crisis. For example, steps were taken to resolve some of the organizational problems that hindered efforts to respond to BW threats. The Department of the Army was designated the executive agent for biological defense, and a Joint Program Office (JPO) was established to provide high-level visibility to the biological defense effort. The JPO was given primary responsibility for implementation of a vaccine program. Other programs were initiated to develop specialized munitions capable of destroying NBC munitions, and efforts were made to develop aircraft bombs capable of penetrating hardened bunkers. Additional funding was devoted to the development of biological sensors. These initiatives, however, were not coherently organized and did not address the broad range of weaknesses revealed during the Gulf War.

THE ASPIN COUNTERPROLIFERATION INITIATIVE

Although the first steps toward developing counterproliferation occurred in the waning days of the Bush administration, it was not until the arrival of the Clinton administration that the effort received high visibility within DOD. The new administration appointed the chairman of the House Armed Services Committee, Congressman Les Aspin, as its first secretary of defense. Aspin came into office with already developed views on the problems posed by proliferation, reflecting both his concerns regarding the collapse of the former Soviet Union and the lessons that he drew from the Iraq experience (Wallerstein, 1995).

Despite the focus given to proliferation in the early days of Aspin's tenure, little progress was made addressing the subject. This was partially a result of the slowness with which the Clinton administration created a team. It was not until nearly the end of the year that the Counterproliferation Initiative was formally launched, during a December 7 speech by Secretary Aspin before the National Academy of Sciences. Aspin argued that the security threat "that most urgently and directly threatens America at home and American interests abroad is the new nuclear danger" (Aspin, 1993a). Aspin noted that two new developments had made the proliferation problem more acute. First, the breakup of the former Soviet Union made it easier for proliferant nations to acquire nuclear-related material. Four factors were identified as enhancing prospects for proliferation as a result of the Soviet collapse.

1. The breakup of the Soviet Union dispersed its nuclear arsenal over the territory of four states rather than just one.
2. Political turmoil in the former Soviet Union could lead to loss of control of nuclear weapons from the Soviet arsenal, so-called loose nukes.
3. Proliferators might hire experts from the weapons establishment of the former Soviet Union.
4. The demise of the Soviet Union eliminated a power that once constrained its client states.

Second, Aspin (1993b) argued that the growth in world trade and the spread of technology "will make it harder and harder to detect illicit diversions of materials and technology useful for weapons development." In addition, the diffusion of weapons technologies was giving proliferators access to technologies once considered state-of-the-art. Thus, such countries were now able to develop the indigenous technology infrastructures required to acquire NBC weapons, making them increasingly independent of foreign support.

Finally, Aspin argued that the inevitable proliferation of nuclear, biological, and chemical weapons required a defense effort that would concentrate on protection: "At the heart of the Counterproliferation Initiative, therefore, is a drive to develop new military capabilities to deal with this new threat." The elements of the Counterproliferation Initiative are

Creating a new mission: This involved a presidential statement authorizing a new defense mission, direction to DOD through the Defense Planning Guidance issued in the late summer of 1993, and the creation of a new organization to address proliferation issues.

Changing acquisition priorities: According to Aspin (1993b), the Defense Department was "reviewing all relevant programs to see what we can do better." As an example, he noted that an effort was being made to explore "improved non-nuclear penetrating munitions to deal with underground installations." Other acquisition initiatives mentioned by Aspin included new systems to locate and destroy mobile missile launchers and a redirection of ballistic missile defense programs away from the previous priority on defense of the continental United States to a new focus on theater missile defenses to protect military forces against ballistic missiles armed with NBC warheads.[4]

Changing the way we fight wars: To enhance the ability of the fighting forces to deal with proliferation threats, Aspin "directed the services to tell us how prepared they are for it." In addition, the chairman of the Joint Chiefs of Staff and the regional commanders in chief were directed to create "a military planning process for dealing with adversaries who have weapons of mass destruction" (Aspin, 1993b).

Improving intelligence: Efforts were being made to improve counterproliferation intelligence. This involved working with the director of the Central Intelligence Agency to create a deputy director for military support in the intelligence community's Nonproliferation Center and by increasing the number of people assigned to the center.

Enhancing international cooperation: Cooperative programs with our North Atlantic Treaty Organization (NATO) allies and with Japan in the defense arena were identified as a priority under the Counterproliferation Initiative. In addition, Aspin reported that DOD was working closely with the new republics of the former Soviet Union to reduce the risk of weapons from the former Soviet arsenal becoming available to proliferant nations.

The Counterproliferation Initiative provided the basis for a variety of activities in the years after it began. In addition to investment in programs intended to enhance the operational capabilities needed to defend against biological attacks, some critical steps have been taken to enhance the organizational structure for addressing such issues.

ORGANIZATIONAL RESPONSES

The Goldwater-Nichols Act defense reforms, adopted by Congress in 1986, give primacy to the role of the regional commanders in chief (CINCs) for defense activities within their theater of operations. This means that the four geographic CINCs (European Command, Central Command for the Middle East, Pacific Command, and Southern Command for Latin America) have a central role in any discussion of defense roles and missions.

In 1994, the chairman of the Joint Chiefs of Staff (CJCS) ordered a missions and functions study to determine who within DOD should be assigned primary responsibility for executing counterproliferation policies. In May 1995, the secretary of defense signed off on a proposal to give the regional CINCs primary responsibility for executing counterproliferation missions. A proposal to give primary counterproliferation responsibility to a function command, Strategic Command (STRATCOM), was rejected because of opposition from most of the other CINCs, who felt that counterproliferation was an integral part of their own responsibilities for regional security matters. However, the Special Operations Command (SOCOM) was assigned responsibility for counterproliferation operations involving special forces (CPRC, 1996). Essentially, these decisions mean that the four

regional CINCS and SOCOM do planning and execution for counterproliferation missions.

The missions and functions study also led to the development of a
Counterproliferation 0400 CONPLAN (concept plan). This CONPLAN
was completed in the summer of 1996, and it directed the CINCs to develop their own CONPLANs consistent with the CJCS guidance. These plans,
although not finalized by early 1997, represent a key step in the integration
of counterproliferation concerns into the routine activities of the CINCs
(CPRC, 1996).

EMERGING CAPABILITIES

As part of the counterproliferation initiative, DOD is attempting to develop
four distinct capabilities in the arena of biological defenses: counterforce,
active defense, biological sensors, and medical treatments.

Counterforce

DOD uses the term "counterforce" to refer to offensive military operations
intended to destroy enemy NBC weapons capabilities before use.
Accordingly, should hostile military forces possess biological munitions,
the U.S. military would prefer to destroy those weapons before the enemy
gets a chance to employ them. This poses certain difficulties, some of them
not unique to the BW threat. U.S. military planners expect that any BW
munitions possessed by an adversary force will be kept in heavily protected
bunkers. To destroy anything stored in such bunkers requires specialized
conventional weapons capable of penetrating into the ground and through
thick concrete walls. Therefore, development of penetration munitions is a
high priority for DOD, and bunker-busting weapons are being built.

There is a uniquely BW element of the problem, however. Attacking
BW munitions could result in the release of agent that could cause casualties among people living in the vicinity of the storage site. If the BW was
stored sufficiently close to friendly territory, it is even possible that friendly
troops and civilians could be exposed. To prevent such collateral damage,
either to civilians (whether friendly or enemy) or to friendly forces, the
United States seeks to develop munitions that will destroy the agent at the
same time as the storage facility. This is not an easy task. The detonation of
conventional high-explosive munitions would not destroy all the biological
agents at the site of the impact. In fact, the detonation of high-explosive
weapons could break apart the BW munitions and lead to venting of agent
outside the bunker as an aerosol (Cochran et al., 1993). Because of this

possibility, DOD is working to develop munitions that will destroy BW agents.

Active Defenses

Iraqi use of ballistic missiles during Desert Storm emphasized the impor- tance of developing defenses capable of shooting down short- and medium- range ballistic missiles. Destroying a ballistic missile carrying biological munitions in flight would pose a significantly more complex challenge than defeating conventionally armed missiles. A sophisticated adversary is likely to rely on BW-filled submunitions, which survive the destruction of the missile warhead even at quite high altitudes. In fact, during the 1960s, before the termination of its offensive BW program, the United States reportedly developed BW submunitions that could be released as high as 50,000 feet. Thus, theater missile defenses must be capable of destroying not only the missile and warhead but also the contents of any submunitions carried by the warhead. This explains some of the interest in destroying missiles just after launch, while still on the ascent, which is known as boost phase intercept.

In addition, there is a growing concern about the possible proliferation of cruise missiles. Cruise missiles have distinct advantages as a delivery system for biological agents, since they can be fitted with spray tanks enabling spraying to disseminate agent as a line source while flying at low altitudes. Currently, DOD is devoting considerable effort to programs designed to shoot down cruise missiles.

Sensors

Since Desert Storm, DOD has assigned a high priority to the development of sensors capable of detecting the presence of aerosol clouds. Such sensors come in two varieties: point detectors that identify aerosol clouds when they pass by the detector, and remote sensors that identify aerosol clouds at a distance from the detector. There are numerous systems in production or under development to achieve these objectives. The United States Army is currently fielding a point-source detector, the biological integrated detec- tion system (BIDS), which will be deployed with field troops. Efforts to enhance the capabilities of the BIDS are already in the works. For example, the United States Navy has developed an interim biological agent detector (IBAD), which is a point-detection system deployed on ships, and has pro- cured twenty-five of the systems. There is also the long-range biological standoff detection system (LR-BSDS), a lidar system for detecting aerosol clouds at a distance (CPRC, 1996).

Originally, these programs were designed to detect and provide early warning of a line source aerosol cloud that might be generated by an aircraft or drone flying parallel to the front line. For this reason, the United States Army believed that its BIDS would provide adequate warning of an attack, even though relatively few systems would be available to the operational forces. The revelation that Iraq was working on artillery and missile delivery systems, however, which would generate point-source agent clouds, has led to a reevaluation of this assumption. The operational effectiveness of these new sensors is not yet clear. Although the systems have been field-tested, no information has been publicly released on the reliability or sensitivity of the sensors they contain. Thus, it is unclear how effectively they will operate in a range of atmospheric conditions against a variety of biological agents. There are no indications as to whether the systems are suitable for use against biological agents disseminated in low concentrations, as might be typical with an aerosol cloud constituted of organisms causing tularemia or Q-fever.

Medical Defenses

Medical responses to agent threats are an important part of the biological defense program and consist of two main elements. First, DOD has long considered vaccines a key element of an integrated biological defense program. It is currently developing new vaccines to protect against anthrax, plague, and Venezuelan equine encephalitis (VEE) and new antitoxins for botulinum and ricin (CPRC, 1996). Second, the DOD has taken steps to enhance the quality of postexposure treatment by improving medical education of military medical personnel and by developing better agent characterization kits to make possible rapid identification of agents in order to enhance treatment of exposed individuals. In addition, the Defense Advanced Research Projects Agency (DARPA) has initiated a number of programs to explore innovative antimicrobial approaches. These DARPA efforts focus on approaches that are technically risky and that are not currently being supported by other government agencies or the pharmaceutical industry.

The most expensive part of the medical defense program is the acquisition of vaccines to immunize military personnel against biological agents. According to press reports, DOD is discussing a program to provide soldiers with anthrax vaccine in peacetime (Graham, 1996). The Joint Chiefs of Staff reportedly recommended adoption of an anthrax vaccine program, but it appears that the secretary of defense has not yet acted on the proposal. In the past, the Department of the Army had argued that the BW defense program needed its own dedicated vaccine production facility, based on the contention that existing suppliers were not willing to provide the vaccines needed to support defense requirements. Until 1994, DOD expected to spend up to $300 million for the construction of such a facility. In 1994, however, this approach was rejected, partly because DOD lacked sufficient numbers of people with the specialized skills needed to establish and operate a vaccine production line. Accordingly, a determination was made that the best approach was to rely on a contractor-owned, contractor-operated production facility. Currently, DOD is stockpiling vaccines needed to support wartime requirements, which means that in a future conflict it should have sufficient quantities of vaccine to protect personnel likely to be assigned to theaters of operation (CPRC, 1996).

INTERNATIONAL COOPERATION

From the beginning, the Counterproliferation Initiative recognized the vital importance of working with other countries in countering NBC threats. DOD recognized that other countries had capabilities that might prove useful to the United States. At the same time, DOD understood that the United States was likely to fight as part of a coalition, and that the effectiveness of the coalition could be undermined if other countries lacked robust chemical and biological defenses. This concern had both a strategic and an operational dimension. Potential coalition partners in the theater of operations might be reluctant to host U.S. and other military forces in the face of chemical and biological threats. Thus, the ability to form coalitions might depend on the state of the chemical and biological defenses available to other countries. In addition, combat effectiveness of military forces lacking capable chemical and biological defenses might be significantly reduced should an adversary employ NBC weapons on the battlefield.

For these reasons, DOD has given considerable attention to international programs. The largest effort involves NATO. At the urging of the United States, NATO established two expert working groups to address proliferation issues, the Senior Political-Military Group on Proliferation (SGP), chaired by NATO's assistant secretary-general for political affairs, and the Senior Defense Group on Proliferation (DGP), co-chaired by an assistant secretary of defense from DOD and a European official of comparable rank. These efforts led to significant changes in NATO approaches to the potential military threat posed by NBC proliferation. Specifically, the SGP concluded that "NATO must address the military capabilities needed to discourage WMD proliferation and use, and if necessary, to protect NATO territory, populations and forces" (NATO, 1994). The DGP has undertaken a comprehensive review of the impact of NBC threats on NATO defense doctrine and has proposed a coordinated alliance response (Joseph, 1996). In addition, the United States has conducted talks with friendly countries in other parts of the world, but these interactions have yet to reach the breadth of the NATO discussions.

CONCLUSION

By early 1997, DOD was investing substantial sums in its efforts to respond to the military challenges posed by BW proliferation. Responding to BW threats has been assigned a higher priority than at any time in the past, and for the first time DOD's senior leadership, both military and civilian, appear committed to rectifying weaknesses in BW defenses (U.S. Department of Defense, 1998).

The challenges, however, are formidable. Great technical challenges are associated with most of the programs intended to counter BW threats, and progress in fielding systems for use in the field has been slow. Ultimately, much will depend on DOD's ability to exploit innovative new technologies emerging from the biotechnology industry, which will permit developments to meet demanding technical criteria at affordable costs. Thus, it is likely that the sensor problem will be solved only when it is possible to develop sensors that are sensitive to a large number of threat agents yet are sufficiently inexpensive that they can be produced and fielded in large numbers. Similarly, DOD efforts to develop innovative new medical therapies, including new vaccines and new antimicrobials, are essential to the ultimate success of the biodefense efforts.

What is unclear, however, is whether the approaches adopted will be any more successful than previous efforts to address BW threats. There are technical problems with virtually every approach to dealing with BW threats. These problems are likely to increase as potential adversaries exploit biotechnology to develop new agents or modify existing ones. Thus, even if the biodefense efforts make it possible to address the existing high priority threats, such as anthrax and botulinum toxin, they may not resolve all the difficulties associated with detection of, characterization of, and medical protection from possible novel agents.

Nevertheless, there appears to be reason for optimism that for the first time it will be possible to provide defenses against the most serious of the existing BW threat agents. DOD now has vaccine stockpiles against anthrax, and the number of vaccines available to the fighting forces will grow over time. In addition, better vaccines are under development, which will further enhance medical defenses against the most likely threat agents.

For the first time, DOD is providing operational forces with sensors that can detect and identify the main threat agents. As a result, it should be possible to determine if forces have been exposed to a range of biological agents within minutes of an attack. This capability will continue to improve over time as the identification technology becomes more robust and the number of agents that can be identified grows. In addition, some innovative approaches to treatment may emerge from some of the efforts undertaken by DARPA, although it will take some time before the success of its programs becomes apparent. At the same time, it is unlikely that the Counterproliferation Initiative will successfully address all the BW challenges. Standoff detection is likely to remain a challenge. Detection of a BW attack requires more point sensors than is currently affordable using existing technology.

If the United States were to go to war today against a BW-equipped adversary, it would be considerably better off than it was during the response to the Iraqi invasion of Kuwait in 1990–1991. The understanding in DOD of BW issues is considerably greater, and at least some of the worst weaknesses have been rectified.

The real problem, however, will come in the future as biotechnology transforms the BW threat. Except for a few initiatives, current DOD efforts target the BW agents that have been the focus of offensive BW programs for decades. As biotechnology makes it possible to engineer novel agents, a new set of challenges will emerge even more daunting than the ones being addressed today.

NOTES

1. The term was introduced into DOD by Captain Larry Seaquist, special assistant to the deputy undersecretary of defense for policy (USDP), who was studying a possible reorganization of the Defense Technology Security Agency, an export control organization under the control of USDP.

2. Proliferation is sometimes defined to include advanced conventional weapons, such as fighter aircraft, missiles, and electronic systems. This broad definition was not accepted within DOD, which in turn affected the focus of counterproliferation activities.

3. Nonproliferation is generally considered to include arms controls, export controls, and diplomatic initiatives intended to prevent, slow, or eliminate existing programs known to possess NBC weapons and missile delivery systems.

4. Theater missile defenses are designed to protect forward deployed military forces against shorter-range missiles likely to be in the arsenal of regional adversaries. Theater missile defenses are compliant with restrictions of the ABM treaty, which limits defenses against intercontinental ballistic missiles.

10

Exploiting Intelligence
in International Organizations

TIM TREVAN

I am not a country. . . . I have no army . . . no land, no police. The importance of the United Nations comes from its moral value, its credibility.
—*Boutros Boutros-Ghali,*
former United Nations Secretary-General

There is nothing wrong with the United Nations—except its governments.
—*Lord Caradon,*
former British delegate to the United Nations

The common perception of intelligence remains that of James Bond and
World War II movies. Images are conjured up of agents being dropped by
parachute in the midst of night behind enemy lines to spy directly on an
enemy's activities or to intervene directly—to overthrow a government, to
assassinate a president, or to steal the latest hi-tech gizmo and thereby save the
world. The spy is the hero or the villain, depending on one's point of view.

But the reality is much more mundane and does not make for James
Bond–style action films. Although cloak-and-dagger activities undoubtedly
continue around the world, the Hollywood interpretation is a somewhat
limited and antiquated one of what intelligence agencies do. Indeed, such
activities should perhaps be termed "espionage" to distinguish them from
"intelligence," which has much more to do with the gathering and analysis
of information to improve decisionmaking and action taking. Espionage
might be defined as the means by which information is collected covertly.
However, most information gathering and analysis does not involve high
drama and secret agents, but depends on technology, contacts, and pen
pushing. And much of the action taken on the basis of intelligence is not

undertaken covertly but rather is factored into the everyday activities of overt branches of government, as well as by businesses.

In this chapter I seek to address how intelligence gathered by national agencies for national purposes might be exploited by international organizations for the general good. I also look at the prospects for persuading states to include in their national intelligence-gathering activities efforts specifically designed to meet international organizations' needs.

To do this, I first discuss in general terms the nature, purpose, and use of intelligence. I then look at the mandate of one United Nations body, the UN Special Commission (UNSCOM), which was established by the UN Security Council to rid Iraq of weapons of mass destruction. I examine that body's problems in obtaining access to intelligence and its experience in and future plans for utilizing it. Finally, I seek to extract general lessons from the UNSCOM experience for the use of intelligence by international organizations.

INTELLIGENCE: NATURE, SOURCES, PURPOSES, AND USE

Nature

Intelligence is information. More particularly, it is data or assessments that, at least in part, incorporate information obtained by covert means. To be good, intelligence must incorporate information obtained from all known sources, both open and secret. If there were no covert component, we could rely on diplomats, analysts, academics, and businesspersons to collect and use the information, and we would have no need for intelligence agencies.

In saying that intelligence is information, I am using the term in its broadest sense. I include documents, records (tape, CD, computer disk, microfilm, microfiche, and any other form of storing information), drawings, imagery, conversations, items, materials, equipment, instrument readings, samples, hardware, software, and even the intentions, plans, objectives, strategies, and tactics of the entity being spied upon. All of these, when examined and analyzed, contain information.

Sources

The traditional role attributed to a spy, of a Scarlet Pimpernel or a James Bond who breaks into offices to steal or photograph secret documents, may still exist; however, other means employed by intelligence agencies yield more useful information by far. Although human intelligence (HUMINT) remains an important source of intelligence, particularly with regard to the more intangible information relating to intentions and objectives, HUMINT presently comes mainly from people other than spies. Defectors or moles, controlled by highly manipulative professionals, are the major sources for HUMINT. To get the most out of these informants, debriefing has become both a science and an art form.

Other significant means of gathering information are through imagery (pictures such as film, photography, or infrared images) obtained from aerial platforms (such as satellites, aircraft, and unmanned aircraft) and through listening in on telecommunications traffic (SIGINT or COMMINT). Vast amounts of information can be and are collected through these means.

Another source of increasing significance as technology improves is what is referred to as "national technical means"—remote sensors that can, from outside the borders of the target country, detect phenomena originating within it. Examples of these include seismic stations that can detect nuclear explosions in the target country and air or water sampling programs that can detect cross-border releases of radiation or chemicals. New technologies might soon be operational that would enable us to analyze from afar the chemical or biological composition of clouds and of plumes from factory chimneys.

But, however important the foregoing sources, the largest source of intelligence is open source data. Numerous data are published or broadcast by individuals, private companies, the media, academia, and governments. And a new source of incredible amounts of data is developing worldwide, albeit in an anarchistic manner—the World Wide Web. There people can input in real time their views and knowledge of events occurring anywhere in the world. Already in electronic form, these data are potentially more amenable to electronic collation and analysis than other data sources.

Purposes

National intelligence gathering has traditionally had many different purposes, but these can be sorted into three broad categories: (1) to obtain "unfair" advantage; (2) to improve knowledge of other countries and, hence, improve foreign policymaking; and (3) to improve national and (sometimes) international security.

The first category can be seen as involving zero sum games. One party's advantage comes at the disadvantage of the other party. Examples of intelligence purposes in this category include political intervention in another country to gain political advantage for one's own, for example, through installation of a friendly government in a strategically important country; gaining a military advantage in an arms race or an armed conflict;

stealing scientific, technological, or commercial information to gain an industrial or trade advantage; or gaining information about another state's negotiating position and objectives in order to obtain one-sided international agreements.

Clearly, as a club of nations come together on a voluntary basis to "establish conditions under which peace and justice and respect for . . . international law can be maintained, and to promote social progress and better standards of life in larger freedom" and to "practice tolerance, and live together in peace with one another as good neighbours" (Preamble, Charter of the United Nations), the UN has no part in intelligence activities of the zero sum kind. Only if the intelligence has a general or public good can the UN sanction and, hence, use it.

The second category might meet this "public good" criterion. If country X obtains information about country Y that enables X to formulate a "better" national policy, that "better" policy might be to the mutual benefit of both X and Y (e.g., if it leads X to decide to improve relations with Y) or only to the benefit of X (e.g., if X decides that its strategic interests will not only be unaffected by reducing aid to Y but enhanced by reallocating the resources thereby freed by discontinuing aid to Y). Sharing intelligence on human rights and humanitarian situations and for environmental monitoring might prove to be to the general good too. In any case, there is, at least theoretically, a category of intelligence generated by national intelligence agencies that would, if available to the UN, increase its understanding of a given situation, thereby enabling it to make better policy decisions to the benefit of all.

The third category is similar to the second. Clearly, intelligence might improve the security of X to the detriment of Y, with no effect on the security of Y, or to the benefit of the entire international community. For example, if Israel were to obtain intelligence that convinced it that Syria genuinely wanted peace and would abide scrupulously by the terms of a peace plan, thereby enabling the conclusion of a comprehensive peace in the Middle East, the entire international community would benefit overall (no doubt there would be some losers, for example, groups whose existence derives from confrontation between the two countries).

This is perhaps the clearest case in which national intelligence can be of direct assistance to the UN and the barriers to the organization receiving intelligence would be the lowest—in the maintenance and restoration of regional and international peace and security. Clearly, this criterion can only be met when the intelligence can be seen to benefit the international community as a whole. And, given its role under the UN Charter, the body to determine whether this criterion is met in a given situation is the UN Security Council.

Use

Anyone wishing to use intelligence faces certain generic problems deriving from the nature and sources of intelligence, particularly the covertly gathered components of it. Much intelligence, especially HUMINT, is vague or not wholly accurate. Corroborating intelligence or matching it to, say, a geographic entity is often problematic. And sometimes the intelligence is little more than gossip or wishful thinking. Furthermore, sources often present their own assessments, suppositions, and interpretations of a situation as facts, which may be false.

Quite apart from the vagueness, intelligence is often of questionable reliability for a variety of reasons. The source may not have understood or observed the information correctly. This is a particular problem when the intelligence relates to high technology, where few observers and hence sources have the requisite knowledge to report accurately and fully. The source may depend on the intelligence agency in some manner (e.g., for income) and therefore might fabricate reports for personal gain or tell the agency what the source thinks it wants to hear in order to ingratiate himself or herself. The source might well have its own political agenda and hence might seek to manipulate the agency in a manner the source deems beneficial, especially if it is an opposition group. Or the source might be an agent provocateur, feeding the agency disinformation on behalf of the target.

A separate problem relates to the releasability of intelligence. There is nothing more frustrating than knowing, through intelligence reports, an important fact but not being able to act upon it. It may, at first glance, seem idiotic to collect intelligence one cannot act upon. However, there are some good reasons that, in certain instances, the release of intelligence beyond a handful of persons (and hence authority to act upon it) might be denied— when acting upon or releasing the intelligence would endanger the future flow of greater quantities of and potentially more valuable intelligence by compromising the source or by allowing the target to evaluate the agency's technical intelligence-gathering capabilities and take effective countermeasures against it.

Given all these considerations, anyone wishing to use intelligence must be able to assess the raw data coming in and to filter out as much as possible of the noise and disinformation. This task should be done within the context of all known data, including the reliability and potential motives of the source. In making the assessment, one must be clear as to which of the data is corroborated fact; which is likely to be fact; and which in reality is assessment, supposition, interpretation, fantasy, or disinformation. The greater one's knowledge is of the subject matter, the easier and more reliable the assessment that can be made. And the more numerous and diverse one's sources of intelligence, the lower the probability that the use of it would compromise the source or capabilities. In short, effective use of intelligence requires a strong analytical capability, a good established database, and many diverse sources.

UNSCOM AND INTELLIGENCE

UNSCOM's Mandate

In 1991, the UN Security Council gave UNSCOM a huge mandate—to track down every banned item, to account for each of Iraq's imports for its banned programs, and to ascertain the current disposition of every item that Iraq ever had that could be used to make banned weapons. Thereafter, the mission was relatively simple—merely to monitor all remaining "dual-use" items in Iraq and all future Iraqi trade in such until further notice, so as to provide the international community with the assurance that Iraq was not rebuilding banned weapons (UN Security Council, 1991). ("Dual-use" items here refer to items that have nonproscribed uses but could be used to acquire or produce banned weapons.)

To fulfill this mammoth mandate, UNSCOM (and the International Atomic Energy Agency [IAEA] in the nuclear area) was given extraordinary powers of investigation. It may conduct any number of unannounced inspections of any site, facility, activity, material, or other item anywhere in Iraq and conduct aerial overflights of any area, location, site, or facility in Iraq for the purpose of inspection, surveillance, transportation, or logistics upon such conditions as UNSCOM may decide. In doing so, it may use its own aircraft and sensors, making use of such airfields in Iraq as it may determine most appropriate for its work. Iraq is obliged to provide (and UNSCOM has the right of access to) information on sites, facilities, materials, equipment, documentation, imports, activities, and intentions. UNSCOM may seize, copy, or photograph any item or record; it may use any sensor; it may take any samples; and it may use any means of analysis it deems necessary. Further, it may search any means of transport and ask any question (with a legal expectation of a full and honest answer).

To encourage Iraqi cooperation, the Security Council devised a carrot-and-stick approach. The carrot was that, once Iraq had completed all of the actions required of it in the disarmament provisions of the cease-fire, the Security Council would lift the oil embargo. The stick consisted of three sets of sanctions imposed on Iraq: a ban on Iraqi imports other than foods, medicines, and essentials; a ban on Iraqi exports of petroleum and natural gas commodities; and a ban on Iraqi arms imports. Sanctions are reviewed every sixty days "in the light of the policies and practices of the Government of Iraq, including the implementation of all relevant resolutions of the Security Council, for the purpose of determining whether to reduce or lift" (UN Security Council, 1991: Resolution 687, para. 21) them. The oil embargo is reviewed every 120 days and "upon Council agreement that Iraq has completed all the actions contemplated [relating to elimination of weapons of mass destruction and ballistic missiles] . . . shall have no further force of effect." The arms embargo is also reviewed every 120 days, "taking into account Iraq's compliance with the [cease-fire] resolution and general progress towards the control of armaments in the region" (UN Security Council, 1991: Resolution 687, para. 28). It can be seen that Iraqi cooperation with UNSCOM is key to lifting the oil embargo and also plays an important role in decisions to lift or ease the sanctions or arms embargo. The stick was multiple: obviously, without cooperation, the oil embargo would remain in force; Iraq would remain isolated internationally; and non-cooperation, such as denial of access to inspection teams, could be deemed by the Security Council to be material breaches of the cease-fire terms, thereby reverting to a situation in which states jointly or individually could use military force to rectify the breach. Most important, Iraqi cooperation in the disarmament area could be a major factor in the Security Council's deciding whether to lift the general sanctions against Iraq.

The problem—quite apart from creating an organization from scratch—was where to start. Powers of search are all very well when officials know where to search. UNSCOM needed to know where Iraq's clandestine programs were located, and because Iraq was not forthcoming, it needed to find out from other sources. Even in the chaos that existed in Baghdad immediately after the war, UNSCOM could not presume upon the willingness of individual Iraqis, in defiance of their government's threats of death to informers, to proffer up such information. UNSCOM did not have the means to ensure the safety of would-be informers. The best sources of such knowledge outside Iraq were the intelligence agencies. UNSCOM needed their help but first had to overcome two sets of problems: convincing national intelligence agencies to share their knowledge and overcoming barriers internal to the UN.

The Intelligence Agencies' Perspective

Identifying national intelligence agencies that would be the best sources of information was not difficult. It was no secret which countries had been close to Iraq politically and militarily in the years during which its government had built up banned programs. Nor was it a secret which of its neighbors had an interest in obtaining quality intelligence on Iraqi missile and weapons of mass destruction capabilities. But there was no history of member states providing the UN with sensitive intelligence about the capabilities of another member state, and there was no assurance that the assistance

UNSCOM required would be forthcoming from all or any of the parties able to assist.

The United States and the United Kingdom, as prime movers in the coalition to oust the Iraqis from Kuwait and as powers with a long history of seeking to prevent proliferation of the weapons banned to Iraq (despite their own possession of them at various stages in their history), were the first to provide UNSCOM with intelligence on the whereabouts of Iraqi capabilities. Clearly, as the drafters of large parts of the cease-fire resolution, both states had a desire to see the successful implementation of the disarmament provisions. However, persuading their intelligence agencies to cooperate in a manner useful to UNSCOM was not a wrinkle-free exercise.

The problems UNSCOM encountered will be familiar to anyone who has been an outside user of intelligence, but were magnified by the fact that the user was not of the same nationality as the providers. Even worse, in the eyes of the providers, the recipient was the UN, staffed by every nationality. There was a presumption that any intelligence supplied would effectively become immediately available to all comers. At that point, UNSCOM had no track record of being able to handle intelligence with confidentiality and to protect it adequately while using it.

Therefore, any intelligence given to UNSCOM had to go through a stringent clearance procedure. The agencies had to be sure that release to UNSCOM would not adversely affect national security, would not compromise sources, and would not reveal information that would facilitate successful countermeasures being taken against the means used to collect intelligence. In addition to such legitimate concerns, one might add more dubious concerns relating to personal empires—by releasing information to other parties, countries reduce their relative power in policy and operational planning discussions. Unless managed well, turf battles get in the way of intelligence sharing. Furthermore, even once parameters have been set for handing over intelligence, there is a human factor involved—those responsible for classifying will generally overclassify intelligence to protect themselves from potential charges of breaching secrecy laws.

The initial instinct of even those with the most desire to see successful implementation of UNSCOM's mandate was to deliver only unclassified information. If UNSCOM were to receive more sensitive intelligence, it would need to convince the providers of its ability to handle intelligence securely, to protect sources, and to act on the intelligence effectively. Without proof of the ability to act on intelligence effectively, there would be no incentive for the agencies to risk compromising intelligence by providing it to UNSCOM, no matter how securely UNSCOM handled it. And to be able to act on it effectively, UNSCOM would have to be able to protect it from Iraqi counterintelligence efforts, at least until it was no longer operationally sensitive.

The UNSCOM Perspective

For its part, UNSCOM faced some barriers to accepting intelligence. For UNSCOM to be able to fulfill its mandate, it needed to be perceived first (by Iraq and member states) as acting solely in accordance with that mandate and second (by those on whose generosity it would depend for personnel and other support, and by the UN Security Council, which would ultimately judge its work) as being dedicated to implementing it fully.

The first was important in securing Iraqi acquiescence to UNSCOM activities. (Cooperation is too strong a word to describe Iraqi relations with UNSCOM—even when it was facilitating access and the installation of the ongoing monitoring and verification system, it was lying about the extent of its past programs.) If Iraq thought that UNSCOM was working on an unstated and hidden agenda, it would have had little incentive to cooperate because the carrot in the carrot-and-stick approach would have been taken away. Iraq probably felt that it could ride out the sanctions and oil embargo until international support for maintaining them crumbled. If Iraq could argue convincingly that UNSCOM was following a hidden agenda, it could gain sympathy internationally, thereby breaking down its isolation and making it more unlikely that the Security Council would find it in material breach of the cease-fire (thereby effectively voting for renewed military enforcement action). Not handing Iraq any cards in this regard was a high priority for UNSCOM.

However, UNSCOM could not give Iraq any favors in implementing the mandate. For the oil embargo to be lifted (which most would agree to be in Iraq's own self-interest), the Security Council would have to be convinced that UNSCOM had diligently fulfilled its mandate. Such a conviction, given the stakes, would not come easily. UNSCOM would have to be able to satisfy Iraq's harshest critics in the Security Council, attesting to an exhaustive knowledge of and accounting for Iraq's capabilities. Iraq's nondisclosure of large parts of its banned programs necessitated that UNSCOM turn elsewhere for the requisite information on those programs. But the mere act of receiving intelligence did not fit well with the traditional UN culture—that of an organization that, because of the debilitating effects the Cold War had had on the ability of the Security Council to undertake enforcement actions, had generally shied away from doing anything that might even potentially upset a member state. Such organizational culture factors should not be underestimated as barriers to action. In addition, to persuade the intelligence agencies to deliver would entail actions by UNSCOM that further clashed with UN culture: establishing procedures for the secure handling of data, which in turn implied some sort of security clearance of personnel and need-to-know procedures, both of which might mean denying access to intelligence to certain UNSCOM (and hence UN) officials on the basis of their nationality or any of a variety of other "need-to-know" reasons; and acting upon data over the objections of a sovereign founder member (Iraq).

In short, for the costs of obtaining intelligence to be of overall benefit to UNSCOM (and hence to both Iraq and the international community), UNSCOM had to be seen by all parties as a credible player. Credibility could only be attained through diligence in its work and through the perception that it was independent of pressures other than those of the mandate. Thus, UNSCOM had to be perceived as being open to all sources and of being capable of distinguishing fact from assessments and of identifying abusive data—maliciously false data aimed at getting UNSCOM to act in a manner designed to serve purposes other than those of the mandate. It also had to make it clear that receiving intelligence from the agencies would not be the traditional two-way street of intelligence sharing between two national agencies: UNSCOM would primarily be a receiver, not a transmitter, of information. Such information that it would pass on to governments would not be part of a barter exchange—it would be provided only to allow the government to be better able to assist UNSCOM in the fulfillment of its mandate. (For example, by telling the Y government of rumors of supplies from a company operating in Y, UNSCOM would enable that government to investigate the rumors fully and to inform UNSCOM of the results of the investigation. If the company had indeed supplied materials of interest to UNSCOM's operations, UNSCOM would then have information on which to act in Iraq.) And, from the UN cultural perspective, UNSCOM's toughness and involvement in intelligence would be tolerable only if it were seen as being scrupulously fair and so as acting in Iraq's ultimate interest.

UNSCOM's Experience with Intelligence

UNSCOM started its operations in April 1991 with no staff, no offices, no equipment, and no information. The plan of operations foresaw, as a first step, Iraq making full disclosures of all holdings and all aspects of its capabilities to acquire, produce, operate, maintain, and test banned weapons systems. Thereafter, UNSCOM would analyze the Iraqi declarations and plan verification inspections of all the declared sites and items and of any additional sites it would designate to ensure that the disclosures were indeed full. (For a description of how UNSCOM was created and operated, see Trevan, 1999.)

In its wisdom, the Security Council decided to establish UNSCOM de novo as an ad hoc subsidiary organ of the Council, reporting to it directly. It also decided that UNSCOM would not be funded from the UN regular budget, nor indeed from the peace-keeping budget or any other assessed budget (i.e., one through which the entire membership contributes on the basis of a formula describing their ability to pay). Rather, the Security

Council decided that Iraq was to be responsible for all UNSCOM's costs. Until Iraq provided funds, UNSCOM would be reliant on donations of cash and in-kind assistance from "supporting governments." Donations in-kind turned out to mean the loan of personnel both for full-time staff and for inspections, the provision of equipment and material, and the provision of information.

For a variety of reasons, these decisions had a fortuitous and beneficial impact on UNSCOM's ability to receive and use intelligence.

• Being the first such enforcement action by the Security Council and having an entirely fresh staff, UNSCOM had to pioneer all its work methods—it could write its own rule book without reference to precedence.

• Many of the persons loaned, either to undertake the assessments of Iraq's declarations or to participate in the inspections teams, had, in their prior national capacity, had access to national intelligence and national intelligence agencies. They brought with them the knowledge and contacts they had previously acquired in their national capacity to UNSCOM, which was inevitably filtered into their work for UNSCOM.

• Because most of the staff of UNSCOM were on loan from outside the UN system, they did not come with the cultural baggage of the organization. Indeed, most of them were arms control or weapons experts and were fully at ease with handling intelligence.

• Because UNSCOM had to establish secure operational procedures to ensure that Iraq could not clean up sites designated for inspection prior to the arrival of the team, UNSCOM had to be housed in secure and hence separate accommodations within the UN Secretariat building. The physical barriers to contact with regular UN Secretariat staff further impeded the assimilation of UNSCOM staff into the traditional UN culture. Indeed, over time it created something of an "us and them" effect that (whatever other positive and negative consequences that entailed) encouraged the opposite—the development of a distinct UNSCOM culture: a somewhat proud, cavalier, "can-do and will-do" attitude.

• Initially, and quite against UNSCOM's wishes to have a qualified staff from as many nationalities as possible, UNSCOM received full-time operations and assessments staff primarily from North Atlantic Treaty Organization (NATO) countries. (The reasons for this fact were no doubt many, including certain states not wanting to admit that they might have expertise in nuclear and other weapons.) Although this state of affairs was strictly unwanted by UNSCOM, it had a direct benefit—agencies saw that essentially only NATO nationals (many of whom, as noted above, were already known to and cleared by the intelligence agencies) competent in the handling of intelligence would have access to the intelligence. This facilitated the provision of intelligence.

• Because most of the personnel were loaned from the supporting governments' arms control or nonproliferation programs, most were personally eager to test whether this new kind of UN enforcement action, as opposed to unilateral or supplier cartel actions, could be successful. They worked with great dedication in their assessments of Iraqi capabilities and declarations, to the extent of using their informal contacts with national intelligence agencies to UNSCOM's benefit, even when no formal arrangements existed. This dedication and evident professionalism over time provided UNSCOM with the track record of using intelligence well, first with intelligence agencies of NATO countries, and then with intelligence agencies of other nations.

By 1996, UNSCOM had established very close relations with a large number of intelligence agencies from different regions, not just NATO agencies. Getting to this position was a long process requiring patient cultivation of trust. That process might be summarized as follows:

• A handful of NATO countries (particularly those that already had extensive intelligence-sharing arrangements) provided proposals for specific sites that UNSCOM should inspect and what it should look for there.
• Once some confidence had been established in UNSCOM's ability to handle confidential information, these same countries provided intelligence assessments of Iraqi capabilities.
• UNSCOM persuaded other NATO as well as certain non-NATO countries that their input was also necessary. The argument used with such countries was that failure to provide input would, through no fault of UNSCOM, preclude its ability to address these countries' concerns. Provision of intelligence would not only ensure that their substantive concerns about Iraqi capabilities were addressed but would also redress concerns about UNSCOM overreliance on NATO or Anglo-Saxon sources.
• Through acquisition of intelligence and information from Iraqi declarations and UNSCOM inspections and through the analysis of these data, UNSCOM developed within its Information Assessment Unit a more profound knowledge of Iraq's weapons programs than that available to any one intelligence agency. And by its conduct of successful inspections, UNSCOM proved that it could act effectively on intelligence. Both these factors facilitated the provision of more sensitive intelligence from those agencies already cooperating with UNSCOM.
• Once UNSCOM had developed both a database and an analytical capability, it organized and presided over seminars at its headquarters of representatives from several key supporting intelligence agencies (not restricted solely to NATO) to share assessments and intelligence in order to

obtain synergies. This generated a new stage in which several agencies might cooperate in developing scraps of intelligence into actionable intelligence to be provided to UNSCOM.

• The track record of successful action on and confidential handling of intelligence was then used with a number of other countries to prove that their national security concerns could be better met by providing intelligence to UNSCOM for action, rather than by trying to use it exclusively through national means. UNSCOM could be trusted not to blow intelligence and, indeed, could be relied on to make better use of it than the providers because, unlike the provider, it had access within Iraq and a mandate to destroy (banned) weapons that threatened the national security of the provider.

• Once UNSCOM could prove that it was better able, because of its accrued knowledge of Iraq, to analyze raw intelligence than were individual intelligence agencies, it was able to persuade some agencies to shift from providing assessments to providing raw intelligence.

• Having proved its ability to handle intelligence in a confidential manner and for the sole purpose of disarming Iraq—to Iraq's ultimate benefit—UNSCOM began, with some success, the process of obtaining the cooperation of the intelligence agencies of other countries whose own national security might be compromised by cooperating with UNSCOM, who might suffer embarrassment in revealing their involvement in Iraqi programs, or who might initially have been hostile to the concept of UNSCOM because it was seen as being anti-Iraq.

Throughout this process, there was an unremitting shift in the relative knowledge of UNSCOM and the agencies. Initially, UNSCOM had only the knowledge that the individual members of staff brought with them from their previous positions, whereas the agencies had a large reserve of high- (and low-) quality intelligence gleaned over many years of observing and cooperating with Iraq. There was also, in the immediate aftermath of the Gulf War, a rash of well-placed defectors possessing high-quality and still valid intelligence on the extent and disposition of Iraqi capabilities. But this stream of defectors soon slowed to a trickle, and the intelligence latecomers brought was often out of date.

Naturally, the highest grade and hence most actionable intelligence was provided by the agencies in the early days. As time went on and Iraq had time to organize its countermeasures and disinformation efforts, this information became less and less valid. Simultaneously, UNSCOM was gaining, through its inspections and aerial surveillance activities, more and more current information. In addition, the relationship with the agencies was not a two-way street. As both the recipient of more information in each individual relationship and as the central information clearinghouse, UNSCOM obtained a steadily greater information advantage over the agencies. Also, with its Information Assessment Unit's resources being dedicated solely to analyzing Iraq's weapons capabilities and with the agencies, over time, increasingly being given newer and higher priority calls on their resources, the analytical abilities of UNSCOM started to overtake those of the individual agencies. At that point, UNSCOM could argue that it was better placed to assess odd scraps of raw intelligence than the agencies themselves—a major turning point in the relationship.

Although UNSCOM benefited greatly from its relationships with the agencies, after 1995 it became far less dependent on their intelligence for the fulfillment of its mandate. Indeed, few inspections were launched on the basis of intelligence received from outside sources—most were initiated on the basis of the decisions by the Information Assessment Unit or on the basis of information that UNSCOM had sought out from open sources or had commissioned national governments to obtain from companies.

In the future, UNSCOM, or its successor agency, will continue to benefit from intelligence. Iraq's mere knowledge that, in order to undertake a clandestine weapons program successfully, it will have to fool not only UNSCOM but all the cooperating intelligence agencies, should be a major deterrent to Iraq's even considering such a course of action.[1] Intelligence will also be a key component of the export/import monitoring mechanism. Here, SIGINT or COMMINT will be vital in ensuring that any undeclared trade with Iraq in banned or dual-use items is spotted and brought under the monitoring regimes.

Because the process has been managed well, the benefits to UNSCOM in receiving intelligence have been clear:

• Intelligence has been of prime importance, particularly in the early days, in tracking down Iraq's undeclared banned capabilities.
• The process of analyzing intelligence to assess whether to act on it improved UNSCOM's understanding of Iraqi capabilities, thus enabling it better to analyze Iraq's declarations and to design its ongoing monitoring and verification system and export/import monitoring mechanism.
• The process of cooperating with intelligence agencies involved states directly in the work of UNSCOM, giving them a stake in UNSCOM's success and thereby helping to ensure that, despite all the financial difficulties of the UN and national budgetary constraints, UNSCOM received the resources it needed to fulfill its mandate. By bringing states into the process, it also precluded the view that UNSCOM, as an entity distinct from member states, had sole responsibility for disarming Iraq, thereby abrogating states' responsibilities and preventing them, should efforts fail,

from using UNSCOM as a scapegoat (the UN's traditional role—hence the quotation from Lord Caradon).

• As noted above, the mere fact that UNSCOM, the monitoring organ, received intelligence was a major deterrent to Iraqi cheating.

LESSONS: INTELLIGENCE AND INTERNATIONAL ORGANIZATIONS

International organizations, whether regional or global, are established for the mutual benefit of the member states. As such, it is inconceivable that the organization per se should create its own capabilities to spy on member states, but the organization could still use intelligence gathered by member states. Indeed, organizations would be better placed to realize the desired mutual benefit if they had better information. Intelligence is only one potential information source. However, in many areas of international cooperation and hence for many international organizations, it is difficult to see why members would need to resort to covert means (intelligence) to collect data for the organization.

In other contexts, it is all too obvious why members would. If an antidumping case comes before the World Trade Organization, it is in the interests of both parties to manage the data to improve their own case, to the extent of not being absolutely forthright in explaining all the facts as they are and selectively omitting some information. Naturally, it could be in the other party's interests to expose by any means, including intelligence, facts favorable to itself that the first party has suppressed. But, in this case, the organization need never know that the information comes from intelligence sources.

The organization is more likely to need to receive and use intelligence

• when it is responsible for taking implementing actions in member state(s);
• when the organization has the teeth to act on intelligence in the furtherance of fulfilling its mandate; and
• when the value to states in cheating derives from not getting caught and hence when there is high opportunity cost to being caught. In such cases, the cheat, in order not to get caught, would be prepared to take steps to thwart or mislead the organization's own information-gathering means. (If it were not concerned about getting caught, as is the case in many human rights or humanitarian situations, the cheat would not see value in such efforts.)

For the organization to be likely to receive intelligence, states would need to see benefits from channeling their national intelligence through the organization, rather than acting on it directly themselves. In other words, the states would have to consider the organization as being better placed to achieve, through fulfilling the organization's mandate, that state's national objectives or believe that sharing intelligence through the organization would result in synergies that, when acted upon by the organization, would derive greater benefit for the state's national objectives than could be obtained by other means, should the state withhold the intelligence. An example would be an organization with access to the target country or a legal mandate that the individual state does not have and the ability to act on the intelligence effectively.

To date, the UN has not conducted many operations that meet all of these criteria, although that might have changed with the Security Council's willingness to consider enforcement and peacemaking actions (as opposed to peacekeeping, which only happens with the agreement of all parties). The main area of international relations where these two criteria might be met is that of arms control agreements and regional security arrangements, which have an executive secretariat responsible for implementing the verification procedures. This rules out all bilateral arrangements and agreements and those regional ones that rely solely on national resources for verification (such as Strategic Arms Reduction Talks and Conventional Forces in Europe). In the future, as states become increasingly aware of the stakes involved in environmental issues and if an international environmental monitoring agency with teeth is established, one could envisage this agency requiring access to intelligence.

For what follows, though, this chapter will concentrate on arms control and disarmament, as it is the area that most resembles the UNSCOM operation. Even here, there is virtually no precedent of an organization that meets both criteria. The IAEA Safeguards Division met these criteria: it was responsible for accounting for fissile material (except that in the military programs of the declared nuclear weapons powers) and the potential payoff for successful cheating was certainly high enough. But its inspection regime was based on bilaterally negotiated safeguards agreements. Although there were provisions for the IAEA to initiate "special inspections" of facilities suspected of being involved in nuclear activities but not declared and hence not subjected to safeguards inspections, these procedures had not been invoked prior to the establishment of UNSCOM, and the IAEA had little power to persist with inspections over the objections of the state to be inspected. And no state, even those with evidence that states were seeking to circumvent safeguards, had come forward to offer the IAEA intelligence about suspected sites. This resistance to sharing intelligence indicated a lack of belief on the state's part in the IAEA's ability to act effectively on the data—and a failure on the part of member states to fulfill their obligations to ensure that it could (Lord Caradon, again). Since its experience in Iraq, the IAEA has sought to incorporate many of the lessons stated below into its operations.

Other global arms control and disarmament agreements did not really have the degree of verification provisions that would meet the above criteria. The Convention on the Prohibition of the Development, Production and Stockpiling of Bacteriological (Biological) and Toxin Weapons, and on Their Destruction (BWC) basically dismissed the idea of a verification inspectorate as not being worthwhile (although, as discussed elsewhere in this volume, efforts are now underway to establish a BWC compliance regime that might include an inspectorate). The Chemical Weapons Convention (CWC) negotiations in Geneva did envisage a verification regime with powers of enforcement (at least until 1990, when the U.S. delegation, responding to congressional concerns about privacy and national security, emasculated President George Bush's own "anytime, anywhere" challenge inspection proposal). But this was still confined to the negotiating rooms at the time UNSCOM was established. Both regimes, if the members are intent on having effective verification, could benefit from UNSCOM's lessons in obtaining and using intelligence.

Benefits

International organizations receiving intelligence from national agencies can derive several major benefits:

- enhancement of the organization's ability to act effectively;
- involvement of member states more closely in the work of the organization and hence an increase in the likelihood that member states will meet their obligations to ensure that the organization has the resources and means to fulfill its mandate; and
- deterrence against cheating.

Management of the Process

Whether an organization receives support from member states is dependent on its credibility and on its dedication solely to the tasks for which it was established. To maintain member states' faith in the organization's credibility and integrity while receiving intelligence, the organization must

- have an independent and internationally respected ability to analyze incoming intelligence so that decisions to act on it are made by the organization, not the provider, and are seen to be made in the interests of fulfilling the organization's mandate, not some other agenda;

- concomitant with this, be seen to be able to filter out mis- and disinformation;
- be able to handle intelligence confidentially, so that providers are not embarrassed and hence deterred from further intelligence sharing;
- as an extension of the previous point, use intelligence only for the purposes of the organization's mandate and in accordance with procedures mutually acceptable to both the organization and the provider and never trade in intelligence provided by one agency (in exchange for additional intelligence from another), even if it appears imperative to do so in order to obtain useful intelligence;
- have sufficient sources of intelligence to counter allegations of bias, a "critical mass" of sources below which most smaller states would believe that the organization was in the pocket of the principal suppliers of intelligence (i.e., the larger states) and above which all parties would think it to be in their interest to provide intelligence, so as not to be left out;
- be open to all potential providers of all types of intelligence in order to preclude allegations that there is within the organization a "rich man's club" of those nations with the privilege of providing intelligence because they are rich enough to afford expensive, sophisticated intelligence-gathering apparatus, such as satellites. True, the superpowers are likely to be better placed to provide intelligence on global issues than smaller states. But where their national interests are directly affected, these smaller states could still have a significant and useful input to make. Indeed, their interest in gathering and hence their ability to provide intelligence might be greater than that of the superpowers.

In conclusion, there are situations, but these are not universal, where being able to obtain and act upon intelligence can make a vital difference in the ability of an international organization to succeed in its mandate—to the benefit of the international community as a whole.

NOTE

1. As the book goes to press, UNSCOM was no longer permitted to enter Iraq and discussions were proceeding in the UN Security Council on approaches for restarting inspections in Iraq. As it looks, UNSCOM will be dissolved and its responsibilities will be taken on by a not yet created UN agency.

11

Bioethics and the Prevention of Biological Warfare

RITA R. COLWELL AND RAYMOND A. ZILINSKAS

The United Nations Special Commission (UNSCOM) and the International Atomic Energy Agency (IAEA), both of which report to the United Nations Security Council, have described the extent and sophistication of Iraq's efforts to acquire weapons of mass destruction (WMD) (UN Security Council, 1995b; UNSCOM, 1999a). These included biological, chemical, and nuclear weapons as well as long-range ballistic missiles developed to serve as delivery systems. Iraq's WMD program was based on advanced engineering capability and strong research and development (R&D) efforts in the biological, chemical, and nuclear sciences. Although our main focus in this chapter is biological warfare (BW), some of the concepts presented and conclusions drawn also apply to Iraq's chemical, nuclear, and engineering capabilities.

UNSCOM reported to the Security Council that Iraq manufactured large quantities of microbial agents and toxins for use as BW agents (UN Security Council, 1995a, 1995b, 1996, 1997; Technical Evaluation Meeting, 1998). These reports made it clear that some Iraqi microbiologists collaborated with military engineers to develop and produce biological weapons systems, including artillery shells, bombs, ballistic missiles, rockets, and aerosol spray devices. BW agents were developed and produced at what were officially portrayed as civilian facilities that employed many Iraqi bioscientists (Barkho, 1995; Barton, 1998). However, since the Iraqi government has made extraordinary efforts to protect its weapons of mass destruction, UNSCOM's knowledge of the Iraqi BW program certainly is incomplete (Ritter, 1999).

Since most of Iraq's biological facilities escaped undamaged from Desert Storm and continue to be led by the same scientific administrators and operated by the same staff members as before the war, it is justifiable to have concerns about future directions of bioscience R&D in Iraq.[1] To secure peace over the long term, we must look beyond UNSCOM, whose presence in Iraq is temporary,[2] and find ways to redirect biological science R&D in Iraq toward peaceful civilian goals, reintegrate Iraqi weapons scientists into the international scientific community, and inculcate Iraqi scientists and scientists-in-training with a professional ethic commensurate with humanitarian values. The question is, how can this be done most effectively and expeditiously?

In Iraq, as in other cases when nations sought to acquire BW capability, scientists, not generals, may have been the most active promoters of the biological weapons acquisition program. The implications of this observation for the international science community are discussed and analyzed in this chapter. Specifically, four questions are considered. First, in general, why do scientists become promoters of biological weaponry, and what are the ethical implications of their activity? Second, how did Iraqi bioscientists come to apply their skills to biological weapons development? Third, what can be done to reintegrate Iraqi scientists into the international scientific community? Fourth, how can members of the scientific community prevent colleagues from fostering BW? The chapter concludes with some observations on the prevention of BW.

BIOSCIENTISTS AND NATIONAL BW PROGRAMS: CASE HISTORIES AND ETHICAL IMPLICATIONS

Its own bioscientists may have initiated Iraq's BW program. During an interview with a German reporter, General Amir Muhammad Rashid, present oil minister of Iraq and former head of the National Monitoring Directorate (the agency that coordinates all Iraqi government activities vis-à-vis UNSCOM), suggested that during the 1980s various experts came up with ideas as to how the Iran-Iraq War, which at the time seemed to be dragging on interminably, might be brought to a quick conclusion (Harrer, 1995). One of the suggestions offered was to develop biological weapons. UNSCOM noted that in 1982 or 1983, "a prominent Iraqi microbiologist wrote a report expressing his concerns on scientific developments relating to biological warfare agents and suggesting that research in this area be commenced in Iraq" (UN Security Council, 1995a: 22). This scientist was subsequently identified as Nassir Hindawi, reportedly a microbiologist by training. He had supposedly been jailed because he was caught trying to leave Iraq illegally while carrying documents (Miller, 1998a).

The impact of Hindawi's report, which was addressed to the ruling Ba'athist Party, cannot be determined. However, the Muthanna State

Establishment (MSE), Iraq's premier chemical weapons facility, commenced BW research shortly afterward, in 1985. It remained the lead agency in biological weapons development until a dedicated BW research laboratory was opened in the Technical Research Center at Salman Pak in 1987. Rihab Rashid Taha has been identified as the head of Iraq's BW program (George, 1995; Safire, 1995; Smith, 1997). Taha earned a Ph.D. at East Anglia University, United Kingdom, and the subject of her doctoral thesis was a toxin produced by a plant pathogen (George, 1995).

If the hypothesis that key Iraqi scientists were promoters of the BW program is correct, developments in Iraq related to acquisition of biological weapons are similar to what is known to have occurred in the past in other countries: namely, that scientists used their influence to encourage military and political leaders to acquire biological weapons for national arsenals. Examples of countries where this occurred include Japan, the Soviet Union, South Africa, Canada, the United Kingdom, and the United States.

In the case of Japan, Ishii Shiro, a specialist in infectious diseases and public health (who later became an army general), was largely responsible for Japan's BW program. Ishii began a campaign in the early 1920s to induce the Japanese military to acquire biological weapons, an effort that ultimately proved somewhat successful. Of all the combatant nations in World War II, Japan operated the largest BW program and was the only one to have used biological weapons in the field (Williams and Wallace, 1989; Yoshio, 1992; Harris, 1994). It is ironic that many of the scientists who took an active part in Japan's BW program were to return to civilian pursuits without having to atone for their sometimes gruesome work and that a substantial number of them attained high positions in academia and industry (TVS Production, 1985).

Little is known about the history of the former Soviet Union's BW program. One source cites evidence that military experts may have initiated such a program in the mid-1920s (Geissler, 1996). A German assessment of Soviet biological and chemical weapons programs performed during World War II stated that Joseph Stalin ordered the institution of a BW program in 1939 (Hirsch, 1951), but precisely who suggested this to him is not known. However, sometime in the late 1970s, it appears that Yuri Ovchinnikov, then vice president of the Union of the Soviet Socialist Republics (USSR) Academy of Sciences and director of the USSR Academy of Sciences' M. M. Shemyakin Institute of Bio-organic Chemistry, initiated an advanced program to develop biological weapon agents using modern biotechnology, including genetic engineering (Kucewicz, 1990; Alibek, 1998a, 1998b, 1998c, 1999). His motivation, apparently, was to persuade the Ministry of Defense to sponsor research in genetics and molecular biology, fields that had, until then, been neglected in the USSR because of the influence of biologist Trofim D. Lysenko and his followers (Zilinskas, 1984). Reaching its peak in the late 1980s, the Soviet program was of substantial size, employing over 25,000 scientific and technical workers and encompassing more than thirty scientific institutes and five production plants (Leitenberg, 1991, 1996a). The existence of the program was a tightly kept secret, and civilian cover was used to conceal the purpose of its facilities. In 1992, President Boris Yeltsin acknowledged the existence of the program and ordered its cessation (Litovkin, 1992). However, the U.S. government, among others, has had, and continues to have, serious concerns about it remaining in operation in present-day Russia (ACDA, 1996b, 1997a, 1998).

The existence of South Africa's BW program has been revealed as a result of a series of hearings carried out by the Truth and Reconciliation Commission, an ad hoc government body that is investigating human rights abuses during the time of apartheid. It is clear from these revelations that South African scientists and medical doctors had important roles in that program and might have been its instigators. Wouter Basson (head of "Project Coast"—the former regime's chemical and biological warfare program), André Immelman (who worked under Basson as head of covert biological and toxin projects at the Roodeplaat Research Laboratory), and Niel Knobel (former surgeon general of the South African Medical Services and Basson's supervisor) appear to have run particularly unsavory projects (Netherlands Institute for Southern Africa, 1997; Beresford, 1998; Murphy, 1998; Potgieter, 1998; van Rensburg, 1998). However, because little is known about South Africa's BW program at the time of this writing, including the extent to which scientists participated in it, only a few aspects of it are noted in this chapter.

Because of the influence of Frederick Banting, corecipient of the Nobel Prize for the discovery of insulin, BW research had begun in Canada even before the larger programs of the United Kingdom and the United States were launched. In 1937, Banting stated that in the eventuality of war, Germany, Italy, and Japan would use tetanus, rabies, and gangrene pathogens, snake venom, or botulinum toxins as weapons (Bryden, 1989). At the beginning of World War II, believing his worst fears were about to be realized, he wrote, "It is a war of scientist against scientist. This war above all in history will be one in which the application of science to warfare will give one side or the other the advantage" (Bryden, 1989: 34).

Acting on this premise, Banting was instrumental in raising money from private sources to begin Canada's BW research program. This effort, which began in 1940, was designed to study "the spread of infectious diseases from aeroplanes and shells" (Bryden, 1989: 43). After consultations among Banting and scientists from the Connaught Laboratories and the University of Toronto on which microorganisms would be most appropriate for warfare, the Canadians decided to develop psittacosis (parrot fever), a zoonotic agent that can be spread by aerosol, as a biological weapon.

In both the UK and the United States, respected scientific organizations, the Royal Society and the U.S. National Academy of Sciences (NAS), respectively, set up committees in 1942 and 1943 to study BW. Both organizations recommended that their countries acquire biological weapons, if for no other reason than to counter what they wrongly perceived to be a significant German program (U.S. Department of the Army, 1977a; Bernstein, 1988). (It should be noted, however, that the UK Medical Research Council was adamantly opposed to biological weapons R&D throughout the war.)

On both sides of the Atlantic, respected scientists promoted biological weapons research. In England, Paul Fildes (fellow of the Royal Society and director of the Medical Research Council Unit in Bacterial Chemistry at the Bland Sutton Institute) and his deputy, D. W. W. Henderson, formed the Biology Department at Porton Down in 1940 (Carter, 1992a, 1992b). There are suggestions that British scientists working at Porton Down, which was the UK's major biological and chemical weapons research and testing facility, favored first use of anthrax-based biological weapons against Germany in 1944 (Bernstein, 1987a). Although initially Prime Minister Winston Churchill supported the idea, logistical problems prevented the British from using biological weapons against the Germans before the war in Europe ended (Bernstein, 1987a).

In the United States, Secretary of War Henry L. Stimson requested that the NAS consider biological warfare. In response, the NAS formed the War Bureau of Consultants (WBC) Committee composed of nine prominent scientists from Rockefeller University, University of Wisconsin, Yale University, and other institutions (Bernstein, 1987b). In February 1942, the WBC Committee issued its report, which recommended that the United States take steps to defend itself against biological weapons by developing appropriate vaccines and protecting water supplies. In addition, the WBC Committee recommended research to develop an offensive biological capability (Cochrane, 1947; Bernstein, 1988). Stimson responded by forming the War Research Service (WRS) to coordinate and supervise the U.S. biological warfare program (Department of the Army, 1977a). In June 1942, George W. Merck, a chemist and president of Merck and Company, was named director of the WRS; eight highly respected scientists were appointed as members. By 1943, twenty-eight major U.S. research universities had been contracted by the WRS to undertake BW-related research, including offense-directed research on anthrax at Harvard University and botulinum toxin at Cornell University and the University of Wisconsin (Bernstein, 1988).

Why did scientists advocate BW acquisition in these cases, and what are the ethical implications? Theodore Rosebury, a microbiologist at Columbia University and an early participant in the U.S. BW program, considered ethical issues associated with the subject (Rosebury, 1949, 1963).

He wrote that most scientists accepted the necessity of doing such work because of the Axis threat. In that way, they "resolved the ethical question just as other equally good men resolved the same question at Oak Ridge and Hanford and Chicago and Los Alamos" (Rosebury, 1963). However, as noted by historian Barton J. Bernstein (1988: 514):

> What Rosebury and the others never understood was that the fateful deci-
> sions about the atomic bomb, as well as biological warfare, were made at
> a much higher level than the laboratory. The ultimate decision-makers
> were civilian leaders and military chieftains in Washington. The scientists
> provided the necessary expertise to conceive and develop the weapons,
> and even to suggest how to deploy them, but they had no controlling
> authority, and even little influence, over when, and under what political
> conditions, the weapons would be used.

Military leaders often know little about biological weapons, at least about the science involved. Generally, those who do become informed about BW are not impressed with the military utility of these weapons. Commanders tend to view them as troublesome to incorporate into a force structure; difficult to integrate into weapons systems already deployed or in the planning stages; and likely to be unpredictable, unreliable, and uncontrollable. For these reasons, military commanders have rarely promoted national programs for biological weapons development.

Since biological weapons essentially have no constituency, other than at most a fairly small group of scientists, it has been relatively easy for governments to eliminate BW programs if it was politically expedient to do so. For example, President Richard M. Nixon experienced no detectable political backlash after he ordered the U.S. defense and intelligence establishments to stop all offensive BW research, development, and production and to destroy all existing stocks of biological and toxin warfare agents (Nixon, 1969, 1970, 1971).[3] In fact, his administration received praise for taking this step. Further, Nixon's initiative provided a significant boost to the international efforts under way at the time to draft what became the 1972 Convention on the Prohibition of the Development, Production and Stockpiling of Bacteriological (Biological) and Toxin Weapons, and on Their Destruction (BWC), which led to the elimination of BW programs in most of the world (ACDA, 1990). As of May 3, 1997, 159 governments had signed the BWC; of these, 141 had ratified the treaty (ACDA, 1997b).

Historically, there have been two distinct phases to bioscientists' involvement in biological warfare activities. The first phase began before World War II and ended in 1969 for U.S. scientists and in 1975 for scientists of the rest of the world. The second phase began in 1969 or 1975 and continues. During the first phase, international law and mores allowed scientists to perform investigative and developmental work that culminated in biological weapons. Although it is true that personal ethics of some scientists led them, individually, to decline to take part in BW-related work, more commonly, biological scientists, like scientists in the nuclear and chemical fields, agreed willingly to partake in weapons-related R&D. We discern that there was a combination of reasons why scientists made this choice, including:

• Scientific interest: Scientists and medical doctors interested in infectious diseases often found it simple to shift the focus of their research from disease processes and development of defensive and preventive measures against infectious diseases to the development of infectious and toxin agents for destructive purposes.

• Scientific challenge: Linked with scientific interest is scientific challenge; that is, scientists were intrigued by the challenge of developing agents and processes for applications that may never have been intended by nature. As is made clear in Part 1 of this volume, there are immense technical difficulties inherent in biological weapons development, which some scientists might have found satisfying to solve.

• Remuneration and other perquisites: Although scientists in Canada, the UK, and the United States who became involved in biological weapons development did not benefit significantly compared to colleagues who remained in civilian life (in fact, some willingly took pay cuts), scientists in totalitarian countries who took part in weapons-related research reaped more economic benefits than did their colleagues in the civilian sector. In Japan during World War II, for example, scientific participants in that country's BW program received significantly higher pay than civilian colleagues, had greater opportunities for performing research in state-of-the-art facilities, and had access to the best equipment and abundant supplies. The situation was similar in the Soviet Union; scientists working in institutes supported by the military had access to equipment and supplies that civilian scientists could only dream about (Alibek, 1998a).

• Job security: In general, employment in government agencies has been considered more secure than in private laboratories. Further, while recognizing that it is difficult to measure excellence and scientific productivity, some scientists hold the opinion, valid or not, that their colleagues performing classified work are of secondary rank; that is, the lack of scientific prowess is easier to conceal when one does not have to expose one's work to peer review and open publication. Biological weapons development typically is a mundane process, calling for engineering skills rather than scientific insight. Therefore, scientists possessing secondary skills might be drawn to this kind of work. (This supposition does not hold true in situations of national emergency because at those times governments call for the services of their nations' foremost scientists.)

• National security: Historically, civilians have made their services available to governments in times of national emergency. Similarly, scientists of all rank have demonstrated their allegiance by doing what their governments call upon them to do, including designing and developing both better offensive weapons and defenses against attack. This fealty can remain in times of lesser stress; scientists often feel duty bound to continue working in defense-related jobs as long as they feel that the security of their country is under threat from proliferant nations and terrorists.

• Explicit and implicit threats: It is possible that there were scientists whose personal ethics would not allow them to take part in weapons-related research and development but who nevertheless were forced to do so after their governments had explicitly or implicitly threatened their, or their families', well-being or freedom. Such situations probably occurred in the Soviet Union under Joseph Stalin and in imperialist Japan.

At the end of the 1960s, several initiatives to abolish chemical and biological weapons were presented by governments and nongovernmental organizations, including scientific societies. A difficult and sometimes strident debate was conducted within the scientific community about the ethics of research on biological weapons. On one side of the debate were those who believed that such research, although legal, was immoral and that all scientists should refuse to participate. Some went as far as to circulate petitions in which the signers pledged to sever any connections with a scientist or institution undertaking BW-related R&D. This was a turbulent period for several scientific societies, including the American Society for Microbiology (ASM). At the annual meeting in 1968 there were discussions and heated debates on the appropriate role for ASM in BW research, particularly whether the ASM should continue its ad hoc Advisory Committee, a committee established in 1955 to advise the Army Chemical Corps on peer review and recruitment of scientific staff for Fort Detrick (Cassell, Miller, and Rest, 1992). Later that year the Advisory Committee was disbanded.

The BW debate continued, however. At its 1970 annual meeting, the ASM Council supported two relevant resolutions—one on secrecy and a second on President Nixon's orders to end the U.S. BW program:

> The Council of the American Society for Microbiology affirms that nonsecret research and free movement of scientists enhance the health of science.
>   Furthermore, the Council affirms support of President Nixon's action on November 25, 1969, and February 14, 1970, to end our involvement in the production and use of biological weapons. Because of our concern for humanitarian application of microbiological science we urge that all nations convert existing offensive biological warfare facilities to peaceful uses. (Cassell, Miller, and Rest, 1992: 232)

The turmoil over the BW issues experienced by the ASM undoubtedly also embroiled other professional societies at national and international levels.[4]

In 1975, the BWC entered into force, thereby becoming international law. In brief, it prohibits its member states (BWC state parties) from developing, producing, testing, and storing biological weapons; it also forbids them from transferring knowledge or technology relevant to biological weapons to non–BWC state parties and subnational groups. Although the BWC is binding on its state parties, it is commonly accepted that it also sets an ethical standard for scientists, namely, that microbiology should not be applied to develop biological weaponry and there can be no justification for any scientist to participate in R&D that aims to develop, produce, and test biological or toxin weapons. By definition, anyone who was to do so would break the law, becoming a criminal. Although nations that have not ratified the BWC technically are not bound by its strictures, scientists who are citizens of nonsignatory states must be guided by the moral force of the convention (Falk, 1986; Flowerree, 1992).

Some scientific activities, however, either are not covered by the BWC, or the treaty is unclear as to their legality. The BWC does not specifically mention "research"; therefore, it can be argued that all research is permissible, even if its findings were used for prohibited activities, such as the development and production of agents for offensive, military purposes. This omission creates serious problems for security experts attempting to verify whether nations are in compliance with the treaty since, under some circumstances, research cannot be differentiated from development. For example, if an outside analyst were to inspect a facility that developed a virus vaccine, when observing research activities that analyst would be faced with two difficult problems: (1) determining if research was aimed at developing an attenuated agent for a vaccine or a more virulent agent for BW and (2) ascertaining when the research phase ceases and the development phase commences (Huxsoll, Parrott, and Patrick, 1989). Further, as the BWC is worded, development and production of "small" quantities of BW agents are permitted if done for defensive purposes. The dilemma is that the BWC does not define what constitutes a "small" quantity, nor does it take into account modern fermentation methods, which enable a fermentation engineer to produce in a matter of days large quantities of many bacterial or toxin agents from small quantities of seed culture. Such loopholes can serve as a cover for unscrupulous scientists to carry out research leading directly to the development of offensive warfare agents. Such research is legal but cannot be considered ethical.

Deficiencies of the BWC, such as those noted above, have been debated in several forums. We refer, in particular, to the Twelfth Kühlungsborn Colloquium entitled "Prevention of a Biological and Toxin Arms Race and the Responsibility of Scientists" (Geissler and Haynes, 1991) and to a conference organized by the Center for Public Issues in Biotechnology at the

University of Maryland Biotechnology Institute entitled "The Microbiologist and Biological Defensive Research: Ethics, Politics, and International Security" (Zilinskas, 1992b). Our analysis of conference proceedings and of other articles and books contributing to the debate leads us to believe that, depending on where they work, scientists may find themselves in difficult and paradoxical situations. In the vast majority of countries that are parties to the BWC, scientists are prohibited from undertaking any activity deemed to be "development" if it is associated with the production of biological weaponry. However, they are permitted to undertake activities deemed to be "research" even if the findings ultimately may be useful for biological weapons development. They also are able to participate in development if the aim of the activity is defense against biological and other weapons, or if it involves only a "small" quantity (undefined) of BW agents.[5] Clearly, it may sometimes be difficult to differentiate between permitted and prohibited activities (Huxsoll, 1992).

Scientists who are citizens of nations outside the BWC face another type of paradox. Legally, they are not prohibited from undertaking biological weapons development and production; nevertheless, they are subject to the moral authority contained in the BWC (Falk, 1986; Flowerree, 1992). This moral authority, which is also articulated in codes of ethics promulgated by professional societies such as the ASM, can be stated simply: microbiology shall not be used in a way that is injurious to humans or the environment.

IRAQI BIOSCIENCE AND BIOLOGICAL WEAPONS

Iraq's former BW program is described in detail elsewhere (Zilinskas, 1997b; Smith, 1997; Broad and Miller, 1998). In this chapter, we consider what may have motivated Iraqi scientists who were involved and explore the mechanisms that the international scientific community might use to prevent recurrence of such a situation elsewhere.

Factors influencing scientists in other nations who in the past contributed to BW R&D may also have applied, with variations specific to the case, to Iraqi scientists. The factors we suggest were most significant in the Iraqi case are as follows:

• Professional challenge: Undoubtedly there were some Iraqi scientists whose professional interests included diseases caused by pathogens and/or toxins. These persons might, for example, have been performing research on organisms and toxins that were selected by Iraq's BW program to be developed for weapons use. In such cases, the interests of scientists dovetailed with the objectives of the program, almost inevitably leading to the scientists' involvement. Similarly, a scientist working on specific organisms or toxins might have come to the realization that they would make effective weapons. Researchers' beliefs that their fields of study had military potential may explain investigations undertaken as part of Iraq's BW program on camel pox and aflatoxin (Zilinskas, 1997b).

• Personal enrichment: The Iraqi BW program was well supported by the government. The program was housed in new, fully equipped facilities, and its staff included a high proportion of doctoral-level scientists trained in industrialized countries. Iraq's main BW development and production plant, the Al-Hakam Single Cell Production Plant, exemplified this situation (Barkho, 1995). The scientists recruited to staff the program were well paid, had use of the best equipment and supplies available in the country, had access to foreign information sources as needed, and enjoyed other generous perquisites, including foreign travel. In a country where scientific research institutions in general were poorly supported, such inducements would have a strong attraction for scientists and engineers who otherwise would have faced the grim economic realities being experienced by other middle-level government scientists (Ibrahim, 1994).

• Implicit threats: Saddam Hussein's dictatorship is widely considered to be ruthless (al-Khalil, 1989). Scientists were subject to scrutiny by all three of the Iraqi security services—the Iraqi Intelligence Service, Special Security Organization, and Ba'athist Party Intelligence. It would have been difficult, therefore, for scientists to refuse to work in a program if the government directly ordered or "requested" them to do so. Further, all positions in universities and research institutions in Iraq are government positions. Permits to emigrate or undertake short-term travel are granted only if the applicant is deemed deserving (and can pay a high exit fee). For these reasons, those who might be brave enough to refuse to comply would, if they survived the refusal, find few, if any, work alternatives, limited emigration possibilities, and an uncertain future.

• Patriotism: Iraqis have been exposed for years to unrelenting propaganda describing their nation as surrounded by enemies. Israel, although not an immediate neighbor, is depicted as an evil usurper of Arab land and property; Iran is characterized as a historical rival and ever-present antagonist; and Saudi Arabia and Kuwait are portrayed as being governed by reactionary leaders whose aim is to impoverish Iraq. Faced with such seemingly implacable foes, average citizens are continually exhorted to do their duty to protect the nation. Some must serve in the armed forces, and others, notably those possessing special skills, must apply their talents as the government deems necessary. Many scientists may have believed adversaries wielding biological weapons threatened their country, a concept taken for granted by Iraqi leaders. When questioned by reporters, high-placed Iraqi officials have alluded to Israel possessing biological weapons and Iran being in the process of acquiring them (Lorieux, 1995). It is likely that some scientists participating in the BW program believed their political leaders' statements and, therefore, willingly contributed their skills to the national BW program.

• Legality of BW-related work: Iraq signed the BWC in 1975 but did not ratify the treaty until 1991, and then only after having accepted the cease-fire conditions imposed after the Gulf War by United Nations Security Council Resolution 687 (UN Security Council, 1991). A condition of the cease-fire was that the Iraqis had to agree to ratify the convention. By signing the convention in 1975, the government of Iraq had indicated its willingness to abide by treaty provisions and signaled its intent to ratify it.[6] However, the Iraqi government and its subjects were not legally obliged to adhere to the treaty until after ratification. Therefore, Iraqi scientists might argue that their involvement in Iraq's BW program was legal since it took place before the nation became a BWC state party.

• Ignorance of the BWC: Some scientists who were employed in the former Soviet Union's BW program claimed to have known nothing about the BWC; others knew of the treaty's existence but not its provisions (Alibek, 1998a). We do not know the extent of knowledge of the BWC among Iraq's scientists, but due to their isolation, many of them might have been as unaware of the treaty as once were their Soviet counterparts.

When comparing the reasons Iraqi scientists might have taken up biological weapons R&D with reasons scientists of other nations did so between 1940 and 1975, we find remarkable consistency. Three factors— professional challenge, personal enrichment, and patriotism—apply to all the cases we have considered. A fourth incentive, implicit threats, did not, as far as we are aware, influence bioscientists in the UK and the United States who participated in their nations' former BW programs. For all practical purposes, UK and U.S. scientists who declined to take up offensive BW work suffered no harm to their careers or personal well-being. That was not the case, however, in Japan before and during World War II or in the USSR from the 1930s through the Cold War years. There is ample evidence that Japanese scientists were forced to take part in BW R&D, including tests on humans, with threats of punishment if they refused (Williams and Wallace, 1989; Tsuneishi, 1982; Harris, 1994). Similar pressures may have been applied in the USSR, especially during the time of Joseph Stalin. So in this regard, the situation for Iraqi scientists was different from that of scientists in the UK and United States but probably similar to that faced by scientists in Japan and the former Soviet Union.

A comparison of Iraq's BW program with those in other countries reveals both similarities and differences relating to the fifth factor affecting the behavior of Iraqi scientists, that based on interpretations of international law. Recall that until the BWC came into force in 1975, offensive BW development, testing, and production were legal and morally acceptable activities. Only the use of these weapons in war was prohibited (by the 1925 Geneva Protocol). Since 1975, only the USSR among BWC state parties is known to have contravened the treaty by conducting a BW program (Smith, 1992b; Leitenberg, 1996a). Even if the convention technically did not apply to Iraq, its moral force should have influenced Iraqi scientists to forgo BW development and production. Therefore, the behavior of Iraqi scientists involved in the program differed from that of scientists in Western countries who more or less willingly abandoned offensive BW research after 1975, but was similar to that of Soviet scientists who participated in an illicit national BW program until 1992, when President Boris Yeltsin finally abolished it (Belitskiy, 1992; *Washington Post,* 1992).[7] Further, both Soviet and Iraqi scientists might have been unaware of the BWC and its prohibitions; thus, they might not have known that what they were doing was against international law.

Obviously, it is not a simple matter to condemn Iraqi scientists for their role in their nation's BW program. Most scientists in the same situation would find it difficult, perhaps impossible, to refuse orders couched in terms of national security and combined with implicit or explicit threats. Nevertheless, it is useful to learn from the Iraqi situation to develop strategies that may reduce or eliminate pressures on scientists to participate in illicit activities in the future.

REINTEGRATING IRAQI BIOSCIENTISTS INTO THE INTERNATIONAL SCIENTIFIC COMMUNITY

The immediate goal of the international community's intervention in the aftermath of the Gulf War was to prevent Iraq from reacquiring WMD capability. To this end, inspections to ensure compliance with UN sanctions and the imposition of import controls on dual-use equipment and supplies are the logical approaches to follow (UNSCOM, 1999b). But equally important in the long run are efforts to reach out to Iraqi scientists and bring them into the fold of the international scientific community (Zilinskas, 1998b). As in the case of eastern bloc scientists during the Cold War, establishing and maintaining communications with individual scientists are valuable ways to encourage acceptance of international norms by building shared values, mutual respect, and friendship.[8] Four approaches for achieving reintegration appear most promising: (1) bringing scientists together at international meetings for professional interchange, (2) fostering formal exchange visits and collaborations, (3) encouraging informal communications between Iraqis and foreign colleagues, and (4) imbuing

Iraqi scientists with an international ethic through discussions of professional ethics.

International Meetings

Regarding freedoms of scientists, the International Council of Scientific Unions (ICSU) states:

> As the intrinsic nature of science is universal, its success depends on cooperation, interaction and exchange, often beyond national boundaries. Therefore, ICSU strongly supports the principle that scientists must have free access to each other and to scientific data and information. It is only through such access that international scientific cooperation flourishes and science thus progresses. (ICSU, 1995)

In this spirit, every effort should be made to include scientists from Iraq (and, if possible, from other countries isolated from the world community, e.g., Iran, Libya, or Syria) in international scientific meetings. The lessons of the Cold War should apply; that is, the participation of scientists of all nations at all international conferences, colloquia, symposia, workshops, and other forums should be actively encouraged.

The effects of economic sanctions on Iraq have been devastating to Iraq's lower and middle economic classes (Ibrahim, 1994). Since most scientists in Iraq are middle-level government servants, they are in dire straits, working at wages too low to secure decent living standards for themselves and their families. Similarly, most scientific research institutions are barely functioning, beset by power outages, few or no expendable supplies, and equipment failures due to lack of spare parts. Even the most basic of daily supplies, such as soap, cannot be secured. This unfortunate situation is likely to persist for some time after economic sanctions are eased or lifted. Therefore, it is not too early to formulate proposals for public and private agencies and foundations to assist Iraqi scientists after international relations are restored. Providing opportunities for Iraqi scientists to pursue civilian research and interact with foreign colleagues would help UNSCOM, or its successor agency, convert military efforts into peacefully directed pursuits. We expect that the need for this type of assistance would diminish as Iraq's economy improves.

Formal Exchanges and Collaborations

Before Desert Shield and Desert Storm cut off communications between Iraqi scientists and the outside world, some of them had been permitted to collaborate with their foreign counterparts. Iraq had also been an active participant in the political process to establish the International Centre for

Genetic Engineering and Biotechnology (see next major section). We assume that once economic sanctions are lifted, similar opportunities for scientific collaborations between Iraqi and foreign scientists will reappear. If so, the international scientific community should be ready to support these endeavors in the overall effort to redirect Iraqi science to peaceful paths.

An appropriate framework for doing so is Article X of the BWC, which calls for international cooperation in applied microbiology. For several reasons, including lack of funding, Article X has yet to be activated (Zilinskas and Hedén, 1991). The lifting of sanctions against Iraq would be an opportune time to activate this provision and use it to facilitate the reentry of Iraqi scientists into the international scientific community. In particular, BWC state parties could fund reciprocal visits in which foreign scientists work at Iraqi research institutions, while scientists from Iraq visit laboratories in other countries. BWC state parties also should consider funding collaborative research projects between Iraqi and foreign laboratories, thus encouraging the development of longer-term associations.

Informal Communications Between Iraqi Scientists and Foreign Colleagues

Even before communications between Iraq and the rest of the world were severed in 1990, informal contacts between Iraqi scientists and foreign colleagues were rare. Even less common were publications by Iraqi scientists in international journals (Canada, 1991b).[9] Unless the ground is prepared now, this situation can be expected to continue for some time after economic sanctions are lifted, possibly leading to Iraqi scientists continuing to feel alienated from the international science community. To counter this tendency, electronic communications, including Internet and e-mail access, should be established to expand opportunities for Iraqi scientists to interact with foreign colleagues and enable them to access international databases. International teams of scientists that include Iraqis will be able to conduct original research and publish the results in internationally recognized publications. International technical assistance agencies, such as the United Nations Development Programme (UNDP), United Nations Educational, Scientific and Cultural Organization (UNESCO), and United Nations Industrial Development Organization (UNIDO) may be able to assist, although they could not act unless formally invited to do so by the Iraqi government. On the nongovernmental level, individual scientists and professional societies could help by prevailing on foundations and nongovernmental organizations to provide the necessary hardware and software support to Iraqi scientists and institutions.

Iraqi Scientists and Professional Conduct

As noted above, some Iraqi scientists probably provided a stimulus for establishing that nation's BW program. There is the risk that, if this pattern were repeated in the future, the scientists involved in international collaborations may misuse information and know-how gathered at international meetings or during visits to foreign laboratories.[10] Nevertheless, on balance, the reintegration of Iraqi scientists into the world community will lessen whatever propensity there might be to utilize knowledge and skills for military purposes. Reintegration would provide constructive avenues for Iraqi scientists to channel their creative energies. Furthermore, Iraqi scientists would be better prepared to resist demands to participate in programs to develop WMD if they had accepted the norms of the international scientific community. Therefore, the participation of Iraqi scientists and scientists-in-training at international forums that include discussions of ethics in science should be encouraged and supported.

THE ROLE OF SCIENTISTS IN PREVENTING BIOLOGICAL WARFARE

Bioscientists, especially microbiologists, grappled with ethical problems associated with BW in the 1960s and early 1970s. In 1975, when the BWC came into force, the problem appeared to have been solved, since the treaty forbade development and production of biological weapons and defined permitted and forbidden activities for scientists. However, biological weapons development and the role of scientists in such activity have reemerged as pressing problems for the international science community as national BW programs once again proliferate and terrorist groups become more likely to arm themselves with biological and toxin weapons. To aid scientists as they confront these issues, we suggest (1) including ethical conduct of science as a component of graduate training of scientists and (2) involving the scientific community directly in efforts to counter BW proliferation.

Ethics and the Training of Scientists

Very few graduate programs in the sciences currently include courses on ethical conduct of science or scientific professional standards. Scientists, therefore, are often unprepared to deal with demands to perform R&D that may contravene international law or generally accepted professional mores. Thus, it is important for the international scientific community to formulate model courses on professional conduct and ethics in science. Although any such course might eventually be offered by research universities throughout the world, an appropriate venue for such offerings might be the highly respected International Centre for Genetic Engineering and Biotechnology (ICGEB). The ICGEB has two components, one in New Delhi, India, and the other in Trieste, Italy. Since February 3, 1994, when Sri Lanka became the thirty-fourth country to ratify the international treaty creating the ICGEB, the center has been formalizing its status as an independent intergovernmental organization. As of 1996, forty countries had joined the ICGEB, and five were awaiting admittance (ICGEB, 1997).

Four major principles guide the ICGEB. First, the organization undertakes R&D on subject matters of high priority for developing countries, especially in areas where researchers in industrialized countries are doing little work. Second, the ICGEB trains scientific and technical personnel from member countries in the advanced techniques of biotechnology. Third, the center provides technical assistance for member countries in establishing and operating national biotechnology centers affiliated with the ICGEB, where R&D of importance to the home nation is performed and local training programs are conducted. Fourth, the ICGEB serves as a central exchange for scientific and technical material, collecting information from books, journals, and databases and sending it to affiliated centers and member governments. In addition, ICGEB offers courses on subjects such as molecular genetics of yeast, computer applications in molecular biology, bacterial genetics, human genetics, techniques in genome research, and environmental biosafety. It would clearly be appropriate for the ICGEB to expand its curriculum by offering courses on ethical conduct of science.

The content of a professional ethics course can be developed effectively by the ICSU; guidance can also be found in publications of the NAS (NAS, 1995) and the Sigma Xi National Honor Society (Sigma Xi, 1993). There are other examples of ethics courses in France, Japan, the UK, and other nations. Curricula may include discussion of a range of issues associated with professional standards, including problems of falsification of data, plagiarism, unsound research practices, and research that contravenes international law.

It could be argued that ethical training would do little for scientists who are coerced by brutal regimes to participate in illicit R&D. Although this may be the case, scientists imbued with a strong sense of ethics who find themselves in this difficult situation might be more likely to try to slow down progress of unethical activities and act as whistle-blowers as opportunities appear than those with little or no training in the ethical conduct of science.

Scientists and BW Counterproliferation

The involvement of scientists and their professional societies in biological arms control processes can be useful in providing technical advice to agencies responsible for the development and monitoring of international arms control treaties and implementation of conforming national legislation. In the United States, two societies have been notably active in performing this function—the ASM and the Federation of American Scientists (FAS).

The ASM, through its Biological Warfare Task Force, has been providing technical assistance to the U.S. government on matters such as legislation that implements the BWC for U.S. nationals and companies and the safe interstate transfer of biological and toxin agents (Atlas and Goldberg, 1993; U.S. Department of Health and Human Services, 1996; Berns et al., 1998). In 1990, the FAS formed a Working Group on Biological and Toxin Weapons Verification to analyze measures for strengthening the BWC and verifying compliance with the treaty. The working group sets up smaller expert groups, as necessary, to investigate technical issues related to verification activities. The working group has published reports pertaining to sampling, microorganism identification, technical cooperation under the BWC's Article X, and other issues that faced the third conference to review the operation of the BWC (FAS, 1990, 1991, 1994, 1995b, 1995c, 1996a). Moreover, the FAS not only publishes technical reports but also works hard to ensure that these reports reach members of national delegations participating in international meetings related to the BWC. Professional societies in countries other than the United States may wish to become similarly involved in political processes related to biological arms control.

Another means by which the scientific community can aid in this regard is for civilian specialists to become involved in the work of national or international agencies responsible for controlling biological weapons proliferation and detecting BW programs (Zilinskas and Hedén, 1991). Since relatively few scientists have expertise in specialized fields such as endo- or exotoxins, specific arboviral strains, or aerobiology, intelligence and security analysts may be unable to analyze technical developments in these fields to differentiate between research intended for development of a vaccine and research to produce an agent suitable for BW. Civilian scientists, working in close cooperation with security analysts, can be helpful in evaluating work in these specialized areas. UNSCOM, for example, employs civilian and military experts to assess and evaluate the work of Iraqi scientists (*Pacific Research,* 1996). This type of collaboration can be equally effective in other international arms control endeavors.

On the international level, the Pugwash Conference on Science and World Affairs has been involved in biological and chemical warfare issues since its founding in 1957 (Perry Robinson, 1998; Kaplan, 1999). Organizers of the Pugwash conference have been able to bridge ideological gaps by bringing together scientists from different political and social systems in neutral settings. Although the major focus of Pugwash has been on nuclear weapons, between 1959 and 1998 it convened forty-two meetings dedicated to biological and chemical arms control (Kaplan, 1999). It was the recipient of the Nobel Peace Prize in 1995. It can be expected that Pugwash will continue its activities that aim to counter the proliferation and use of weapons of mass destruction; it could play a valuable future role by including scientists from nations such as Iraq and North Korea in its activities.

CONCLUSION

Biological weapons acquired by aggressive national leaders and terrorist organizations will continue to pose a serious threat to international security for the foreseeable future. Although access to pathogenic strains of microorganisms and toxic materials is restricted, covert traffic in such material is as difficult to control as traffic in illegal drugs. In addition, international travel of scientists qualified to perform applied microbiological research is not restricted; thus, desperate or unprincipled microbiologists may sell their services to those willing to pay for work to develop biological weaponry (*Science,* 1996). The sophistication of modern research in microbiology and its applications makes it difficult to determine whether a given set of scientific activities is legitimate or related to biological weapons acquisition. Further, as demonstrated by Aum Shinrikyo's scientific programs, small-scale BW R&D undertaken to support terrorism or other illegal endeavors can easily be concealed (Taylor, 1996; Henderson, 1999). Although these trends cannot be reversed, the bioscientific community nevertheless can do its part in the effort to limit proliferation of biological weaponry. Most important, scientists in democratic countries can take the lead in promoting the development of mutual trust and friendship among all their professional colleagues at both national and international meetings and by way of person-to-person communication to ensure a shared commitment by all microbiologists to the health and well-being of humankind. In addition, where appropriate, scientists can apply their special skills and knowledge to assist governments and intergovernmental organizations in strengthening international biological arms control activities.

NOTES

1. Iraq's premier biological weapons development and production plant, the Al-Hakam Single Cell Production Plant, escaped unharmed from Desert Storm. However, it was totally demolished by Iraqi workers under UNSCOM supervision during May-June 1996. Although its most important attribute, namely its human resources, was dispersed, it easily could be reassembled should the government so command (Zilinskas, 1997b).

2. As this book goes to press, UNSCOM is no longer able to operate in Iraq. However, it is most probable that eventually an accord will be reached between the UN Security Council and the Iraqi government that will include provisions for inspecting Iraq's biological, chemical, missile, and nuclear facilities. Whether inspectors will be working under the authority of UNSCOM or a yet to be determined agency makes little difference in regard to the thrust of this chapter (i.e., there will be a need for methods to reintegrate Iraqi scientists into the international scientific community).

3. Anti-BW activities conducted by scientists and their professional societies significantly influenced President Nixon's decision; see Geissler and Haynes (1991).

4. In 1985 the society published a code of ethics (ASM, 1985). Although BW is not mentioned in the code, it has two applicable provisions:

Microbiologists . . . will discourage any use of microbiology contrary to the welfare of humankind. . . . Microbiologists are expected to communicate knowledge obtained in their research through discussions with their peers and through publication in the scientific literature.

Note should also be made of how industry in the United States views the issue of BW. Thus, the foremost industrial interest organization, the Biotechnology Industry Organization (BIO), adopted a statement of principles in 1997 that includes the following:

We respect the power of biotechnology and apply it only for the benefit of mankind. We will pursue applications of biotechnology that promise to save lives or improve the quality of life. We will avoid applications of our technology that would infringe upon human rights or carry risks that outweigh the potential benefits. . . .
We oppose the use of biotechnology to develop weapons. We support the Biological Weapons Convention, a treaty signed by the United States and many other nations banning the development of biological weapons. We will not undertake any research intended for use in developing, testing or producing such weapons. (BIO, 1997)

5. The issue of whether research and development to defend against biological weapons is ethical has caused considerable controversy among scientists and their professional societies. The statement by philosopher Douglas MacLean (1992) offers a useful premise for decision:

Defensive BW research is not the same as offensive BW research, even if they are indistinct in their earliest stages. The claim that defensive BW research inevitably supports offensive BW programs is empirically false. Defensive BW research cannot be morally prohibited for this reason.

6. Article 18 of the Vienna Convention on the Law of Treaties, which the United States recognizes as a codification of customary international law, includes the following language:

A State is obliged to refrain from acts which would defeat the object and purpose of a treaty when: (a) it has signed the treaty or has exchanged instruments constituting the treaty subject to ratification, acceptance or approval, until it shall have made its intentions clear not to become a party to the treaty.

7. There are indications that work contravening the BWC may be continuing in Russia (Smith, 1992a; ACDA, 1996b, 1997a). If so, scientific personnel involved in that work would be contravening both national and international law.

8. For a thorough discussion of the roles of scientists in mitigating discords between nations, see de Cerreño and Keynan, 1998.

9. This situation was similar to that pertaining to developing countries generally; that is, comparatively few scientists from developing countries publish in international journals. Several reasons can be offered, including rudimentary level science or problems of language and costs, such as page charges. The inability of developing country scientists to publish internationally prevents those in the industrialized world from knowing scientists in the Third World and learning of their research and, simultaneously, promotes a sense of isolation on the part of scientists in developing countries.

10. This concern, of course, is equally worrisome when considering scientists from the several countries identified as possessing BW programs (U.S. Congress, 1993c).

Conclusion

RAYMOND A. ZILINSKAS

Advances achieved in the biosciences since the early 1970s have profoundly affected most fields of human endeavor. Scientists have used newly discovered genetic and molecular biology techniques to unravel and understand many previously unknown processes that define life in humans,
animals, plants, and microorganisms; some of these findings have been
applied to improve agricultural yields, develop and produce unique pharmaceuticals and specialty chemicals, and restore the environment. In fact,
so much new knowledge has been gained and so many unique applications
have been generated within a comparatively short time that many speak of
a "biotechnology revolution" having occurred and, as the twenty-first century commences, of our society entering an "era of biology."

When most of us think of revolutionary advances and anticipate the era
of biology, we are, of course, contemplating pursuits that will benefit all of
humanity. But is it possible that persons or entities may develop and apply
findings from biosciences research for their benefit and in doing so deliberately seek to injure or kill people, animals, or plants? In other words, is it
possible that there is a dark side to modern biosciences, in which the powers of the new biotechnologies are applied for purposes of war, terrorism,
and criminality?

Of course, the history of warfare demonstrates that microbiological
techniques have been applied to develop and produce biological weapons.
Further, these techniques were the same as those developed by industry and
applied for civilian purposes. We must assume that a similar progression is
occurring now and will continue in the future, that is, that the newly developed molecular biology techniques, presently used in research to extend the
frontiers of knowledge and in industry to develop and produce new

247

processes and products, will be used to fight wars, terrorize, and perpetrate crimes. Advanced biotechnologies, including genetic engineering, already have been used by scientists who operated the Soviet Union's research in biological warfare (BW) that aimed to enhance the military value of classical BW agents and develop new strains of microorganisms. Similarly, the Japanese sect Aum Shinrikyo employed at least one molecular biologist in its program to develop biological weapons. However, as far as is known, neither of these two BW programs had actually deployed biological weapons containing genetically engineered microorganisms. In fact, the mainstays of both were "traditional" or wild pathogens and toxins, agents that had been developed and produced through the application of classical microbiological research and production methods. Similarly, Iraq's BW program was entirely based on traditional agents and methods. This implies that although advanced biotechnological techniques are used in BW-related research, to date there have been no practical results from such research.

When I began this project, I hypothesized that the work by Soviet and Aum Shinrikyo scientists would be likely to serve as precedents for other nations and groups. In other words, ongoing and future BW programs, whether operated by a government or subnational group, would attempt to apply advanced biotechnologies in research to perfect agents for use in biological weapons but would depend on classical biotechnologies to actually get the work done. However, a corollary to this hypothesis is that sometime in the not-too-distant future, the advanced technologies will become ever more important to BW programs and eventually will be used by weapons scientists to develop and produce agents particularly well suited for biological weapons. Thus the question is, are we almost there, or do we have some time before the full impact of advanced biotechnologies on BW is realized?

With this question in mind, I asked the contributors to this volume to consider the extent to which the advanced biotechnologies presently affect the topics they address and what might be expected for the future. From their writings, I have attempted to estimate how advanced biotechnologies have affected or will affect biological weapons development and their use by military forces and terrorists; methods whereby nations and societies defend themselves against biological weapons; and international biological arms control.

BIOLOGICAL WEAPONS DEVELOPMENT AND USE

From the information presented in Part 1, I estimate that it will be at least five years before scientists working for proliferant governments or subnational groups will be able to apply the new biotechnologies so as to qualitatively change biological weapons development and usage. However, after approximately five years we can expect major advances in two weapons-related developments: (1) "improving" wild microbial species for weapons use and (2) enabling better "targeting."

Engineering Wild Species

By about 2005, military scientists will have gained sufficient knowledge to genetically engineer a bacterial or viral species to overcome the severe technical limitations that limit the utility of "wild" microorganisms for use in weapons. These limitations, generally ascribing biological weapons as being undependable, unpredictable, and uncontrollable, are believed to cause military commanders to shun them. Thus, as far as I am aware, in the past, no biological weapons system has ever been included in plans made by the military for force structure or operations. However, if weapons scientists were able to design and produce virulent bacteria and viruses that could be depended on to fulfill strategic and tactical objectives with at least as much certainty as chemical weapons, the military's attitude toward biological weapons would likely change. For example, if it was possible for military scientists to genetically engineer a virulent bacterium so that it attacked only young males and, further, died after having undergone a set number of divisions, this bacterium would be largely predictable and controllable. Then, if field-testing demonstrated that it also was dependable, the military would be likely to include this system in its force structure.

Scientists in the Soviet Union's BW programs appear to have genetically engineered various types of bacteria and viruses for military ends. A former assistant director of Biopreparat (the cover name for the civilian component of the Soviet Union's BW program), Ken Alibek, tells of research that produced a hybrid virus strain containing genetic characteristics of the smallpox and Ebola viruses (Alibek, 1999). The reason why this research was undertaken has not been made clear, but it could be that the Biopreparat scientists sought to combine in one virus certain desirable characteristics of both—the smallpox virus's hardiness and ability to spread via aerosol and the Ebola virus's extreme virulence. Even if the Soviet Union's BW program had not reached the point where it could field the smallpox-Ebola hybrid virus in a weapons system, it nevertheless gives an indication of how the advanced biotechnologies might be applied to develop microbial strains uniquely suited for weapons.

Targeting Specific Groups

When the Human Genome Project is completed, sometime before 2005, the 80,000 to 100,000 genes constituting the human genome will have been mapped. Already data generated by the Human Genome Project have given rise to a new scientific field called genomic information technology, more commonly known as functional genomics. Functional genomics attempts to correlate the activity of a gene with specific functions, such as protein production, disease processes, and signaling between body cells. By using functional genomics, scientists are also beginning to clarify how genes interact with one another, interactions that probably constitute the molecular basis of health and disease.

If we accept that information can be used for good or bad, another area of concern is the possibility that bioweaponeers will utilize functional genomics to identify genetic markers possessed by populations of interest to them. There has been the occasional article in the arms control literature about so-called ethnic weapons, that is, weapons targeted to affect only a population possessing a specific genetic marker. But such ideas have seemed farfetched until now. At the present state of knowledge, we do not know how to genetically differentiate one human population (say, an Australian Aborigine) from another (say, a Maya Indian). The genetic differences between the two are so small that present-day scientific techniques cannot detect them. Yet, we can infer that they are genetically unlike because they evidence more differences than can be explained by environmental effects, for example, the types and number of hereditary diseases that afflict them. It is not farfetched to hold that soon sufficient data will become available from the Human Genome Project to enable researchers to identify genetic differences between populations. This knowledge will be exceedingly useful to those who are attempting to devise better ways to prevent, diagnose, and treat disease. However, referring again to the dark side of biotechnology, it might also be utilized by those who harbor ill will toward a population group and who will try to design biological or toxin agents that selectively harm only that designated population.

As this book was being written in late 1998 and early 1999, press reports appeared that accused Israel of working on biological weapons that would target Arabs without hurting Jews and of biological studies done by white South African scientists to identify genetic characteristics of black Africans. Although these allegations were denied by the respective governments, the notion of an ethnic weapon was given credence by the British Medical Association's 1999 report *Biotechnology, Weapons and Humanity.* Although one of the report's conclusions was that an ethnic weapon was not a practical possibility at this time, it did say that genetic differences between populations do exist and are being identified. Therefore, the report concludes, it would be complacent to assume that ethnic weapons would never be developed in the future.

NATIONAL BIOLOGICAL DEFENSE AND RESPONSE

The major reason why both our military and civilian populations are vulnerable to biological attacks is that we lack the means to accurately detect pathogens and toxins in a timely manner. Thus, a crucial question is, will the biosciences produce biological and toxin detectors capable of functioning in real time, that is, devices that immediately signal the act of having captured a pathogen or toxin particle from the environment? Without having real-time detectors in place and immediately available at all times, a military formation cannot know when it is under biological attack, nor can a civilian population know that a bioterrorist attack is underway. In either case, the fact of a biological attack having occurred would not become manifest until days later, when hundreds to thousands of sick victims present themselves to aid posts or emergency rooms.

The answer is that no application of advanced biotechnologies is likely to become available within five years that would enable analysts to detect and identify pathogens and toxins in real time. Now, as in the past and for the foreseeable future, the mainstay of clinical and public health laboratories will be classical techniques that allow investigators to identify bacterial species in a few days and viruses in days to months. Therefore, the best way to defend against biological attack is to be forewarned, which is unlikely unless good intelligence is received in a timely manner by military or civilian authorities. Inherent to this conclusion is that intelligence agencies must have the expertise to assess biotechnological capabilities of adversaries; something most nations now lack.

It is reasonable to expect that within five years military and public health authorities will be in the possession of several types of kits and devices based on advanced biotechnologies and electronics. These new kits and devices will be a significant improvement over what now is available for the detection and identification of BW agents because they will be easier to take into the field, will be simple to set up and operate, and will be capable of providing definitive results within fifteen minutes of the time when the sample was collected. Detection and identification kits most likely will contain an array of immunological sensors; devices will include laptop-size mass spectrometers, colorimeters, and fluorometers. Although these technologies and techniques will not be sufficient to provide timely warning to threatened populations of impending or actual biological attack, they will be adequate for the thorough investigation of such events, by either local or international authorities. On the local level, investigations utilizing advanced biotechnologies will provide information that military or public health officials can use to alleviate or foreshorten the ill effects from a biological attack, that police will employ to track and capture the perpetrators, and that prosecutors will utilize to convict the guilty parties. The same biotechnological tools would also have utility to international investigators who will be called on to perform the technical studies necessary to determine if the health event in question resulted from natural forces or were deliberately brought about by human action. If the latter, the government of the affected population might seek political action under the provisions of the Convention on the Prohibition of the Development, Production and Stockpiling of Bacteriological (Biological) and Toxin Weapons, and on Their Destruction (BWC).

INTERNATIONAL ARMS CONTROL

By 2005, advanced biotechnologies can be expected to considerably improve existing capabilities to mount meaningful investigations of events and activities alleged to contravene the BWC. As discussed by Chevrier in Chapter 7, an immense international effort is under way to develop a protocol to the BWC that specifies the establishment of an international inspectorate. The major issue yet to be settled by BWC state parties concerns intrusiveness, that is, to what extent will the future inspectorate be able to intrude on facilities and sites in the performance of its mission? It is almost a truism that the more power of intrusion the inspectorate has, the greater the ability of the inspectorate to thoroughly investigate allegations; however, the greater the intrusion, the more risk that the secrets or confidential business information of inspected facilities will be revealed.

In this regard, the problem of sampling looms. Should the inspectorate be able to take samples from the production line of inspected facilities, and if so, where and how might analysis of samples be performed? This issue might be settled to the satisfaction of both the inspectorate and the biotechnology industry if detection devices, such as those described in the foregoing section, were available to inspectors on-site, thus enabling them to carry out analysis without removing samples from the inspected facility. Obviously, the risk of the inspected facility losing intellectual property or proprietary information is substantially decreased if no samples are removed from its premises. Thus, advanced biotechnologies can be expected to help improve the operation of the BWC in two ways: (1) by significantly enhancing the ability of inspectors to detect and identify substances indicative of prohibited activities and (2) by enabling inspectors to do their work adequately while protecting confidential information possessed by the inspected facility.

Future developments in advanced biotechnologies can be expected to be applied for both defense and offense. In defense, they will enable the fielding of exceedingly accurate detection and identification devices, which will be used by military and public health officials, police forces, and the judicial system in the furtherance of their work. Those intent on developing biological weapons undoubtedly will use the advanced biotechnologies to develop and produce pathogens uniquely suited for use in warfare or for terrorism.

In the race between the defense and the offense, a race so often seen before in military history, the defense seems to be leading for the moment. This being the case, the international arms control community has a small window of opportunity to design and put into place mechanisms to meet the threat of advanced bioweaponry. The primary mechanism could be the inspectorate that will be established when BWC state parties adopt the protocol to the BWC. I say "could" because it is not yet certain if it will be done. Russia, in particular, seems to be working against the realization of an effective protocol. However, if a meaningful protocol were adopted, with or without Russia, it would be imperative to equip the inspectorate with the latest kits and devices for detection and identification of microorganisms and toxins. Further, financial and logistic steps would have to be taken by BWC state parties to make certain that as science advances, the inspectorate can immediately incorporate new developments in his/her investigations.

The BWC encompasses only the nations that have chosen to adhere to it. Therefore, the problem remains of what to do about the biological threats posed by nations outside the treaty and by subnational groups. Possibly the only way to meet these threats is to have good intelligence; that is, there must be penetration by human agents of suspect governments and terrorist groups technically capable of acquiring and deploying biological weapons. Further, once intelligence has been secured in the field, it must be properly analyzed at headquarters. As this intelligence probably will be of a technical nature, its examination must be done by analysts who are well trained in the biosciences. If done in this way, it is likely that a biological threat assessment will be delivered in understandable language to decisionmakers. Intelligence agencies do not give out information about their assets, so one can only hope that they are aware of the need to have the requisite expertise for biological analysis and have taken steps to fulfill that need.

I have argued before for the need of the civilian scientific community to become actively involved in international biological arms control endeavors (Zilinskas and Hedén, 1991; Zilinskas, 1998b). If the BWC protocol is adopted, scientists can assist by investing the inspectorate with the expertise it requires to fulfill its mission. Scientists can help in this regard by willingly serving on the inspectorate's scientific advisory board and providing expert advice to those inspections that require it. If the BWC protocol is not adopted, or if the process of having it adopted is lengthy, scientists can still assist in endeavors that strengthen international biological arms control by lobbying their governments to activate Article X of the BWC. This article, which enjoins state parties to cooperate in peacefully directed applied microbiology, has never been put into operation. The main reason is that the BWC, unlike the CWC, is not funded. The BWC state parties could easily remedy this situation by asking the UN Secretary-General to take such steps as necessary to activate Article X and pledge the funding to cover the costs of doing so.

The UN Department of Disarmament Affairs could be given responsibility for carrying out this task, which would mean that it would have to be expanded. Alternatively, the International Centre for Genetic Engineering and Biotechnology, which is headquartered in Trieste and New Delhi, could be requested and funded by the BWC state parties to set up a two-component program. One component would comprise exchanges between scientists of state parties, where scientists from one country go and spend time in a laboratory of a second country. The second component would fund collaborative research projects between scientists of different countries, with findings to be published freely. The major effect of such exchanges and collaborative research would be to shed light on biosciences-related activities undertaken in the involved countries, which would lower the probability of activities occurring that contravene the BWC.

Acronyms &
Abbreviations

ACDA	U.S. Arms Control and Disarmament Agency
AFMIC	U.S. Armed Forces Medical Intelligence Center
AHG	Ad Hoc Group of the States Parties to the BWC
AIDS	acquired immunodeficiency syndrome
ARDS	acute respiratory distress syndrome
ASM	American Society for Microbiology
BIDS	biological integrated detection system
BIO	Biotechnology Industry Organization
BPI	bactericidal permeability increasing
Bt	*Bacillus thuringiensis* (a biological pesticide)
BW	biological warfare
BWC	Convention on the Prohibition of the Development, Production and Stockpiling of Bacteriological (Biological) and Toxin Weapons, and on Their Destruction (for short, the Biological and Toxin Weapons Convention)
CBD	Convention on Biological Diversity
CBI	confidential business information
CBMs	confidence-building measures
CCC	Convention on Climate Change
CDC	U.S. Centers for Disease Control and Prevention
cDNA	complementary deoxyribonucleic acid
CIA	Central Intelligence Agency
CINC	commander in chief
CJCS	chairman of the Joint Chiefs of Staff
CLISA	chemiluminescence immunosorbent assay

CN	cyanide gas
CONPLAN	concept plan
CW	chemical warfare
CWC	Convention on the Prohibition, Development, Production, Stockpiling and Use of Chemical Weapons and on Their Destruction (for short, Chemical Weapons Convention)
DARPA	U.S. Defense Advanced Research Projects Agency
DFA	direct fluorescent antibody examination
DIA	U.S. Defense Intelligence Agency
DNA	deoxyribonucleic acid
DOD	U.S. Department of Defense
DOE	U.S. Department of Energy
ELIFA	enzyme-linked immunofiltration assay
ELISA	enzyme-linked immunosorbent assay
FAS	Federation of American Scientists
FBIS	U.S. Foreign Broadcast Information Service
FDA	U.S. Food and Drug Administration
GC/MS	gas chromatography/mass spectrometry
GLC-MS	gas liquid chromatography–mass spectroscopy
GP	Geneva Protocol (1925)
HCT	hematocrit (a measurement for blood cell volume)
HEPA	high-efficiency particulate air
HF	hemorrhagic fever
HIV	human immunodeficiency virus
HPLC	high-performance liquid chromatography
HUMINT	human intelligence
IAEA	International Atomic Energy Agency
IBAD	interim biological agent detector
IC	U.S. intelligence community
ICGEB	International Centre for Genetic Engineering and Biotechnology
ICSU	International Council of Scientific Unions
IEM	immunoelectron microscopy
IMAGINT	imaging intelligence
IOE	International Office of Epizootics
JPO	U.S. Joint Program Office
LR-BSDS	long-range biological standoff detection system
MALDI	matrix-assisted laser desorption ionization
MASINT	measurement and signal intelligence
MS	mass spectrometry

MSE	Muthanna State Establishment (Iraq)
NAS	U.S. National Academy of Sciences
NATO	North Atlantic Treaty Organization
NBC	nuclear, biological, or chemical
NGO	nongovernmental organization
NMRC	U.S. Naval Medical Research Center
OSI	on-site inspection
PCR	polymerase chain reaction
ProMED	Program on Monitoring Emerging Diseases
R&D	research and development
rDNA	recombinant deoxyribonucleic acid
RFIS	Russian Foreign Intelligence Service
RFLP	restriction fragment length polymorphism
RNA	ribonucleic acid
RT-PCR	reverse transcriptase polymerase chain reaction
SEB	staphylococcal enterotoxin B
SIGINT (or COMMINT)	signals intelligence
SIPRI	Stockholm International Peace Research Institute
SLTEC	shiga-like toxin-producing *Escherichia coli*
SOCOM	U.S. Special Operations Command
STRATCOM	U.S. Strategic Command
T2	a type of trichothecene mycotoxin
TRC	Technical Research Center
UNDP	United Nations Development Programme
UNEP	United Nations Environment Programme
UNESCO	United Nations Educational, Scientific, and Cultural Organization
UNIDO	United Nations Industrial Development Organization
UNSCOM	United Nations Special Commission
USAMRIID (RIID)	U.S. Army Medical Research Institute of Infectious Diseases
USSR	Union of Soviet Socialist Republics
VEE	Venezuelan equine encephalitis
VEREX	Ad Hoc Group of Government Experts to Identify and Examine Verification Measures from a Scientific and Technical Standpoint
WBC	War Bureau of Consultants
WBC	white blood count
WHO	World Health Organization
WMD	weapons of mass destruction
WRS	War Research Service

Glossary

Aerobic   requiring oxygen.

Aerosol   a colloidal suspension of liquid droplets or solid particles in air.

Amino acid   any of a group of twenty chemicals that are linked together in various combinations to form peptides or proteins.

Antibody   a specific protein molecule produced by an organism's immunological defense system when it is challenged by a foreign substance (the antigen). The antibody neutralizes the antigen by binding to it.

Antigen   a substance that when introduced into an organism elicits from it an immunological defensive response. Living microorganisms or chemical agents can, under appropriate circumstances, become antigens.

Applied research   experimental or theoretical work directed toward the application of scientific knowledge for the development, production, or utilization of some useful product or capability.

Authenticate   to confirm that a declaration about strategic weapons is true.

Bacteriophage (phage)   a virus that attacks or colonizes a bacterium. Bacteriophages are specific; one type of phage will attack only one species of bacteria.

Basic research   experimental or theoretical work that is undertaken to acquire knowledge of fundamental principles of phenomena and observable facts and that may not be directed toward a specific application.

Bioaerosol   an aerosol whose components contain, or have attached to them, one or more microorganisms.

Biodegradation   the natural process whereby microorganisms break down organic molecules.

259

Bioremediation a technology that uses biological activity to treat contaminated soil or water in order to reduce or eliminate the contaminant(s).

Biosafety in activities involving life forms or their parts, the observance of precautions and preventive procedures that reduce the risk of adverse effects.

Biosecurity activities designed to secure for humans, animals, and plants freedom from possible hazards attending biological activities, such as research, development, testing, and applications; measures taken by governments to guard against damage that may be brought about by accidental or intentional exposure to biological agents or toxins.

Biotechnology a collection of processes and techniques that involves the use of living organisms or substances from those organisms to make or modify products from raw materials for agricultural, industrial, or medical purposes.

Capability the ability to produce or apply a particular set of scientific techniques or technologies.

Catalyst a substance that affects the rate of a chemical reaction but remains itself unaltered in form or amount.

Cell culture the propagation of cells removed from a plant or animal in culture.

Cell fusion combining nuclei and cytoplasm from two or more different cells to form a single hybrid cell.

Clone a group of genetically identical cells or organisms asexually descended from a common ancestor. In the case of a cloned organism, all cells making up that organism have the same genetic material and are exact copies of the original.

Cloning the use of genetic engineering to produce multiple copies of a single gene, a segment of DNA, or an entire organism.

Containment the act, process, or means of restricting the spread of a population of organisms either within the laboratory or to a specified site in the environment.

Conversion to completely remanufacture a weapon by substituting a treaty-noncompliant design by a treaty-compliant one.

Culture the growth of cells or microorganisms in a controlled artificial environment.

Data authentication steps taken to ensure that data collected in the course of monitoring activity are not corrupted, by design or inadvertence, before presentation to the inspector.

Database a collection of data, defined for one or more applications, which is physically located and maintained within one or more electronic computers.

Development the process of applying scientific and technical knowledge to the practical realization or enhancement of a specific product or capability.

DNA   deoxyribonucleic acid; the carrier of genetic information found in all living organisms (except for a small group of RNA viruses). Every inherited characteristic is coded somewhere in an organism's complement of DNA.

Elimination   the irreversible alteration of a treaty-limited item such that it no longer has military value.

Enzyme   a special protein produced by cells that catalyze the chemical processes of life.

Escherichia coli (E. coli)   a species of bacteria that commonly inhabits the human lower intestine and the intestinal tract of most other vertebrates as well. Some strains are pathogenic, causing urinary tract infections and diarrheal diseases. Weakened strains are often used in laboratory experiments.

Expression   the translation of a gene's DNA sequence by RNA into protein.

Fermentation   the anaerobic bioprocess by which yeasts, bacteria, or molds convert a raw material into products such as alcohols, acids, or cheeses.

Fraction   a chemical agent or compound that may be recovered by chemical or physical methods from a solvent containing a mix of substances.

Gene   the fundamental unit of heredity. Chemically, a gene consists of ordered nucleotides that code for a specific product or control a specific function.

Gene splicing   the use of site-specific enzymes that cleave and reform chemical bonds in DNA to create modified DNA sequences.

Genetic engineering   a collection of techniques used to alter the hereditary apparatus of a living cell, enabling it to produce more or different chemicals. These techniques include chemical synthesis of genes, recombinant DNA or recombinant RNA, cell fusion, plasmid transfer, transformation, transfection, and transduction.

Hazard   the likelihood that an agent or substance will cause immediate or short-term adverse effects or injury under ordinary circumstances of use.

Host   a cell whose metabolism is used for growth and reproduction of a virus, plasmid, or other form of foreign DNA, or an organism that is invaded and infected by a parasite.

Host-vector system   compatible host-vector combinations that may be used for the stable introduction of foreign DNA into host cells.

Hybridoma   a special cell produced by joining a tumor cell (myeloma) and an antibody-producing cell (lymphocyte). Cultured hybridomas produce large quantities of a particular type of monoclonal antibodies.

Hydrocarbon   one of a large and diverse group of compounds, consisting of only carbon and hydrogen, constituting petroleum.

ID_{50}   the number of organisms or spores required to establish an infection in 50 percent of exposed hosts.

Infection   the invasion and settling of a pathogen within a host.

Intellectual property   the area of the law encompassing patents, trademarks, trade secrets, copyrights, and plant variety protection.

Interferon   a type of cytokine discovered in the 1950s having potential as anticancer and antiviral agents. Three types of interferons are known, alpha (IFN-α), beta (IFN-β) and gamma (IFN-γ).

In vitro   literally, "in glass"; pertaining to biological processes or reactions taking place in an artificial environment, usually the laboratory.

In vivo   literally "in the living"; pertaining to biological processes or reactions taking place in a living system such as a cell or tissue.

Metabolism   the sum of the chemical and physiological processes in a living organism in which foodstuffs are synthesized into complex biochemicals (anabolism), complex biochemicals transformed into simple chemicals (catabolism), and energy is made available for the organism to function and procreate.

Metabolite   a substance vital to the metabolism of a certain organism, or a product of metabolism.

Microorganism   any of a number of microscopic organisms, such as bacteria, fungi, microalgae, plankton, and viruses.

Monitoring   collecting, analyzing, and reporting information on the activities of another party related to provisions of arms control agreements.

Monoclonal antibody   an antibody produced by a hybridoma that recognizes only a specific antigen.

nanogram   one millionth of a gram.

ng/ml   nanograms per milliliter

Nonroutine inspection   a generic term for when inspectors visit a designated treaty-related site to investigate a probable treaty violation or to exercise treaty visitation protocols. A nonroutine inspection may include a suspect site inspection, special access visit, short-notice inspection, or challenge inspection.

Nucleotide   the fundamental molecule that makes up DNA and RNA. Each nucleotide constituting DNA consists of one of four amino acids (adenine, guanine, cytosine, or thymine) linked to the phosphate-sugar group deoxyribose; each nucleotide constituting RNA consists of one of four amino acids (adenine, guanine, cytosine, or uracil) linked to the phosphate-sugar group ribose.

Pathogen   an organism that causes disease in humans, animals, or plants.

Peptide   a linear polymer of amino acids. A polymer consisting of many amino acids is called a polypeptide.

Plasmid   small, circular, self-replicating forms of DNA often used in recombinant DNA experiments as vectors of foreign DNA.

Plasmid transfer   the use of genetic or physical manipulation to introduce a foreign plasmid into a host cell.

Polymer   a linear or branched molecule of repeating subunits.

Polymerase chain reaction   a method for amplifying (making multiple copies of) a selected piece of DNA.

Production   the conversion of raw materials into products or components thereof through a series of manufacturing processes.

Real time   a characteristic of a system that makes information available about a process so quickly it allows the operator to act to change the outcome of the process while it is still under way.

Recombinant DNA   rDNA; the hybrid DNA resulting from the joining pieces of DNA from different sources.

Risk   the probability of injury, disease, or death for persons or groups of persons undertaking certain activities or being exposed to hazardous substances. Risk is sometimes expressed in numeric terms (in fractions) or qualitative terms (low, moderate, or high).

Risk management   the process of determining whether or how much to reduce risk through regulatory action. Decisions usually depend on data from risk assessment and take into account economic, ethical, legal, political, and social factors.

RNA   ribonucleic acid; found in three forms—messenger, transfer, and ribosomal RNA. RNA assists in translating the genetic code of a DNA sequence into its complementary protein.

Safe   not threatened by danger, or freed from harm, injury, or risk.

Security   being secure from danger; freedom from fear and anxiety; measures taken by governments to guard against espionage, sabotage, and surprises.

Species   a population that is genetically isolated from other species; that is, a population of genetically similar organisms that normally does not exchange genes with other populations of organisms.

Synthesis   the production of a compound by a living organism.

Technology   the scientific and technical information, coupled with know-how, that are used to design, produce, and manufacture products or generate data.

Threat   an indication of something impending and usually undesirable or dangerous; something that by its very nature or relation to another threatens the welfare of the latter.

Toxicity   the quality of being poisonous or the degree to which a substance is poisonous.

Toxin   a toxic substance produced by living organisms.

Trait   a characteristic that is coded for in an organism's DNA.

Transduction   the transfer of one or more genes from one bacteria to another by a vector, such as a bacteriophage.

Transfection   the process in which a bacterium is modified in a way which allows the cell to take up purified, intact viral, or plasmid DNA.

Transformation   the introduction of new genetic information into a cell using naked DNA (i.e., without using a vector).

Transgenic organism   an organism bearing within its DNA copies of genetic constructs from another organism introduced through recombinant DNA technology.

Transparency   intentional openness with the intent to enhance mutual predictability, confidence building, and cooperation.

Treaty-limited item   a weapon or weapon component that is identified and controlled by an international treaty.

Vector   a transmission agent, usually a plasmid or virus, used to introduce foreign DNA into a host cell.

Verification   a policy function related to the process of judging compliance to an arms control treaty.

Virus   an infectious agent, containing either DNA or RNA as its genetic material, which requires a host cell for its replication.

Warhead   the part of a bomb, missile, or shell that houses the explosive charge, or in the case of biological or chemical weapons, the pathogenic or toxic agent.

Bibliography

Abramova, F. A., L. M. Grinberg, O. V. Yampolskaya, and D. H. Walker (1993). Pathology of inhalation anthrax in 42 cases from the Sverdlovsk outbreak of 1979. *Proceedings of the National Academy of Sciences* 90:2291–2294.

Abramowitz, S. (1996). Towards inexpensive DNA diagnostics. *Trends in Biotechnology* 14:397–401.

ACDA (U.S. Arms Control and Disarmament Agency) (1976). *Verification: The critical element of arms control.* Washington, D.C.: U.S. Arms Control and Disarmament Agency.

——— (1983). *Annual report, 1982.* Washington, D.C.: United States Government Printing Office.

——— (1990). *Arms control and disarmament agreements: Texts and histories of the negotiations.* Washington, D.C.: U.S. Arms Control and Disarmament Agency.

——— (1993). *Adherence to and compliance with arms control agreements and the president's report to Congress on Soviet non-compliance with arms control agreements.* Washington, D.C.: U.S. Arms Control and Disarmament Agency, January 14.

——— (1996a). *Adherence to and compliance with arms control agreements: 1996 annual report.* Washington, D.C.: U.S. Arms Control and Disarmament Agency.

——— (1996b). *Threat control through arms control: Annual report to Congress 1995.* Washington, D.C.: U.S. Arms Control and Disarmament Agency.

——— (1997a). *Threat control through arms control: Annual report to Congress 1996.* Washington, D.C.: U.S. Arms Control and Disarmament Agency.

——— (1997b). Parties and signatories of the Biological Weapons Convention. Web site: http://www.acda.gov/treaties/bwcsig.htm.

——— (1998). *Threat control through arms control: Annual report to Congress, 1997.* Washington, D.C.: U.S. Arms Control and Disarmament Agency.

Adams, James (1994). *The new spies: Exploring the frontiers of espionage.* Hutchinson: London.

——— (1995). South Africa: Libya said seeking secret biological weapons. *Sunday*

Times (London), February 26. See also http://web.lexis-nexis.com/universe/docu...a3&_mds=2177267ab92b392733f352219dbe26.

Adesiyun, A. A., M. Eschbach, W. Lenz, and K. P. Schaal (1992). Detection of enterotoxigenicity of *Staphylococcus aureus* strains: A comparative use of the modified ouchterlony precipitation test, reversed passive latex agglutination test, and avidin-biotin ELISA. *Canadian Journal of Microbiology* 38:1097–1101.

AFMIC (U.S. Armed Forces Medical Intelligence Center) (1992a). Translation of *Manual no. 469: Mobilization use of arms of mass destruction, vol. II, part I: Principles of using chemical and biological agents in warfare*, by the Iraqi General Staff, 1987. Fort Detrick, Md.: AFMIC-HT-099-92.

——— (1992b). Translation of *Manual: Chemical, biological and nuclear operations*, by Col. Sameem Jalal Abdul Latif, Training Department, Iraqi Chemical Corps, 1984. Fort Detrick, Md.: Foreign Armies Studies Series No. 21, AFMIC-HT-101-92.

Aggarwal, V. K. (1985). *Liberal protectionism: The international politics of organized textile trade.* Berkeley: University of California Press.

Aldinger, C. (1996). Libya getting aid on chemical arms—Pentagon. *Reuters News Service*, April 11.

Algeria et al. (1995). Draft Resolution, NPT/CONF.1995/L.7, May 9, 1995. In *1995 review and extension conference of the parties to the Treaty on the Non-Proliferation of Nuclear Weapons, final document part II: Documents issued at the conference*, pp. 241–242. New York: United Nations.

Alibek, K. (1998a). Presentation at the Carnegie Endowment for Peace. Washington, D.C., May 22.

——— (1998b). Presentation at the annual meeting of the Association for Politics and the Life Sciences. Boston, Mass., September 5.

——— (1998c). Russia's deadly expertise. *New York Times*, March 27, p. A1.

———. (1999). *Biohazard.* New York: Random House.

ASM (American Society for Microbiology) (1985). Code of ethics for microbiologists. *ASM News* 51:35.

Al-Anbari, A. A. A. (1991). Letter to H.E. Javier Pérez de Cuéllar, Secretary-General of the United Nations, from Abdul Amir A. al-Anbari, Ambassador and Permanent Representative of Iraq. April 18.

Anderson, K. (1992). Letter from Human Rights Watch to Rolf Ekéus enclosing copies of Iraqi documents and English translations, December 29.

Aspin, L. (1993a). Remarks by the Honorable Les Aspin to the U.S. National Academy of Sciences' Committee on International Security and Arms Control. Washington, D.C., December 3.

——— (1993b). Remarks by the Honorable Les Aspin to the U.S. National Academy of Sciences' Committee on International Security and Arms Control. Washington, D.C., December 7.

Atlas, R. M. (1998). The medical threat of biological weapons. *Critical Reviews in Microbiology* 24:157–168.

Atlas, R. M., and M. Goldberg (1993). Biological warfare: Examining verification strategies. *ASM News* 59(8):393–396.

Australia (1991). National position paper: Australia. Unpublished paper, Seminar on the Biological and Toxin Weapons Convention. Noordwijk, the Netherlands.

Ausubel, F. M., R. Brent, R. E. Kingston, D. D. Moore, J. A. Seidman, and J. A.

Smith, eds. (1994 et seq.). *Current Protocols in Molecular Biology.* New York: J. Wiley.

Baghdad Radio (1990). Translated in FBIS-NES-90-135, June 19.

Baker, J. A., with T. M. DeFrank (1995a). *The politics of diplomacy: Revolution, war, and peace, 1989–1992.* New York: G. P. Putnam's Sons.

Baker, J. A. (1995b). The politics of diplomacy. *Newsweek,* October 2, p. 57.

Barbas, C. F., III, and D. R. Burton (1996). Selection and evolution of high-affinity human anti-viral antibodies. *Trends in Biotechnology* 14:230–234.

Barkho, L. (1995). Iraq shows foreign reporters main biological site. *Reuters News Service,* April 22.

Barry, J. (1993). Planning a plague. *Newsweek,* February 1, pp. 40–41.

Barry, T., and F. Gannon (1991). Direct genomic PCR amplification from autoclaved infectious microorganisms using PCR technology. *PCR Methods and Applications* 1(1):75.

Barton, R. (1998). The application of the UNSCOM experience to international biological arms control. *Critical Reviews in Microbiology* 24:219–233.

Baselt, D. R., G. U. Lee, K. M. Hansen, L. A. Chrisey, and R. J. Colton (1997). A high-sensitivity micromachined biosensor. *Proceedings of the IEEE* 85 (4):672–680.

Belgium (1991). Belgian contribution. Unpublished paper, Seminar on the Biological and Toxin Weapons Convention. Noordwijk, the Netherlands.

Belgrader, P., W. Benett, D. Hadley, J. Richards, P. Stratton, et al. (1999). PCR detection of bacteria in seven minutes. *Science* 284:449–450.

Belitskiy, B. (1992). Yeltsin's biological weapons decree assessed. *Radio Moscow World Service,* May 15.

Beresford, D. (1998). Poison, cholera, anthrax: Apartheid's deadly arsenal. *Guardian* (Canberra), June 11. Web site: http://www.smh.com.au/news/9806/11/text/world2.html.

Bernauer, T. (1993). *The chemistry of regime formation: Explaining international cooperation of a comprehensive ban on chemical weapons.* Dartmouth: United Nations Institute for Disarmament Research (UNIDIR).

Berns, K. I., R. M. Atlas, G. Cassell, and J. Shoemaker (1998). Preventing the misuse of microorganisms: The role of the American Society for Microbiology in protecting against biological weapons. *Critical Reviews in Microbiology* 24:273–280.

Bernstein, B. J. (1987a). Churchill's secret biological weapons. *Bulletin of the Atomic Scientists* 43(1):46–50.

——— (1987b). The birth of the U.S. biological warfare program. *Scientific American* 256:116–121.

——— (1988). America's biological warfare program in the Second World War. *Journal of Strategic Studies* 11:292–317.

Bhatia, S. (1992). Iraqi scientist tells 10-year secret. *The Observer* (London), August 9, p. 1.

BIO (Biotechnology Industry Organization) (1990). *Biotechnology in Perspective.* Washington, D.C.: Biotechnology Industry Organization.

——— (1997). *Biotechnology Industry Organization: Statement of principles.* Washington, D.C.: Biotechnology Industry Organization.

Borysiewicz, L. K., et al. (1996). A recombinant vaccinia virus encoding human papillomavirus types 16 and 18, E6 and E7 proteins as immunotherapy for cervical cancer. *Lancet* 347(9014):1498–1499.

Boulden, L. H. (1996). CIA, DIA provide new details on CW, BW programs in Iran and Russia. *Arms Control Today* 26:32–33.

Brackett, D. W. (1996). *Holy terror: Armageddon in Tokyo.* New York: Weatherhill.

Brazil (1994). *Strengthening the BWC: Elements for a possible verification system.* Working paper presented to the Special Conference of the States Parties to the Convention on the Prohibition of the Development, Production and Stockpiling of Bacteriological (Biological) and Toxin Weapons, and on Their Destruction. BWC/SPCONF/WP.4. United Nations.

Brès, P. (1986) *Public health action in emergencies caused by epidemics.* Geneva: World Health Organization.

British Medical Association (1999). *Biotechnology, weapons, and humanity.* London: Harwood Acadamic Publishers.

Broad, W. J. (1998). Sowing death: A special report; How Japan germ terror alerted world. *New York Times,* May 28, p. A1.

Broad, W. J., and J. Miller (1998). How Iraq's biological weapons program came to light. *New York Times,* February 26, p. A1.

Brochier, B., D. Boulanger, F. Costy, and P. P. Pastoret (1994). Toward rabies elimination in Belgium fox by using vaccinia-rabies glycoprotein recombinant virus. *Vaccine* 12(15):1368–1371.

Brown, F. J. (1968). *Chemical warfare: A study in restraints.* Princeton, N.J.: Princeton University Press.

Bryden, J. (1989). *Deadly allies: Canada's secret war 1937–1947.* Toronto: Canadian Publishers.

Bryden, W. A., R. C. Benson, S. A. Ecelberger, T. E. Phillips, R. J. Cotter, and C. Fenselau (1995). The tiny-TOF mass spectrometer for chemical and biological sensing. *Johns Hopkins APL Technical Digest* 16:296–310.

BWC (Convention on the Prohibition of the Development, Production and Stockpiling of Bacteriological (Biological) and Toxin Weapons, and on Their Destruction) (1975). *Treaties and Other International Acts, series 8062.* Washington, D.C.: U.S. Department of State.

——— (1980). First Review Conference of the Parties to the Convention on the Prohibition of the Development, Production and Stockpiling of Bacteriological (Biological) and Toxin Weapons, and on Their Destruction. *Final Document.* BWC/CONF.I/10.

——— (1986a). Second Review Conference of the Parties to the Convention on the Prohibition of the Development, Production and Stockpiling of Bacteriological (Biological) and Toxin Weapons, and on Their Destruction. *Final Document.* BWC/CONF.II/13/2.

——— (1986b). Second Review Conference of the Parties to the Convention on the Prohibition of the Development, Production and Stockpiling of Bacteriological (Biological) and Toxin Weapons, and on Their Destruction. *Final Document.* BWC/CONF.II/13.

——— (1986c). Second Review Conference of the Parties to the Convention on the Prohibition of the Development, Production and Stockpiling of Bacteriological (Biological) and Toxin Weapons, and on Their Destruction. Summary Records of the 3rd, 4th, and 5th Meetings. BWC/CONF.II/SR.3, BWC/CONF.II/SR.4, BWC/CONF.II/SR.5.

——— (1991). Third Review Conference of the Parties to the Convention on the Prohibition of the Development, Production and Stockpiling of Bacteriological (Biological) and Toxin Weapons, and on Their Destruction. *Final Document.* Geneva. BWC/CONF.III/22/Add.2.

──── (1992). The Third Review Conference of the States Parties to the Convention on the Prohibition of the Development, Production and Stockpiling of Bacteriological (Biological) and Toxin Weapons, and on Their Destruction. *Final Document.* September 9–27, Geneva. BWC/CONF.III/23.

──── (1993). United Nations Ad Hoc Group of Governmental Experts to Identify and Examine Potential Verification Measures from a Scientific and Technical Standpoint. *Summary Record. Fourth Session.* BWC/CONF.III/VEREX/8.

──── (1994a). Special Conference of the States Parties to the Convention on the Prohibition of the Development, Production and Stockpiling of Bacteriological (Biological) and Toxin Weapons, and on Their Destruction. *Final Report.* BWC/SPCONF/1.

──── (1994b). Special Conference of the States Parties to the Convention on the Prohibition of the Development, Production and Stockpiling of Bacteriological (Biological) and Toxin Weapons, and on Their Destruction. *Final Declaration.* BWC/SPCONF/FD.

──── (1995a). United Nations Ad Hoc Group of the Parties to the Convention on the Prohibition of the Development, Production and Stockpiling of Bacteriological (Biological) and Toxin Weapons, and on Their Destruction. *Procedural Report.* BWC/AD HOC GROUP/28.

──── (1995b). United Nations Ad Hoc Group of the Parties to the Convention on the Prohibition of the Development, Production and Stockpiling of Bacteriological (Biological) and Toxin Weapons, and on Their Destruction. *Procedural Report.* BWC/AD HOC GROUP/29.

──── (1996a). Fourth Review Conference of the States Parties to the Convention on the Prohibition of the Development, Production and Stockpiling of Bacteriological (Biological) and Toxin Weapons, and on Their Destruction. *Final Document.* BWC/CONF.IV/9.

──── (1996b). Fourth Review Conference of the States Parties to the Convention on the Prohibition of the Development, Production and Stockpiling of Bacteriological (Biological) and Toxin Weapons, and on Their Destruction. *Final Document.* BWC/CONF.IV/9.

──── (1996c). United Nations Ad Hoc Group of the Parties to the Convention on the Prohibition of the Development, Production and Stockpiling of Bacteriological (Biological) and Toxin Weapons, and on Their Destruction. *Procedural Report.* BWC/AD HOC GROUP/31.

──── (1996d). Fourth Review Conference of the States Parties to the Convention on the Prohibition of the Development, Production and Stockpiling of Bacteriological (Biological) and Toxin Weapons, and on Their Destruction. *Final Document.* BWC/CONF.IV/9.

──── (1997). United Nations Ad Hoc Group of the Parties to the Convention on the Prohibition of the Development, Production and Stockpiling of Bacteriological (Biological) and Toxin Weapons, and on Their Destruction. *Procedural Report.* BWC/AD HOC GROUP/34,27.

──── (1998a). United Nations Ad Hoc Group of the Parties to the Convention on the Prohibition of the Development, Production and Stockpiling of Bacteriological (Biological) and Toxin Weapons, and on Their Destruction. *Procedural Report. Annex I. Rolling text of a protocol to the Convention on the Prohibition of the Development, Production and Stockpiling of Bacteriological (Biological) and Toxin Weapons, and on Their Destruction.* BWC/AD HOC GROUP/39.

──── (1998b). United Nations Ad Hoc Group of the Parties to the Convention on the Prohibition of the Development, Production and Stockpiling of Baceriological (Biological) and Toxin Weapons, and on Their Destruction. *Rolling text of a protocol to the Convention on the Prohibition of the Development, Production and Stockpiling of Bacteriological (Biological) and Toxin Weapons, and on Their Destruction.* BWC/AD HOC GROUP/41.

———— (1998c). United Nations Ad Hoc Group of the Parties to the Convention on the Prohibition of the Development, Production and Stockpiling of Baceriological (Biological) and Toxin Weapons, and on Their Destruction. *Proposed elements of clarification visits.* Working paper prepared by the United States. BWC/AD HOC GROUP/WP.294.

———— (1999). United Nations Ad Hoc Group of the Parties to the Convention on the Prohibition of the Development, Production and Stockpiling of Bacteriological (Biological) and Toxin Weapons, and on Their Destruction. *Procedural Report. Annex I.* BWC/AD HOC GROUP/44.

Cao, L. K., G. P. Anderson, F. S. Ligler, and J. S. Ezzell (1995). Detection of *Yersinia pestis* fraction 1 antigen with a fiberoptic biosensor. *Journal of Clinical Microbiology* 33:336–341.

Canada (1991a). Strengthening the Biological and Toxin Weapons Convention: Observations on confidence-building measures and verification. Unpublished paper, Seminar on the Biological and Toxin Weapons Convention. Noordwijk, the Netherlands.

———— (1991b). *Collateral analysis and verification of biological and toxin research in Iraq.* Toronto: External Affairs and International Trade Canada.

Carl, M., R. Hawkins, N. Coulson, J. Lowe, D. L. Robertson, W. N. Nelson, R. W. Titball, and J. N. Woody (1992). Detection of spores of *Bacillus anthracis* using the polymerase chain reaction. *Journal of Infectious Diseases* 165:1145–1148.

Carter, G. B. (1992a). *Biological warfare and biological defence in the United Kingdom 1940–1979.* Porton Down, UK: Chemical and Biological Defence Establishment.

———— (1992b). *Porton Down: 75 years of chemical and biological research.* London: Her Majesty's Stationery Office.

Carter, G., and G. S. Pearson (1996). North Atlantic chemical and biological research collaboration: 1916–1995. *Journal of Strategic Studies* 19(1):74–103.

Carus, W. S. (1991). *"The poor man's atomic bomb?" Biological weapons in the Middle East.* Policy papers no. 23. Washington, D.C.: Washington Institute for Near East Policy.

———— (1998a). Biological warfare threats in perspective. *Critical Reviews in Microbiology* 24:149–155.

———— (1998b). *Bioterrorism and biocrimes: The illicit use of biological agents in the 20th century.* Washington, D.C.: Center for Nonproliferation Research, National Defense University.

Cassell, G. H., L. A. Miller, and R. F. Rest (1992). Biological warfare: Role of scientific societies. In R. A. Zilinskas, ed., *The microbiologist and biological defense research: Ethics, politics and international security. Annals of the New York Academy of Sciences* 666:230–238.

CBD (Convention on Biological Diversity) (1994). United Nations, *Convention on Biological Diversity.* UNEP/CBD/94/1. The text of the convention can be found at Web site http://www.biodiv.org/chm/conv/dbc_text_e.htm.

Centers for Disease Control and Prevention (1996). *Addressing emerging infectious disease threats: A prevention strategy for the United States.* Web site: http://www.cdc.gov/ncidod/publications/eid_plan/home.htm.

Chemical Warfare Review Commission (1985). *Report.* Washington, D.C., June 11.

Cheng, J., P. Fortina, S. Surrey, L. J. Kricka, and P. Wilding (1996). Microchip-based devices for molecular diagnosis of genetic diseases. *Molecular Diagnosis* 1:183–200.

Chevrier, M. I. (1990). Verifying the unverifiable: Lessons from the Biological Weapons Convention. *Politics and the Life Sciences* 9(1):93–105.

———— (1992). The Biological Weapons Convention: The Third Review Conference. *Politics and the Life Sciences* 11(1):86–92.

———— (1995a). BW arms control: Countering proliferation by changing incentive structure. *Political Economy Working Paper* 95-14. Dallas: University of Texas, April.

———— (1995b). From verification to strengthening compliance: Prospects and challenges of the Biological Weapons Convention. *Politics and the Life Sciences* 14(2):209–219.

Chevrier, M. I., and A. E. Smithson (1996). Preventing the spread of arms: Chemical and biological weapons. In J. A. Larsen and G. J. Rattray, eds., *Arms control: Toward the 21st century,* pp. 201–227. Boulder: Lynne Rienner Publishers.

Chopra, I., J. Hodgson, F. Metclaf, and G. Poste (1996). New approaches to the control of infections caused by antibiotic-resistant bacteria: An industry perspective. *Journal of the American Medical Association* 275(5):401–403.

Claydon, M. A., S. N. Davey, V. Edwards-Jones, and D. B. Gordon (1996). The rapid identification of intact microorganisms using mass spectrometry. *Nature Biotechnology* 14:1584–1586.

Cochran, Alexander S., L. M. Greenberg, K. R. Guthe, W. W. Thomson, and M. J. Eisenstadt. (1993). Planning. In Eliot A. Cohen, director, *Gulf War air power survey, volume II: Planning and command and control.* Washington, D.C.: Government Printing Office.

Cochrane, R. C. (1947). *History of the chemical warfare service in World War II (1 July 1940–15 August 1945): Biological warfare research in the United States, volume II.* Washington, D.C.: U.S. Chemical Corps.

Cohen, A. (1998). Israel and the evolution of U.S. nonproliferation policy: The critical decade (1958–1968). *Nonproliferation Review* 5(2):1–19.

Colby, W. E. (1983). *The nuclear freeze and arms control.* Proceedings of a symposium held at the American Academy of Arts and Sciences, January 13–15. Cambridge, Mass.: Center for Science and International Affairs, John F. Kennedy School of Government, Harvard University; American Academy of Arts and Sciences.

Collins, J. M., Z. S. Davis, and S. R. Bowman (1994). *Nuclear, biological and chemical weapon proliferation: Potential military countermeasures.* Washington, D.C.: Congressional Research Service, Report no. 1994-528S.

Cordesman, A. (1990). *Weapons of mass destruction in the Middle East.* London, UK: Brassey's.

Cordingley, P. (1996). *In the eye of the storm.* London: Hodder and Stoughton.

Cornell, B. A., V. L. B. Braach-Maksvytis, L. G. King, P. D. J. Osman, B. Raguse, L. Wieczorek, and R. J. Pace (1997). A biosensor that uses ion-channel switches. *Nature* (London) 387:580–583.

CPRC (Counterproliferation Program Review Committee) (1996). *Report on activities and programs for countering proliferation.* May. Washington, D.C.: Counterproliferation Program Review Committee.

Czechoslovakia (1991). Approach of the Czech and Slovak Federative Republic to the present state of the Biological Weapons Convention. Unpublished paper,

Seminar on the Biological and Toxin Weapons Convention. Noordwijk, the Netherlands.

Dando, M. (1994). *Biological warfare in the 21st century.* London: Brassey's.

Danzig, R. (1996). *Biological warfare: A nation at risk—A time to act.* Institute for National Strategic Studies, National Defense University, Washington, D.C., Strategic Forum no. 58, January, pp. 1–4.

Davis, D. (1996). Statement, Biological Weapons Convention Fourth Review Conference, November 26.

Davis, L. G., W. M. Kuehl, and F. J. Battey (1994). *Basic methods in molecular biology,* 2nd ed. Norwalk, Conn.: Appleton and Lange.

Davis, S. H. (1977). *Victims of the miracle: Development and the Indians of Brazil.* New York: Cambridge University Press.

De Cerreño, A. L. C., and A. Keynan, eds. (1998). *Scientific cooperation, state conflict: The roles of scientists in mitigating international discord.* Annals of the *New York Academy of Sciences* 866:1–284.

Defense Intelligence Agency (1986). Iraqi CW and BW. GulfLINK document no.001mc.90. (GulfLINK is a DOD Internet Web site containing declassified intelligence documents relating to the 1991 Gulf War.)

Denmark, Finland, Iceland, Norway, and Sweden (1998). Report of a trial random visit to a biopharmaceutical production facility. Working paper from the Twelfth Session of BWC Ad Hoc Group, September 14–October 9, Geneva. BWC/AD HOC GROUP/WP.298.

Der Spiegel (1996). Computer für die Giftküche [Computers for the Poison Kitchen], no. 35 (August 26), pp. 22–25.

Dettmer, J. (1995). Tehran building deadly gas plant. *Washington Times,* January 30, p. A1.

Deutch, John (1996). Worldwide threat assessment brief, Senate Select Committee on Intelligence, February 22.

Diab, M. Z. (1997). Syria's chemical and biological weapons: Assessing capabilities and motivations. *Nonproliferation Review* 5(1):104–111.

DuPont, H. L. (1990). *Shigella* species (bacillary dysentery). In G. L. Mandell, R. G. Douglas Jr., and J. E. Bennett, eds., *Principles and practice of infectious diseases,* pp. 1716–1722. New York: Churchill Livingstone.

Dupont, H. L., J. Therasse, J. M. Pinon, and P. Binder (1990). Detection of staphylococcal enterotoxin B: A comparative study of ELISA and ELIFA systems. *Journal of Immunological Methods* 128:287–291.

Dunn, I. S. (1996). Phage display of proteins. *Current Opinion in Biotechnology* 7:547–553.

Dyson, F. (1984). Weapons and hope: III—people. *The New Yorker,* vol. 60, February 20, pp. 52–103.

The Economist (1995a). Disease fights back. May 20, p. 15.

——— (1995b). The hobbled horseman. May 20, p. 83.

Einhorn, R. J. (1982). Treaty compliance. *Foreign Policy* 45: 29–47.

Eisenstadt, M. (1990). *"The sword of the Arabs": Iraq's strategic weapons.* Policy Papers no. 21. Washington, D.C.: Washington Institute for Near East Policy.

——— (1993). Syria's strategic weapons. *Jane's Intelligence Review* 5: 168–173.

——— (1995). Prepared testimony before the House International Relations Committee, Hearing on Iran's military capabilities and intentions: An assessment, November 9.

——— (1996). *Iranian military power: Capabilities and intentions.* Policy Papers No. 42. Washington, D.C.: Washington Institute for Near East Policy.

Falk, R. A. (1986). Inhibiting reliance on biological weaponry: The role and relevance of international law. *American University Journal of International Law and Policy* 1:17–34.

Falk, R. A., and S. Wright (1990). Preventing a biological arms race: New initiatives. In S. Wright, ed., *Preventing a Biological Arms Race*, pp. 330–351. Cambridge, Mass.: MIT Press.

FAS (Federation of American Scientists) Working Group on Biological and Toxin Weapons Verification (1990). *Proposals for the Third Review Conference of the Biological Weapons Convention.* Washington, D.C.: Federation of American Scientists.

——— (1991). *Implementation of the proposals for a verification protocol to the Biological Weapons Convention.* Washington, D.C.: Federation of American Scientists.

——— (1994). *Beyond VEREX: A legally binding compliance regime for the Biological and Toxin Weapons Convention.* Washington, D.C.: Federation of American Scientists.

——— (1995a). Beyond VEREX: A legally binding compliance regime for the Biological and Toxin Weapons Convention. *Contemporary Security Policy* 16(2):103–146.

——— (1995b). *Potential for new approaches to microorganism identification.* Washington, D.C.: Federation of American Scientists.

——— (1995c). *Proposals for technological cooperation to implement Article X of the Biological Weapons Convention.* Working paper. Washington, D.C.: Federation of American Scientists.

——— (1996a). *Report of the subgroup on investigation of alleged use or release of biological or toxin weapons agents.* Washington, D.C.: Federation of American Scientists.

——— (1996b). *Report of the subgroup on investigation of alleged use or release of biological or toxin weapons agents.* Available at Web site http://www.fas. org/bwc/report.html.

——— (1997). Estimate of the number of declared facilities. Working paper, September. Available at the FAS Web site: www.fas.com.

——— (1998). The structure and cost of a BWC organization. Washington, D.C.: Federation of American Scientists.

Feldman, S. (1982). *Israeli nuclear deterrence: A strategy for the 1980s.* New York: Columbia University Press.

Fenselau, C. (1994). Mass spectrometry for characterization of microorganisms: An overview. In C. Fenselau, ed. *Mass spectrometry for the characterization of microorganisms,* ACS Symposium Series 541, pp. 1–7. Washington, D.C.: American Chemical Society.

Fetter, S. (1991). Ballistic missiles and weapons of mass destruction: What is the threat? What should be done? *International Security* 16(1): 5–21.

Fever, P. (1992–1993). Command and control in emerging nuclear nations. *International Security* 16(3):160–187.

Fisher, L. (1996). Biotech counterattack on resistant bacteria. *New York Times,* April 26, p. D1.

Flowerree, C. C. (1992). The biological weapons convention and the researcher. In R. A. Zilinskas, ed., *The microbiologist and biological defense research: Ethics, politics and international security. Annals of the New York Academy of Sciences* 666:113–130.

Franz, D. R. (1997). Defense against toxin weapons. In F. R. Sidell, E. T. Takafuji, and D. R. Franz, eds., *Medical aspects of chemical and biological warfare.* Washington, D.C.: Office of the Surgeon General, pp. 603–619.

Fraser, D. W. (1980). Legionellosis: Evidence of airborne transmission. In R. B. Kundsin, ed., *Airborne contagion. Annals of the New York Academy of Sciences* 353:61–66.

Fraser, D. W., T. R. Tsai, W. Orenstein, W. E. Parkin, et al. (1977). Legionnaires' disease: Description of an epidemic of pneumonia. *New England Journal of Medicine* 297:1189–1197.

Freedman, L. (1983). *The evolution of nuclear strategy.* New York: St. Martin's Press.

Frenc, N. M. (1994). Mid-south cotton insect control with MVP, an encapsulated *Bacillus thuringiensis* (BT) bioinsecticide. In *Proceedings, Beltwide Cotton Conference,* vol. 2. Memphis, Tenn.: National Cotton Council of America, pp. 1049–1051.

Fritz, D. L., N. K. Jaax, W. B. Lawrence, K. J. Davis, et al. (1995). Pathology of experimental inhalation anthrax in the rhesus monkey. *Laboratory Investigation* 73:672–691.

Fulop, M., D. Leslie, and R. Titball (1996). A rapid, highly sensitive method for the detection of *Francisella tularensis* in clinical samples using the polymerase chain reaction. *American Journal of Tropical Medicine and Hygiene* 54:364–366.

Fulop, M., T. Webber, R. J. Manchee, and D. C. Kelly (1991). Production and characterization of monoclonal antibodies directed against the lipopolysaccharide of *Francisella tularensis. Journal of Clinical Microbiology* 29:1407–1412.

Gallate, R., P. Beauverger, and T. Wild (1995). Passively administered antibody suppresses the induction of measles virus antibodies by vaccinia-measles recombinant viruses. *Vaccine* 13(2):197–201.

Garrett, L. (1994). *The coming plague: Newly emerging diseases in a world out of balance.* New York: Farrar, Straus and Giroux; Penguin Books.

Gayler, N. (1986). Verification, compliance and the intelligence process. In K. Tsipis, D. W. Hafemeister, and P. Janeway, eds., *Arms control verification: The technologies that make it work.* Washington, D.C.: Pergamon-Brassey's, pp. 3–7.

Geisbert, T. W., and P. B. Jahrling (1990). Use of immunoelectron microscopy to show Ebola virus during the 1989 United States epizootic. *Journal of Clinical Pathology* 43:813–816.

Geisbert, T. W., P. B. Jahrling, and J. W. Ezzell Jr. (1993). Use of immunoelectron microscopy to demonstrate *Francisella tularensis. Journal of Clinical Microbiology* 31:1936–1939.

Geissler, E. (1984). Implications of genetic engineering for chemical-biological warfare. *World Armament and Disarmament: SIPRI Yearbook 1984.* Philadelphia: Taylor and Francis, pp. 421–451.

——— (1986). A new generation of biological weapons. In E. Geissler, ed., *Biological and toxin weapons today.* New York: Oxford Press, pp. 21–35.

——— (1990a). The first three rounds of information exchanges. In E. Geissler, ed., *Strengthening the Biological Weapons Convention by confidence-building measures,* pp. 71–79. SIPRI Chemical and Biological Warfare Studies. Oxford: Oxford University Press.

———, ed. (1990b). *Strengthening the Biological Weapons Convention by confidence-building measures,* SIPRI Chemical and Biological Warfare Studies. Oxford: Oxford University Press.

——— (1996). BW activities in Germany before and during World War II. Unpublished document.

Geissler, E., and R. H. Haynes, eds. (1991). *Prevention of a biological and toxin arms race and the responsibility of scientists.* Berlin: AkademieVerlag Berlin.

Gelman, I. H., J. Zhang, E. Hailman, H. Hanafusa, and S. S. Morse (1992). Identification and evaluation of new primer sets for the detection of lentivirus proviral DNA. *AIDS Research and Human Retroviruses* 8:1981–1989.

George, A. (1995). Head of Saddam's germ warfare program received her education and experience in British university (in Arabic). *Al-Sharq Al-Awsat,* January 29, p. 2.

Gerbrandy, J. L. (1996). The value of declarations and notifications. Unpublished paper. Budapest, Hungary.

Gertz, B. (1992). Defecting Russian scientist revealed biological arms effort. *Washington Times,* July 4, p. A4.

——— (1996). Weapons spread seen as "urgent threat." *Washington Times,* April 12, p. A3.

Gil-Grande, R., J. M. Aguado, C. Pastor, and M. Garcia-Bravo (1995). Conventional viral cultures and shell vial assay for diagnosis of apparently culture-negative *Coxiella burnetii* endocarditis. *European Journal of Clinical Microbiology and Infectious Diseases* 14:64–67.

Graham, B. (1996). Chiefs back anthrax inoculations. *Washington Post,* October 2, p. A1.

Gregg, M. B. (1985). The principles of an epidemic field investigation. In W. W. Holland, R. Detels, and G. Knox, eds., *Textbook of public health.* Oxford: Oxford University Press, pp. 284–299.

Grompe, M. (1993). The rapid detection of unknown mutations in nucleic acids. *Nature Genetics* 5:111–117.

Grmek, M. (1990). *History of AIDS: Emergence and origin of a modern pandemic.* Trans. R. Maulitz and J. Jacalyn. Princeton, N.J.: Princeton University Press.

Hamza, I. (1995). Syria links Israel joining NPT to peace talks. *Reuters News Service,* February 22.

Harrer, G. (1995). Interview with Iraqi oil minister 'Amir Muhammad Rashid by Gudrun Harrer in Vienna (in German). *Frankfurter Rundschau,* November 29, p. 7.

Harris, E. D. (1990). *New threats: Responding to the proliferation of nuclear, chemical and delivery capabilities in the Third World.* Lanham, Md.: University Press of America and Aspen Strategy Group.

Harris, S. H. (1994). *Factories of death: Japanese biological warfare 1932–45 and the American cover-up.* New York: Routledge.

Hemsley, John (1987). *The Soviet biochemical threat to NATO.* London: Macmillan Press.

Henderson, D. A. (1999). Biological terrorism—the looming threat of bioterrorism. *Science* 283:1279–1282.

Hendricks, M. (1989). The doomsday gene. *Washington Post.* January 1, p. A27.

Hersh, S. M. (1991). *The Samson option: Israel's nuclear arsenal and American foreign policy.* New York: Random House.

Hewetson, J. F., V. R. Rivera, D. A. Creasia, P. V. Lemley, et al. (1993). Protection of mice from inhaled ricin by vaccination with ricin or by passive treatment with heterologous antibody. *Vaccine* 11:743–746.

Hewlett, E. L. (1995). Toxins and other virulence factors. *Principles and practice of infectious diseases.* New York: Churchill Livingstone, pp. 2–8.

Hine, Patrick (1991). Joint commander Operation Granby. *London Gazette*, second supplement, June 28, p. G39.

Hinnebusch, J., and T. G. Schwan (1993). New method for plague surveillance using polymerase chain reaction to detect *Yersinia pestis* in fleas. *Journal of Clinical Microbiology* 31:1511–1514.

Hirsch, W. (1951). *Soviet BW and CW preparations and capabilities* (Hirsch Report) (translated from German). Edgewood, Md.: United States Army Chemical Warfare Service.

Holum, J. D. (1996). Statement, Biological Weapons Convention Fourth Review Conference, November 26.

Howey, D. C., R. R. Bowsher, R. L. Brunellel, et al. (1995). Pro(B29)0 human insulin: Effect of injection time on postprandial glycemia. *Clinical Pharmacology Therapy* 58(4):459–469.

Hunger, I. (1996). Article V: Confidence building measures. In G. S. Pearson and M. R. Dando, eds., *Strengthening the Biological Weapons Convention: Key points for the Fourth Review Conference*. Geneva: Quaker United Nations Office, pp. 77–92.

Hunt, E. H. (1998). Israel's biological and chemical research and development—potential menace at home and abroad. *Washington Report on Middle East Affairs*:84, 93.

Hurst, C. J., G. R. Knudsen, M. J. McInerney, L. D. Stetzenbach, and M. V. Walter, eds. (1996). *Manual of environmental microbiology*. Washington, D.C.: American Society for Microbiology.

Hurst, R. E., and J. Y. Rao (1993). Molecular biology in epidemiology. In P. A. Schulte and F. P. Perera, eds., *Molecular epidemiology: Principles and practices*, pp. 45–78. Academic Press: New York.

Hutchinson, A. M. (1995). Evanescent wave biosensor. Real time analysis of biomolecular interactions. *Molecular Biotechnology* 3:47–54.

Huxsoll, D. L. (1992). Narrowing the zone of uncertainty between research and development in biological warfare defense. In R. A. Zilinskas, ed., *The microbiologist and biological defense research: Ethics, politics and international security. Annals of the New York Academy of Sciences* 666:177–190.

———— (1994). The nature and scope of the BW threat. In Kathleen C. Bailey, ed., *Director's Series on Proliferation no. 4*. Livermore, Calif.: Lawrence Livermore Laboratory, p. 24.

———— (1995). On-site inspection measures and interviews. *Politics and the Life Sciences* 14(2):238–240.

Huxsoll, D. L., C. D. Parrott, and W. C. I. Patrick (1989). Medicine in defense against biological warfare. *Journal of the American Medical Association* 262(5):677–679.

Ibrahim, Y. M. (1994). Iraq is near economic ruin but Hussein appears secure. *New York Times*, October 25, pp. A1, A12.

ICSU (International Council of Scientific Unions) (1995). *ICSU Statement on freedom in the conduct of science*. Paris: International Council of Scientific Unions.

ICGEB (International Centre for Genetic Engineering and Biotechnology) (1997). *Activity report 1996*. Trieste, Italy: International Centre for Genetic Engineering and Biotechnology.

Inbar, E. (1996). Contours of Israel's new strategic thinking. *Political Science Quarterly* 111(1):41–64.

India (1991). Statement by ambassador from India. Unpublished paper, Seminar on the Biological and Toxin Weapons Convention. Noordwijk, the Netherlands.

Innis, M. A., D. H. Gelfand, and J. J. Sninsky, eds. (1995). *PCR strategies*. San Diego: Academic Press.

IOM (Institute of Medicine) (1996). Committee to Review the Health Consequences of Service During the Persian Gulf War. *Health consequences of service during the Persian Gulf War: Recommendations for research and information systems*. Washington, D.C.: National Academy Press.

Iovine, J. (1994). Genetically altering *Escherichia coli*. *Scientific American* 270:108–111.

Interdepartmental Political-Military Group (1969). *U.S. policy on chemical and biological warfare and agents: Report to the National Security Council*. Washington, D.C.: National Security Council.

Jackson, P. J., M. E. Hugh-Jones, D. M. Adair, G. Green, et al. (1998). PCR analysis of tissue samples from the 1979 Sverdlovsk anthrax victims: The presence of multiple *Bacillus anthracis* strains in different victims. *Proceedings of the National Academy of Sciences USA* 95:1224–1229.

Jacobs, G. (1986). Third World ballistic missiles: A cause for concern. *Jane's Defence Weekly,* November 15, p. 1179.

Jahrling, P. B., T. W. Geisbert, N. K. Jaax, M. A. Hanes, et al. (1996). Experimental infection of cyanomologous macaques with Ebola-Reston filoviruses from the 1989–1990 U.S. epizootic. *Archives of Virology Supplement* 11:115–134.

Jaurin, B., I. Bolin, M. Forsman, et al. (1987). *Genetic engineering and biological weapons*. Umea, Sweden: National Defense Research Institute.

Johannes, L. (1996). Biotech goat is created to produce drug. *Wall Street Journal,* April 9, p. B1.

Johnson, E. D., B. K. Johnson, D. Silverstein, P. Tukei, et al. (1996). Characterization of a new Marburg virus isolated from a 1987 fatal case in Kenya. *Archives of Virology Supplement* 11:101–114.

Johnson, K. M. (1990). Marburg and Ebola viruses. In G. L. Mandell, R. G. Douglas Jr., and J. E. Bennett, eds., *Principles and practice of infectious diseases,* pp. 1303–1306. New York: Churchill Livingstone.

Johnson-Winegar, A. (1995). The role of declarations in UNSCOM's program in Iraq. *Politics and the Life Sciences* 14(2):236–238.

Jones, P. (1998). Israel's nuclear option plays large regional role. *Washington Times,* June 3, p. A17.

Joseph, R. (1996). Proliferation, counter-proliferation and NATO. *Survival* 38 (1):111–130.

Kaplan, D. E., and A. Marshall (1996). *The cult at the end of the world: The incredible story of Aum*. London: Hutchinson, and New York: Crown.

Kaplan, M. M. (1999). The efforts of WHO and Pugwash to eliminate chemical and biological weapons—a memoir. *Bulletin of the World Health Organization* 77(2):149–155.

Kemp, G. (1991). *The control of the Middle East arms race*. Washington, D.C.: Carnegie Endowment for International Peace.

Keeny, S. M. J. (1995). NPT endgame '95: Finish strong. *Arms Control Today* 25(2):2.

al-Khalil, S. (1989). *Republic of fear: The inside story of Saddam's Iraq*. New York: Pantheon Books.

Köster, H., K. Tang, D.-J. Fu, A. Braun, et al. (1996). A strategy for rapid and efficient DNA sequencing by mass spectrometry. *Nature Biotechnology* 14:1123–1128.

Kozal, M. J., N. Shah, N. Shen, R. Yang, et al. (1996). Extensive polymorphisms observed in HIV-1 clade B protease gene using high-density oligonucleotide arrays. *Nature Medicine* 2:753–766.

Kramer, F. R., and P. M. Lizardi (1989). Replicatable RNA reporters. *Nature* 339:401–402.

Krasner, S. D. (1983). Structural causes and regime consequences: Regimes as intervening variables. In S. D. Krasner, ed., *International Regimes*. Ithaca: Cornell University Press.

Ksiazek, T. G., C. J. Peters, P. E. Rollin, S. Zaki, et al. (1995). Identification of a new North American Hantavirus that causes acute pulmonary insufficiency. *American Journal of Tropical Medicine and Hygiene* 52:117–123.

Ksiazek, T. G., P. E. Rollin, P. B. Jahrling, E. Johnson, et al. (1992). Enzyme immunosorbent assay for Ebola virus antigens in tissues of infected primates. *Journal of Clinical Microbiology* 30:947–950.

Kucewicz, W. (1990). Lead scientist in scourge search. *Wall Street Journal,* May 1, p. 6.

Kumaraswamy, P. R. (1996). Marcus Klingberg and Israel's "biological option." *Middle East International* 532: 21–22.

——— (1998). Has Israel kept its BW options open? *Jane's Intelligence Review* 10(3): 22.

Lederberg, J. (1993). Viruses and humankind: Intracellular symbiosis and evolutionary competition. In S. S. Morse, ed., *Emerging Viruses,* pp. 3–9. New York: Oxford University Press.

Lehman, R. F. (1996). Foreword. In J. A. Larsen and G. J. Rattray, eds., *Arms control: Toward the 21st century,* pp. vii–ix. Boulder: Lynne Rienner Publishers.

Leitenberg, M. (1991). Soviet activities related to biological weapons. *Arms Control* 12(2):161–190.

——— (1992). Anthrax in Sverdlovsk: New pieces to the puzzle. *Arms Control Today* 22(3):10–13.

——— (1996a). Biological weapons arms control. *Contemporary Security Policy* 17(1):1–79.

——— (1996b). *Biological weapons arms control.* Project on Rethinking Arms Control, PRAC Paper no. 16. College Park, Md.: Center for International and Security Studies at Maryland.

——— (1998). Resolution of the Korean War biological warfare allegations. *Critical Reviews in Microbiology* 24:169–194.

Lemley, P. V., P. Amanatides, and D. C. Wright (1994). Identification and characterization of a monoclonal antibody that neutralizes ricin toxicity in vitro and in vivo. *Hybridoma* 13:417–421.

Lewis, F. (1987). Moscow at the crossroads. *New York Times,* December 11, p. 39.

Ligieza, J., J. Reiss, and M. Michalik (1994). Chemiluminescence immunosorbent assay (CLISA) and a possibility of the specific detection of soluble antigens of *Clostridium botulinum* type A. *Archivum Immunologiae et Therapiae Experimentalis* (Warsaw) 42:129–133.

Litovkin, V. (1992). Yeltsin bans work on bacteriological weapons. This means: Work was underway, and we were deceived (in Russian). *Izvestiya,* April 24:1.

London *Sunday Times* (1995). Article on August 27, cited in the *Chemical Weapons Convention Bulletin* (30):17.

Lorieux, C. (1995). Interview with Iraqi deputy prime minister Tariq 'Aziz by Claude Lorieux in Baghdad (in French). *Le Figaro* (Paris), September 30, p. 2.

Lowe, K., G. Pearson, and V. Utgoff (1996). Potential values of a simple BW protective mask. Institute for Defense Analyses IDA Paper P-3077.

MacEachin, D. J. (1998). Routine and challenge: Two pillars of verification. *CBW Conventions Bulletin* (39):1.

MacLean, D. (1992). Ethics and biological defense research. In R. A. Zilinskas, ed., *The microbiologist and biological defense research: Ethics, politics and international security. Annals of the New York Academy of Sciences* 666:100–112.

Mahnaimi, U., and J. Adams (1996). Iran builds biological arsenal. *Sunday Times* (London), August 11. See also Web site http://web.lexis-nexis.com/universe/docu...a3&_md5=f317decdb3975b80cdb7805a3f5b425d.

Marcus, A. D. (1996). U.S. drive to curb doomsday weapons in Mideast is faltering. *Wall Street Journal,* September 6, pp. A1, A6.

Marrie, T. J. (1990). *Coxiella burnetii* (Q fever). In G. L. Mandell, R. G. Douglas Jr., and J. E. Bennett, eds., *Principles and practice of infectious diseases.* New York: Churchill Livingstone, pp. 1472–1476.

Marwick, C. (1994). Vaccinia-based immunization may be on the way. *Journal of the American Medical Association* 272(23):1810.

Massung, R. F., J. J. Esposito, L. I. Liu, J. Qi, T. R. Utterback, et al. (1993). Potential virulence determinants in terminal regions of variola smallpox virus genome. *Nature* 366(6457):748–751.

Massung, R. F., L. I. Liu, J. Qi, J. C. Knight, et al. (1994). Analysis of the complete genome of smallpox variola major virus strain Bangladesh—1975. *Virology* 201(2):215–240.

Matzusawa, M., R. S. Potember, D. A. Stenger, and V. Krauthamer (1993). Containment and growth of neuroblastoma cells on chemically patterned substrates. *Journal of Neuroscience Methods* 50:253–260.

McDade, J. E., C. C. Shepard, D. W. Fraser, and T. R. Tsai, et al. (1977). Legionnaires' disease: Isolation of a bacterium and demonstration of its role in other respiratory disease. *New England Journal of Medicine* 297:1197–1203.

Medical Management of Chemical Casualties Handbook (1993). U.S. Army Medical Research Institute of Chemical Defense, Aberdeen Proving Ground, Md.

Medical Management of Biological Casualties Handbook (1996). U.S. Army Medical Research Institute of Infectious Diseases, Fort Detrick, Frederick, Md.

Meselson, M. (1999). The challenge of biological and chemical weapons. *Bulletin of the World Health Organization* 77(2):102–103.

Meselson, M., J. Guillemin, M. Hugh-Jones, A. Langmuir, I. Popova, A. Shelokov, and O. Yampolskaya (1994). The Sverdlovsk anthrax outbreak of 1979. *Science* 266:1202–1208.

Meselson, M. S., and J. Perry Robinson (1996). Criminalizing BW. *Chemical Weapons Convention Bulletin* 31:1.

Miller, J. (1993). Evidence grows on biological weapons. *New York Times Magazine,* January 3, p. 33.

——— (1998a). Iraq arrests scientist viewed as father of its germ war effort. *New York Times,* March 24, p. 6.

Miller, J., J. Broad, and W. J. Broad (1998b). New York girding for grim fear: Deadly germ attack by terrorists. *New York Times,* June 19, p. A1.

Ministry of Defence (1991). *Statement on the Defence Estimates, Britain's Defence for the '90s,* CM 1559-I, Her Majesty's Stationery Office, London, July.

MMWR (*Morbidity and Mortality Weekly Report*) (June 9, 1995). Enhanced detection of sporadic *Escherichia coli* O157:H7 infections—New Jersey, July 1994. Vol. 44:417–418.

—— (July 14, 1995). Outbreak of acute gastroenteritis attributable to *Escherichia coli* serotype O104:H21—Helena, Montana, 1994. Vol. 44:501–503.

—— (October 6, 1995). Venezuelan equine encephalitis—Colombia, 1995. Vol. 44:721–724.

—— (March 22, 1996). *Shigella sonnei* outbreak associated with contaminated drinking water—Island Park, Idaho, August 1995. Vol. 45:229–231.

Moelans, I. I., J. Cohen, M. Marchand, C. Molitor, et al. (1995). Induction of *Plasmodium falciparum* sporozoite-neutralizing antibodies upon vaccination with recombinant Pfs16 vaccinia virus. *Molecular Biochemical Parasitology* 72(1–2):179–192.

Mohr, A. J. (1995). Biological sampling and analysis procedures for the United Nations Special Commission (UNSCOM) in Iraq. *Politics and the Life Sciences* 14(2):240–243.

Monath, T. P., and L. K. Gordon (1998). Biological warfare—strengthening the Biological Weapons Convention. *Science* 282:1423.

Moodie, M. (1993). Arms control programs and biological weapons. In B. Roberts, ed., *Biological weapons: Weapons of the future?* vol. 15, Significant Issues Series, pp. 47–57. Washington, D.C.: Center for Strategic and International Studies.

Morgan, C. L., D. J. Newman, and C. P. Price (1996). Immunosensors: Technology and opportunities in laboratory medicine. *Clinical Chemistry* 42:193–209.

Morse, S. S. (1992). Epidemiologic surveillance for investigating chemical or biological warfare and for improving human health. *Politics and the Life Sciences* 11:28–29.

—— (1996). Importance of molecular diagnostics in the identification and control of emerging infections. *Molecular Diagnosis* 1:201–206.

Morse, S. S., B. H. Rosenberg, and J. P. Woodall (1996). ProMED global monitoring of emerging diseases: Design for a demonstration program. *Health Policy* 38:135–153.

Mukerjee, M. (1994). Little winners: Bioprospectors reap rewards from Third World microbes. *Scientific American* 270(6):105.

Mullis, K. B., and F. A. Faloona (1987). Specific synthesis of DNA *in vitro* via a polymerase-catalyzed chain reaction. *Methods in Enzymology* 155:335–350.

Murphy, D. E. (1998). U.S. had a role in S. African biological warfare, witness alleges. *Detroit News.* Web site: httm://detnews.com:80/1998/nation/9808/01/08010066.htm.

Murray, P. R., E. J. Baron, M. A. Pfaller, F. C. Tenover, and R. H. Yolken, eds. (1999). *Manual of clinical microbiology,* 7th ed. Washington, D.C.: American Society for Microbiology.

Myers, G., K. MacInnes, and L. Myers (1993). Phylogenetic moments in the AIDS epidemic. In S. S. Morse, ed., *Emerging viruses.* New York: Oxford University Press, pp. 120–137.

NAS (National Academy of Sciences) (1995). *On being a scientist: Responsible conduct in research.* Washington, D.C.: National Academy Press.

NATO (North Atlantic Treaty Organization) (1994). Alliance policy framework on the proliferation of weapons of mass destruction. Press release M-NAC-

1(94)45, issued at the Ministerial Meeting of the North Atlantic Council, Istanbul, June 9.

Nature (1994). India ponders the flaws exposed by plague. *Nature* 372:119.

——— (1995). Indian confirms identity of plague. *Nature* 373:650.

Netherlands (1991). National position paper: The Netherlands. Unpublished paper, Seminar on the Biological and Toxin Weapons Convention. Noordwijk, the Netherlands.

Netherlands and Canada (1993). Bilateral trial inspection in a large vaccine production facility: A contribution to the evaluation of potential verification measures. Paper submitted to the Ad Hoc Group of Governmental Experts to Identify and Examine Potential Verification Measures from a Scientific and Technical Standpoint, Third Session. Geneva.

Netherlands Institute for Southern Africa (1997). *Questions about the involvement of the South African apartheid regime and its secret services in external operations like hit squads, chemical and biological warfare. Submission to the Research Department of the Truth and Reconciliation Commission by the Netherlands Institute for Southern Africa.* Web site: httm://www.contrast.org/truth/html/chemical_biological_weapons.html.

New York Times (1991). January 13, p. A9.

Nichol, S. T., C. F. Spiropoulo, S. Morzunov, P. E. Rollin, et al. (1993). Genetic identification of a Hantavirus associated with an outbreak of acute respiratory illness. *Science* 262:914–917.

Nielsen, F. S., L. N. Jorensen, M. Ipsen, A. I. Voldsgaard, and H. H. Parring (1995). Long-term comparison of human insulin analogue B10Asp and soluble human insulin in IDDM patients on a basal/bolus insulin regime. *Diabetologia* 38(5):592–598.

Nigeria (1991). Statement by Ambassador E. A. Azikiwe of Nigeria at the Seminar on the Biological Weapons Convention in the perspective of the forthcoming Third Review Conference. Unpublished paper, Seminar on the Biological and Toxin Weapons Convention. Noordwijk, the Netherlands.

Nixon, R. M. (1969). *Statement by the president.* Washington, D.C.: Office of the White House Press Secretary.

——— (1970). *The White House.* Key Biscayne, Fla.: Office of the White House Press Secretary.

——— (1971). Statement on chemical and biological defense policies and programs, November 25, 1969. In *Public papers of the presidents of the United States: Richard M. Nixon, 1969.* Washington, D.C.: U.S. Government Printing Office.

Norway (1991). Biological Weapons Convention: Position paper, Norway. Unpublished paper, Seminar on the Biological and Toxin Weapons Convention. Noordwijk, the Netherlands.

Novick, R., and S. Shulman (1990). New forms of biological warfare? In Susan Wright, ed., *Preventing a Biological Arms Race.* Cambridge, Mass.: MIT Press, pp. 103–119.

Odom, W. (1989). Soviet military doctrine. *Foreign Affairs* 67(2):114–134.

Old, R. W., and S. B. Primrose (1994). *Principles of gene manipulation: An introduction to genetic engineering,* 5th edition. Cambridge, Mass.: Blackwell Science.

Olson, Kyle B. (1994). *The Matsumoto incident: Sarin poisoning in a Japanese residential community.* Alexandria, Va.: Chemical and Biological Arms Control Institute.

Ottaway, D. B. (1989). U.S. gave Iraq bacteria, senator charges. *Washington Post,* January 26, p. A16.

Ou, C.-Y., C. A. Ciesielski, G. Myers, C. I. Bandea, et al. (1992). Molecular epidemiology of HIV transmission in a dental practice. *Science* 256:1165–1171.

Pacific Research (1996). The one that nearly got away: Iraq and biological weapons, an interview with Rod Barton. *Pacific Research* 9:31–35.

Patrick, W. C. III (1994a). Biological warfare: An overview. *Director's Series on Proliferation no. 4.* Livermore, Calif.: Lawrence Livermore Laboratory, pp. 2–3.

————— (1994b). A history of biological and toxin warfare. In Kathleen C. Bailey, ed., *Director's Series on Proliferation, no. 4.* Livermore, Calif.: Lawrence Livermore National Laboratory, Report no. UCRL-LR-114070-4, pp. 9–20.

Pearson, G. S. (1993a). Biological weapons: Their nature and arms control. In E. Karsh, M. S. Navias, and P. Sabin, eds., *Non-conventional weapons proliferation in the Middle East: Tackling the spread of nuclear, chemical and biological capabilities.* Oxford: Clarendon Press, pp. 99–133.

————— (1993b). Prospects for chemical and biological arms control: The web of deterrence. *Washington Quarterly* 16(2):145–163.

————— (1995). Chemical and biological defence: An essential national security requirement. *RUSI Journal* 140 (4):20–27.

————— (1997). Environmental and security regimes for toxic chemicals and pathogens: A useful synergy. In R. Guthrie, ed., *Verification 1997, the VERTIC yearbook.* Boulder, Colo.: Westview Press, pp. 131–158.

Pearson, G. S., and M. R. Dando (1997). *The necessity for non-challenge visits.* Strengthening the Biological Weapons Convention, Briefing Paper no. 2. Bradford: Department of Peace Studies, University of Bradford.

————— (1998). *An optimum organization.* Strengthening the Biological Weapons Convention, Working Paper no. 5. Bradford: Department of Peace Studies, University of Bradford.

Perry Robinson, J. P. (1980). East-West fencing at Geneva. *Nature* 284:393.

————— (1981). Environmental effects of chemical and biological warfare. In W. Barnaby, C. Erikson, and A. Fraser, eds., *War and environment.* Stockholm: Environmental Advisory Council, Ministry of Agriculture.

————— (1996). Some political aspects of the control of biological weapons: Address to the Parliamentary and Scientific Committee. *Science in Parliament* 53(3):6–11.

————— (1998). The impact of Pugwash on the debates over chemical and biological weapons. In A. L. C. Cerreño and A. Keynan, eds., *Scientific cooperation, state conflict: The roles of scientists in mitigating international discord. Annals of the New York Academy of Sciences* 866:224–252.

PhRMA (Pharmaceutical Research and Manufacturers of America) (1996a). Statement of principle on the Biological Weapons Convention, May 16.

————— (1996b). Reducing the threat of biological weapons—A PhRMA Perspective.

————— (1996c). Correspondence from PhRMA president Gerald Massinghof, to John Holum, director of the U.S. Arms Control and Disarmament Agency, June 12.

Poli, M. A., V. R. Rivera, J. F. Hewetson, and G. A. Merrill (1994). Detection of ricin by colorimetric and chemiluminescence ELISA. *Toxicon* 32:1371–1377.

Potgieter, D. W. (1998). Apartheid's poison legacy: South Africa's chemical and biological warfare program. *Covert Action Quarterly.* Web site: http://caq.com: 80/CAQ/caq63/caq63apartheid.html.

Potter, W. C. (1982). *Nuclear power and nonproliferation: An interdisciplinary approach.* Cambridge, Mass.: Oelgeschlager, Gunn and Hain.

——— (1995). The politics of nuclear renunciation: The cases of Belarus, Kazakhstan, and Ukraine, Occasional Papers no. 22 (April). Washington, D.C.: Henry L. Stimson Center.

Poupard, J. A., and L.A. Miller (1992). History of biological warfare: Catapults to capsomeres. In R. A. Zilinskas, ed., *The microbiologist and biological defense research: Ethics, politics, and international security. Annals of the New York Academy of Sciences* 666:920.

Powell, C. (1993). Statement before the House Armed Services Committee, U.S. Congress, March 30.

Primakov, Yevgeni (1993). *A new challenge after the Cold War: The proliferation of weapons of mass destruction.* Moscow: Foreign Intelligence Service of the Russian Federation, pp. 1–30.

Rabbany, S. Y., B. L. Donner, and F. S. Ligler (1994). Optical immunosensors. *CRC Critical Reviews in Biomedical Engineering* 22:307–346.

Rattray, G. J. (1996). Introduction. In J. A. Larsen and G. J. Rattray, eds., *Arms control: Toward the 21st century,* pp. 1–18. Boulder: Lynne Rienner Publishers.

Raviv, D., and Y. Melman (1990). *Every spy a prince: A complete history of Israel's intelligence community.* Boston: Houghton Mifflin.

Reed, J. (1993). *Defence exports: Current concerns.* London: Jane's Consultancy Services.

Relman, D. A., and D. H. Persing (1996). Molecular methods for pathogen identification. In D. H. Persing, ed., *PCR protocols for emerging infectious diseases.* Washington, D.C.: American Society for Microbiology.

Rennie, J. (1994). Borrowed savagery: Interloping viral genes may cause lethal strep infections. *Scientific American* 271(2):26.

Reuters News Service (1988). Egyptian says Arabs should acquire chemical weapons, July 27, P.M. cycle.

——— (1995). Iraq targeted enemy capitals if Baghdad nuked, September 21.

——— (1996). Gaddafi says Arabs have right to germ warfare arms, March 30.

Richman, D. D. (1993). Virus detection systems. In S. S. Morse, ed., *Emerging viruses.* New York: Oxford University Press, pp. 91–99.

Rimmington, A. (1996). From military to industrial complex? The conversion of biological weapons facilities in the Russian Federation. *Contemporary Security Policy* 17:80–112.

Ritter, S. (1999). *End game: Solving the Iraqi problem—once and for all.* New York: Simon & Schuster.

Roberts, B. (1994). Controlling the proliferation of biological weapons. *The Nonproliferation Review* 2:55–59.

——— (1998). Export controls and biological weapons: New roles, new challenges. *Critical Reviews in Microbiology* 24:235–254.

Rodan, S. (1996). Chemical, biological threats loom large in U.S.-Israeli talks. *Defense News,* December 2–8, p. 6.

Rosato, R. R., F. F. Macasaet, and P. B. Jahrling (1988). Enzyme-linked immunosorbent assay detection of immunoglobulins G and M to Venezuelan equine encephalomyelitis virus in vaccinated and naturally infected humans. *Journal of Clinical Microbiology* 26:421–425.

Rose, N. R., E. Conway de Macario, J. D. Folds, H. C. Lane, and R. M. Nakamura, eds. (1997). *Manual of clinical laboratory immunology,* 5th ed. Washington, D.C.: American Society for Microbiology.

Rosebury, T. (1949). *Peace or pestilence: Biological warfare and how to avoid it.* New York: Whittlesey House.

——— (1963). Medical ethics and biological warfare. *Perspectives in Biology and Medicine* 6:512–523.

Rosenberg, B. H. (1993). North vs. South: Politics and the Biological Weapons Convention. *Politics and the Life Sciences* 12(1):69–77.

Royal Society (1994). *Scientific aspects of control of biological weapons.* London: The Royal Society.

Russian Foreign Intelligence Service (1993). *A new challenge after the Cold War: Proliferation of weapons of mass destruction,* trans. in U.S. Foreign Broadcast Information Service, *JPRS Report: Proliferation Issues,* JPRS-TND-93-007, March 5.

Safire, W. (1995). Iraq's ton of germs. *New York Times,* April 13, p. A25.

Saiki, R. K., D. H. Gelfand, S. Stoffel, R. Higuchi, et al. (1988). Primer-directed enzymatic amplification of DNA with a thermostable DNA polymerase. *Science* 239:487–491.

Saluzzo, J. F., and B. Le Guenno (1987). Rapid diagnosis of human Crimean-Congo hemorrhagic fever and detection of the virus in naturally infected ticks. *Journal of Clinical Microbiology* 25:922–924.

Sambrook, J., E. F. Fritsch, and T. Maniatis (1989). *Molecular cloning: A laboratory manual,* 2nd ed. Cold Spring Harbor, N.Y.: Cold Spring Harbor Laboratory Press.

Sano, T., C. L. Smith, and C. R. Cantor (1992). Immuno-PCR: Very sensitive antigen detection by means of specific antibody-DNA conjugates. *Science* 258:120–122.

Schelling, T. C. (1984). Confidence in crisis. *International Security* 8(4):55–66.

Schelling, T. C., and M. H. Halperin, assisted by D. G. Brennan (1961). *Strategy and arms control.* New York, N.Y.: Twentieth Century Fund.

Schmaljohn, A. L., D. Li, D. L. Negley, D. S. Bressler, et al. (1995). Isolation and initial characterization of a newfound Hantavirus from California. *Virology* 206:963–972.

Schwarz, T. F., H. Nsanze, M. Longson, H. Nitschko, et al. (1996). Polymerase chain reaction for diagnosis and identification of distinct variants of Crimean-Congo hemorrhagic fever virus in the United Arab Emirates. *Archivum Immunologiae et Therapiae Experimentalis* 55:190–196.

Science (1996). Libya and Iran seek ex-Soviet scientists. *Science* 271:1485.

Seiff, Martin (1996). "Devastating" reply to gas attack vowed. *Washington Times,* March 29, p. A6.

Shchelkunov, S. N., R. F. Massung, and J. J. Esposito. (1995). Comparison of the genome DNA sequences of Bangladesh-1975 and India-1967 variola viruses. *Virus Research* 36(1):107–118.

Sigma Xi (1993). *1993 Sigma Xi forum proceedings ethics, values, and the promise of science.* Research Triangle Park, N.C.: Sigma Xi Publications.

Shepherd, A. J., D. E. Hummitzsch, P. A. Leman, R. Swanepol, and L. A. Searle (1986). Comparative tests for detection of plague antigen and antibody in experimentally infected wild rodents. *Journal of Clinical Microbiology* 24:1075–1078.

Sims, N. A. (1988). *The diplomacy of biological disarmament: Vicissitudes of a treaty in force. 1975–1985.* London: MacMillan Press, p. 356. New York: St. Martin's.

Sinai, J. (1997). Libya's pursuit of weapons of mass destruction. *Nonproliferation Review* 4(3):92–100.

———— (1998). Ghadaffi's Libya: The patient proliferator. *Jane's Intelligence Review* 10:27.

SIPRI (Stockholm International Peace Research Institute) (1971). *The problem of chemical and biological warfare*, vol. 1: *The rise of CB weapons*. New York: Humanities Press.

———— (1973a). *The problem of chemical and biological warfare*, vol. 2: *CB weapons today*. New York: Humanities Press.

———— (1973b). *The problem of chemical and biological warfare*, vol. 3: *CBW and the law of war*. New York: Humanities Press.

Smith, G., M. Mackett, and B. Moss (1983). Infectious vaccinia virus recombinants that express hepatitis B surface antigen. *Nature* 32(5908):490–495.

Smith, L. M. (1996). Sequence from spectrometry: A realistic prospect? *Nature Biotechnology* 14:1084–1085.

Smith, R. J. (1992a). Russia fails to detail germ arms. *Washington Post*, August 31, pp. A1, A15.

———— (1992b). Yeltsin blames '79 anthrax on germ warfare efforts. *Washington Post*, June 16, pp. A1, A15.

———— (1994). Russia's germ warfare program is alive, U.S. says. *International Herald Tribune*, September 4, p. 1.

———— (1997). Iraq's drive for a biological arsenal. *Washington Post*, November 21, pp. A1, A48.

South Africa (1995a). United Nations Ad Hoc Group of the Parties to the Convention on the Prohibition of the Development, Production and Stockpiling of Bacteriological (Biological) and Toxin Weapons and on Their Destruction. *The relationship between investigations of alleged use of BTW and unusual outbreaks of disease and challenge inspections*. Working paper prepared by South Africa. BWC/AD HOC GROUP/WP. 16.

———— (1995b). United Nations Ad Hoc Group of the Parties to the Convention on the Prohibition of the Development, Production and Stockpiling of Bacteriological (Biological) and Toxin Weapons and on Their Destruction. *Use of investigative epidemiology as a tool in the investigation of unusual outbreak of disease and alleged use of biological weapons*. Working paper prepared by South Africa. BWC/AD HOC GROUP/WP. 11.

———— (1996a). United Nations Ad Hoc Group of the Parties to the Convention on the Prohibition of the Development, Production and Stockpiling of Bacteriological (Biological) and Toxin Weapons and on Their Destruction. *Difference between investigation of alleged use of BTW and investigation of unusual outbreaks of disease*. Working paper prepared by South Africa. BWC/AD HOC GROUP/WP. 54.

———— (1996b). United Nations Ad Hoc Group of the Parties to the Convention on the Prohibition of the Development, Production and Stockpiling of Bacteriological (Biological) and Toxin Weapons and on Their Destruction. *Systems and tools for an investigation of the alleged use of biological or toxin weapons*. Working paper prepared by South Africa. BWC/AD HOC GROUP/WP. 55.

———— (1996c). United Nations Ad Hoc Group of the Parties to the Convention on the Prohibition of the Development, Production and Stockpiling of Bacteriological (Biological) and Toxin Weapons and on Their Destruction. *Unusual outbreaks of disease and their investigation*. Working paper prepared by South Africa. BWC/AD HOC GROUP/WP. 62.

South Centre. (1996). *For a strong and democratic United Nations: A South perspective on UN reform.* Geneva: South Centre.

Stafford, R. G., and H. B. Hines (1995). Urinary elimination of saxitoxin after intravenous injection. *Toxicon* 33:1501–1510.

Starr, B. (1996). Impenetrable Libyan CW plant progresses. *Jane's Defence Weekly,* April 17, p. 3.

Stein, A., and D. Raoult (1992). Detection of *Coxiella burnetii* by DNA amplification using polymerase chain reaction. *Journal of Clinical Microbiology* 30:2462–2466.

Steinberg, G. M. (1994). Middle East arms control and regional security. *Survival* 36(1):126–141.

St. Onge, A. A. (1995). United Nations biological warfare inspectors in Iraq: Implications for biological arms control—One Canadian's perspective. *Politics and the Life Sciences* 14(2):259–262.

Suplee, C. (1996). Epidemiology: Elusive bacteria adopt disguises. *Washington Post,* May 13, p. A2.

Sweden (1991). Verification of the Biological Weapons Convention: A Swedish position paper. Unpublished paper, Seminar on the Biological and Toxin Weapons Convention. Noordwijk, the Netherlands.

Taylor, P. (1995). Toxic S. African arms raise concern. *Washington Post,* February 28, p. A14.

Taylor, R. (1996). All fall down. *New Scientist* 150:32–37.

Technical Evaluation Meeting (1998). *Report of the United Nations Special Commission's Team to the Technical Evaluation Meeting on the Proscribed Biological Warfare Program,* Vienna, March 20–27. Vienna: United Nations Special Commission.

Tehran IRNA (1988). Broadcast in English, transcribed in *Foreign Broadcast Information Service Daily Report: Near East and South Asia,* October 19, pp. 55–56.

Terrill, W. A. (1991). The chemical warfare legacy of the Yemen War. *Comparative Strategy* 10(2):109–119.

——— (1994). Libya and the quest for chemical weapons. *Conflict Quarterly* 14:47–61.

Titball, R. W., and G. S. Pearson (1993). BWC verification measures: Technologies for the identification of biological warfare agents. *Politics and the Life Sciences* 12 (2):255–263.

Townes, J. M., P. R. Cieslak, C. L. Hatheway, H. M. Solomon, et al. (1996). An outbreak of type A botulism associated with commercial cheese sauce. *Annals of Internal Medicine* 125:558–563.

Trainor, B. (1996). Interview during the Public Broadcasting Service *Frontline* special, The Gulf War, Part I, broadcast on January 9.

Trevan, T. (1999). *Saddam's secrets: The hunt for Iraq's hidden weapons.* London: HarperCollins.

Tsuneishi, K. (1982). *The germ warfare unit that disappeared: The Kwantung Army's 731st unit.* Tokyo: Kaimeisha.

Tucker, J. B. (1992). The future of biological warfare. In W. T. Wander and E. H. Arnett, eds., *The proliferation of advanced weaponry: Technology, motivations, and responses,* pp. 53–73. Washington, D.C.: American Association for the Advancement of Science.

——— (1993). Lessons of Iraq's biological weapons programme. *Arms Control/Contemporary Security Policy* 14:229–271.

—— (1994). Dilemmas of a dual-use technology: Toxins in medicine and warfare. *Politics and the Life Sciences* 13(1):51–62.

—— (1996). Chemical/biological terrorism: Coping with a new threat. *Politics and the Life Sciences* 15(2):167–183.

——, ed. (1997). *The utility of sampling and analysis for compliance monitoring of the Biological Weapons Convention.* Proceedings of a workshop held in Washington, D.C., October 7–8, 1996. Monterey Institute of International Studies and L.L.N.L. Center for Global Security Research.

—— (1998). Strengthening the BWC: Moving toward a compliance protocol. *Arms Control Today* 28:20–27.

Turner, A. P. F. (1997). Switching channels makes sense. [News and Views]. *Nature* (London) 387:555–557.

TVS Production (1985). *Did the emperor know?* A television documentary film presented on British Broadcasting Company's channel 1, United Kingdom.

Twing, S. L. (1996). Is Iran's military buildup purely defensive or potentially destabilizing? *Washington Report on Middle East Affairs* 14:7–8.

United Kingdom (1994). Special Conference of the States Parties to the Convention on the Prohibition of the Development, Production and Stockpiling of Bacteriological (Biological) and Toxin Weapons, and on Their Destruction. *United Kingdom BTWC practice compliance inspection (PCI) programme. Summary Report.* Working paper prepared by the United Kingdom. BWC/SPCONF/WP.2.

United Nations (1969). Report of the Secretary-General, *Chemical and bacteriological (biological) weapons and the effects of their possible use.* A/7575/Rev.1, S/9292/Rev. 1.

—— (1992). Conference on Environment and Development, Rio de Janeiro 1992, United Nations Conference on Environment and Development, A/CONF. 151/26, August 12, 1992. Also available as *Earth Summit '92,* Regency Press Corporation, London.

—— (1995). *Verification in all its aspects, including the role of the United Nations in the field of verification.* A/50/377.

UN Environment Programme (1995). Decision II/5: Consideration of the need for and modalities of a protocol for the safe transfer, handling and use of modified living organisms. *Report of the Second Conference of the Parties to the Convention on Biological Diversity,* Jakarta, November 6–17. UNEP/CBD/COP/2/19, Annex II.

UN General Assembly (1972). *Convention on the Prohibition of the Development, Production and Stockpiling of Bacteriological (Biological) and Toxin Weapons, and on Their Destruction,* Resolution 2826 (XXVI). The convention is reproduced in U.S. Department of State (1975), *Treaties and Other International Acts,* series 8062, and in Her Majesty's Stationery Office, Cmnd. 5053.

—— (1996a). Letter dated July 5, 1996, from the Permanent Representative of France to the United Nations addressed to the Secretary-General, A/51/208, S/1996/543.

—— (1996b). Letter dated August 1, 1996, from the Permanent Representative of France to the United Nations addressed to the Secretary-General, measures to eliminate international terrorism, A/51/261.

—— (1996c). Address by President Bill Clinton, fifty-first Session, 6th Plenary Meeting, September 24, A/51/PV.6.

UNSCOM (UN Special Commission) (1999a). *Report: Disarmament.* New York: UN Special Commission.

────── (1999b). *Iraq: Ongoing monitoring and verification*. New York: UN Special Commission.

UN Security Council (1990). *Resolution 660 (1990)*. S/RES/660.

────── (1991). *Resolution 687 (1991)*. S/RES/687.

────── (1992). Third 6-monthly report of the Executive Chairman of UNSCOM, S/24984, December 17.

────── (1995a). *Eighth report of the Secretary-General on the status of the implementation of the Special Commission's plan for the ongoing monitoring and verification of Iraq's compliance with the relevant parts of section C of Security Council resolution 687 (1991)*. S/1995/864.

────── (1995b). *Tenth report of the Executive Chairman of the Special Commission established by the Secretary-General pursuant to paragraph 9(b)(i) of Security Council resolution 687 (1991), and paragraph 3 of resolution 699 (1991) on the activities of the Special Commission*. S/1995/1038.

────── (1996). *Report of the Secretary-General on the activities of the Special Commission established by the Secretary-General pursuant to paragraph 9(b)(i) of resolution 687 (1991)*, S/1996/848.

────── (1997). *Report of the Secretary-General on the activities of the Special Commission established by the Secretary-General pursuant to paragraph 9(b)(i) of resolution 687 (1991)*, S/1997/301.

────── (1998). *Report of the Secretary-General on the activities of the Special Commission established by the Secretary-General pursuant to paragraph 9(b)(i) of resolution 687 (1991)*, S/1998/332.

Urban, M. (1993). The Cold War's deadliest secret. *Spectator Magazine*, Jan. 23, 1993, pp. 9–10.

U.S. Congress (1993a). Committee on Armed Services, House of Representatives. *Countering the chemical and biological weapons threat in the post-Soviet world*. Report of the special inquiry into the chemical and biological threat. 102nd Congress, 2nd session. Washington, D.C.: U.S. Government Printing Office.

────── (1993b). Committee on Armed Services, House of Representatives, Report on special inquiry into the chemical and biological threat. 102d Congress, 2d session, no. 15, February 23.

────── (1993c). Office of Technology Assessment. *Proliferation of weapons of mass destruction: Assessing the risks*. OTA-ISC-559, S/N 052-003-01335-5. Washington, D.C.: U.S. Government Printing Office.

────── (1993d). Office of Technology Assessment. *Technologies underlying weapons of mass destruction*. OTA-BP-ISC-115, S/N 052-003-01361-4. Washington, D.C.: U.S. Government Printing Office.

────── (1993e). Committee on Armed Services, House of Representatives. Statement by General Colin Powell made during Full Committee Hearings on Authorization and Oversight, National Defense Authorization Act for Fiscal Year 1994, March 30, 1993. In H.R 2401, HASC No. 103-9. Washington, D.C.: U.S. Government Printing Office.

────── (1996). Conference Report on S. 735, Terrorism Prevention Act, House of Representatives, House Report 104-518, April 15, 104th Congress, 2nd session. Web site: http://rs9.loc.gov/cgi-bin/query/D?r104:3:./temp/ˆr104mx97g8: e207.

U.S. Department of Defense (1987). *Soviet military power 1987*. Washington, D.C.: U.S. Department of Defense.

────── (1992). *Conduct of the Persian Gulf War*. Final Report to Congress Pursuant to Title V of the Persian Gulf Supplemental Authorization and Personnel Benefits Act of 1991 (Public Law 102-25).

——— (1996). *Proliferation: Threat and response.* Washington, D.C.: U.S. Government Printing Office.

——— (1997). Office of the Secretary of Defense. *Proliferation: Threat and response.* Washington, D.C.: Department of Defense.

——— (1998). Department of Defense nuclear/biological/chemical (NBC) defense. *Annual report to Congress.* Washington, D.C.: U.S. Department of Defense.

U.S. Department of Health and Human Services (1996). Public Health Service, Additional requirements for facilities transferring or receiving select infectious agents (proposed rulemaking). *Federal Register* 61(112):29327–29332.

U.S. Department of State (1992). Office of Assistant Secretary/Spokesman, Joint U.S./U.K./Russian statement on biological weapons, statement by Richard Boucher, spokesman, September 14.

——— (1995). *Report on the extent of compliance of the independent states of the former Soviet Union with the Biological and Toxin Weapons Convention and other international agreements relating to the control of biological weapons.* Washington, D.C.: United States Department of State.

U.S. Department of the Army (1977a). *U.S. Army activity in the U.S. biological warfare programs 1942–1977,* vol. 2: *Annexes.* Washington, D.C.: U.S. Department of Defense.

——— (1977b). *U.S. Army activity in the U.S. biological warfare programs,* vols. 1 and 2. Washington, D.C.: U.S. Department of Defense.

U.S. Federal Register (1996). Proposed Rules for Section 511 of Public Law 104–132, vol. 61, no. 112, June 10.

U.S. Senate (1989). Committee on Foreign Relations, Hearing, *Chemical and biological weapons threat: The urgent need for remedies,* January 24, March 1, and May 9. Washington, D.C.: U.S. Government Printing Office.

——— (1994). Committee on Banking, Housing, and Urban Affairs, Hearing, *United States dual-use exports to Iraq and their impact on the health of the Persian Gulf War veterans,* May 25 (S. Hrg. 103-900). Washington, D.C.: U.S. Government Printing Office.

——— (1995). Permanent Sub-Committee on Investigations (Minority Staff), *Hearings on global proliferation of weapons of mass destruction: A case study on Aum Shinrikyo,* staff statement, October 31, 1995.

Usleber, E., E. Schneider, G. Terplan, and M. V. Laycock (1995). Two formats of enzyme immunoassay for the detection of saxitoxin and other paralytic shellfish poisoning toxins. *Food Additives and Contaminants* 12:405–413.

USSR (Union of Soviet Socialist Republics) (1950). *Materials on the trial of former servicemen of the Japanese army charged with manufacturing and employing bacteriological weapons.* Moscow: Foreign Languages Publishing House.

Utgoff, V. A. (1993). The biotechnology revolution and its potential military implications. In B. Roberts, ed., *Biological weapons: Weapons of the future?* Washington, D.C.: Center for Strategic and International Studies, pp. 28–31.

van Rensburg, S. J. (1998). The science of apartheid: Testimony by Dr. S. J. van Rensburg before the Truth and Reconciliation Commission. *Harper's Magazine* 297(1780):19–25.

Vasiliev, N. (1991). A few proposals on strengthening the 1972 Convention and establishing a verification mechanism. Unpublished paper, Seminar on the Biological and Toxin Weapons Convention. Noordwijk, the Netherlands.

Vorobiev, A. V. (1996). Working on the compliance regime for the BWC. *Chemical Weapons Convention Bulletin* 31:2–4.

Waller, R. (1996a). The Libyan threat to the Mediterranean. *Jane's Intelligence Review* 8:225–229.

—— (1996b). Libyan CW raises the issue of preemption. *Jane's Intelligence Review*:522–526.

Wallerstein, Mitchell B. (1995). Concepts to capabilities: The first year of counter-proliferation. In S. E. Johnson and W. H. Lewis, eds., *Weapons of mass destruction: New perspectives on counterproliferation.* Washington, D.C.: National Defense University Press, pp. 27–38.

Wall Street Journal (1996). Patent is received for use of bacteria-killing protein. June 5, p. B4.

Washington Post (1992). Russia denies it is building germ weapons. September 1, p. A14.

Watts, B. D., and T. A. Kearney (1993). Effects and effectiveness. In E. A. Cohen, director, *Gulf War air power survey,* vol. 1: *Operations and effects and effectiveness.* Washington, D.C.: Government Printing Office.

Webster, R. (1993). Influenza. In S. S. Morse, ed., *Emerging viruses.* New York: Oxford University Press, pp. 37–45.

Weir, S., H. Lee, and J. Trevors (1996). Survival of free and alginate-encapsulated *Pseudomonas aeruginosa* UG2Lr in soil treated with disinfectants. *Journal of Applied Bacteriology* 80:19–25.

Wells, R. M., S. S. Estani, Z. E. Yadon, D. Enria, et al. (1997). An unusual Hantavirus outbreak in southern Argentina: Person-to-person transmission. *Emerging Infectious Diseases* 3(2):171–174.

Wheelis, M. L. (1991). The role of epidemiology in strengthening the Biological Weapons Convention. In E. Geissler and R. H. Haynes, eds., *Prevention of a biological and toxin arms race and the responsibility of scientists.* Berlin: Akademie-Verlag, pp. 277–284.

—— (1992). Strengthening the Biological Weapons Convention through global epidemiological surveillance. *Politics and the Life Sciences* 11:179–189.

—— (1999). Biological warfare before 1914: The prescientific era. In E. Geissler and J. v. C. Moon, eds., *Biological and toxin weapons research, development and use from the Middle Ages to 1945.* Oxford University Press: London.

WHO (World Health Organization) (1970). *Health aspects of chemical and biological weapons.* Geneva: World Health Organization.

—— (1995). Forty-eighth World Health Assembly, *Communicable diseases prevention and control: New, emerging and re-emerging infectious diseases,* Resolution WHA 48.13, May 12.

—— (1996a). *The world health report 1996: Fighting disease, fostering development.* Geneva: World Health Organization.

—— (1996b). Emerging and other communicable diseases (EMC). Web site: http://www.who.org/programs/WHOprograms.html.

Wiefels, K., A. Hubinger, K. Dannehl, and F. Gries (1995). Insulin kinetic and dynamic in diabetic patients under insulin pump therapy after injections of human insulin or the insulin analogue (B28 Asp). *Hormone Metabolic Research* 7(9):421–424.

Wiener, S. L. (1986). Biological warfare defense, and toxin warfare. In S. L. Wiener and J. Barrett, eds., *Trauma management for civilian and military physicians.* Philadelphia: W. B. Saunders.

—— (1987). Strategies of biowarfare defense. *Military Medicine* 156:321–327.

———— (1996). Strategies for the prevention of a successful biological warfare aerosol attack. *Military Medicine* 161:251–256.

Wiener, S. L., and J. Barrett (1986). *Trauma management for civilian and military physicians*. Philadelphia: W. B. Saunders.

Wilhelmsen, C. L., and M. L. Pitt (1996). Lesions of acute inhaled lethal ricin intoxication in rhesus monkeys. *Veterinary Pathology* 33:296–302.

Williams, B., M. Fojtasek, P. Connolly-Stringfield, and J. Wheat (1994). Diagnosis of histoplasmosis by antigen detection during an outbreak in Indianapolis, Ind. *Archives of Pathology and Laboratory Medicine* 118:1205–1208.

Williams, P., and D. Wallace (1989). *Unit 731: The Japanese Army's secret of secrets*. London: Hodder and Stoughton.

Winter, H., and R. M. Pfisterer (1991). Inhalation anthrax in a textile worker; non-fatal course. *Schweizerische Medizinische Wochenschrift* 121:832–835.

Woodall, J. P. (1998). The role of computer networking in investigating unusual disease outbreaks and allegations of biological and toxin weapons use. *Critical Reviews in Microbiology* 24:255–272.

Woodall, J. P., and E. Geissler (1990). Information on outbreaks of infectious diseases and intoxinations. In E. Geissler, ed., *Strengthening the Biological Weapons Convention by confidence-building measures*. Oxford: Oxford University Press, pp. 105–124.

Woodward, Bob (1991). *The commanders*. New York: Simon and Schuster.

Woollett, G. (1998). Industry's role, concerns, and interests in the negotiation of a BWC compliance protocol. In A. E. Smithson, ed., *Biological weapons proliferation: Reasons for concern, courses of action*. Washington, D.C.: Stimson Center, pp. 39–52.

Wyllie, J. (1995). Libya—Regime stress. *Jane's Intelligence Review* 7:554–555.

Yeltsin, B. (1992). President of Russian Federation Decree no. 390, April 11.

York, H. (1973). The elusive nuclear airplane. Reprinted in Morton H. Halperin and Arnold Kanter, eds., *Readings in American foreign policy: A bureaucratic perspective*. Boston: Little, Brown, pp. 353–363.

Yosiho, T. (1992). Unit 731. In H. T. Cook and T. F. Cook, eds., *Japan at war: An oral history*. New York: New Press, pp. 158–168.

Yost, M. (1996). China's deadly trade in the Mideast. *Wall Street Journal*, December 4, pp. 1, 18.

Zanders, J. P. (1995). The chemical threat in Iraq's motives for the Kuwait invasion. *POLE-PAPERS* 2(1), Centrum voor Polemologie, Vrije Universiteit, Brussel.

Zelicoff, A. P. (1995). The Biological Weapons Convention: When does sampling make sense? *Politics and the Life Sciences* 14(1):79–86.

Zilinskas, R. A. (1984). Biotechnology in the USSR, Part 2. *Bio/Technology* 2:686–692.

———— (1986). Recombinant DNA research and biological warfare. In R. A. Zilinskas and B. K. Zimmerman, eds. *The gene-splicing wars: Reflections on the recombinant DNA controversy*. New York: Macmillan, pp. 167–203.

———— (1990). Biological warfare and the Third World. *Politics and the Life Sciences* 9:59–76.

———— (1992a). Confronting biological threats to international security: A biological early warning program. In R. A. Zilinskas, ed., *The microbiologist and biological defense research: Ethics, politics, and international security. New York Academy of Sciences* 666:146–176.

————, ed. (1992b). *The microbiologist and biological defense research: Ethics,* politics and international security. *Annals of the New York Academy of Sciences* 666:1–249.

—— (1995). UNSCOM and the UNSCOM experience in Iraq. *Politics and the Life Sciences* 14(2):230–235.

—— (1997a). The other biological weapons worry. Op-Ed. *New York Times*, November 28, p. A39.

—— (1997b). Iraq's biological weapons: The past as future? *Journal of the American Medical Association* 278(5):418–424.

—— (1998a). Verifying compliance to the Biological and Toxin Weapons Convention. *Critical Reviews in Microbiology* 24:195–218.

—— (1998b). Bioethics and biological weapons (editorial). *Science* 279:635.

Zilinskas, R. A., and C. G. Hedén (1991). The Biological Weapons Convention: A vehicle for international cooperation. In S. J. Lundin, ed., *Views on possible verification measures for the Biological Weapons Convention*. New York: Oxford University Press, pp. 71–97.

The Contributors

Will D. Carpenter is a former vice president and general manager of Monsanto Company. He served as the Chemical Manufacturers Association's representative to the U.S. Government in negotiations leading to the Chemical Weapons Convention and is a member of the Center for Strategic and International Studies Congressional Study Group on Chemical Arms Control. He is on the Harvard-Sussex Program Advisory Board on CBW Armament and Arms Limitation.

W. Seth Carus is a senior research professor at the National Defense University, Washington, D.C. He formerly served on the Policy Planning Staff in the Office of the Under Secretary of Defense for Policy. The views expressed in his article do not necessarily represent the positions of the National Defense University, the Department of Army, or the Department of Defense.

Marie I. Chevrier is an associate professor of political economy at the University of Texas at Dallas. She has published widely on the Biological Weapons Convention, is a member of the Federation of American Scientists' Working Group on Biological and Toxin Weapons Verification, and has participated in a Pugwash Conference on Strengthening the BWC. She was the associate director of the Harvard-Sussex Program on Chemical and Biological Warfare Armaments and Arms Limitation at the Belfer Center for Science and International Affairs, Kennedy School of Government, Harvard University.

Rita R. Colwell, former president of the University of Maryland

Biotechnology Institute, is a professor of microbiology at the University of Maryland. She has served as president of the National Science Board, the American Society for Microbiology, the International Union of Microbiological Societies, and the American Association for the Advancement of Science. In 1998, President Bill Clinton appointed her as director of the National Science Foundation.

Robert P. Kadlec, a physician in the U.S. Air Force, currently is on assignment as a senior assistant for counterproliferation policy in the office of the Secretary of Defense for International Security Policy. He has served as a United Nations Special Commission biological weapons inspector in Iraq and was the secretary of defense's representative on the U.S. delegation to the Convention on the Prohibition of the Development, Production and Stockpiling of Bacteriological (Biological) and Toxin Weapons, and on Their Destruction in Geneva, Switzerland.

Michael Moodie is president of the Chemical and Biological Arms Control Institute (CBACI), a nonprofit research organization established to promote the goals of arms control and nonproliferation. During the Bush administration, he served as assistant director for multilateral affairs at the U.S. Arms Control and Disarmament Agency where his responsibilities included, among others, chemical and biological weapons and arms control issues.

Stephen S. Morse is a program manager at the Defense Advanced Research Projects Agency, where his responsibilities include the advanced diagnostics area. Before coming to Washington, he was director of the Program in Emerging Diseases at the Joseph L. Mailman School of Public Health of Columbia University. Previously, he was assistant professor of virology at Rockefeller University and was principal organizer and chair of the Conference on Emerging Viruses held by the National Institutes of Health in 1989. Among other activities, he has served as a temporary adviser to the World Health Organization on emerging infections and surveillance, and is chair of the international Program for Monitoring Emerging Diseases (ProMED). The views expressed in his chapter do not necessarily represent the views of the Department of Defense or the U.S. government.

Graham S. Pearson is a visiting professor in international security in the Department of Peace Studies at the University of Bradford, West Yorkshire, United Kingdom. He was previously the director general of the Chemical and Biological Defense Establishment, Porton Down, Salisbury, United Kingdom. He is on the advisory board of the Harvard-Sussex Program on CBW Armament and Arms Limitation.

Tim Trevan is a former British diplomat, having served in the Arms Control and Disarmament Department of the Foreign Office, the Embassy in Yemen, the United Nations Department of the Foreign Office, and as head of the chemical warfare section of the UK delegation to the Conference on Disarmament in Geneva. From 1992–1995 he was special adviser to, and spokesperson for, the executive chairman of the United Nations Special Commission. He now concentrates on writing on international security and consulting on strategic risk. His latest book is *Saddam's Secrets,* an account of the hunt for Iraq's biological weapons.

Jonathan B. Tucker has worked as a policy analyst in the international security division of the congressional Office of Technology Assessment, as a specialist in chemical and biological arms control at the U.S. Arms Control and Disarmament Agency, and as a senior policy analyst with the Presidential Advisory Committee on Gulf War Veterans' Illnesses. Currently, he is director of the Chemical and Biological Weapons Nonproliferation Project at the Center for Nonproliferation Studies, Monterey Institute of International Studies, California.

Mark L. Wheelis is a senior lecturer in the Department of Microbiology, University of California at Davis. His research interests include the history of biological weapons use and the control of biological weapons.

Stanley L. Wiener is professor of medicine at the College of Medicine, University of Illinois, and on the faculty in emergency medicine and internal medicine at the Rush-Presbyterian Saint Luke's Medical Center in Chicago. He also is an infectious disease specialist and retired colonel with over twenty years of experience in the U.S. Army's biological defense program, and for the last three years has worked as an emergency physician in civilian health delivery facilities dealing with many varieties of acute infectious diseases. He is the coauthor of *Trauma Management for Civilian and Military Physicians* (1986).

Alan P. Zelicoff, a physicist and board certified physician in internal medicine, currently is a senior scientist at the Sandia National Laboratory in Albuquerque, New Mexico. His professional interests include arms control verification technologies, counterproliferation systems, and telecommunications. For the past six years, he has been a member of the U.S. delegation to the Convention on the Prohibition of the Development, Production and Stockpiling of Bacteriological (Biological) and Toxin Weapons, and on Their Destruction.

Raymond A. Zilinskas is senior scientist in residence at the Monterey Institute of International Studies, and adjunct associate professor at the School of Hygiene and Public Health, Johns Hopkins University. He has been a William Foster Fellow at the U.S. Arms Control and Disarmament Agency, a biological analyst at the UN Special Commission, and participated in two biological warfare–related inspections in Iraq. His current research focuses on biological arms control, the former Soviet Union's biological warfare program, and defenses against bioterrorism.

Index

investigation of outbreaks and,
105–108, 113–114; on-site inspections, 156, 159–163; First Review
Conference (1981), 15, 106,
173(n25); Second Review
Conference (1987), 77, 106, 156;
Third Review Conference (1991),
156–157, 183; Fourth Review
Conference (1996), 115, 162–163,
166; Special Conference of States
Parties, 115, 157, 165; verification
and, 30, 96–97, 114–115; violations,
164–165. *See also* Ad Hoc Group
Counterforce, 200–201
Counterinsurgency, 33
Counterproliferation, 50; active defenses, 201; Aspin initiative, 197–199,
203; counterforce, 200–201; defini-
tions, 193–194; international cooper-
ation and, 203–204; limitations, 204;
military preemption, 7, 195, 200–
201; origins, 194–197; scientists and,
241–243; sensors, 96, 127, 201–202,
204. *See also* Proliferation
Counterproliferation 0400 CONPLAN,
200
Counterproliferation Initiative, 197–199,
203
Coxiella burnetii, 62, 132
Cruise missiles, 201
Cuba, 164
CW. *See* Chemical weapons
CWC. *See* Chemical Weapons
Convention
Cyanide, 140–141

DARPA. *See* Defense Advanced
Research Projects Agency
Decapitation of command structure, 35,
38
Declaration of Principles, UNCED, 66
Declarations, 156–159, 174(n28),
186–187
Decontamination, 71
Defense Planning Guidance, 198
Delivery systems, 21–22, 37, 38, 39,
60–69; attack methods, 107–110;
Iraq and, 72, 74; missiles, 37, 38, 42,
43, 44, 72, 74, 201, 205(n4). *See also*
Aerosol delivery
Democratization, 51

Department of Disarmament Affairs,
UN, 254
Desert Shield, 71, 194–196
Desert Storm, 4, 60, 71, 72, 194–196
Detection, 6, 25, 71, 85, 116; arms control and, 96–99; array-based assays,
101–102; in battlefield, 94–96,
100–101, 121–123, 196, 197, 251;
BIDS, 96, 127, 201–202; of chemical
weapons, 92, 99–100; classical biological assay, 87; epidemiological
analysis, 110–113; immunoassay,
87–89, 100; limitations, 95; medical
diagnostics, 96, 101, 102;
microscopy, 86–87; nucleic acid
analysis, 89–92, 102, 111; particle
agglutination, 88–89, 95, 102; physical and chemical analysis, 92–93;
practical considerations, 94; sample
collection, 95, 98–99, 110, 188, 252;
sensors, 96, 127, 201–202, 204; terrorism and, 99–100. *See also* Threat
assessment
Deterrence, 43, 126, 164; limited value,
34; nuclear weapons use and, 29–30,
51–52
DIA. *See* U.S. Defense Intelligence
Agency
Diarrheal agents, 137–138
Division of Emerging and Other
Communicable Diseases, WHO, 58
DNA, 11; detection, 89–92, 93, 111. *See
also* Recombinant DNA (rDNA)
techniques
DOD. *See* U.S. Department of Defense
Dual-use issue, 13–14, 154, 155, 177,
233

Earth Summit, 66
East Asia, 27, 166
Ebola virus, 19, 57, 86, 87, 113, 137, 249
E. coli. See Escherichia coli
Egypt, 30, 36–37, 46, 154, 172(n14)
Eisenstadt, Michael, 45
Ekéus, Rolf, 195
Electrophoresis, 91, 101
ELIFA. *See* Enzyme-linked immunofil-
tration assay
ELISA. *See* Enzyme-linked immunosor-
bent assay
Environment, 83, 178

About the Book

Recent revelations about Iraqi and Soviet/Russian biological weapons programs and highly publicized events such as the deployment of anthrax and botulinum by the Aum Shinrikyo sect in Japan have made clear the necessity for addressing the issues of biological warfare and defense. In a comprehensive analysis of this imminent threat to global security, fourteen internationally recognized authorities consider the motivations of governments and terrorist groups seeking to acquire biological weapons; managing the consequences of a biological attack; techniques for weapons development; methods for detection of pathogens and toxins; defense against biological weapons; and international efforts to counter their proliferation.

Raymond A. Zilinskas, a former UN weapons inspector, is senior scientist in residence at the Monterey Institute of International Studies. His publications include *The Microbiologist and Biological Defense Research: Ethics, Politics and International Security.*